# THE COMPLETE IDIOT'S GUIDE™ TO

# The Beatles

## *by Richard Buskin*

## alpha
## books

A Division of Macmillan Reference USA
A Simon and Schuster Macmillan Company
1633 Broadway
New York, NY 10019-6785

*This book is dedicated with gratitude to my parents, Harry and Raymonde Buskin, for their love, support and patience, and to the memory of my late brother Paul.*

Macmillan Publishing books may be purchased for business or sales promotional use. For information please write: Special Markets Department, Macmillan Publishing USA, 1633 Broadway, New York, NY 10019-6785.

International Standard Book Number: 0-02-862130-1
Library of Congress Catalog Card Number: 97-80970

01  00  99  98    4  3  2  1

Interpretation of the printing code: The rightmost number of the first series of numbers is the year of the book's printing; the rightmost number of the second series of numbers is the number of the book's printing. For example, a printing code of 98-1 shows that the first printing occurred in 1998.

*Printed in the United States of America*

# Alpha Development Team

### Brand Manager
*Kathy Nebenhaus*

### Executive Editor
*Gary M. Krebs*

### Managing Editor
*Bob Shuman*

### Senior Editor
*Nancy Mikhail*

### Development Editors
*Jennifer Perillo*
*Amy Zavatto*

### Editorial Assistant
*Maureen Horn*

# Production Team

### Production Editor
*Phil Kitchel*

### Illustrator
*Jody Schaeffer*

### Designer
*Glenn Larsen*

### Cover Designer
*Mike Freeland*

### Indexer
*Tim Wright*

### Production Team
*Kim Cofer, Aleata Howard*

# Contents at a Glance

# Contents

# Foreword

I have an admittedly unscientific theory that for anyone born in or after the 1960s, The Beatles' music is part of what philosophers used to call "innate knowledge," that welter of collective memory and instinct that all children bring into the world.

There is, in fact, anecdotal evidence to support this notion. Friends report with astonishing consistency that their children respond immediately to The Beatles—and not just "Yellow Submarine" and "Octopus's Garden." And if you've prowled the children's sections of big record stores, you've no doubt seen tapes of Beatles songs reconfigured into everything from gentle lullabies and Sesame Street songs for toddlers to versions sung by Bugs Bunny and Friends for... well, actually, I know some adults who listen to that one. Let's face it: The people who produce and market these things usually have scads of behavioral data to back up their repertory decisions.

True, one could argue that kiddie versions are just another drop in a vast ocean of Beatles reinterpretations. The songs written and recorded by John Lennon, Paul McCartney, George Harrison, and Ringo Starr have been recast every which way. There are country, soul, ultra-folksy, and heavy metal versions of Beatles songs, as well as comic send-ups, Baroque and symphonic arrangements, and avant-garde deconstructions. What other pop music—of any era—is this durable? And what better proof can there be that this music, for some reason, resonates across the spectrum of human experience and taste?

Of course, it's likely that the almost universal response that people have to The Beatles is nothing more than the natural consequence of their music being so good, varied, inventive, and full of surprises. The Beatles, of course, were not just about music, and anyone who looks behind the curtain at the lives and times of the four young men who created this music will find an incredible world of colorful characters who in some ways are larger than life and in other ways just like us.

In *The Complete Idiot's Guide to The Beatles*, Richard Buskin presents the story of The Beatles' climb from unpromising backgrounds in Liverpool to their dominance of the pop music world, and he does so in a fascinatingly accessible, humorous way that is very much in keeping with the subject at hand. The Beatles, after all, were known for an iconoclastic wit that could turn press conferences and interviews into provocative streams of wordplay, and particularly in their later years, they took a real pleasure in toppling accepted myths—even their own myths.

So their story, in Mr. Buskin's telling, is not a star-struck parable, propelled by great strokes of luck. Sure, there are a few, and he notes them; but what he offers here is the somewhat more realistic story of how the young Beatles pursued and eventually surpassed their original goal of "making it big" through hard work, passion, and dedication to their blossoming art. He tells you what the common myths are, and the way he deflates them makes it clear that the reality is actually much more interesting. Along the way, he conveys plenty of detail about how they made the innovative albums and singles that changed absolutely everything about pop music, from the way it was composed and recorded to the aesthetics of composition.

For the neophyte, a series of boxes provide a crash course in everything from studio and musical terminology to famous (and obscure but telling) remarks by The Beatles and those around them. For those who have already explored this world—even those of us who have made a specialty of keeping tabs on the Fab Four and the stacks of books and articles that have been written about them over the last three and a half decades—Mr. Buskin has brought together an array of facts, details, and informed opinion not otherwise to be found between the covers of a single, concise volume.

Mr. Buskin recognizes, for example, that The Beatles' world has taken on a life of its own, and has spawned a world beyond that of The Beatles themselves. There are tidbits and arcana that have spawned endless discussions among Beatles fans over the years. At the elementary level, there are questions about song authorship: If Lennon and McCartney did not always collaborate on the songs that bear both their names, who wrote what? A few steps beyond that are performance details: Harrison was the group's lead guitarist, but Lennon played lead now and then, and McCartney's lead guitar lines enliven quite a few songs, including Harrison's own "Taxman." All this is sorted out herein, along with such peculiar byways as the 1969 rumor—itself a minor industry—that McCartney had died in 1966, and that the others peppered their album covers and lyrics with clues.

Also covered here is the sometimes wacky business of memorabilia and trinkets—the Beatles wigs, dolls, gum cards, and toys that poured onto the market in the 1960s, and since. Mr. Buskin, having written another book on this very subject, offers a glimpse of this world, and useful pointers about how to tell the real thing from the fly-by-night imitation. There is a useful appendix for those who want to track down all the recordings and the most useful books, publications, and videos.

There is even a section in the book devoted to Beatles look- and sound-alike bands, groups of often quite talented musicians who have sublimated their own creative impulses in favor of recreating The Beatles experience for listeners who missed the group in its original incarnation. Silliness? Okay. That's an important aspect of Beatling in itself. But ask yourself: Is this really that much different, in spirit, from what a symphony orchestra does when it plays the 19th-century classics? And, for the sake of Beatles' imitators everywhere, Mr. Buskin even takes the trouble to analyze the differences between the real Beatles' accents.

Given my "innate knowledge" theory, I'm not sure it's possible for anyone to be a *complete* idiot about The Beatles. But anyone who feels intimidated by the vast amount of information their local Beatle Brain can produce at the slightest prompting, and for anyone who knows the stuff intimately but wants a handy resource to help them verify a half remembered factoid using the latest in Beatles scholarship, this is the place to look.

—Allan Kozinn
music critic, *The New York Times*

# Introduction

What are the necessary ingredients for superstar status? Unique talent or a generous smattering of charm? Likeability or sheer magnetism? The ability to influence and inspire or the knack of capturing people's attention?

Well, the truth is that, in today's famous-for-15-minutes world, any one of these attributes could help you qualify. (After all, certain lucky devils appear to get by with none at all.) That's right, no one has the complete package of superstar goodies, but when complementary forces come together, great things can happen... and one of the greatest was a supergroup by the name of The Beatles.

Four seemingly ordinary guys from an industrial city in northwestern England, as a united force John, Paul, George, and Ringo basically had it all: unique talent, incredible charm, charismatic personalities, and an ability to influence, inspire, and entertain that resonates to this day.

There has never been anyone or anything quite like The Beatles. So many great songs, so much teen adulation, such widespread acclaim. But how did it all happen? What inspired the Fab Four in the first place and brought them together? What did they have to do in order to become the most successful act in the history of popular entertainment? And what is it about their music, their lives, their every word that, nearly 30 years after the band's demise, continues to attract new generations of fans, not to mention collectors, critics, and news-hungry media hounds? This book answers all of the questions, telling it how it was... and how it is.

As a four-year-old, I was swept up in the first tidal wave of Beatlemania when it flooded Britain back in 1963, and I've been trying to clear my eyes, ears, and nostrils ever since. Nothing works. Once you've been bitten by the Beatle bug it's impossible to shake off, so why bother? Better to listen to those records, watch those movies and TV appearances, and indulge in "Beatle small-talk" with like-minded victims.

You see, there is a *lot* to talk about. Aside from the group's history, its vast catalogue of work, and that of its individual members, there's also the memorabilia, the fan clubs, and tourist haunts; the inner circle of family, friends, and helpers; and, of course, all of those rumors that need confirming or denying. It can get very interesting... and pretty complicated.

Which is where this book comes in. I'll supply all of the vital stories and statistics, while negotiating the minefield of facts, fiction, and fab or fake collectibles, so that even those of you who are complete novices will soon be able to consider yourselves Beatle-know-it-alls!

# What You'll Learn in This Book

This book is divided into six parts that tell you all that there is to know about being a Beatle, a fan, or a collector. You'll learn how the group really struggled hard for its success, how talent and luck combined to achieve it, how the world reacted, and, in the wake of Beatlemania, what memorabilia items are worthy of being in your collection.

**Part 1, "All Together Now,"** discusses the social and cultural conditions that aided The Beatles in their rise to prominence, their social impact, their record-breaking achievements, and the reasons for the group's lasting popularity. We take a look at the people who have been most clearly influenced by the Fab Four, as well as the personal and professional qualities of John, Paul, George, and Ringo. Lastly, I provide you with details of the trends that they set and just about everything you need to know about the people in their "inner circle."

**Part 2, "Crying, Waiting, Hoping—Years of Struggle,"** tells you about The Beatles' birthplaces and families, as well as their major influences on radio and on record during their formative years. You'll then read about their adventures as students, their earliest musical performances, and their initial successes in Germany and in Liverpool. I'll also tell you about the Pre-Fab Three's search for a name as well as for a drummer, their musical collaborators, and their life in Hamburg—on the streets, in the clubs, and in the recording studios.

**Part 3, "A Taste of Honey—The Rise of The Beatles,"** starts off with a look at The Beatles' manager, Brian Epstein, and his efforts to clean up their stage appearance and gain them a recording contract. After recounting Ringo's replacement of Pete Best on drums, I describe the contribution of producer George Martin, as well as that of his sound engineer colleagues, before illustrating how The Beatles began playing in front of more prestigious audiences.

**Part 4, "To the Toppermost of the Poppermost,"** tells you how The Beatles presented themselves on radio and television, and to the press. I then provide the main events of the Beatlemania years and a breakdown of the group's big-screen efforts, before you learn about their final concerts, individual activities, and the era in which they reigned.

**Part 5, "Upsetting the Apple Cart,"** looks at the reasons for some of the more negative publicity that was attracted by the group, Brian Epstein's tragic death, and the subsequent rift between his charges. You'll then read about the solo careers of John, Paul, George, and Ringo.

**Part 6, "Oldies But Goldies,"** describes the activity surrounding the *Beatles Anthology* project, and then helps you discern between valuable and fake collectibles. Lastly, I tell you about fan clubs to join, conventions to attend, magazines to read, and places of interest to visit. To round out this *Complete Idiot's Guide*, there's a chronology of events in

Appendix A, chart positions in Appendix B, a comprehensive list of films, videos, and biopics in Appendix C, and details of the best and most interesting Beatles books in Appendix D.

# Every Little Thing

Just to ensure that no stone is left unturned, this book contains other types of information to help you become an expert on all things Beatle. Here's how to recognize these features:

### Do You Want to Know a Secret?

Here are some great anecdotes to amuse and elevate you to the heights of a true Beatle Brain!

### I Want to Tell You

The Beatles in their own words and in the words of others. Memorable quotes that will inform and entertain you.

### Say the Word

Check out these definitions to understand terms that are used by recording industry aficionados or connoisseurs of Beatle small-talk.

### I Should Have Known Better

Once and for all I will nail those rumors, lies, and misconceptions. No one will be able to pull the wool over *your* eyes!

### With a Little Help

Handy tips to help you find the best collectibles and better appreciate the Fab Four.

# Acknowledgments

For their help during the research and writing of this book I would like to thank the following people: Allen J. Wiener, Mark Lewisohn, Allan Kozinn, Bob Iuliucci, David Stark, and James Leasing (who are all honorary members of the Beatles Idiot Society) as well as Kerry Faulkner at Tony Stone Images, and Dorothy-Jean Lloyd.

# Special Thanks from the Publisher to the Technical Editor

*The Complete Idiot's Guide to The Beatles* was reviewed by an expert in the field who not only checked the technical accuracy of what you'll learn here, but also provided insight to help us ensure that this book tells you everything you need to know about The Fab Four. Our special thanks are extended to Allen J. Wiener.

Allen J. Wiener, author of *The Beatles: The Ultimate Recording Guide*, which is now in its third revised edition, is one of the world's most reputed Beatles scholars. His articles have appeared in *Goldmine*, *The Washington Post*, and *People* magazine.

# Part 1
# All Together Now

When The Beatles were performing live on the rooftop of the Apple office building in London towards the end of the Let It Be movie, it was very nice of that old guy in the street down below to assert, "The Beatles are classic, y'know. You can't beat 'em." But when he went on to say, "They've got a style of their own," and "They can sing well," he was only telling part of the story.

Obviously talent played a large part in the group's massive success, but then so did a slew of other factors that I'll tell you about soon enough. You're embarking on a very rewarding journey, but don't think that you're alone. As you're about to find out, millions of other people have been Beatle-mad for many years.

If you haven't climbed aboard yet, there's still plenty of time. So, are you ready? All right, cue the music—"One-two-three-faw!"...

# Twilight of the Gods: The Fab Four Phenomenon

In 1970, John Lennon described The Beatles as "just a band who made it very, very big." Well, I'm pretty sure *that* could go down as one of the great understatements of our time!

Basically, the group's success and influence was such that, for more than 30 years, it has managed to transcend changing tastes and trends. Today their music, their statements, their personalities, and—in the case of the three surviving members—their every movement continue to excite, amuse, and inspire.

Yet, it took more than the talents of The Beatles and those around them to achieve success on the scale that they did. In this chapter we'll explore the factors that were beyond their control—the state of the music business and events going on in the world around them—setting off the biggest pop-culture explosion of the 20th century. This resulted in record-breaking achievements that were not even a pipe dream when our heroes were singing for someone else's supper during the late-1950s and early 1960s.

# Britain: Post-War Blues

Post-war, pre-Beatle Britain was a pretty drab place to be, especially if you were a teenager. The nation may have been one of the chief victors in the fight against Hitler, but you could have been forgiven for not knowing it, especially if you compared the general standard of living with that of the United States.

Food rationing continued in Britain for several years after the war, and the sight of bombed-out craters and prefabricated housing lasted a lot longer. The 1953 coronation of Queen Elizabeth II may have helped to lift the gloom (and sell tens of thousands of TV sets), but unfortunately, the Monarch and her family also appeared to lead the nation's fashion sense. Now that *was* depressing! Still, things could only get better… and they soon did.

The arrival of rock and roll during the mid-1950s certainly helped wake up the kids and wind up their parents. While America blazed the trail, the Brits responded with cover versions of U.S. hits and a few dozen Elvis clones, complete with moody expressions, curled upper lips, and an ability to sing, "I lurv ya, baybeh," in an accent that would put true Americans to shame. This was just the beginning.

**I Want to Tell You**

"As kids we were all opposed to folk songs because they were so middle-class. It was all the college students with big scarves and a pint of beer in their hands singing folk songs in what we call la-di-da voices—'I worked in a mine in New-cast-le' and all that s—t."

—John Lennon, 1980

By the early 1960s, the first generation of Brit rockers—names such as Billy Fury and Marty Wilde—were about to be overtaken by "respectable" teen crooners who had the parents' stamp of approval. (Much the same was happening in the United States.) Young musicians such as Mick Jagger and Keith Richards, for instance, were beginning to adapt the material from across the Atlantic and perform it in their own style. Others, such as Lennon and McCartney, were even writing their own songs.

Enter The Beatles. Having been used to American domination of the film and music scenes for years, Britain's teens (1963 model) were ecstatic that they finally had worthy idols of their very own to scream about. What's more, while their parents rolled their eyes and snickered among themselves, it was pretty obvious that they were won over by The Beatles as well. After all, these four "youngsters with the scraggy hairdos" all appeared to be nice, clean-cut boys-next-door. Cheeky, charming, and not at all impressed by the fame and fortune—unlike those glossy Hollywood types!

Instead of trying to escape for a while by taking bland trips to Elvis' *Blue Hawaii*, Mr. and Mrs. Brit and the kids could now all sit back and watch some homegrown talent live out their own fantasies on foreign shores.

*The Beatles, 1963: Ringo Starr, George Harrison, Paul McCartney, John Lennon.*
©Hulton Getty

As for the British press, they were more than willing to promote some innocent fun after all of the sleaze and scandal surrounding the resignation of Government Defense Minister John Profumo. (Mr. Profumo, you see, had sent the sleaze-o-meter into the red by confessing to sharing a mistress with—tut, tut—a Russian spy!)

### Do You Want to Know a Secret?

Many male fans who attended The Beatles' 1963 concerts often complained that they couldn't hear the music for all the screaming, and John, Paul, George, and Ringo hardly fared better themselves. In the days before artists had monitors facing them from the front of the stage, the Fab Four and their audiences had to make do with a few Vox AC30 amplifiers on either side of Ringo's drum kit. At the end of November, the band doubled their output with some Vox AC60s—but they still couldn't hear a thing over the teen screams.

Money, music, and fun would be on the agenda from now on, and London and the rest of Britain were ready to swing.

# Stateside—The Right People at the Right Time

America was still the unrivaled leader in Western pop music at the end of 1963, and most of its entertainers and entrepreneurs would have been very happy if things had stayed that way. However, certain events that had already taken place were about to drastically and irreversibly alter the status quo.

American rock and roll had suffered some serious blows: the deaths of stars such as Buddy Holly and Eddie Cochran; the U.S. Army's transformation of Elvis Presley into Perry Como; Little Richard's conversion to a life of religion; Chuck Berry's imprisonment for statutory rape; and the furor over Jerry Lee Lewis' marriage to his 13-year-old cousin. These events had virtually stopped the rock and roll revolution in its tracks. In its place came a succession of insipid, approved-by-parents smoothies with names like Fabian, Frankie Avalon, and Troy Shondell. Nice boys with smiles more dazzling than their talent. Thankfully, they were soon countered by the groundbreaking recordings from Berry Gordy Jr.'s Motown label; the superior sounds of producer Phil Spector; and the California surf 'n' hot-rod bands, led by The Beach Boys.

During this period of transition, American records no longer dominated the British pop charts. The new wave of Liverpool acts, led by The Beatles and backed up by Gerry and the Pacemakers, The Searchers, Billy J. Kramer with the Dakotas, Cilla Black, The Swinging Blue Jeans, The Fourmost, and The Merseybeats, scored some hits and created a new and exciting sound of their own. But would this trend ever cross over the Great Pond to America? Few thought so—no British pop acts had yet made a lasting impression on America's youth.

Then an incident occurred that would shock America and the world, and unwittingly pave the way for the British Invasion. On November 22, 1963, just hours before The Beatles stepped onto the stage of the Globe Cinema in Stockton-on-Tees, Durham, England, President John F. Kennedy was assassinated in Dallas, Texas. America mourned the loss of its youngest and perhaps most charismatic president.

**Say the Word**
The **Mersey sound** and **Merseybeat** were terms applied to the similar sound produced by bands from Liverpool and the areas surrounding the River Mersey. A local pop paper was named *Mersey Beat*.

Britons may have been coming to terms with their shock (and titillation) over the Profumo scandal, yet this was small-fry compared to the mass American depression after Kennedy's slaying. Clearly something, or someone, was needed to help revive the spirits of the people. The Brits, however, had a *Merseybeat* tonic up their sleeves!

Eleven weeks to the day after the death of the president, The Beatles arrived at New York's newly re-christened Kennedy Airport. Now *that's* what you call good timing…

# That Was Then—Their Social Impact

During the early years of their success, The Beatles charmed virtually everyone, while also representing the voice of youth. Then, later on, they led the way in redefining their own generation. As a result, they managed to wreak havoc on society across two broad fronts. Let's take a look at these in greater detail.

# Those Adorable Moptops

Never mind the effect that The Beatles' music had on the public consciousness during their early years of megastardom. Just about everything else to do with the group seemed to be of incredible importance as well.

First off, aside from the "yeah, yeah, yeah" refrain in "She Loves You," which the press immediately tagged right onto, there was that unmistakable hairstyle that helped launch a million wigs. That's right, the *moptop*, so called because of the shaggy way it was combed from the top of the head to create bangs just above the eyebrows (or below them, should you need to dust your eyelids). What a fuss over a *coiffure* similar to the one sported by Julius Caesar a few thousand years before!

According to the press, parents, headmasters, and heads of state, to have a moptop was to have long hair. Apparently none of them noticed that it was way shorter than the pompadour style that had been preferred by Elvis, Tony Curtis, and millions of their followers until then (including the pre-fame Beatles).

Whatever! During those early years, John, Paul, George, and Ringo were basically the "Apple" of the eyes of much of the world. Even royalty joined in the adulation. In 1965, the Queen awarded each of The Beatles with an MBE (the Membership of the Most Excellent Order of the British Empire). This had apparently been recommended by Prime Minister Harold Wilson, a "fellow Liverpudlian" with a sharp eye for self-promotion. While fans were proud of their heroes' accomplishment, many soldiers and bona fide war heroes had their noses put out of joint. I mean, imagine Elvis Presley having been rewarded for his efforts with the Congressional Medal of Honor! (In 1970 he did receive a special narcotics agent's badge from Richard Nixon, but that wasn't quite the same thing.)

**Say the Word**

The word **moptop** refers to The Beatles' famous early haircut. The style, long for the time, only meant that the hair was combed forward to create bangs just above the eyebrows. As the ones who sparked the trend, The Beatles were affectionately dubbed the **Moptops**.

**With a Little Help**

If you're looking to invest in an authentic 1960s Beatles Wig, you should search out one manufactured in Britain by the Bell Toy Company. In its original packaging, which carries the slogan "Be With It, Wear a Beatles Wig," it could be worth up to five times as much as its American counterpart, which was made in much larger quantities by Lowell Toy Manufacturing.

### I Should Have Known Better

Contrary to a popular rumor that would later help to eradicate their moptop image, The Beatles did *not* share a joint in the visitors' restroom at Buckingham Palace while waiting to be invested with their MBEs. The truth is that they were slightly nervous, smoked cigarettes, and were all stone-cold sober when they each went down on one knee in front of Her Majesty.

A couple of years earlier, Leeds University Law Society had elected Ringo its vice-president. (No doubt his vocal performance of "Boys" had contributed to this historic decision.) Then, in 1964, some American students campaigned to have him elected U.S. President. Hey, if he'd stood against Lyndon Johnson he probably would have fared better than Senator Barry Goldwater!

The strength of The Beatles' impact in America was that not only did they pave the way for other British pop acts, they also opened up the doors to their fellow countrymen and women in other fields: Cockney-accented film star, Michael Caine; Sean Connery as super-spy James Bond; super-skinny supermodel, Twiggy; fashion designer, Mary Quant; celebrity photographer, David Bailey…British was best, London was supposedly swinging, and even the Union Jack became a fashion symbol, adorning clothes, bags, and wristwatches. Suddenly, it had become cool in America to have a British accent.

It's not overstating the facts to say that, thanks to The Beatles' global impact, there was a boom in the domestic fashion industry and a sharp rise in the number of tourists from overseas. No wonder they officially received their MBEs for "services to British export."

## The Generation Game

The 1960s weren't like any other decade in the 20th century. Initially a time of hope and innocence, it rapidly developed into an age when anything seemed possible and a lot of it actually happened: landing a man on the moon, wide-scale music festivals, student protests, frozen TV dinners—you name it. As a result, those of us who grew up during this era were likely to take even the most ridiculous things for granted.

### Say the Word

Fab is an abbreviation of "fabulous" that became extremely popular among British and American teenagers during the early to mid-1960s. Its use became synonymous with The Beatles when they were nicknamed the **Fab Four**.

The phantasmagorical, psychedelic, peace 'n' love, flower-power era had arrived, and leading it were, of course, The Beatles. By now their concert tours had come to an end and the teen screaming had stopped, to be supplanted by more way-out clothes and less happy-go-lucky attitudes. The glossy "Fab Four" image was being shed in favor of the band members' true personalities, and they began to be more outspoken in their political and social beliefs. One result was that they adopted their rightful position at the forefront of the burgeoning counter-culture movement. No longer did they keep quiet about the war in Vietnam, apartheid in South Africa, or even the hallucinogenic drugs in their bloodstream. They'd achieved all of the fame and fortune that they needed, thank you very much, and now they felt entitled to… well, to quote a Buck Owens song covered by Ringo, act naturally.

In the July 24, 1967 edition of *The Times* of London, John, Paul, George, Ringo, and Brian Epstein all lent their names to a petition calling for the legalization of marijuana. Of course, this immediately set them apart from many of the moms and pops who, until now, had considered them "adorable." Yet it also helped to reaffirm their credibility with many people of their own rebellious generation.

> **I Want to Tell You**
> "The taking of drugs expands the consciousness, but it's like taking an aspirin without having a headache."
>
> —Paul McCartney, 1967

The clean-cut, teen sensibilities of the first half of the decade were now considered completely out of step with what was going on in the world. In this respect, The Beatles could easily have become overnight has-beens, and it's a testament to their power, astuteness, and strength of character that they didn't. What's more, they actually continued to set the trends, sing the songs, and say the words that their contemporaries wanted to hear.

*May 19, 1967: Paul, Ringo, George, and John show off their* Sergeant Pepper's Lonely Hearts Club Band *album at its launch party in the London home of manager Brian Epstein.* ©Hulton Getty

The new *Sergeant Pepper's Lonely Hearts Club Band* album (I'm hoping you'll bear with me if I use the abbreviated name, *Sgt. Pepper*, from here on in) was virtually a manifesto for their generation, as was the single "All You Need Is Love." George's visit to the Haight-Ashbury district of San Francisco in August 1967 was viewed as an official endorsement of the hippie movement on America's West Coast, and the whole concept of transcendental meditation was popularized when The Beatles studied TM under Maharishi Mahesh Yogi.

Where they went, millions of others followed, for as John Lennon once said, "One thing The Beatles did was to affect people's minds."

# This Is Now—The Record-Breaking Statistics

During the years 1963 to 1970, The Beatles not only sold millions of records but, while vinyl was a lot more flexible than shellac, they also managed to break quite a few—sales figures, the speed of sales, the number of prints of *A Hard Day's Night* that were distributed to movie theaters, TV viewing figures, the amount of merchandise, and on and on. The entertainment industry had never known anything quite like it.

## Do You Want to Know a Secret?

When The Beatles filmed the TV-performance segment of *A Hard Day's Night* at the Scala Theatre in London on March 31, 1964, one of the songs they performed was "You Can't Do That." This was cut before the film's release, but was nevertheless seen by American viewers of *The Ed Sullivan Show* on May 24. United Artists had supplied the clip, but it wouldn't see the light of day until the 1994 documentary *You Can't Do That: The Making of A Hard Day's Night.* Incidentally, this show proves that in the audience at the Scala Theatre on March 31 was a 13-year-old actor (and future drummer, singer, and songwriter) by the name of Phil Collins.

Some of the group's achievements were so staggering that they stand to this day, while others were only surpassed in 1996…by The Beatles themselves! Here are the Fab Four's current record-breaking statistics:

➤ The greatest sales of any group, estimated by EMI at over one billion discs and tapes worldwide.

➤ The most multi-platinum albums (13 in the U.S.).

➤ The most platinum albums by a group (18 in the U.S., tied with Chicago and The Rolling Stones).

➤ The most number-one singles (22 in the U.S.).

➤ The biggest first-week sales of a double album (*The Beatles Anthology Volume 1*, which sold 855,473 copies in the U.S. from November 21 to 28, 1995).

➤ The most successful songwriters (Lennon and McCartney) in terms of number-one hits. (In the U.S., Paul takes the credit for 32 and John for 26, with 23 of these having been written together; in the UK, John takes credit for 29 and Paul for 28, with 25 of these having been written together.)

➤ The most covers of any song (over 3,000 versions of "Yesterday").

➤ The fastest-selling single ("I Want To Hold Your Hand," which sold 250,000 copies within the first three days of its U.S. release, one million after two weeks, and a staggering 10,000 copies per hour in New York City alone after 20 days).

➤ The biggest advance orders for a single (2.1 million copies of "Can't Buy Me Love" in the U.S.).

Another record that still stands is held by Paul McCartney for the largest paying audience attracted by a solo performer. Between 180,000 to 184,000 people went to see his concert at the Maracana Stadium in Rio de Janeiro, Brazil, on April 21, 1990.

As for The Beatles' own records in relation to their long list of achievements, here are some of the leading statistics:

➤ Their biggest-selling single was "Hey Jude," which sold more than 8 million copies in the U.S. and UK.

➤ Their most-played song is "Yesterday," which has so far been broadcast more than 6 million times on U.S. radio alone.

➤ Their greatest volume of sales within a 12-month period is, due to the popularity of all three *Anthology* albums, an estimated 33 million during 1996/97.

So, those are the facts—but now that you know them don't get too cocky. All of The Beatles' albums continue to be steady sellers, so the stats are constantly changing.

> **I Should Have Known Better**
> Contrary to what Bob Dylan once thought, The Beatles do actually sing, "I can't hide," at the end of the bridge section of "I Want To Hold Your Hand." On meeting the group for the first time in their New York hotel room in 1964, the folk-music poet congratulated them on the "sly drug reference" in which he assumed they sang, "I get high!"

# The Least You Need to Know

➤ Talent, favorable circumstances, and fortunate timing all contributed towards The Beatles' unprecedented success.

➤ The band managed to appeal to all sections of society.

➤ Their success opened the way for many fellow British artists.

➤ Once The Beatles became successful, they were able to voice their political and social views, influencing a generation.

➤ The Beatles set many records that stand to this day.

# Chapter 2

# Four Little Lord Fauntleroys— All Bow Down

## In This Chapter

➤ A look at the crazy world of the Fab Four's fans

➤ Meet the performers most influenced by The Beatles

➤ Beatles imitators: homage or rip-off?

➤ Tributes to The Beatles

With the possible exception of Elvis Presley, no other popular entertainment act has been as influential or as idolized on a long-term basis as The Beatles.

The fans range from the Interested to the Obsessive (with the Adoring somewhere in between), but almost without exception their motives are genuine. They have been taken by the group's music, their personalities, their clothes, you name it.

Then there are the musicians who impersonate The Beatles, as well as those who are influenced by them to the point of looking and sounding like imitators. These comprise a mixture of admirers and profiteers, and there's little middle ground with regard to what they produce. It will either entertain or annoy you, especially if you're an astute or paranoid Beatle Brain, in which case you may well feel inclined to shout, "Rip-off!"

In this chapter I'll provide you with a potted history of the Beatles' fans and describe their behavior so that you'll be able to spot them a mile away. Then we'll take a look at the professional admirers and imitators, after which I'll give you a run-down of some of the more notable (or notorious, depending on your point of view) "tribute" records.

# The Beatlemaniacs

The Beatles had fans in Liverpool and Hamburg, Germany (where they played during the early 1960s) even before they were world-famous. Many of those who regularly watched "the boys" playing in their hometown in 1961 and '62 even belonged to the original fan club, yet this was all small-fry compared to the numbers who made up the Official Beatles Fan Club of Great Britain by September 1964. By that time there were 58,000 of them, along with a special telephone number (COVent Garden 2332) set up to handle up to 100 inquiries per hour. (What everyone had to inquire about is anyone's guess.)

Meanwhile, there were more than a million registered fans in clubs all over North America, Europe, Africa, Asia, and the Pacific Rim. Rabid Beatlemaniacs from the Netherlands to Nigeria, Mauritius to Mozambique, would do practically anything to get close to their idols, if and when the Fab Four were anywhere near them. So it was that, as the band left the stage of the Seattle Coliseum on August 21, 1964, a girl fell from an overhead beam and landed at Ringo's feet.

On another occasion, at a Dallas hotel on September 18 of that year, a chambermaid was kidnapped by a frantic female and urged at knifepoint to divulge which suite The Beatles were staying in. Apparently the chambermaid held out, but there was also drama elsewhere in the same hotel when several other Beatle maidens had to be fished out of the air-conditioning shaft. These were the kind of lunatics who were prepared to shell out money to buy bogus merchandise such as "Bottled Beatle Breath"!

**I Want to Tell You**

"Dear George, I recently read that while you were in America you were asked if you were going to buy any American clothes. You answered, 'Yes, only what I need.' They asked, 'What's that?' and you said, 'Underwear, the American kind.' Well, what's the difference between American and English underwear? Our fan club needs this information before our next meeting."

—Joan B, President, Beatle Fan Club, New York City, 1964

Quite a few American teenagers who ran away during the Beatlemania years were simply en route to London in the hope of catching a glimpse of John, Paul, George, or Ringo. Others were even more persistent, and when the band's company, Apple, established a London office in the latter part of the 1960s, these fans would wait outside for days and even weeks on end to say, "Hi," "Bye," or perhaps a few more words to their heroes. The Beatles dubbed them the *Apple Scruffs* and George even wrote a song of the same name in tribute to them (released on his solo *All Things Must Pass* triple album). Others would simply turn up wherever The Beatles went—familiar faces with names such as Big Sue, Little Sue, Margo Stevens, Carole Bedford, Gayleen, Willie, and Knickers. (There's an obvious joke to be had with these last two names, but don't tempt me!)

**Say the Word**

The **Apple Scruffs** were the dedicated female fans who waited night and day outside the Apple offices to get a glimpse of John, Paul, George, or Ringo.

*October 26, 1965: Oh no, it's those rabid girls again! The London bobbies clearly had their hands (and mouths) full outside Buckingham Palace, when The Beatles turned up to receive their MBEs from the Queen.*
©Hulton Getty

Today, the really mad behavior has obviously subsided. After all, the "spot-a-Fab" opportunities are few and far between compared to the old days. Nevertheless, you'll still see countless people risking their lives on the "zebra" crossing in front of London's Abbey Road Studios. If they survive the speeding cars, chances are they'll also scribble messages on the regularly whitewashed wall there. Others hang around outside the various Beatle homes in London, Sussex, New York, Monte Carlo, and Henley-on-Thames; take the "Magical History Tours" around Liverpool (I'll tell you about that in Chapter 28); and scream as their idols appear on screens at fan conventions around the world. Now, if you spot this kind of behavior you can be sure of one thing: You're face to face with the current generation of Beatlemaniacs!

**With a Little Help**

If you wish to emulate The Beatles' *Abbey Road* album cover by walking along the same zebra-striped pedestrian crossing as the group, be warned: Make certain that you select the crossing nearest to the front wall of the studio in St. John's Wood, North London. There are two others close by, but neither has any Beatles connection whatsoever. So tread carefully, and watch out for the traffic!

# The Beatles Impersonators

While some bands have copied or been clearly influenced by the Fab Four, others have actually made a living by being straight imitators. They impersonate their sounds, their look, and often even their speaking voices...with varying degrees of success.

The trend really got underway during the 1970s, when public demand for the *real* Beatles to reunite was not met by the people in question. Others rushed forward to try to fill the void ("try" being the operative word), taking names from albums such as *Abbey Road* and *Revolver*. Then there were the fully fledged stage shows, such as *John, Paul, George, Ringo...and Bert*, *Sgt. Pepper's Lonely Hearts Club Band on the Road*, and the Broadway show *Beatlemania* (later adapted to the film).

**I Should Have Known Better**

If you're thinking of putting together your own Fab-Four lookalike band, be careful to avoid legal entanglements. The Beatles name is trademarked, and the group's company, Apple, does not take kindly to names containing the words "Beatles" or "Beatlemania." The band's trademark logo, "Beatles" with a long "T" (as it appeared on Ringo's bass drum), is also copyrighted.

Unabashed imitation aside, in 1978 there was that brilliant spoof of the whole Beatles legend in the form of The Rutles and their TV "rockumentary," *All You Need Is Cash*. Musically this was the brainchild of Neil Innes of The Bonzo Dog Band, who, aside from assuming the Lennonish role of Ron Nasty, ingeniously concocted Beatlesque numbers that made reference to specific Beatles songs without actually infringing copyright. The script was co-written by *Monty Python* team member Eric Idle, who also starred as both the show's narrator and as McCartney parody Dirk McQuickly. A cameo appearance by George Harrison (a pal of the *Monty Python* team) was the ultimate endorsement.

John Lennon's death in December of 1980 finished off any hopes of a full Beatles reunion. What it *did* do, on the other hand, was elevate the group's status to mythical proportions and ensure a steady living for enterprising imitators. So it is that today there are virtually hundreds of these bands, with names such as 1964 The Tribute, Long Live The Beatles, Yesterday—A Tribute to The Beatles, Beatle Magic, and, at the top of this particular tree, Rain, Liverpool, and The Bootleg Beatles.

The last band, originally formed in 1978, are Britain's premiere Beatles imitators. Their *schtick* is to appear in four different sets of costumes: Velvet-collared *A Hard Day's Night*-style suits; black suits and dark glasses similar to those worn by the band in 1966; *Sgt. Pepper* uniforms (of course); and clothes that are similar to those worn by the group on the *Abbey Road* album cover. Needless to say, each era also calls for the appropriate wigs! The Bootleg Beatles tour Europe, play to capacity crowds in venues such as the London Palladium and the Royal Albert Hall, and have even supported groups like Oasis, appearing before outdoor crowds of 125,000 in the UK.

Unlike the original Beatles, the Bootleg ones have the luxury of performing with a 20-piece orchestra, and they also enjoy the kind of audience feedback that even the real Paul McCartney hasn't experienced since the mid-1960s. That's right—when Bootleg Lennon announces (in a thick Liverpudlian accent) that the next song will be sung by Bootleg McCartney, the kids in the audience actually scream! Now, how's that for authenticity?

# The Beatle-like Bands

The accusation of trying to look and/or sound like the Fab Four has been leveled at countless bands up to the present day. This trend started way before The Monkees were assembled as an American "answer" to The Beatles, echoing the way the Brits manufactured their own "Elvises" during the preceding decade.

In fact, it even started before West Coast folk-rock group The Byrds went to see *A Hard Day's Night* and emerged from the movie theater with a definite idea as to their own future direction. ("Hey, dig those moptop hairstyles, man, and go for that cool *Rick 12-string* sound!").

**Say the Word**
**Rick 12-string** refers to the Rickenbacker guitar, which, unlike conventional six-string guitars, has two strings for each note. This creates the resonant, jangling sound that characterized George Harrison's solos on the *A Hard Day's Night* album.

*The Beatles' favorite mid-1960s American band, The Byrds: Chris Hillman, Roger McGuinn, Michael Clarke, David Crosby, Gene Clark.*
©Hulton Getty

Such was The Beatles' impact on the British scene during the summer of 1963, and so clearly different were they from anyone who had come before, there was almost immediately a glut of domestic artists trying to jump on the Beatle-buggy. One way, of course, was to be a beat group with that Mersey Sound; another was to just look like the Fab Four. You could, for instance, don those distinctive Pierre Cardin collarless jackets, as worn by The Beatles during the first half of 1963. Then there were the shaggy hairstyles, which acts such as The Dave Clark Five—and, the following year, The Kinks and Herman's

Hermits—were quick to latch onto; or the waistcoat, shirt, and tie look that even The Rolling Stones decided to adopt for a short while.

A few years later (just to digress for a brief moment), Mick and the boys would take yet another, equally unsuccessful stab at trying to match John, Paul, George, and Ringo. After the release of The Beatles' landmark *Sgt. Pepper* album, the Stones recorded what amounted to a psychedelic mishmash entitled *Their Satanic Majesties Request*, complete with overt drug references and "far-out" sounds. Basically, beads 'n' bells never suited the Stones as much as rhythm and blues.

Meanwhile, on the other side of the Atlantic, some groups gave a nod in the direction of the "Liverpoplians" (as UK newspaper *The Daily Mirror* idiotically nicknamed The Beatles) by simply christening themselves with a Brit-sounding title. How about The Beau Brummels, or even The Buckinghams. (As in the Queen's palace. Get it?)

Seemingly going along with the attitude of "If you can't beat 'em, join 'em," The Beatles themselves even got in on the act by the end of the decade. The Iveys were a soundalike band who they signed to their Apple label and who, as Badfinger, also had releases—such as "Come and Get It" and "Day After Day"—composed and produced by members of the Fab Four.

### Do You Want to Know a Secret?

While numerous people have tried to imitate The Beatles, the Fab Four themselves have often gone in the opposite direction by adopting assumed names when working on their own solo projects or those of other artists. Here are a few:

John—Joel Nohnn, John O'Cean, Dr. Winston O'Boogie, Dr. Winston O'Reggae, Dr. Winston O'Ghurkin, Rev. Thumbs Ghurkin, Rev. Fred Ghurkin, Hon. John St. John Johnson, Kaptain Kundalini, Dr. Dream, Dwarf McDougal, Mel Torment.

Paul—Bernard Webb, Apollo C. Vermouth, Paul Ramon, Percy "Thrills" Thrillington.

George—L'Angelo Misterioso, George O'Hara, George O'Hara Smith, George Harrisong, George Harrysong, Son of Harry, Hari Georgeson, P. Roducer, Jai Raj Harisein, Nelson Wilbury.

Ringo—Richie, Richie Snare, English Ritchie.

So, that was the way of things while The Beatles were together, and since then it's been a similar story. Sample the *Revolver*-type sounds of early '80s outfit The Jam, or the "Rain"-soaked psychedelia of '90s "supergroup" Oasis. Then there are the unmistakably Lennonish voice and production values of producer/composer/musician Jeff Lynne.

Actually, as things have turned out, Lynne's tastes and talents have benefited not only his former band, Electric Light Orchestra, but also Paul, George, and Ringo. George was the first to sit up and take notice, collaborating with Lynne on a number of projects during the past decade, including Harrison's smash-hit album, *Cloud Nine*, and two records by all-star group The Traveling Wilburys. This band featured Messrs. Harrison and Lynne playing alongside Bob Dylan, Roy Orbison, and Tom Petty, but even this lineup paled in comparison to the one featured on one of Jeff's more recent production assignments—namely, the two new Beatles singles, "Free As A Bird" and "Real Love."

**I Want to Tell You**
"Anytime you spell Beatle with an 'a' in it, we get some money."

—Ringo Starr, 1964

Now, even Paul McCartney has been won over, entrusting Lynne to take care of some of the production chores for his 1997 solo album, *Flaming Pie*. Sometimes it pays to emulate your idols!

## We Love You Beatles: The Tribute Records

Never mind that there have been more than 3,000 cover versions of "Yesterday." Can you believe that, up to 1981, there were no less than 357 records produced as "tributes" or novelty items relating to The Beatles? (And that was just in English, because the Swedes, the Germans, and seemingly everyone else on the planet has got in on the act too. But hey, who's counting?)

Now, we all know that, given a particularly strong fad, there will always be eagle-eyed entrepreneurs who are hot out of the starting blocks. Comedienne Dora Bryan had started the whole cash-in craze in Britain with "All I Want For Christmas Is a Beatle." There the Vernon Girls recorded "We Love the Beatles," while in the States, Allan Sherman stood defiant with "I Hate The Beatles." Still, for all of the admirable effort, the only song to crack the Top 80 in the U.S. charts was The Carefrees' "We Love You Beatles," which climbed to the dizzy heights of No. 39 in 1964.

**I Should Have Known Better**
During the 1970s, when "Beatles to reunite" rumors were all the rage, there was even false speculation that they had already collaborated under assumed names. The top contender was a 1976 album by a Canadian "soundalike" band named Klaatu. The fact that it was released on Capitol Records and that no musicians were credited helped spark the rumor, and as a result it was a million-seller.

However, not all of the tributes came from a bubblegum wrapper. In fact, you may be surprised at the caliber of some of the other artists who jumped on the imitation bandwagon during the height of Beatlemania. I mean, how about Ella Fitzgerald recording "Ringo Beat"? Or Cher (under the assumed name of Bonnie Jo Mason) warbling "Ringo I Love You," produced by the legendary Phil Spector? (In

1964, Mr. Starr evidently served as a magnet; in Britain, TV entertainer Rolf Harris even recorded "Ringo for President.") Then there was singer/composer and sometime-member of The Crickets, Sonny Curtis, with "A Beatle I Want To Be," and, in 1967, TV talk-show host Steve Allen with "Here Comes Sgt. Pepper"(!)

The following year, the sight of John Lennon and Yoko Ono standing naked on the cover of their *Two Virgins* album distracted future actress Sissy Spacek from her drama lessons long enough to sing, "John, You Went Too Far This Time."

These days, Beatle "tribute" songs are practically non-existent, which is a blessing to say the least. (The last flurry of activity was immediately after John Lennon's death.) Nevertheless, some of those old discs are still worth searching out, even if their value is more novelty than monetary.

As for my own favorite tribute? Well, I suppose that would have to be cartoon character Huckleberry Hound and his fab rendition of "Bingo Ringo"! After all, who ever said that a dog can't carry a tune?

## The Least You Need to Know

- ➤ In the 1960s, Beatlemaniacs would go to almost any lengths to be near their idols.
- ➤ To this day, there are many Beatles impersonators who attempt to sound and/or look like the original band.
- ➤ The Beatles influenced more rock musicians than any other band.
- ➤ The flood of tribute records in the 1960s demonstrates the appeal and influence of The Beatles, but few of these records stand the test of time.

# Chapter 3

# The Band You've Known For All These Years

## In This Chapter

➤ Defining The Beatles' individual accents and personalities

➤ How The Beatles charmed us and made us laugh

➤ The lowdown on Beatle-related fads and fashions

Like the four points of the compass, The Beatles managed to cover all bases. They had the perfect combination of unique talents and winning personalities with which to conquer the masses, as well as the determination, imagination, and uncanny sense of timing that enabled them to sustain their success.

In this chapter we'll take a brief look at the personal characteristics of John, Paul, George, and Ringo, as well as the trends they set both before and after they established themselves at the top of the pop tree. The Beatles were primarily musicians, yet their charm, sense of humor, and outward appearance all played a very large part in winning over the masses.

## Tip of My Tongue

Whether talking or singing, there can be little mistaking the very identifiable voices of John, Paul, George, and Ringo. Many people—often professional actors and musicians—have attempted to impersonate them down the years, and even though some have managed to get fairly close, there's nothing like the real thing.

### Do You Want to Know a Secret?

In the full-length animated feature, *Yellow Submarine*, what Paul McCartney has since referred to as "those dreadful, bloody voices" belong not to The Beatles themselves, but to a set of actors. Producer Al Brodax and director George Dunning had previously worked on a Beatles cartoon series for ABC-TV. Less than impressed with the way they were drawn and characterized, John, Paul, George, and Ringo refused to contribute their own voices. Equally skeptical of the *Yellow Submarine* project, they again were not interested, although by this time Al Brodax had no intention of even asking them. Nevertheless, they did make a cameo appearance towards the end of the film.

As far as Liverpool accents go, The Beatles' regional nuances have become less pronounced in the more than 35 years since they left their home city. Accents are very important in England, and in the British Isles in general. A miniscule piece of land when compared to the United States, England has a very large population that's about one fifth of America's. Nevertheless, British accents differ sharply every few hundred miles.

Not only does an accent indicate where you come from in the UK, but, in an extremely class-conscious society, your social standing as well. Liverpool is an industrial city. Not everyone who lives there works in industry or is poor, yet those with the thickest local accents are generally perceived to be "working class." In this respect, the speaking voices of both George and Ringo are a dead giveaway as to their humble background.

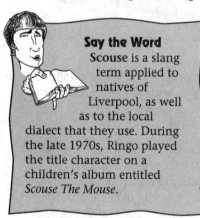

### Say the Word

**Scouse** is a slang term applied to natives of Liverpool, as well as to the local dialect that they use. During the late 1970s, Ringo played the title character on a children's album entitled *Scouse The Mouse*.

During the early years of The Beatles' success, George still had a *Scouse* accent. To a lesser extent so did Ringo, although his voice is altogether deeper and somehow suits his sad-eyed face. Paul, on the other hand, has always spoken with less of an edge or an accent than his three colleagues, while John's voice also betrayed little of his Liverpool surroundings when he was a child, if his Aunt Mimi is to be believed. This would have reflected his middle-class upbringing, but, according to Mimi, he cultivated a stronger accent when he became a Beatle. Whether this was true or not, the native accent remained until the end of John's life, even though, during his final years, it was tinged with the faintest of American inflections.

## The Four Up Close—Tell Me What You See

Just as with their voices and their individual musical talents, John, Paul, George, and Ringo had four very distinct personalities. Of course, given the nature of the press and media, this led to stereotyping along the lines of the animated Beatles who appear in the

*Yellow Submarine* cartoon. Still, these simplistic characterizations did have some basis in truth. I'll provide you with a brief run-down.

## John—The Cynic

John Lennon was a man who could annihilate an opponent with a razor-sharp put-down, and fend off all comers with his stoic, myopic glare. There was little point in crossing verbal swords with him; he would usually win.

### Do You Want to Know a Secret?

Since his childhood John Lennon was extremely nearsighted. During his teens he wore thick, black-framed glasses similar to those of his idol, Buddy Holly, yet he would often take them off in public, with sometimes dangerous consequences. Not only could he not see where he was going, but an innocent squint in the wrong direction could be mistaken for a "hard stare" by a local thug! As a Beatle, John took to wearing contact lenses away from home and the recording studio, but on stage he could still hardly see beyond the first couple of rows. Consequently, once the band abandoned its "moptop" image, he adopted the circular "granny" glasses that would become his trademark.

Intolerant of ignorance and bigotry, John was a broad-minded thinker who ingested everything around him, from music, art, books, and magazines, to radio, film, and—one of his pet loves—television. Still, he was a mass of contradictions—a hard-edged cynic who would regularly display a heart of gold, and an alert skeptic who would often leave himself wide open to masters of exploitation. Impulsiveness was one of his chief traits—Beatles producer, George Martin, likened him to someone "driving without a clutch"—and even though he worked extremely hard at his career, John was, by his own admission, inherently lazy. Indeed, on several occasions he asserted that he "would probably still be a bum hanging around Liverpool," if The Beatles hadn't been successful.

At the same time, John also spent the better part of his life trying to improve himself as a human being, evolving from a physically aggressive youth into a man of peace, from a chauvinist into a househusband. He had, to use his own words, "a grasshopper mind," and to the end of his short life he was an interviewer's dream, full of strong opinions and witty insights. After all, nearly everything that John Lennon ever said or wrote for public consumption made for a great quote.

## Paul—The Baby-Face

Adored by female fans as the handsome, "baby-faced" Beatle, Paul McCartney has gentle looks that hide an iron will and a steely determination. He's a "workaholic" with a strong

### I Should Have Known Better

Contrary to popular rumor, Paul's wife Linda has no connections to the Eastman-Kodak photographic empire. Her late father, Lee Eastman, was one of New York City's most powerful lawyers, and he has been followed into the profession by her brother John. When the three other Beatles decided to enlist Allen Klein as the group's manager, Paul counter-proposed Lee Eastman. He was out-voted.

sense as to how things should be done, and while this has led to friction in some of his professional relationships, it has also ensured that he has remained firmly in the public spotlight for nearly four decades.

Paul was always the Beatle most in love with being a member of the Fab Four. He enjoyed performing concerts more than the other three, and he was the last to want to quit touring. His competitive nature spurred both John and himself to greater heights as songwriters, and it was he who struggled to keep the band together when cracks started to appear. On the other hand, he's also apt to tread carefully: He was the last member of the group to experiment with drugs, the last one to get married, and the only one to be wary of manager Brian Epstein's eventual successor, Allen Klein.

"Macca," as he's fondly known, is also the only Beatle not to have been divorced. He is a publicity man's dream—extremely courteous to fans and eager to do interviews—yet he treasures the simple privacy of his Sussex country-side home and his farm in Scotland's Mull of Kintyre. An astute businessman (at least since his Beatle days), he's one of Britain's wealthiest citizens. What's more, he and wife Linda are among the nation's most celebrated environmentalists and animal-rights activists.

## George—The Quiet One

Behind the lop-sided grin and understated manner, George Harrison is a man of strong opinions and long-standing, deep-rooted beliefs. During the mid-1960s, he was the Beatle who first turned his fellow band members—and then countless others in and out of the entertainment industry—onto Indian music and culture. For most this was just a passing fad, but George has never wavered. He's been a constant follower and supporter of Hindu philosophy, while sustaining a personal and professional relationship with legendary sitar player, Ravi Shankar.

While John was largely perceived as the intellectual member of The Beatles and Paul was the pin-up, George charmed the masses with his apparent shyness. However, while he often left much of the talking during interviews to his three more outgoing colleagues, he rarely missed an opportunity to make an incisive comment or funny aside. At the same time, he was also Paul's polar opposite in several respects.

For one thing, George almost immediately resented the intrusion on his privacy and freedom exacted by The Beatles' fame. As a result, he was the first member of the Fab Four to make a case for quitting live performances. He now shuns interviews and public appearances, unless he feels that he really needs to (which these days is not very often).

When he does talk about The Beatles, his memories are, well, let's just say they're laced with a little cynicism.

## Ringo—The Clown

Ringo Starr was the oldest Beatle, the last to join the group and, at five foot eight, also the shortest by three inches. Ringo ensured a place in everybody's hearts thanks to his sad eyes, ready smile, and good-natured willingness to be the butt of his colleagues' jokes.

This is not to say that he won't stand up for himself when the going gets tough. Ringo came closest to John when it came to producing laughs, and it was for that reason—as well as his innate ability to win the sympathy of an audience—that he was singled out for his performance in *A Hard Day's Night*, and then given the central role in *Help!*

During the Beatlemania years, Ringo was perhaps the most popular—and certainly most recognizable—member of the group among the general public. However, within the group itself he fully acknowledged John and Paul's greater talents as both singers and composers, and he accepted his more limited role while taking full advantage of whatever opportunities came his way. As a result, through all of the ups and downs of The Beatles' relationships with one another, Ringo ranks far and away as the best team player.

**I Want to Tell You**
"I'd like to end up sort of unforgettable."
—Ringo Starr, 1963

# Don't You Know the Joker Laughs at You?

The Fab Four were no slouches when it came to wisecracks. Neither, for that matter, are their fellow Liverpudlians, who are noted in Britain for their ability to see the funny side in even the most depressing situations. And they have seen their fair share, given the social and economic status of the industrial city that they live in.

The Beatles grew up in an environment where one-liners flew at them from every direction. Their minds quickly became attuned to dealing with quips and put-downs, and to doling out more than a few of their own. The expert was one John Winston Lennon, who not only had a quick brain and a sharp tongue, but also loved nonsensical wordplay. This was inspired by the radio characters he heard during his youth, including the anarchic British comedy team, The Goons (comprising Peter Sellers, Spike Milligan, and Harry Secombe), and he was already putting it to good use by the time he was in his early teens.

At school John would amuse his fellow classmates with his exercise books, which he would fill with cartoons, nonsense verse, and drawings of the teachers. On the cover of each book he would write the title, *The Daily Howl*, and inside there would be send-ups of popular characters of the day: Davy Crockett, for example, was immortalized in "The Story of Davy Crutch-Head." John would mess with words—switching letters or changing

**With a Little Help**
If you'd like to get hold of one of John's original *Daily Howl* school books, you'll have to shell out some serious money. During the very early 1960s his fellow college student, Rod Murray, found a copy in an apartment that they had shared. On August 30, 1984, Rod sold this at a Sotheby's auction in London for about $30,000!

their sound so that they had a double meaning—and his special talent for this would later be fully revealed in his best-selling books of poetry and nonsense prose, *In His Own Write* and *A Spaniard in the Works*, as well as classic Beatles numbers such as "I Am The Walrus" and "Come Together."

Lennon's humor was often incredibly funny, sometimes cruel—he had a lifelong obsession with (and fear of) physical disabilities—but always distinctive. Meanwhile, an ability that all of The Beatles shared was the remarkable speed with which they could fire off the one-liners. They ruled supreme in press conferences, especially the one held at Kennedy Airport just minutes after their initial arrival in the States on February 7, 1964. It was hard to believe that the questions and answers hadn't been rehearsed beforehand, but they hadn't—and America was won over before The Beatles had even played a note on U.S. soil.

Here are some samples of The Beatles' press conference quips:

Q: Do you wear wigs?
John: If we do they must be the only ones with real dandruff.

Q: What did you think when your airline's engine began smoking as you landed today?
Ringo: Beatles, women, and children first!

Q: How does it feel, putting on the whole world?
John: How does it feel to be put on?

Q: Paul, you look like my son.
Paul: You don't look a bit like my mother.

Q: Ringo, why do you wear two rings on each hand?
Ringo: Because I can't fit them through my nose.

Q: What's your reaction to a Seattle psychiatrist's opinion that you are a menace?
George: Psychiatrists are a menace.

Q: Would you like to walk down the street without being recognised?
John: We used to do this with no money in our pockets. There's no point in it.

Q: You were at the Playboy Club last night. What did you think of it?
Paul: The Playboy and I are just good friends.

**Q:** Does all the adulation from teenage girls affect you?

**John:** When I feel my head start to swell, I look at Ringo and know perfectly well we're not supermen.

**Q:** Do teenagers scream at you because they are, in effect, revolting against their parents?

**Paul:** They've been revolting for years.

**Q:** What is the biggest threat to your careers? The atom bomb or dandruff?

**Ringo:** The atom bomb. We've already got dandruff.

**Say the Word**

Gear was a Liverpudlian expression, meaning terrific, that was popularized by The Beatles during 1963 and 1964. For a while both "gear" and "fab" (short for fabulous) were hip words among teenagers, but not for long.

**Q:** The French have not made up their minds about The Beatles. What do you think of them?

**John:** Oh, we like The Beatles. They're *gear*.

**Q:** Do you like topless bathing suits?

**Ringo:** We've been wearing them for years.

**Q:** There's a "Stamp Out The Beatles" movement underway in Detroit. What are you going to do about it?

**Paul:** We're going to start a campaign to stamp out Detroit.

**Q:** Sorry to interrupt you while you are eating, but what do you think you will be doing in five years time when all this is over?

**Ringo:** Still eating.

# Nothing Is Real—Changing Tastes and Trends

Just as quickly as The Beatles' music progressed from album to album, so the guys themselves developed new tastes, changed their look, and seemingly led the world in whatever direction they chose to take.

When John, Paul, George, and Ringo expressed their liking for recordings by the black Tamla Motown artists, this gave a tremendous boost to the fledgling Detroit label. The same could be said for The Byrds when, in 1965, The Beatles proclaimed them to be their favorite American group, and for the Indian sitar music of artists such as Ravi Shankar. Basically, if The Beatles liked these people it had to be worth giving them the time of day!

Lark cigarettes, scotch whisky, and Coca-Cola—whatever they fancied was all right with practically everyone else. Not so, perhaps, when they began to replace the sugar in their tea with some LSD, but then there were people who chose, rightly or wrongly, to follow their example.

Nevertheless, among all of the opportunists who profited from our heroes changing like the British weather, perhaps the ones who owed them the most were those in the fashion industry. Admittedly, The Beatles were not reluctant to copy an appearance that someone else had started, from the greasy ducktail hairstyles and leather outfits they started with in the 1960s, to the dishevelled scarecrow look they ended the decade with. Whatever they did was viewed as some sort of endorsement, while in between they set trends that were a sensation, not least among fashion designers, manufacturers, and retailers. Let's take a quick look at some of them.

### Do You Want to Know a Secret?

The Beatles' moptop hairdos were first fashioned by Astrid Kircherr, a photographer they befriended while in Hamburg, Germany. In 1961 Astrid cut the hair of her boyfriend—the band's recently departed bassist, Stuart Sutcliffe—in a style sported by a group of German students known as "Exis" (existentialists). When John, Paul, and George first saw Stuart's new look, they broke up with laughter. As Elvis-style rockers, they thought his hair looked ridiculous. In spite of their cackling, they soon grew to like and adopt it themselves...and, within a few years, so would the rest of the world.

First off, having refashioned their retro hairstyles into those revolutionary moptops, The Beatles agreed to go along with their manager Brian Epstein's advice and smarten their physical appearance. This initially took the form of the kind of mohair suits that were worn by countless pop smoothies of the era. Okay, so now at least you could bring them home to meet the folks. Then, from April to October of 1963, there were those Pierre Cardin collarless jackets that took the world by storm, even though the Fab Four only wore them in Britain and on their trip to Sweden. Still, at least everyone got to see their Cuban-heeled boots!

While 1964 ushered in the era of suits with velvet collars, 1965 was the year of military-style uniforms with "Nehru collars," as worn by "the boys" in their movie, *Help!* By then, the hair was perilously close to covering their ears, but they still wore a variety of matching suits for their final world tour the following year. The mustaches that sprouted shortly thereafter marked the last time that they really all conformed to a particular image. Sure, they all hopped into elaborate uniforms for the *Sgt. Pepper* cover shots, but, in line with their different personalities, these were each a different color. (Being that his outfit was pink, I'm not sure what Ringo would make of this analysis.)

*Eeek! The photographer's placed a plastic beetle on Ringo's nose! The Fab Four in 1963, sporting the moptop hairstyles and collarless jackets that sparked a twin craze.*
©Hulton Getty

The psychedelic, flower-power era was now underway, and the clothing industry no longer needed to look to The Beatles to gain "an early clue to the new direction" (to quote from *A Hard Day's Night*—but more on that later).

Still, there was one more major fashion statement to be made, and this would last a lot longer than all of the others. Yes, it was those circular "granny glasses," as worn by Mr. Lennon and available from your neighborhood optometrist. The fact that this was one of the styles subsidized by Britain's National Health Service made them easily affordable. The fact that John inadvertently caused a run on them probably accounted for the tax rises that took place shortly afterwards.

## The Least You Need to Know

➤ Each of The Beatles had a distinctive, recognizable speaking voice.

➤ John, Paul, George, and Ringo had very different personalities that perfectly complemented one another.

➤ Their quick-fire humor was yet another key to their massive success.

➤ The Beatles set fashion trends as much as they followed them.

# Chapter 4

# Reelin' and Rockin': The Beatles' Artistry

## In This Chapter

➤ The low-down on The Beatles' singing abilities

➤ The Beatles as composers/songwriters

➤ The inside track on John, Paul, George, and Ringo's talents as musicians

➤ The Beatles' amazing technological and recording accomplishments

Few people would dispute that The Beatles were musical pioneers. However, if the band members had pursued separate careers right from the start, it's fairly certain that none of them would have made as big a splash as they did together. The Fab Four have each met with varying measures of success in their solo work, and the fewer sparks of creative genius lend credence to that saying about the whole being greater than the sum of its parts.

There's a game that some fans like to play in which they try to estimate how successful the band would have been had its lineup been different. How about John, Paul, Eric Clapton, and Ringo, for instance? Or perhaps John, Paul, and George, together with The Who's flamboyant drummer, Keith Moon?

Well, there'll never be an answer to that kind of speculation, but we do know that the four very different characters who made up The Beatles complemented each other brilliantly. In the end, those differences caused tension, but when they clicked there was magic in the air and on record. Let's take a look at their natural gifts and the advancements that they made.

# And Your Bird Can Sing

Just as The Beatles had distinctive speaking voices, when they sang each of them were very recognizable.

John, with his harsh, razor-sharp tones, was by far the easiest to identify, whether singing lead or backing vocals. With his tremendous range and incredible power, he was undoubtedly the Beatle—and arguably the artist—with the best rock and roll voice, ripping into numbers like "Twist And Shout," "Slow Down," and "Rock And Roll Music." At the same time, while his voice couldn't exactly be described as pretty, it had a sincerity and depth of feeling that enhanced the tenderest of love songs.

John himself never really rated his own singing. In fact, when he eventually produced his own solo recordings, he often tried to cover up what he considered flaws by smothering his vocals in echo. Those who worked with John, however, had a completely different opinion, asserting—like Beatles producer George Martin—that he had "a tremendous voice."

If any of the Fab Four did have a "pretty" voice, it had to be Paul, the Beatle best suited to singing romantic ballads like "A Taste Of Honey" and "Till There Was You." Like his speaking voice, Paul's singing sounded altogether smoother than his colleagues, but when he sang rock numbers such as "Long Tall Sally," "Oh! Darling," and "Helter Skelter," he had all of the edge that he needed. What a combination for one band: two lead singers who could rock and serenade with the best of them.

George's voice was not as powerful as John's or as melodic as Paul's, nor could he boast the dexterity or range of either one. Nevertheless, he was still able to inject energy into his performance of a rock standard like "Roll Over Beethoven," and also summon up the necessary wistfulness for tracks such as "While My Guitar Gently Weeps" and "Here Comes The Sun."

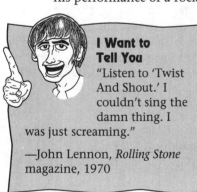

**I Want to Tell You**

"Listen to 'Twist And Shout.' I couldn't sing the damn thing. I was just screaming."

—John Lennon, *Rolling Stone* magazine, 1970

Having been heavily influenced by The Everly Brothers, John and Paul learned to harmonize perfectly with each other, whether sharing the lead vocal or blending together for the backing. Paul would take the high harmonies, John would handle the low, and they were ably accompanied by George. Indeed, songs like "Help!," "The Night Before," and "If I Needed Someone,"—where one would perform the lead vocal and the other two would back him—comprised a large part of The Beatles' unmistakable and much-imitated sound. When all three harmonized together, such as on the track "Because" on *Abbey Road*, the effect was sublime.

As for Ringo, well, his voice was even more limited than George's. Its sound, however, was undoubtedly as distinctive as his style of drumming, whether he was rocking his way through "Boys," crooning "Goodnight," or getting by "With A Little Help From My Friends."

There aren't many four-piece rock bands that share the vocal spoils. The Beatles were an exception. Still, I can't end this description of their singing talents without mentioning the intonation of their voices. You see, as rock and roll was originally an American art form, many non-American performers—whether British, Swedish, Australian, you name it—tend to acquire a pseudo-American accent when they sing in English. Just listen to Paul's rendition of Carl Perkins' "Sure To Fall (In Love With You)," featured on The Beatles' *Live at the BBC* album. Macca sounds like he just stepped out of hillbilly country: "Lovin' yooo, is the natural *thang* t'dooo…"

John, George, and Ringo, on the other hand, were invariably British in terms of their vocal style, and George sometimes made little attempt to disguise his Liverpudlian roots. In the song "Do You Want To Know A Secret?" he sings, "You'll never know how much I really *cur*." That last word was his way of saying "care." Now *that's* pure Liverpool!

# Songs That Fill the Air

In the annals of 20th-century popular music, John Lennon and Paul McCartney composed an unparalleled body of work, ranging from the early naiveté of "Ask Me Why" to the worldly sophistication of "Girl"; from the catchy melody of "Misery" to the meandering nature of "She Said She Said"; from the slickness of "All My Loving" to the disjointed character of "Happiness Is A Warm Gun"; and from the straightforward subject-matter of "I'll Follow The Sun" to the quasi-religious psychedelia of "Tomorrow Never Knows."

## All Together Now

While John and Paul evolved and progressed as songwriters, they also turned their hands to many different styles of composing. However, when listening to a Beatles recording of a Lennon-McCartney song, have you ever wondered which one of them played a bigger part in writing it? After all, contrary to the public perception, once they tasted success (and often even beforehand) it was only on rare occasions that John and Paul sat down together and composed a number from beginning to end. Usually, one of them would write most—if not all—of a song, and then the other would perhaps contribute the odd musical or lyrical idea.

Sgt. Pepper's
*mustachioed maver-
icks, turning the
musical world on its
head, 1967.*
©Hulton Getty

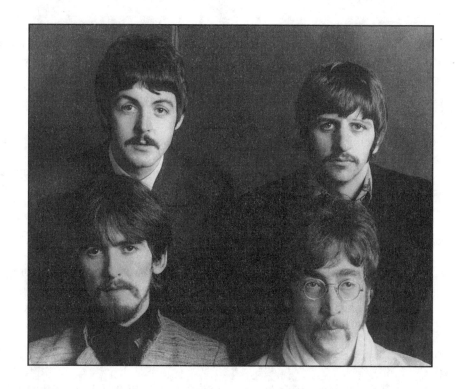

**I Want to
Tell You**

"You hear lots of
McCartney-
influenced songs
on the radio
now. These stories about
boring people doing boring
things; being postmen and
secretaries and writing home.
I'm not interested in writing
third-party songs. I like to
write about me, 'cause I *know*
me."

—John Lennon, *Playboy*
magazine, 1980

The easiest way to tell who wrote a particular song is to
listen to who actually performed the lead vocal. I've already
told you how to identify each of the voices, so this should
make things pretty straightforward. "Ticket To Ride," for
example, is basically John's song. "I Saw Her Standing
There" is Paul's. As for some early numbers on which the
two shared the vocal spoils, such as "Misery," "From Me To
You," "Thank You Girl," "She Loves You," "I'll Get You," "I
Want To Hold Your Hand," and "Baby's In Black," these
were true collaborative efforts. They *did* sit down and write
together. On the other hand, numbers like "We Can Work It
Out," "A Day In The Life," and "I've Got A Feeling," each
consist of incomplete compositions that were slotted
together—John and Paul therefore sing the sections that
they themselves wrote. Fairly logical, eh?

Otherwise, another way of identifying who wrote what is to
listen to the lyrics. This applies specifically to numbers *not*
dealing with the standard "I love you, I've lost you," pop
format. In such cases John would often write in the first person, relating his own experiences—"I'm A Loser," "Help!," "You've Got To Hide Your Love Away," "In My Life,"

"Strawberry Fields Forever," and so on. Paul, on the other hand, seemed to enjoy constructing scenarios about other people, as with songs like "Penny Lane," "Rocky Raccoon," "Ob-La-Di, Ob-La-Da," and "Maxwell's Silver Hammer."

While the different composing styles were evident right from the start, these became more marked as time went on and John and Paul (and George, for that matter) became more accomplished tunesmiths and lyricists. John's songs usually retained a harder edge, and, in the case of numbers such as "I Am The Walrus" and "Happiness Is A Warm Gun," became more unconventional and lyrically complex.

Paul's songs sometimes matched John's for rawness—"Why Don't We Do It In The Road" is a prime example—but he also composed upbeat pop ditties that his erstwhile writing partner grew increasingly disenchanted with. "Ob-La-Di, Ob-La-Da" and "Maxwell's Silver Hammer" may have been catchy enough, but they certainly weren't John's cup of tea.

For his part, some of George's earlier compositions were awkward both melodically and lyrically. John and Paul would sometimes help him out, but he had no real writing partner and no huge cache of songs to fall back on. He basically had to do much of his learning in public, but the opportunity to do so, coupled with the hothouse atmosphere of sharing a creative environment with Lennon and McCartney, eventually paid off. George carved out his own niche with Indian-flavored numbers such as "Love You To" and "Within You Without You," before his Western pop sensibilities blossomed in the form of "While My Guitar Gently Weeps," "I Me Mine," "Something," and "Here Comes The Sun," among other notable "Harrisongs" of the era.

In this climate, even Ringo caught the songwriting bug, penning the solo compositions "Don't Pass Me By" and "Octopus's Garden," which appeared on the *White Album* and *Abbey Road,* respectively. Still, in the *Let It Be* film George can be seen assisting Ringo while he tries to work out the melodic structure of "Octopus's Garden" on a piano. "Don't Pass Me By" was recorded in 1968, yet poor Ringo had referred to it a full five years earlier when he talked about his new song to press and radio interviewers. Obviously, the competition was hot!

> **With a Little Help**
> Until 1967, none of the Beatles albums released by Capitol Records in the U.S. had the same track listings as those released by EMI in the UK. Most of them also had completely different names, except for *A Hard Day's Night, Help!, Rubber Soul,* and *Revolver.* Today, all of the albums that were originally released in Britain are also available in America as CDs on Capitol Records.

## Getting Better All the Time

Overall, you can gauge the progress in The Beatles' songwriting from album to album. At the same time, the band's entire body of compositions can be broken down into several distinct periods. First there is the straightforward, boy-loves-girl, boy-loses-girl era, stretching from 1962 to 1965 and winding down with the *Help!* album. Then *Rubber Soul,* recorded and released later that year, signals a definite transition, with serious, intricately crafted numbers such as "Nowhere Man," "Norwegian Wood (This Bird Has Flown)," "Girl," and "In My Life," (all John's songs), as well as "You Won't See Me" and "I'm Looking Through You" (both Paul's).

*Rubber Soul* almost serves as a bridge between *Help!* and *Revolver*, the remarkable 1966 album that signals the start of The Beatles' experimental/psychedelic songwriting period. This would flourish with the release of *Sgt. Pepper's Lonely Hearts Club Band* in 1967 and basically end with the tracks recorded for the *Magical Mystery Tour* TV movie later that year. Thereafter, through 1968 and 1969, the floodgates really burst open, with songs ranging from commercial pop to hard rock, country & western to the *avant-garde*.

It's incredible to think that the same guys who sang "Love Me Do" and "Baby's In Black" were going into the studio with material such as "Eleanor Rigby," "Tomorrow Never Knows," "A Day In The Life," "I Am The Walrus," and "While My Guitar Gently Weeps" just a few years later. But then again, that's a large part of what made The Beatles great!

# Movin' And Groovin': The Musicianship

Individually, The Beatles weren't the world's greatest musicians, yet the effect of their combined playing, together with their unbridled willingness to keep pushing back the boundaries in this respect, helped make them world-beaters.

The only one of the four to really rank in the upper echelons was Paul McCartney, whose bass playing, although fairly average at the start, became truly innovative by the mid-1960s. A major turning point was the recording of "Paperback Writer" in 1966, on which Paul utilized a Rickenbacker bass instead of his usual Hofner, and played melodic lines that, until then, would have normally been left to a lead guitarist. What's more, just to ensure that everybody shared in the excitement of what he was doing, engineer Geoff Emerick recorded Paul's bass so that it was far louder than any previous pop record. It was almost as if Paul was playing "lead bass," and much the same applied on tracks such as "With A Little Help From My Friends" and "Lucy In The Sky With Diamonds" the following year.

At around the same time, Geoff Emerick was also boosting the sound of Ringo's bass drum to unprecedented heights on songs like "Tomorrow Never Knows" and "Sgt. Pepper's Lonely Hearts Club Band." In a technical sense, Ringo's drumming wasn't in the same league as some of his contemporaries, yet John and Paul always asserted that he was the best drummer in the world for The Beatles. In a 1987 interview, their producer, George Martin, told me why: "Ringo gets a sound out of his drums which is all Ringo," he explained. "Although his time-keeping isn't rigid, clinical,

**I Want to Tell You**

"We were always pushing ahead; 'louder, further, longer, more different.' I always wanted things to be different because we knew that people, generally, always want to move on."

—Paul McCartney, 1987

and of quartz-controlled accuracy, he's got tremendous feel. He always helped us to hit the right tempo for a song, and gave it that support—that rock-solid backbeat—that made the recordings of all The Beatles' songs that much easier."

While acknowledging that Ringo's tempos would vary, George Martin also pointed out that they would "go up and down in the right way to help the song. His use of tom-toms was also very inventive. The 'A Day In The Life' timpani sound on the toms was very characteristic."

## Do You Want to Know a Secret?

John's main instrument was rhythm guitar, Paul's was bass, George's was lead guitar, and Ringo's was drums, but in several instances The Beatles switched roles during recording sessions. Here are just a few:

"Love Me Do" (album version), "PS I Love You": Drums—session man Andy White.

"Ticket To Ride," "Taxman," "Good Morning, Good Morning": Lead guitar—Paul.

"While My Guitar Gently Weeps": Lead guitar—Eric Clapton.

"Back In The USSR": Lead guitar—Paul, George; drums—Paul, John, George (it isn't clear who contributed what to the finished drum track).

"Dear Prudence": Drums—Paul.

"Get Back": Lead guitar—John.

"Helter Skelter": Bass—John.

"Honey Pie," "Golden Slumbers": Bass—George.

"The Ballad Of John And Yoko": Guitars—John; piano, bass, drums—Paul.

So was George Harrison's lead guitar playing; inspired by Nashville session man and producer Chet Atkins, George excelled on the Fab Four's more country-flavored performances for the *Beatles For Sale* album. At times, George's shortcomings could be exposed in a live situation or in a recording setup that didn't permit more than one take. This is evident on several tracks on The Beatles' *Live At The BBC* album. However, when he got it right in the studio, he *really* got it right, and standout examples of this are his solos on songs such as "And Your Bird Can Sing" and "I Feel Fine," as well as the innovative backwards solo that the two Georges (Harrison and Martin, that is) contrived for "Tomorrow Never Knows." (This was achieved by George Martin notating the musical chart for the solo, then writing it out in reverse. George Harrison was recorded playing to this backwards score, and then, when the tape itself was subsequently played back in reverse, the result was a backwards-sounding guitar playing a normal tune.)

The sounds that musicians produce are often an extension of their personalities. This is true with regard to George, whose careful, precise guitar playing doesn't have the loose feel associated with, say, an Eric Clapton or a Jimi Hendrix. Likewise, and similar to his vocal delivery, John Lennon's guitar style was altogether more raw than George's. His usual role was to play rhythm and this he did quite adequately. One of his more notable performances was his distinguished, super-fast strumming on "All My Loving." You have to remember that, despite their shortcomings, The Beatles each contributed unique sounds that have served to influence and inspire.

And just in case you want to compare the guitar styles of Messrs. Lennon, McCartney, and Harrison, listen to the instrumental break in "The End" on *Abbey Road*. Along with featuring the only drum solo of Ringo's Beatle career, Paul, George, and John (in that order) can be heard trading guitar solos several times in quick succession. A fitting end to a fantastic career!

## Recordings and Technology

As The Beatles took giant strides in their songwriting, they also became more adept as studio musicians, capitalizing on the talents of their producer, George Martin, and engineers such as Norman Smith and Geoff Emerick, in order to realize their artistic visions. What's more, together with the technical staff at EMI Studios in North London, they conspired to break the rules and push back the boundaries of recording technology.

**I Want to Tell You**

"We didn't set out to specifically give an album a different sound from the last one, but there was this eternal curiosity that the boys had, to try something new. They were growing up, and they were like plants in a hot-house... They were thirsty for knowledge, curious to find out what else they could have, and with their fame came the opportunity to experiment."

—George Martin (Beatles producer), 1987

These days, most major artists only release an album every few years, and when they do, the progression in the sound and the material is often marginal. In The Beatles' case, however, the differences were enormous, and so was the amount of product: two albums each in 1963, 1964, and 1965, and one each in 1966, 1967, 1968, 1969, and 1970. This, however, does not include the *Long Tall Sally* EP (elongated play record) in 1964 that contained four new tracks; the 1967 *Magical Mystery Tour* EP that featured six new tracks; or the *Yellow Submarine* album in 1969 that included four new songs.

Then there were the UK singles themselves—22 of them from 1962 to 1970, featuring 44 songs, 25 of which were never included on albums at that time. (In America, Capitol released many more singles, but The Beatles had little say in the matter.) These included such gems as "She Loves You," "I Want To Hold Your Hand," "I Feel Fine," "We Can Work It Out," "Penny Lane," "Lady Madonna," "Hey Jude"... the list goes on and on. So does the one comprising the incredible album tracks that were not even offered up as singles in the UK. Would you believe "I Saw Her Standing There,"

"All My Loving," "Eight Days A Week," "Yesterday," "Nowhere Man," "Back In The USSR," and "The Long And Winding Road," for example? All could have very easily topped the British charts, giving you just some idea as to how prolific and steeped in quality The Beatles were.

Equally remarkable was the difference in sound from album to album. Easily the most old-fashioned by today's standards was the first one, *Please Please Me*, released in March of 1963, and full of heavy echo and "sha-la-la"-style backing vocals. Yet, just eight months later, there was *With The Beatles*, a record that sounds just as fresh and full of life today as it did on the day of its release. Of course, the band had producer George Martin and engineer Norman Smith largely to thank for this, but the power of their performances and their own determination to improve also moved things forward.

Likewise, *A Hard Day's Night, Beatles For Sale, Help!*, and *Rubber Soul* each had their own distinctive sounds and advancements—not least the inclusion of a string quartet on "Yesterday," and George playing an Indian sitar on "Norwegian Wood (This Bird Has Flown)." At the time these were ground-breaking innovations for a rock and roll band.

The next *really* major breakthrough came with *Revolver*, and, most specifically, tracks such as "Tomorrow Never Knows," with its multi-recorded effects, distorted guitars, and John Lennon's voice being fed through the revolving speaker inside a Hammond organ!

"Once you started something, for a while it almost became the fashion," The Beatles' record producer, George Martin, recalled in my 1987 interview with him. "For example, once I'd turned John's voice around on 'Rain,' played his voice backwards to him, and put it on the track, it was, 'Great! Let's try everything backwards!' So, George started doing backwards guitar solos, and there was backwards cymbal on 'Strawberry Fields,' until that was exhausted and it was on to the next gimmick. It was a healthy curiosity to find new sounds and new ways of expressing themselves."

"Tomorrow Never Knows" was, in fact, the first Beatles track on which 20-year-old Geoff Emerick served as the recording engineer. For his work on their next album—the landmark *Sgt. Pepper's Lonely Hearts Club Band*—he would receive a Grammy Award. A large part of what turned the musical world on its head about *Sgt. Pepper*, aside from the breathtaking vision of songs such as "A Day In The Life," was the way it was assembled as a

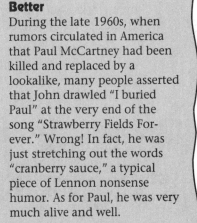

**I Should Have Known Better**

During the late 1960s, when rumors circulated in America that Paul McCartney had been killed and replaced by a lookalike, many people asserted that John drawled "I buried Paul" at the very end of the song "Strawberry Fields Forever." Wrong! In fact, he was just stretching out the words "cranberry sauce," a typical piece of Lennon nonsense humor. As for Paul, he was very much alive and well.

concept instead of as a random collection of individual tracks. In this case, the concept was a supposed stage show, and to this end there were numerous sound effects—audience laughter and applause, even a cock crowing, courtesy of the EMI Studios effects library—as well as the device of having some songs fade directly (or "segue") into one another.

**Say the Word**
The **mellotron**
was a forerunner
of the synthesizer;
a keyboard with
tapes inside that can
imitate the sounds of other
instruments. **Double tracking** is
the process of recording the
same voice or instrument twice
onto the same track in order to
reinforce the sound, and **ADT**
(artificial double tracking) is a
process whereby the doubling of
a sound is achieved by electronic means. **Flanging** is a
variation of ADT, whereby the
tape speed is constantly altered
in order to produce a phasing
sound.

Just a few years before, all that The Beatles needed to make
a record was bass, drums, two guitars and, on occasion, a
keyboard. Now here they were, enlisting the services of
a 40-piece orchestra while utilizing instruments such as a
*mellotron*. Then there were the innovative techniques that
the EMI technical staff came up with in order to meet their
recording demands, including *ADT, flanging*, and the
linking of tape machines to enable more sounds to be
committed to tape. Never had so much care been taken
over the recording and mixing of an album, or so much
time (just under five months).

After *Sgt. Pepper*, The Beatles continued to toy with different sounds and techniques. Then, as a reaction to the
seemingly endless recording sessions for the *White Album*,
they decided to revert to the methods of the good old
days, when they had completed all of the tracks for *Please
Please Me* in about 17 hours. All of the songs were to be
recorded live in the studio, with no additional overdubbed
effects. However, group squabbles ensured that the new
project lasted months rather than mere hours, while the
shoddy state of the recorded material necessitated editing
and overdubbing, as well as changing the name of the album (and film) from the hopeful
*Get Back* to the more philosophical *Let It Be*.

And in the end... there was *Abbey Road*, a polished production and one of The Beatles'
finest works. Still, producer George Martin did have to strike a compromise between the
artistic desires of Lennon and McCartney.

"One side of the album [was] very much the way John wanted things—'Let it all hang
out, let's rock a little,'" Martin explained in 1987, "and the other was what Paul had
accepted from me; to try to think in symphonic terms, and think in terms of having a
first and second subject, put them in different keys, bring back themes and even have
some contrapuntal [intricate vocal harmony] work. Paul dug
that, and that's why the second side sounds as it does."

**Say the Word**
The **White Album**
is the nickname
of the 1968 two-
record set entitled
*The Beatles*. Pack-
aged in a plain white cover,
it's easier to refer to this than
to confuse the album with the
group's name.

John, however, wasn't quite so enthused. "*Abbey Road* was
really unfinished songs all stuck together," he told *Playboy*
magazine in 1980. "Everybody praises the album so much,
but none of the songs had anything to do with each other,
no thread at all."

Oh well, you can't please everyone!

# The Least You Need to Know

➤ The Beatles are as easy to identify when they are singing as when they are talking.

➤ You can often tell whether John or Paul wrote a song by identifying the singer or listening to the lyrics.

➤ The Beatles were innovators rather than virtuoso musicians.

➤ The Beatles were aided by their producer and engineers in making rapid advancements in the recording studio.

➤ As both songwriters and recording artists, The Beatles made a marked—and unrivaled—progression from album to album.

# All These Friends and Lovers

While there are obviously four central characters in the story of The Beatles, they are easily outnumbered by the cast of supporting players. So outnumbered, in fact, that it would be almost impossible—and just plain boring—to list them all here.

Therefore, in this chapter I plan to start off by telling you how some of the band members' friends actually played a role in the shaping of their career. Many of these people can only be credited with cameo appearances; others remained on the Fab Four scene a little longer, and a few lasted through the halcyon years and beyond.

Next, I'll explain the functions of two of The Beatles' closest and most faithful assistants: Mal Evans and Neil Aspinall. Of course, countless other helpers served the group in a variety of ways: press officers such as Derek Taylor, Tony Barrow, and Brian Sommerville; their driver, Alf Bicknell; and associates of manager Brian Epstein, such as Peter Brown and Alistair Taylor. Yet, Mal and Neil were the two men who through the years were seemingly always by their side, both on the road and in the studio.

Finally, this chapter will wind down with brief summaries of how John, Paul, George, and Ringo met their various wives, and what has become of them and the children that these unions produced.

# Buddies, Friends, and Pals

None of the young Beatles were classmates or childhood chums. Paul and George certainly knew each other from an early age and they both attended the Liverpool Institute during their teens. A year apart, they eventually struck up a friendship of sorts by way of their mutual love of rock and roll. As for the rest of the group, they all eventually became firm friends, but only as a *result* of having formed a musical alliance, rather than the other way around.

During the first explosion of rock music in the mid-1950s, thousands of British teenagers decided to form their own bands, and it was easy to collaborate with close friends or casual acquaintances. Ringo, for example (then still going by his real name of Richard—or "Ritchie"—Starkey), got together with a fellow engineering apprentice named Eddie Miles and assembled the Eddie Clayton Skiffle Group.

Sixteen-year-old John Lennon, on the other hand, was truly the founder of the musical unit that would become known as The Beatles. The first person he turned to in his new venture was his best buddy at Quarry Bank High School, Pete Shotton.

In 1957, Lennon and Shotton were, in fact, already notorious at school as two of its most disruptive and unruly students. (Don't take the word "students" too literally here—neither of them did that much studying.) Other mates would join The Quarry Men (so named because of a line in the school song, "Quarry Men, old before our birth..."), among them Bill Smith, Rod Davis, Colin Hanton, Eric Griffiths, Len Garry, Nigel Whalley, and John "Duff" Lowe. Yet, although Pete would be among the first to leave, he would also be one of the very few to remain in John's circle of friends.

George Harrison knew the meaning of loyalty—throughout the years he would stay in touch with boyhood acquaintances such as Arthur Kelly and Tony Bramwell—and in 1965 he and John set Pete Shotton up in a supermarket business. Later on, Pete would also be employed within The Beatles' Apple empire and as John's personal assistant. For his part, Tony Bramwell worked for Brian Epstein before being appointed Apple's head of production.

Meanwhile, filling Pete's shoes as John's fellow crony when he went to art college was a classmate named Jeff Mohammed. Yet, it was with another college student that John would form one of his very closest friendships: Stuart Sutcliffe. An artist of prodigious talent, Stu would become John's trusted confidant and, at John's insistence (and in spite of his total lack of musical ability), even a member of

**Say the Word**
**Skiffle** was a simply structured form of music that blended jazz, folk, and blues. It was an overnight sensation with British teenagers in 1956 and 1957, but quickly faded in the shadow of rock and roll.

the fledgling Beatles. Unfortunately, what looked like being a lifelong friendship was cut short by Sutcliffe's premature death from a brain hemorrhage.

Stu's girlfriend, photographer Astrid Kircherr, has remained in touch with the group over the years, as has another friend from their Hamburg days, artist Klaus Voormann. In fact, Voormann has put his talents to good use for The Beatles, coming up with the imaginative sleeve designs for their 1966 *Revolver* album and the recent *Anthology* box-set. Meanwhile, as a bass guitarist, the groups he played for in the 1960s and '70s included John and Yoko's Plastic Ono Band and Manfred Mann.

For all that, perhaps the person who could claim to have made one of *the* most significant contributions to the whole Beatles story was yet another of the part-time Quarry Men. His name was Ivan Vaughan. A pal of Paul McCartney as well as John Lennon, Ivan was the one who took Paul to see John's group playing at a church fete in Liverpool on June 6, 1957. That was the day when Lennon and McCartney first met. Within a couple of weeks they had joined forces, and the rest of the story…well, I'll be telling you about that a little later on.

**I Want to Tell You**

"We took it out on people like Neil, Derek [Taylor], and Mal, and that's why, underneath their facade, they resent us…. It was hard work and somebody had to take it…. You have to be a bastard to make it and that's a fact, and The Beatles are the biggest bastards on earth."

—John Lennon, *Rolling Stone* magazine, 1970

# Helping Out—Mal and Neil

If you watch The Beatles' first film, *A Hard Day's Night*, you'll see John, Paul, George, and Ringo being con-stantly ordered about by their on-screen "road man-ager," Norm (played by Norman Rossington). Partly aided by his dimwitted but likable sidekick, Shake (John Junkin), Norm struts about like a principal badgering a bunch of naughty schoolboys. Back in the real world, there was no way The Beatles would have put up with this kind of nonsense, yet the roles of Norm and Shake were undeniably based on a pair of individuals who were far more competent in real-life: Malcolm (Mal) Evans and Neil Aspinall.

Big Mal Evans was working as a bouncer at Liverpool's Cavern Club when he first encountered the band. On August 11, 1963, he quit his day job as a post-office engineer to become their assistant, and, during the next three years, he could be seen setting up their amplifiers and instruments on concert stages all over the world. At the same time, Mal also doubled as The

**I Should Have Known Better**

In the film *Let It Be*, Mal Evans can be seen banging a hammer onto an anvil when The Beatles rehearse the song "Maxwell's Silver Hammer." As a result, it's been widely assumed that Mal also played the hammer and anvil when the track was properly recorded for the subsequent *Abbey Road* album. However, studio session sheets confirm that it was, in fact, Ringo.

Beatles' personal bodyguard, and he often accompanied one or more of them when they went on private vacations. (As long as they went to the same place together. It could have proved a little tricky otherwise.)

In the studio, Mal was called upon not only to help set up the equipment (as is evident in the *Let It Be* documentary), but also make cups of tea and even help out on some of the recordings. What's more, he made cameo appearances in the movies *Help!* (in which he portrays a long-distance swimmer who has trouble finding his way) and *Magical Mystery Tour*, as well as in the *Strawberry Fields Forever* promo film.

## Do You Want to Know a Secret?

Although he was only a general assistant, Mal Evans probably appeared on more Beatles records than anyone outside of the Fab Four themselves. Handclaps, tambourine shakes, various background noises—all were part of Big Mal's repertoire. He was credited with playing Hammond Organ on the *Rubber Soul* album track, "You Won't See Me"; contributed some harmonica to *Sgt. Pepper*'s "Being For The Benefit Of Mr. Kite"; played a little piano for that album's closer, "A Day In The Life"; (on which he can also be heard counting the bars); and blew into a trumpet on the *White Album's* "Helter Skelter." In 1973, Mal co-wrote "You And Me (Babe)" with George Harrison, for the album *Ringo*.

In 1968, Mal was appointed assistant general manager of The Beatles' company, Apple, and, after their split, he both managed and produced the group Badfinger. On January 5, 1976, Los Angeles police were called to Mal's home when, due to mounting problems in his personal life, he was threatening suicide. In his confusion, Mal allegedly turned a gun on the six officers, and the result was that they shot him dead. Mal Evans was just a few months short of his fortieth birthday.

When Mal took over the chore of lugging The Beatles' equipment from one venue to the next, he was also giving a well-earned break to Neil Aspinall. Neil had been doing this job in the less-than-savory atmosphere of Liverpool's dingier clubs. There, local thugs would keep a beady eye on him as he walked to and from the van that he also drove the group around in.

Having attended the Liverpool Institute with Paul and George, Neil was also a close friend of The Beatles' drummer, Pete Best. When Pete was fired in August of 1962, Neil was so outraged that he considered turning his back on the band, which had, at long last, just signed a recording contract. In the end, however, he made what turned out to be a profitable decision. He quit his accountancy studies and went to work for The Beatles full-time as their chief road manager. In turn, his loyalty and intellect were rewarded in 1968 when he was appointed managing director of their Apple Corps company. It's a position Neil (or "Nell" as John liked to call him) holds to this day.

# Fab Wives

Four Beatles, seven wives. That's the tally; two each, save for Paul, who took the longest to make up his mind before he finally settled down. Still, when he did, he evidently made the right decision.

The first—and youngest—Beatle groom was John Winston Lennon. He married Cynthia Powell on August 23, 1962, when he was still 21 and she was 22. The two had met just a little under five years earlier at Liverpool College of Art, and it really had been a case of opposites attracting. For one thing, Cyn was a diligent student. She spoke nicely, dressed conservatively, and was seemingly no match for loudmouthed Lennon, with his greasy, Elvis-style hairdo, devil-may-care attitude, and bunch of equally rowdy friends. At first, sending up her air of quiet civility, John referred to Cynthia as "the posh Miss Powell," but soon they hit it off and their friendship turned into love.

> **With a Little Help**
> If you want to gain good insight into what it was like being married to a member of the Fab Four at the height of Beatlemania, read the paperback memoir *A Twist of Lennon* by John's ex-wife, Cynthia. In June 1978, John tried unsuccessfully to prevent a British newspaper, the *News of the World*, from publishing some extracts.

John relied on Cyn's emotional strength and honesty, yet it's arguable whether they would have ever married had she not become pregnant. Basically, it was a sign of the times, and of John's honorable instincts, that he viewed marriage as the only option in such circumstances. At the subsequent civil ceremony, Paul and George were the only friends in attendance. That night, the band fulfilled a concert booking in nearby Chester.

Cynthia set the tone for the "first generation" of Beatle wives, in that she stayed largely out of the spotlight. In fact, at first there was a concerted effort to keep the marriage a secret. After all, in those pre-liberation days there was a fear that, if John wasn't "free and single," it might hurt his reputation with the female fans! That soon proved to be a joke, as word leaked out and the press spread the news. The adoring girls didn't seem to care either way.

Stability was, seemingly, the main feature of the Lennon marriage, but in many ways John came to realize that he was looking for more; he wanted someone less conventional and more in tune with his wayward tastes and ideas. Enter Yoko Ono, the Japanese avant-garde artist who John first met in December of 1966, when he visited an exhibition of her work in London. He didn't initially view Yoko as the realization of his dreams, but when he did—some 18 months later—the resultant explosion blew away the union with Cynthia and, eventually, put an immense strain on The Beatles. Anyway, let's not get into *that* can of worms right now...at least not until Chapters 23 and 24.

Let's just say that John and Yoko's love for one another was all-consuming and made them inseparable. He grew his hair long to resemble hers, and, soon after their wedding on March 20, 1969 (it was Yoko's third), even changed his middle name from Winston to

### I Should Have Known Better

After having his name changed in a ceremony on the roof of The Beatles' Apple building on April 22, 1969, John always referred to himself as John Ono Lennon. The truth, however, is that he should have been calling himself John Winston Ono Lennon, as in Britain there is no legal means of fully revoking a middle name that is given to you at birth.

Ono. Except for a 15-month "trial separation" that, according to John, "didn't work out" during the mid-1970s, the union would last until John's tragic death in December 1980.

During their last years together Yoko, nearly seven years John's senior, took care of all of the couple's financial dealings, while he stayed at home to tend to their baby, Sean. Born into a wealthy banking family, Yoko's background has served her well since her husband's death, as she has kept a tight rein on the multi-million dollar Lennon estate. For her part, Cynthia has since been twice married and divorced.

Ringo's first wife, Maureen Cox, was only 18 when she married The Beatles' 24-year-old drummer on February 11, 1965. Previously, she had been among the locals who watched the group performing at Liverpool's Cavern Club, and she and Ringo started dating in 1962. While the Fab Four toured the world, "Mo" stayed in Liverpool and worked as a hairdresser. Then, after their marriage, she and Ringo moved to a house situated close to John and Cynthia, in Weybridge, Surrey.

Maureen answered her husband's fan mail and attended Beatle concerts whenever possible. She's the one Paul is talking to when he says, "Thanks, Mo," at the end of "Get Back" on the *Let It Be* album. Nevertheless, by 1973 the marriage was faltering, and Ringo spent a lot of time in Los Angeles while Maureen stayed at home in England with their three children. The couple divorced in 1975, but they remained friends up until her death from cancer on December 30, 1994.

During the interim, Ringo had taken glamorous actress Barbara Bach as his second wife. Bach's biggest claim to fame was her starring role opposite Roger Moore in the 1977 James Bond movie, *The Spy Who Loved Me*. Three years later, she met Ringo on the set of the film, *Caveman*. Having survived a really bad car crash without injury in London on May 19, 1980, Ringo and Barbara evidently felt that they were destined to be together. They were married on April 27 of the following year, and, despite some difficult times (including Ringo's much publicized—and winning—battle with alcoholism), they have remained together ever since.

### I Want to Tell You

"I don't think I could have named five of [The Beatles'] songs a year ago. I was never really into music, though I am now...up to my ears!"

—Barbara Bach, interviewed by *Playboy* magazine, 1980

Present at Ringo and Barbara's London wedding in 1981 were the two other surviving Beatles and their wives. Like Ringo, George was with his second wife, his first marriage having been to Patricia Ann Boyd, a London model who had a bit-part in the film *A Hard Day's Night*. Beatlemania was at its height, yet in the beginning Pattie actually had the cheek to reject George's advances; she was engaged to somebody else, but the youngest Beatle was nothing if not determined.

*July 29, 1965: Fab couples—Cynthia and John Lennon, alongside Ringo and a pregnant Maureen, arriving for the royal charity world premiere of The Beatles' film, Help!, at the London Pavilion cinema in Piccadilly Circus.* ©Hulton Getty

Both George and John, you see, shared a passion for the actress Brigitte Bardot, and Cynthia had even dyed her dark hair blonde to please goggle-eyed Lennon. Well, when George caught a glimpse of Pattie he was convinced that she actually bore a resemblance to the French sex kitten. Enough said! On January 21, 1966, the two of them "tied the knot," with Paul and manager Brian Epstein sharing best-man honors while John and Ringo were away in Trinidad.

Pattie became just as involved as George in the study of Indian culture—in fact, it was she who first introduced her husband to the Transcendental Meditation teachings of the Maharishi Mahesh Yogi. Still, while they seemed perfectly compatible as the archetypal swinging-yet-mystical '60s couple, Pattie began to feel alienated when George became more and more obsessed with the pursuit of "spiritual enlightenment." Eventually she embarked on an affair with his friend, guitarist Eric Clapton, and in 1974 George and Pattie split up. Five years later she and Clapton began a short-lived marriage, yet any bitterness on George's part was also short-lived. At the wedding party, he, Paul, and Ringo reunited for an impromptu jam session.

### Do You Want to Know a Secret?

One of Eric Clapton's biggest hit songs, the 1970 Derek and the Dominoes track, "Layla," was actually written as a direct plea to Pattie Harrison. In the lyrics, Eric tells the woman who has "got me on my knees," about how he tried to "console" her when her "old man" had let her down, and then unwittingly fell in love. Now he's desperate! Pattie eventually responded to Eric's charms by walking out on her marriage, but this then prompted George to launch an attack on his out-of-favor buddies in the form of the Everly Brothers song, "Bye Bye Love," on his 1974 album Dark Horse. Oh well, at least it made for some decent music!

In the meantime, George had hooked up with Olivia Trinidad Arias, a secretary for his Dark Horse record label in Los Angeles. The two of them first met in 1974, and shortly afterwards Olivia moved to England and into the Harrison residence at Henley-on-Thames. The couple's plans to marry in May 1978 were cancelled due to the death of George's father, and so the wedding was rescheduled for September 2, a month after the birth of their son, Dhani.

In the marital sweepstakes, that's three Fabs down and one to go: Paul, the longest-lasting bachelor Beatle, and, to date, also the longest-married ex-Beatle. Throughout much of the 1960s his most serious relationship was with British actress Jane Asher, leading to constant rumors that they were about to get married or had already done so. The speculation appeared to be at an end when they became engaged on Christmas Day of 1967, but then, just seven months later, Jane announced on TV that their relationship was over. This paved the way for Linda Louise Eastman.

Born into a wealthy Jewish family in Scarsdale, New York, Linda had already been married and had a child by the time she first came face-to-face with Paul. That was in her capacity as a rock photographer—The Beatles, The Rolling Stones, Traffic, Jimi Hendrix, and Jim Morrison were just some of the famous names that Linda would eventually be able to count among her subjects. Nevertheless, on May 15, 1967 it was a social encounter at London's Bag O'Nails nightclub that initially stirred up interest between her and Paul, and four nights later they met again at the launch party for the *Sgt. Pepper* album. Still, this didn't dissuade him from getting engaged to Jane Asher, so in May of 1968 Linda tried again.

At a New York press conference held by John and Paul to announce the setting up of their Apple business venture, Linda slipped the baby-faced Beatle her phone number. This time he took the bait, and in October of 1968, with Jane Asher firmly off the scene, Linda moved permanently to England. She and Paul were married on March 12, 1969, with Paul's brother Mike as best man. None of the other Beatles attended.

**I Want to Tell You**

"It's all over now. It's the end in a way, isn't it?"

—Fifteen-year-old Londoner Diane Robbins on the day Paul was married.

Paul and Linda have stuck together through thick and thin. Some of the thinnest moments have included drug busts, and press and public criticism for her inclusion in Paul's musical ventures, despite her obvious "lack of experience." On the up side, Linda continues to take great photos—she took the official pics when Paul, George, and Ringo reunited for the *Beatles Anthology* project—and she and "Macca" are also among Britain's leading spokespeople when it comes to preserving the environment and eating vegetarian food. Indeed, she has published two best-selling vegetarian cookbooks, and Findus launched a line of frozen veggie food with her face on the packet.

Recently, Linda has had to battle breast cancer, an illness that took the life of Paul's mother when he was in his early teens. Linda was not even able to stand by her husband's side when, on March 11, 1997, he went to Buckingham Palace to receive his Knighthood from the Queen. Thankfully, at the time of this writing, her cancer appears to be in remission.

# Gear Kids

Well, being that all four Beatles can never get back together, how about forming a group consisting of some of their kids? Say, John's oldest son Julian on rhythm guitar, Paul's son James on bass, George's son Dhani on lead guitar, and Ringo's oldest son Zak on drums. Now, doesn't that sound like a good idea? I hope not, and I'm sure it doesn't to the parents concerned (or concerned parents). But believe me, it has been suggested...by certain hacks in the media, not by The Beatles themselves.

John, Paul, George, and Ringo have all kept their children from the full glare of the publicity spotlight. The first to be born, on April 8, 1963, was Julian (named in honor of John's late mother, Julia). Aside from some official family photographs, his parents made every effort to keep Julian away from the press, yet during his early years he actually had a hard time gaining the attention of John himself. Too busy recording and touring with The Beatles to be a constant presence in his son's life, John only wanted to deal with the youngster on his own terms when he did return home. Later on, after his parents' divorce, Julian lived with Cynthia and visited John during school holiday periods, although this became a little more difficult when John and Yoko moved to America in 1971.

**With a Little Help**

If you want to compare how similar Julian Lennon can sound to his father when singing, check out the former's 1984 debut album, *Valotte*. Cannily produced to ensure Lennonish vocal mannerisms, it sold fairly well and even spawned a couple of hit singles. The novelty soon wore off, however, and in May 1986 Julian's first UK concert tour had to be canceled due to poor ticket sales.

Towards the end of that decade, however, John and Julian were growing increasingly close, which made it even more difficult for the son when the elder Lennon was gunned down in December 1980. Julian subsequently enjoyed short-lived chart success as a musician in his own right, but it appears that the interest that he initially sparked was due more to his name than anything else. He now lives in Los Angeles.

Meanwhile, over on the East Coast, there is another junior Lennon attempting to step out of his father's musical shadow. This is Sean, who was born on October 9, 1975, John's 35th birthday. Sean is the Irish version of the name John (Julian's first name is also John), and the first five years of the infant's life coincided with his father's temporary retirement.

Having been absent for much of Julian's childhood, and having tried so hard with Yoko to actually have a child, John was determined to make a better effort the second time around. In fact, this effort extended to not only being at home more, but actually being ever-present. Yoko went out and took care of business while the former chauvinist Beatle assumed the role of househusband, cooking the food and taking care of the baby.

From Sean's perspective, John's death not only deprived him of a doting father, but it also served to bring him to the public's attention on a scale unmatched by any of the other Beatle kids. (Sporting round glasses and center-parted hair, he has recently been performing in a band with Yoko.) Sure, Zak Starkey is now a successful professional drummer in his own right (he has toured with his father and with The Who), James McCartney played guitar on his dad's 1997 *Flaming Pie* album, and Paul's daughter Stella is making a name for herself as a fashion designer. But, on the whole, most of the Fab Four's offspring could walk down any street largely unnoticed.

Now, reputable journalist that I am, I'm not about to disrupt the kids' privacy by giving you a full physical description of each and every one of them. What I will do, however, is provide you with a comprehensive list of names and birth dates. (This does not include stepchildren or any "unofficial" claimants to The Beatles' dynasty.)

## Beatle Parents and Kids

| The Parents | The Kid | Birth Date |
|---|---|---|
| John and Cynthia | John Charles Julian | 4-8-63 |
| John and Yoko | Sean Taro Ono | 10-9-75 |
| Paul and Linda | Mary | 8-28-69 |
| | Stella Nina | 9-13-71 |
| | James Louis | 9-12-77 |
| George and Olivia | Dhani | 8-1-78 |
| Ringo and Maureen | Zak | 9-13-65 |
| | Jason | 8-19-67 |
| | Lee Parkin | 11-11-70 |

As you can see, coincidence was certainly on the menu when Sean Lennon was born on John's birthday, just as it was when Stella McCartney came into the world precisely six years after the grand entrance of Zak Starkey. James was just a day too early to turn Zak and Stella's shared anniversary into a triple-play, yet he did ensure the continuance of a particular family tradition. James, you see, was the name of Paul's father, who died on March 18, 1976, and it is also the first name of...yes, that's right, Paul himself. Not that this has ever been a really big secret; in 1973, he made a song-and-dance TV special entitled *James Paul McCartney*.

# The Least You Need to Know

➤ The Fab Four could always count on two particularly loyal helpers, Mal Evans and Neil Aspinall.

➤ The Beatle wives: John's first wife was Cynthia Powell, his second Yoko Ono; George's first wife was Pattie Boyd, his second (and current) Olivia Arias; Ringo's first wife was Maureen, his second (and current) Barbara Bach; and Paul's sole marriage has been to Linda Eastman.

➤ Some Beatle kids are following in their fathers' musical footsteps.

# Part 2
# Crying, Waiting, Hoping— Years of Struggle

*And in the beginning… Yep, there were four young guys, born into a depressed city, but not altogether miserable surroundings. The Beatles had close family relatives who cared, some who didn't, and the limited prospects of many war babies growing up in the north of England during the 1940s and early '50s—a basic education and, hopefully, a steady job. That is, unless they had the talent to "make something of themselves," or perhaps even the luck to…no, Liverpudlians didn't take too much stock in luck back in those days.*

*Well, in the story that shall now unfold before your very eyes, talent certainly played a part. First, however, we must look at the other factors that grabbed the spotlight before talent took center-stage: the social and cultural influences, the barely adequate early musical excursions, the disappointments, the disasters, and the people who never quite made it. The Beatles had to go through all of these phases before they began to taste the fruits of their labors.*

*And now, I'm glad to say, you're going to relive those escapades with them!*

# Chapter 6

# The Baby Beatles

---

## In This Chapter

➤ The Beatles' home city, Liverpool

➤ What it was like for The Beatles growing up

➤ The truth about The Beatles' respective backgrounds

➤ The Fab Four's relatives

---

Outside of India and its caste system, Britain is one of the most class-conscious societies in the world. The majority of the population consists of the working and lower-middle-classes, with the remainder comprising the affluent upper-middle-class (millionaire businessmen, for instance), privileged upper-class (such as the late Princess of Wales when she was Lady Diana Spencer), and, of course, the aristocracy.

Now, a working-class Brit can certainly climb up the ladder, just as an upper-class one can slide down the slippery slope. Yet, among many citizens, there is an underlying belief that, while you can take the person out of the social class, you can't take the social class out of the person. I'm not about to discuss the rights and wrongs of that philosophy, but it helped shape the social attitudes of John, Paul, George, and Ringo. However much success changed their lifestyle, it didn't really alter their take on the world around them, and in 1970 John even wrote and recorded a song in which he referred to himself as a "Working Class Hero." While that may have reflected how he felt, his self-appraisal—as you are about to discover—was a little wide of the mark.

# There's a Place (Up and to the Left a Bit): Liverpool

Located in the northwest corner of England, Liverpool is positioned above Wales and across the sea from Ireland. Consequently, there's plenty of Welsh and Irish blood to be found in Liverpudlians, as well as some sharp tongues and a sardonic sense of humor.

Among the city's major claims to fame during the 19th century were the world's first passenger railway, in 1830, and the world's first ocean liners, which were launched by the Cunard Steamship Company at the start of the following decade. (In time, the local sailors who traveled back and forth between Liverpool and the United States would become known as "Cunard Yanks.") Lancashire, the county in which Liverpool is situated, was then a center of the thriving cotton industry, and so the ships served everybody's purposes by bringing in the cotton for the mills.

For the next 100 years, as one of the world's major seaports, Liverpool thrived with activity, yet to Londoners and others living close to Britain's seat of Government it was still just "up north"; one of the cities—along with places such as Newcastle and Manchester—in which many of the country's biggest wheels of industry turned, yet where few southerners would care to visit. After all, what was the point? There were plenty of jobs down in London, and that's where all national decisions were made.

Liverpool, like many British cities, suffered the effects of heavy German bombing during the Second World War, and that period also coincided with the decline of the cotton industry. Therefore, by the time John, Paul, George, and Ringo had joined the local scene, large sections of it were already run down.

In the city center, imposing but grimy-looking 19th-century public buildings reflected Liverpool's declining fortunes. Nearby, the endless rows of *terraced* public housing symbolized the cramped living conditions that were afforded the industrial classes. At the front, the main door opened directly onto the sidewalk; at the back, a tiny yard accommodated an outside toilet.

**Say the Word**

**Terraced** homes in Britain are the rows of identical houses that are attached to one another like a chain. Two adjoining houses are known as **semi-detached**, while stand-alone houses are **detached**.

To people living "down south," Liverpool was the place that spawned many of the nation's best-loved comedians, yet for Liverpudlians the early post-war years were not always a laughing matter. A focal point where they would gather was the Pier Head. There, lining up at the central bus terminal, they could see ships sailing across to Ireland and America, and a few of them would dream—dream about someday leaving their home city and making a name for themselves out there in the big, wide world. A fleeting thought, perhaps, but some sort of ambition nonetheless.

# Those Were the Days: The Historical Perspective

Though no one could have known it at the time—and few would have believed it—the end of World War II signaled the start of the longest period of peace Western Europe has known in centuries. For once this meant that young men wouldn't grow up just to die at a front where their ruling elders sent them. In the meantime, however, there was the Cold War to contend with, and fear of the hydrogen bomb, which was one thousand times more powerful than the one dropped on Hiroshima.

Still, while the Cold War raged on throughout the 1950s, there was also a general rise in the standard of living. This was more true for America than Britain, and still more true for Britain's southern and rural areas than its industrial north. There were more cars on the road and more TV sets in the homes, while advances in medical science—such as the development of a polio vaccine—meant that people in the West now had the chance to lead healthier lives. As an added bonus, lucky Brits also benefited from the free medicine, attention, and facilities provided by the new state-run National Health Service.

This was all good news, yet for Western teenagers there could be no denying that the early 1950s were also pretty boring. I mean, think about it: All that the "hit parade" had to offer were antiseptic records like "How Much Is That Doggie in the Window?" And as for sex—well, the basic message from parents, TV, and the movies seemed to be that it didn't even exist! Could every birth be the result of an "immaculate conception"? Yes, during the 1950s, "repression" was a key word, but things were about to change. Dr. Alfred Kinsey's reports on sexual behavior, and the surgical transformation of Denmark's George Jorgenson into Christine Jorgenson, were bringing sex out into the open. And so, for that matter, was a kid with sideburns from Memphis, Tennessee. His name, of course, was Elvis Aaron (Aron on the birth certificate), and I'll be telling you more about him in the next chapter.

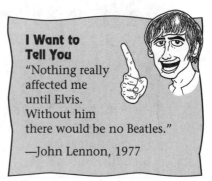

**I Want to Tell You**

"Nothing really affected me until Elvis. Without him there would be no Beatles."

—John Lennon, 1977

# Cry Baby Cry?—Childhood Days

Like most cities, Liverpool has its good areas and its tough areas, its blue-collar districts and its white-collar neighborhoods. All of The Beatles were born into working-class surroundings during the years that German bombs were raining down on the city, yet in three of the four cases—and one in particular—their living conditions definitely improved as time went on.

The one whose lot in early life remained the same was Ringo. The area where he was brought up, the Dingle, was by far the worst of any of the neighborhoods in which The Beatles were raised, and also among the roughest in Liverpool. Situated in the center, not far from the docks, the Dingle was drab compared to the newer suburbs where his future colleagues grew up.

The house in Madryn Street where Richard Starkey spent about the first five years of his life was a terraced three-up, three down (rooms, that is). However, the rent was too much for his single mother, and so they then moved around the corner to a two-up, two-down in Admiral Grove. They were still living there when The Beatles took Britain by storm in 1963.

When he was five, "Ritchie" enrolled at nearby St. Silas' Junior School, but after only a year he was hospitalized when his appendix burst and he came down with peritonitis. Two operations followed at Myrtle Street Children's Hospital, and then a 10-week spell when Ritchie was in a coma. He would remain in the hospital for just over a year. At that point he was still not able to read and write.

At 11, Ritchie wasn't even allowed to take the "eleven-plus" exam which, at that time, would entitle those who passed to enter the higher caliber "grammar schools." Instead he went to Dingle Vale Secondary Modern, and within two years he was back in the Myrtle Street hospital with pleurisy and a shadow on the lung. From there he was moved to Hezzle Children's Hospital, and, when 15-year-old Ritchie finally emerged after two years, his school days were at an end.

## Do You Want to Know a Secret?

As the Fab Four and many other celebrities have found out, there's nothing like a spot of fame and success to jog people's memories. Suddenly, even the vaguest of acquaintances turn into "friends," and long-lost relatives come crawling out of the woodwork. In Ringo's case, when he went back to Dingle Vale Secondary Modern School for a job reference after having spent two years in the hospital, his teachers couldn't remember him. However, years later, when he was Ringo Starr of The Beatles, their memories magically returned and they even managed to drum up "his old desk," charging people sixpence apiece to sit behind it and have their photos taken!

Meanwhile, George was born into yet another tiny two-up, two-down terraced home, although in the relatively better neighborhood of Wavertree. Just like Ringo's house and many others across Britain in those days, 12 Arnold Grove had very little in the way of heating. In fact, in the winter it was freezing. The family was on a seemingly endless re-housing list, and when George was six they finally reached the top of it and were moved to Upton Green in Speke. The home there was on an estate owned by the Liverpool Corporation, and although it was larger and more comfortable than the one on Arnold Grove, the area was still rough. The Harrisons eventually went back onto the housing list, and subsequently moved to 174 Mackett's Lane near Woolton. This was the pleasant family home where the fledgling Beatles would often rehearse.

Mackett's Lane was not far from Menlove Avenue where John grew up, and, as a five-year-old in Wavertree, George also happened to go to the same Infant and Junior School as John, in Dovedale Road near Penny Lane. (Yes, *the* Penny Lane.) Not that they met then, since George was three years younger. A person he *did* meet at his next school—Liverpool Institute—was Paul, who was a year above him. Paul was fairly studious until rock and roll took over his life, but George—who, like Paul, had passed the eleven-plus—never really studied and left school with no qualifications.

**Say the Word**
Council properties in Britain are the subsidized homes owned by the local government (or "council"), that are rented out to low-income families in return for monthly payments that are well below the normal market value.

During his earliest years, Paul had also lived in Speke, in a small *council* house on Western Avenue. At five, he went to the nearby Stockton Wood Road Primary School, and then Joseph Williams Primary in an area named Gateacre. In 1955, the McCartneys moved to a semi-detached council home at 20 Forthlin Road in the more pleasant Allerton. This brought him into the orbit of one John Winston Lennon.

Paul was the only Beatle baby born into the luxury of a private ward. This was at Walton Hospital, where his mother had earned the privilege because she had previously been a nurse there. John, on the other hand, was born into a general ward at Liverpool Maternity Hospital, and from there he went to his mother's tiny terraced house in Newcastle Road, near Penny Lane. (Yep, that name keeps cropping up!) Again, it was the kind of place where the front door opens onto the street; but he wasn't there for very long. When he moved it was to a distinctly middle-class area, and would be the only privately owned home that any of The Beatles ever lived in as children.

This was "Mendips," the spacious semi-detached house on Menlove Avenue in Woolton, where John lived with his Aunt Mimi and Uncle George after his parents had split up. Quite simply, this home is in a different league to those of Paul, George, and Ringo. So much for Mr. "Working Class Hero"! As John's Art College friend, Bill Harry, told me in 1992, "He didn't know what it was like to live in a really tough area. I mean, Menlove Avenue?"

Despite his genteel upbringing, young Lennon "fought all the way through Dovedale [Primary School]," and relied on his innate intelligence to get him through the eleven-plus exam. This would have qualified him for the highly respected Liverpool Institute, but Aunt Mimi opted instead for Quarry Bank Grammar School, partly because it was nearer to home, and also due to the fact that it was in a nicer area than the bohemian city-center district where the Institute was located. None of that altered her nephew's attitude, however.

"I looked at the hundreds of new kids," John told Beatles biographer Hunter Davies in 1968, referring to his first day at Quarry Bank, "and thought, 'Christ, I'll have to fight my way through all this lot!'"

*The Maternity Hospital in Oxford Street, Liverpool, where John Winston Lennon entered the world at 6:30 in the evening of October 9, 1940.*
©Richard Buskin

He never quite managed that feat, but, together with Pete Shotton, his friend from Dovedale, Lennon did cause untold mayhem. The offenses are too numerous to list here, but among some of the charges on Lennon's school reports were "insolence," "cutting class," and "throwing blackboard out of window"!

John had the ability to succeed as a student, but not the initiative. During his first year at Quarry Bank he was high up in the A-stream class, but by the end of his graduation year he was 20th in the C-stream. That meant bottom of the bottom class. Things wouldn't exactly get better at the College of Art.

# The Family Way—Who's Who Among the Relatives

The only Beatle who had a musician for a parent was Paul. His father, James McCartney, had played the piano in a ragtime outfit named Jim Mac's Band during his late teens and early twenties, and he appears to have passed onto his son the ability to pick up an instrument and produce a tune.

Jim married Mary Patricia Mohinn when he was 39 and she was 30. Jim was a cotton salesman, Mary was a nurse. Both were of Irish descent. The following year, 1942, Paul was born, and he was followed two years later by his brother Michael. Jim was too old to fight in the war, and so when the Cotton Exchange closed he took a day job at the engineering works and served as a firefighter at night. Next he was employed as a garbage inspector (checking up on the collectors, not the trash), and, as he was now bringing in a fairly small pay-packet, Mary paid the larger portion of the bills by becoming a midwife.

This was a settled, tight-knit family home—an atmosphere that Paul would later recreate with his own wife and children. Then, one day in 1956, Mary felt pains in her chest. She went to the doctor, was diagnosed as having breast cancer, and within a month she was dead. Jim, Paul, and Michael were devastated.

While Jim somehow managed to support the household on his meager wage, Paul found solace in music. In fact, his father bought him a trumpet for his birthday, but when the budding vocalist realized that he couldn't sing with the brass instrument stuck in his mouth, he traded it in for a guitar.

Jim McCartney lived to see his eldest son become a world-famous superstar, and his other son find British chart success during the 1960s as Mike McGear, lead singer with the Liverpudlian novelty group, The Scaffold. Under his real name, Mike McCartney, he has since had his photos of Paul and The Beatles

**I Should Have Known Better**

In the song "Let It Be," when Paul describes "Mother Mary" still coming to him in "times of trouble," he isn't referring to the Virgin Mary, but to his own mother who died when he was 14. Paul has since stated that one of the great regrets of his life is that his mother never lived to enjoy his fame, or even to see him become a musician.

during the 1950s and early '60s published in book form. James McCartney eventually remarried and had a stepdaughter, Ruth McCartney. He died in 1976.

The two other Beatle dads to remarry did so after deserting and divorcing a pair of Beatle mums. One of these was Ringo's father, Richard Starkey, who married Elsie Gleave in 1936 when they were both working at a bakery. He was 24, she was 22. Four years later, little Richard (as in the future Beatle, not the singer of "Tutti Frutti") was born, and, three years after that, the elder Richard was out of there. He would come back into his son's life on just a handful of occasions.

Elsie, one of 14 children, was used to poverty, and to make ends meet she worked as a barmaid while Grandma Starkey often looked after young Ritchie. Then, when her son was 12, Elsie married Londoner Harry Graves, a painter and decorator who immediately hit it off with the only child and bought him his first drum kit. Both Harry and Elsie would be around to witness Ringo's fame and fortune. They are also in the photographs of his 1965 wedding to Maureen Cox.

The other deserter-divorcee Beatle dad was Alfred Lennon. The son of an Irishman named Jack who had toured America as a Kentucky minstrel, Freddy had been orphaned at the age of five. Ten years later, while he was an office boy, he met John's mother, Julia Stanley. That was in 1928, and they would continue to see each other on and off for the next ten years. The reason for the off periods was that in 1929 Freddy went to sea, working first as a waiter. He sometimes sang on board and, according to him, taught Julia to play the banjo during one of his visits home.

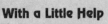

**With a Little Help**

If you go to see "Mendips," the house at 251 Menlove Avenue where John grew up with his Aunt Mimi and Uncle George, you'll be able to see a couple of notable features from the sidewalk: The window above the front porch belongs to John's former bedroom, while the porch itself is where Mimi would often confine him when he was practicing on his guitar.

In December 1938, the two of them married, and a couple of years later John was born, but still Freddy sailed the seven seas. While he was away, it appears that Julia was hardly a stay-at-home wife. She enjoyed going out, meeting other men, and generally having a good time, and so she handed over the responsibility of raising John to her sister Mimi and brother-in-law George Smith.

When John was five, Freddy returned and tried to "save" his faltering marriage. This attempt quickly failed, so he took John to the nearby coastal resort of Blackpool with the intention of emigrating to New Zealand. Julia followed them there and the two grown-ups proceeded to squabble over who had rights to the child. Their solution? They asked the five-year-old who he wanted to be with! John, sobbing and confused, initially opted for his dad, but then, when he saw his mother walk out of the door and down the street, he chased after her.

Julia had won the battle with Freddy, and she celebrated by promptly handing John back over to Aunt Mimi and Uncle George. Mimi was a strict but loving woman, and with Julia only making the odd visit from where she lived around the corner, things ran fairly smoothly for John until George died in 1952. (It was this gentle man who had bought John his first musical instrument, the harmonica.)

Thereafter, Julia began to show up more and more, and John would also visit her at the home that she shared with John Dykins, who, due to an unfortunate facial tic, was promptly given the charming nickname "Twitchy" by Master Lennon. She taught her son to play the banjo, and she also encouraged him to be more rebellious like her. They clearly shared the same offbeat, wayward sense of humor, yet any fears that Mimi had of her sister unsettling the child were compounded when Julia was killed in a road accident in 1958. A speeding car driven by a drunk, off-duty policeman knocked Julia down as she walked across Menlove Avenue after visiting Mimi. It was a loss that John never really got over.

Freddy, meanwhile, was off on his travels, and after 20 years he made his grand return. By then, of course, John was a famous Beatle and Freddy was washing dishes in a hotel not far from where his son lived just outside of London. Looking like a hobo, he turned up on the younger Lennon's doorstep one day and tried to angle for some cash. At the same time, he told a tale of misery and woe to the national newspapers and, wouldn't you know it, was quickly hustled into a studio to record an idiotic song entitled, "That's My Life (My Love And My Home)"! It bombed, but John's embarrassment was complete. So was his resentment: Although he appeared to have patched things up with "The Ignoble Alf" (as he nicknamed him), a few years later John took his father by surprise and unleashed all of his bottled-up anger in a scathing verbal attack.

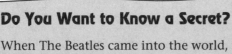

## Do You Want to Know a Secret?

When The Beatles came into the world, it was a working-class tradition in England to name the eldest son after the father, and this was upheld in three of the four Beatle families. Both Richard Starkey and James Paul McCartney took their fathers' names, while George's eldest brother, Harold, did the same in the Harrison household. The only exception was John, who appears to have been named after his paternal grandfather, Jack Lennon. (Jack being a derivative of John.) In turn, John named Julian after his mother, and Sean after himself. Paul's only son is called James. As for Ringo's eldest and George's only child—Zak and Dhani, respectively—they're complete originals!

Meanwhile, 56-year-old Freddy had married 19-year-old Pauline Jones, and in 1969 they had a son, David Henry Lennon. John bought them a home and set them up with a modest weekly allowance. Four years later, Robin Francis Lennon was born, but when John died in 1980 he had still never met his seven-year-old half-brother. Freddy passed away in 1976. For her part, Mimi outlived them all, dying on December 5, 1991, at the age of 88.

And so we arrive at the happy Harrisons, and happy is just about right, for at least George didn't suffer any of the childhood traumas that his fellow Beatles experienced. Furthermore, his mother, Louise, could certainly be described as jolly and outgoing, for among all of the Beatle parents and guardians, she was the one who supported the whole notion of a musical career the most. Not surprisingly, it was often a case of "Let's go over to George's" when the pre-fame Beatles needed a place to rehearse.

### I Want to Tell You

"We used to have a zinc bath, a big one, hanging on the wall outside. We used to bring it in and put it in front of the kitchen fire and then fill it from pans and kettles with hot water. Good place to wash your hair, Liverpool. Nice soft water."

—George Harrison, 1980

Yet another Fab Four relative with Irish blood in the veins, Louise French was a greengrocer's assistant when she met Harold Harrison in 1929. He was a steward in the merchant navy, and they were married the following year. In 1931, their first child, Louise, was born, and three years later came a son, Harold. Peter was born in 1940, and George in 1943. Peter, in fact, was in the same year as Master John Lennon at Dovedale Primary School.

Harry senior left the navy in 1936, and, after being out of a job for 15 months, he became a bus conductor, taking the passengers' money and handing out the tickets. Then, in 1938, he actually got to drive the bus. Years later, when George was fantasizing about what he would do with his money were he to become famous, he said that he would actually like to buy his father his own bus!

Fortunately for all concerned, that little idea was dropped, but both parents did get satisfaction in seeing their youngest kid make it to the top of the showbiz tree. Louise, who had sprung for her son's first guitar, died in 1970, but Harry visited the United States during George's 1974 concert tour and even accompanied him to see President Gerald Ford at the White House. He died in 1978.

### Do You Want to Know a Secret?

In case you want to celebrate The Beatles' birthdays, here are the all-important dates:

John—October 9, 1940
Paul—June 18, 1942
George—February 25, 1943
Ringo—July 7, 1940

# The Least You Need to Know

➤ Liverpool was a depressed city when The Beatles lived there.

➤ They Beatles grew up during the sexually repressed 1950s and the Cold War.

➤ The Fab Four's family homes ranged from the cramped (George and Ringo) to the comfortable (John and Paul).

➤ George's childhood was the only one not be disrupted by death or divorce.

➤ John and Paul both lost their mothers while they were teens.

# Chapter 7

# Long Distance Information: Early Influences

## In This Chapter

➤ How radio helped shape The Beatles' tastes

➤ Some of the rock and rollers The Beatles idolized

➤ Understanding the roots and dynamics of skiffle music

➤ How The Beatles had access to American records not generally available in British stores.

These days, your trusty TV set is practically a member of the family, always sitting in the corner (although, unlike with Grandma, there are no arguments, no fuss). Still, in the decades before TV took over as a multi-purpose medium, radio was king. A lot of people got their entertainment and up-to-the-minute information by way of the "wireless," as it was then known, and John, Paul, George, and Ringo were no exceptions.

That well-known Beatle sense of humor came about partly because of the radio comedians they listened to as kids. At the same time, it was also via the airwaves that they first heard the strains of rock and roll. In this chapter I'll tell you about some of the personalities The Beatles idolized during the 1950s, as well as the effect these people had on our Fab heroes. Next I'll explain why and how they initially got caught up in the skiffle music craze that swept Britain in 1956 and 1957.

Lastly, I'll leave you feeling smug and satisfied after I reveal how The Beatles came to know all the songs they covered during the early part of their career; not just the oldies, but also the numbers from the 1950s and early '60s that they didn't write, but you probably don't recall hearing elsewhere. Well, after a few more pages, you won't have to admit to this failing, because you'll be able to talk with authority on the subject…

# From Luxembourg to The Goons—Radio in the '50s

Okay, let's face it; none of The Beatles' families were exactly made of money, were they? Food, clothing, and roofs over their heads were the first priorities, and everything after that was a bonus. Public transport was often a necessity and TV sets were a definite luxury, but one commodity that found its way into all of their homes was the radio.

Now, if you were George or Ringo, that radio probably consisted of a small wooden box with a pair of "twiddly" knobs, a cloth-covered speaker, and a large tuning dial. Over at the McCartney household things were a little more up-market, with Jim accommodating his sons by rigging up the radio to two pairs of headphones in their bedroom. Meanwhile, at "Mendips," Master Lennon would sit in his bedroom listening to the flashy *radiogram* located in the living room downstairs. This was achieved by way of an extension speaker that was connected to a wire running down the staircase.

John would sit in his room for hours, reading the *Just William* series of mischievous-schoolboy books by Richmal Crompton, Lewis Carroll novels such as *Alice in Wonderland*, and the writings of Balzac. At other times he would shout out, "Change the program on the wireless, Mimi," and have her tune the radio to *Up the Pole*, featuring British vaudeville-style comedians Jimmy Jewel and Ben Warris, the thriller serial *Dick Barton, Special Agent*, or his all-time favorite, *The Goon Show*.

Showcasing the talents of Peter Sellers, Spike Milligan, Harry Secombe, and, on occasion, Michael Bentine, *The Goon Show* was an inspiration to millions of Brits, both old and young alike. Certainly, its outrageous characters, way-out scenarios, and anarchic humor were a revelation to The Beatles and others of their generation. John would often mimic the characters' voices, but neither he nor Paul, George, or Ringo could have ever dreamed that one day they would be collaborating with the man who produced The Goons' comedy records. (In case you don't know, I'm referring to Beatles' producer George Martin. He'll have his very own chapter later on, so be patient.)

**Say the Word**
**Radiogram** refers to the large wooden unit that housed a radio, record player, and speakers, together with storage space for the discs. Basically, it was the '50s and '60s predecessor to today's "music center."

Another influence on John, both in terms of his humor and his penchant for word play, was comedian Stanley Unwin, who almost created his own language by converting English into gobbledygook. It's important to highlight this, because later on such influences would be evident in his books of poetry and nonsense prose, *In His Own Write* and *A Spaniard in the Works*, as well as in the words to several of his songs. As a lyricist, John Lennon was far and away the most imaginative of The Beatles.

Meanwhile, all four got their first taste of rock and roll via the airwaves, and that's where Radio Luxembourg came in. During the mid-'50s the only British channels that people could tune into were those of the government-controlled British Broadcasting Corporation. Now, the BBC may have produced some classic comedy shows, but when it came to "popular" music, they basically transmitted what the adults wanted to hear—"easy listening," all the way from Vera Lynn to Frankie Laine. No way was there going to be any of that new-fangled rock and roll nonsense! Why, one could hardly even call it music!

## Do You Want to Know a Secret?

For many years, the BBC monopolized British broadcasting. Unless people tuned in to overseas radio stations, everything was run by "the Beeb," yet this setup was threatened in the 1960s when "pirate" stations began broadcasting illegally from ships sailing around the British Isles. Banning them only seemed to increase their popularity, so in the 1970s the Government bowed to public pressure and the independents entered the fray. Meanwhile, from 1936—when it made the world's first television broadcast—until 1955, the BBC also ran Britain's only TV channel. Then the Independent Television Authority was established and ITV began broadcasting. Now, of course, there are dozens of cable channels, but the BBC is still commercial-free.

So, what to do? Well, if you turned that dial really carefully to 208 meters, at night you could just about pick up the pop sounds being broadcast from the tiny European state of Luxembourg. I say "just about" because the reception was poor and the sound would fade in and out, but at least the music was popular with the people who mattered as far as future record sales were concerned: the kids.

It was on Radio Luxembourg that John, Paul, George, and Ringo almost certainly heard Elvis Presley singing "Heartbreak Hotel" for the first time. After that, nothing would ever be the same again, either for themselves or for the world around them.

# Rock and Roll—Grow Those Sideburns!

As children, The Beatles grew up listening to the music of their parents' generation and those before them. It was all they knew, and it was pleasant enough. Then came the first flourishes of rock and roll in the form of Bill Haley and His Comets. The use of his smash-hit recording, "Rock Around The Clock," over the opening credits to the 1955 juvenile delinquency picture, *The Blackboard Jungle*, immediately aligned Haley's rhythmic

jazz-based music with rebellious youth. Yet, when the pre-Fab Four first caught sight of this chubby man, sporting a plaid sports jacket and hair styled into an old-fashioned "kiss-curl" at the front, they didn't exactly feel inspired to completely throw themselves into it—yet.

No, it was Elvis Presley who started the ball rolling, and his thousands of teenage disciples including John, Paul, George, and Ringo, ran with it. At the same time, courtesy of their talents, their music, and the sexual innuendo inherent in many of the songs they performed, many other rock artists had a major impact on The Beatles during these formative years. These ranged from Fats Domino—whose "I'm In Love Again" was the first rock and roll record that George Harrison recalls hearing—to Eddie Cochran, Carl Perkins, and Gene Vincent, not to mention non-rock acts such as Ray Charles. The list goes on and on, and it would be impossible to prioritize them in the order of importance to each Fab member. However, I *will* provide you with a handful of acts The Beatles were undoubtedly influenced by and in each case I'll point out the major reasons for that influence.

## Elvis Presley

The King. The teenage Messiah. The guy who lit The Beatles' fuse. He had the sound, the look, the hip clothes, the stage moves—the whole nine yards as far as John, Paul, George, and Ringo were concerned.

When, around May of 1956, they each heard the strains of "Heartbreak Hotel" coming over their radios, it was like a call to arms. I mean, who was this guy, his voice swamped in echo, singing as if he were stuck in the most desolate place on earth? "Waaall since ma baybeh left me, ah foun' a noo place to dwell …" Yeah, down at the end of some lonely street—possibly he was singing about one of those back roads near the Liverpool docks. Unlikely. Could he be referring to the darkest recesses of his mind? Whoa! Compared to telling people to "catch a falling star and put it in your pocket," this was pretty heavy stuff!

Many people thought Elvis had to be black. None of those insipid white artists would ever have the *nerve* to sing like that, with that kind of pain. This guy knew what it was like to feel lonely, to feel depressed, to feel angry. So did plenty of white kids living in an environment where parents and teachers made the rules, but they could never translate their frustrations into music. No, he had to be black.

*Elvis in the 1950s. "It was Elvis who got me hooked for beat music," John said in 1963. "When I heard 'Heartbreak Hotel' I thought, 'this is it,' and I started to grow sideboards [sideburns] and all that gear."*
©Hulton Getty

Then they saw his picture—in a magazine, on a poster, somewhere—and they were hit with shock number two: He was white. Unbelievable! What's more, he was white with plenty of attitude—hair slicked back into a *DA*, long greasy sideburns like some truck driver, lip curled into a sneer that said, "Go hang yourself," and moody, heavy-lidded eyes that were clearly inviting all of womanhood into *his* bed! Oh, brother, this was the way to be!

When Elvis sang "Good Rockin' Tonight," he was clearly alluding to more than just a spot of dancing, and when he belted out the lyrics to "Hound Dog," it was with a venom and a spirit that were completely liberating. Almost instantly, kids all around Britain began styling their hair like his, wearing flashy clothes (or, at least, what they *considered* to be flashy clothes), taking an insolent attitude towards the adults, and trying to play a musical instrument. Among them were Messrs. Lennon, McCartney, Harrison, and Starkey.

Elvis was taking the Western world by storm, but he was also laying the foundations for those who would succeed him.

## Chuck Berry

To The Beatles, Elvis may have represented the whole nine yards, but he wasn't *quite* the complete package. He sang brilliantly, he looked fantastic, and he delivered great songs, but he didn't actually write them. That task was taken care of by professional composers, some of them specially commissioned. However, there were now other artists coming onto the scene who also wrote their own material, and this kind of self-sufficiency really appealed to the young Lennon and McCartney.

**I Should Have Known Better**

The Beatles were unique, but it's a mistake to think everything they did was 100% original. In The Beatles' number "Come Together," John slipped in the line "Here come old flat-top" from Chuck Berry's "You Can't Catch Me," and that prompted Berry's publisher, Morris Levy, to threaten legal action for plagiarism. John subsequently agreed to earn Levy royalties by recording some Berry songs on his 1975 *Rock 'n' Roll* album.

At the top of that particular tree was one Charles Edward Berry, out of St. Louis, Missouri. Chuck, as he was known, was one of the few black performers to get across to white teenage audiences during the 1950s, and he did so largely on the strength of charismatic stage demeanor (including his trademark "duck walk"), his distinctive, rocking, and widely imitated guitar licks, and his ingenious songs. "Maybellene," "Roll Over Beethoven," "Johnny B. Goode," "Sweet Little Sixteen," "Memphis Tennessee," "Brown Eyed Handsome Man"—each featured witty, sometimes acerbic lyrics, and, thanks to the uncluttered instrumentals and Berry's clear vocal delivery, you were actually able to understand them.

The subject matter often dealt with young love and teen rebellion, and it did so in a poetic style that particularly appealed to John Lennon. In fact, if any one aspect of Chuck Berry's tremendous influence should be highlighted, then it's the way he introduced a more sophisticated and disciplined form of lyricism to rock music. He also inspired the likes of Lennon and McCartney to write their own songs and become a self-contained unit.

# Buddy Holly

Whereas Elvis Presley had looks to die for, Buddy Holly gave Joe Average a sense of hope. As Paul McCartney recently stated, "Suddenly, here was a rock and roll hero who had glasses."

That's right: black, horn-rimmed glasses that near-sighted John Lennon normally only wore in private. And they sat on a face that, well, belonged more to your next-door neighbor than some matinee idol. Yet, that was part of the Holly charm—the everyman who proved that talent alone could sometimes be enough.

Charles Harden Holley—he dropped the "e" as part of his stage name—had plenty of talent, and with that gift he helped craft some of the late '50s' best pop songs. Infectious, catchy tunes with a driving beat, such as "Rave On," "Peggy Sue," and "Maybe Baby"; simple teen ballads like "Everyday"; and, towards the end of his tragically short career, the melodic string arrangements of "True Love Ways" and "It Doesn't Matter Anymore."

When Buddy and his band, The Crickets, appeared on British TV's *Sunday Night at the London Palladium* in 1957, thousands of budding Brit rockers paid close attention to the modern, solid-bodied Fender Stratocaster guitar he was playing. It would help inspire a craze for that instrument that lasts to this day. Holly died in a plane crash at the age of 22 in February of 1959, yet this only served to heighten his popularity, especially in Britain. The Beatles' name would be a play on the insect-like Crickets (more on that later), and they would cover his songs; their earliest known recording is a 1958 rendition of "That'll Be The Day" (on *Anthology 1*). During the 1970s, Paul actually acquired the publishing rights to Buddy's music, and since 1976 his "Buddy Holly Week" celebrations have been an annual tradition in the UK.

# The Preacher and The Killer: Little Richard and Jerry Lee Lewis

Two men—one black, one white. Both from the American South. Both innately religious, yet compelled to perform what was initially touted as "the devil's music." In their individual ways, Little Richard and Jerry Lee Lewis were the wild men of early rock and roll. The hit records and on-stage energy of these two dynamic performers left a lasting impression on the Fab Four.

Richard Penniman, from Macon, Georgia, honed his rasping gospel style singing in church choirs, and this was what helped electrify songs such as "Tutti Frutti," "Good Golly Miss Molly," "Rip It Up," "The Girl Can't Help It," "Lucille," and "Long Tall Sally." Likewise, his live performances were completely irrepressible. White crooners such as Pat Boone had far greater chart success than Richard did with his own songs. They recorded insipid, toned-down versions that were "more acceptable" to—and therefore encouraged by—white parents, yet The Beatles never paid attention to them. It was Richard's, not Pat's version of "Long Tall Sally" that they emulated on stage and on record. In 1962, they also shared the concert bill with Little Richard in Liverpool and in Hamburg; Richard

**I Want to Tell You**

"I still love Little Richard and I love Jerry Lee Lewis. They're like primitive painters ... Chuck Berry is one of the all-time great poets, a rock poet you could call him. He was well advanced of his time lyric-wise. We all owe a lot to him..."

—John Lennon, *Rolling Stone* magazine, 1970

claims he taught Paul McCartney to sing those high-pitched "ooohs," which were definitely in evidence on The Beatles' smash, "She Loves You."

Louisiana's Jerry Lee Lewis, on the other hand, was certainly not in the Pat Boone mold. A one-time student minister, Jerry Lee displayed an aggression and an arrogance never before seen in a white performer. Combining raucous, country-flavored vocals with manic, boogie-style piano playing, "The Killer" (as he came to be known) would tear his way through songs such as "Whole Lotta Shakin' Goin' On" and "Great Balls Of Fire," and leave the listeners almost more exhausted than he was.

As John Lennon asserted in 1970, "There is nothing conceptually better than rock and roll. No group, be it Beatles, Dylan, or [the] Stones has ever improved on 'Whole Lotta Shakin,' for my money."

## The Everly Brothers

Don and Phil, from Brownie, Kentucky, were always more country than rock. However, during the late 1950s and very early '60s, their wonderfully tight vocal harmonies made them one of the most important acts in the evolution of rock and roll.

### Do You Want to Know a Secret?

When his interest in rock and roll took off, Paul McCartney initially tried out his vocal talents in an Everly Brothers-style pop duo with his younger brother, Michael. In Paul's estimation, he was better suited to the higher harmonies as performed by Phil. Well, these abilities were put to the test when the two young Macs took part in an amateur talent contest in the summer of 1957. This was at Butlin's holiday camp in Filey, Yorkshire, where Paul and Mike gave their rendition of "Bye Bye Love." Very nice, but it was perhaps fortunate that they didn't win and take their act on the road. Only a few weeks later, Paul joined The Quarry Men.

A string of perfectly produced pop hits, including "Bye Bye Love," "Wake Up Little Susie," "All I Have To Do Is Dream," and "Cathy's Clown," had a major impact on fledgling artists on both sides of the Atlantic. These ranged from Simon and Garfunkel to Lennon and McCartney, all of whom clearly learned a thing or two listening to the way the Everlys' voices blended so perfectly with each another. Just listen to any of the aforementioned Everly Brothers hits, and then play The Beatles' recordings of, say, "If I Fell" and "Baby's In Black." You'll hear what I mean.

So, there it is—the demeanor of Elvis Presley, the lyricism of Chuck Berry, the commercial appeal of Buddy Holly, the unbridled energy of Little Richard and Jerry Lee Lewis, and the vocal harmonizing of The Everly Brothers. In a nutshell, some of The Beatles' major musical influences...but not all of them!

# All Fingers and Thumbs—The Skiffle Boom

At around the same time that rock and roll hit Britain in early 1956, a similar form of music came along and simplified the task of forming a band for cash-strapped Brit teenagers. For that matter, it also did the same for *talent*-strapped Brit teenagers.

Skiffle was really an amalgam of American jazz, blues, and folk music, and it had been surfacing in various guises for quite a few years. The reason money and skill weren't of paramount importance is that band members only needed a cheap acoustic guitar ("guaranteed not to split"), and a bunch of items that were still common in households across Britain during the 1950s: some thimbles, a broom handle, a length of string, and a tea-chest.

One "musician" would wear the thimbles on the fingers and thumb of one hand, and run these up and down the washboard in order to create a percussive rhythm. Meanwhile, the broom handle would be poked through a hole in the upturned tea-chest, and the cord attached between the two, in order to create a crude imitation of an upright bass, known in this case as a "tea-chest bass." As for the guitar: Donegan had a basic three-chord style, but even that wasn't important. For most newcomers, the instrument was little more than a prop.

So, that was the core of the skiffle band—guitar, percussion, bass—and then, if money really was growing on trees, you could also add a set of drums, an accordion, a ukulele, you name it.

In January 1956, the Lonnie Donegan Skiffle Group's recording of the old Huddie "Leadbelly" Ledbetter blues song, "Rock Island Line," entered the British charts and took the teen scene by storm. Other acts quickly followed in Donegan's wake: among them, Tommy Steele, The Vipers Skiffle Group, and the Chas McDevitt Skiffle Group featuring Nancy Whiskey.

The real skiffle craze only lasted about 18 months or so, from the start of 1956 until the latter part of 1957. Yet, during that relatively short time, more than 5,000 such groups came into existence around Britain,

**With a Little Help**
If you're interested in listening to the kind of skiffle material that influenced The Quarry Men (and which they then performed), try to locate some of the following recordings: "Rock Island Line," "The Cumberland Gap," and "Railroad Bill" by Lonnie Donegan and his Skiffle Group; "Worried Man Blues" by The Vipers Skiffle Group; and "Freight Train" by the Chas McDevitt Skiffle Group featuring Nancy Whiskey.

several hundred of which were in Liverpool, and one of which—The Quarry Men—instigated the events that are now enabling me to write this book!

# Back in the USA—Imported Records

Remember those "Cunard Yanks" I told you about in Chapter 6? That's right, the sailors who, in the old days, used to spend their time traveling between Liverpool and the United States. Well, the reason I'm mentioning them once again is that they also had a hand in influencing The Beatles.

No, the Cunard Yanks didn't sing "Ferry 'Cross The Mersey." (That was Gerry and the Pacemakers, and they had a hit with that song *after* the Fab Four had become famous...Oh, never mind!) What they *did* do was bring American records with them when they returned to Merseyside, and some of these were by artists who were less than mainstream: bluesmen such as Muddy Waters and Big Bill Broonzy; country guitarists like Chet Atkins and Jimmie Rodgers; and, as the 1950s turned into the '60s, the acts out of Detroit who were recording for a small, independent label named Tamla Motown.

Many of these records would get sold or passed around, and among those who either heard or laid their hands on them were you-know-who. (And if you don't know who, maybe you should go back to the beginning of this book and start all over again.) The likes of Atkins and Rodgers were big influences on George's guitar playing. He has often sounded more comfortable when dealing with country material, as is evident by his consummate solo work on *Beatles For Sale*, the group's most country-flavored album.

At the same time, Ringo has always been a very big fan of C&W, from Gene Autry and Hank Williams through to a couple of singer-composers whose songs he recorded (and sang lead vocals on) with The Beatles: Buck Owens and Carl Perkins. In interviews, John Lennon alluded to Perkins' influence in the fields of both country and rock and roll, with "Sure To Fall (In Love With You)" (which the Fab Four perform on the album *Live at the BBC*) and "Matchbox" (which is on their *Long Tall Sally* EP) as respective examples of each genre. John also stated that Hank Williams' "Honky Tonk Blues" was a favorite of his, but that he could never quite achieve the unique Williams yodeling effect.

**I Want to Tell You**

"At one point, Liverpool—maybe it still is—was the capital of country and western music in England ... Johnny Ray was my first real hero, but that was after Gene Autry, the singing cowboy. What a great voice."

—Ringo Starr, 1992

Now, I've only mentioned a tiny fraction of the recorded talent that The Beatles were exposed to during their pre-fame days, but here's the point: In spite of the fact that none of them could read or write music, John, Paul, George, and Ringo had a pretty comprehensive musical education. They breathed in the sounds and the *feel* of all of the different influences that came their way, and, when they exhaled, the result was a remarkable depth and variety to their work, both as composers and as performers.

Furthermore, there were the songs of other artists that The Beatles chose to record on their earlier albums. These were often lesser-known B-sides of singles or just tracks that many of their fans were plain unfamiliar with. "Anna (Go To Him)" by Arthur Alexander, "Chains" by The Cookies, "Devil In Her Heart" (originally "Devil In His Heart") by The Donays, "Bad Boy" by Larry Williams—none of these were massive hits. Yet, The Beatles' had the ability to interpret this material and turn in a performance that was often better than the original. No easy task, but hey, wasn't this just one of the Fab Four's talents?

# The Least You Need to Know

➤ Radio helped to shape The Beatles' musical tastes and their sense of humor.

➤ Different rock stars—including Elvis, Chuck Berry, Little Richard, and Buddy Holly, to name a few—inspired the Fab Four in a number of ways.

➤ A large part of skiffle music's charm lay in its simplicity.

➤ The Beatles had a comprehensive knowledge of different forms of music.

# Chapter 8

# The Pre-Beatles: Thinking of Linking

## In This Chapter

➤ John's first group, The Quarry Men

➤ The historic first meeting between Lennon and McCartney

➤ How George was recruited into the group

➤ The band's first performances and its various names

Imagine going to see one or more of The Beatles perform at your local church or social club, and watching them do so with cheap or battered instruments. Well, everyone has to start somewhere, and there was a time when our not-yet-Fab heroes would take any gigs that were offered to them. Sometimes there were a few hundred people in attendance, sometimes only a handful, but they all shared one thing in common: No one there could have realized that they were witnessing the birth of a phenomenon that would forever change the course of popular music. Believe me, those earliest efforts were nothing to write home about, but they were the vital starting point.

In this chapter, we'll take a look at how John, Paul, and George each started playing music, how they met, and how they joined forces. These three were the nucleus of The Beatles; as Ringo doesn't enter the picture until a bit later, we'll get to him in a later chapter. The story begins a full six years before the band rose to national prominence, and seven years before they hit the States. During that time they really struggled for their success, and, in spite of what the media may have said when Beatlemania finally exploded, they were certainly *not* "overnight sensations."

No, when they started out, John, Paul, and George were simply concerned with learning their instruments, finding venues that would book them, people who would play with them, and a name that would suit them. After all, it just wouldn't be the same if I had to tell you about a craze known as "Quarrymania," now would it?

## Quarry Men, Old Before Our Birth

Although John Lennon's life turned around the moment he heard Elvis Presley sing "Heartbreak Hotel" in May 1956, it wasn't until the following year that he actually did something about it. First, he persuaded Aunt Mimi to shell out £17 (equal to about $50) for an acoustic guitar. Then he turned to his mother, Julia—who he was now beginning to see more often—for instruction on how to play it. The fact that she taught him banjo chords didn't seem to matter at that point. He practiced like a madman and drove Mimi so crazy that she would banish him to the front porch of their house. There he could strum tunelessly to his heart's content.

Next, in March 1957, John teamed up with his best high school friend, Pete Shotton, and formed a skiffle group named The Black Jacks. That lasted for all of a week, then they decided to re-christen the band The Quarry Men in recognition of their school, Quarry Bank High, and its song, which contained the line, "Quarry Men, old before our birth." Friends and acquaintances soon joined the lineup—John on guitar and vocals, Pete on washboard, Rod Davis on banjo, Eric Griffiths on guitar, Colin Hanton on drums, and Bill Smith, Len Garry, Ivan Vaughan, and Nigel Whalley all taking turns on tea-chest bass.

**I Should Have Known Better**

Beware of quotes from John and Paul in which they claim to have first met in 1955 or 1956. There is now documented proof of the precise date in 1957 when this took place, shortly after the very first Quarry Men performances. Beatle memories are often inaccurate, largely because they don't need to remember all of the details—writers and researchers do that for them.

The first proper rehearsal took place in Eric Griffiths' house, and then afterwards the location shifted to the upstairs bathroom at the home of John's ever-encouraging mother, Julia. Although a few engagements were quickly secured, these largely consisted of parties and school dances. Yet, by the start of June, with barely three months of experience under their belts, The Quarry Men evidently felt ready for the big time.

Caroll Levis was then the host of a popular talent show on British TV, and in order to discover budding jugglers, magicians, singers, sword-swallowers, or whoever, he would run *TV Star Search* shows up and down the country. A preliminary audition took place at the Empire Theatre in Liverpool on June 9, 1957, and among the long list of hopefuls were The Quarry Men. Unfortunately, by the end of the try-out, they were not on the short list of qualifiers for the finals.

Still, even though fame and fortune didn't exactly come knocking on their door (it didn't even make it to the sidewalk!), John and his fellow band members stuck with it. A couple of weeks later, on June 22, they found themselves performing on top of a stationary coal truck at an outdoor party in Roseberry Street, Liverpool 8. Everything was going fine until a couple of local thugs decided that, instead of listening to the music, it would be more fun to "get that Lennon"! Obviously, John's loudmouth reputation preceded him, and so after the gig he and a few other Quarry Men took refuge in the party organizer's house. They were then given a police escort to the nearby bus stop.

Ah well, these were the risks of being famous. Next up was a gig at a church fete. Nothing *that* exciting was likely to take place there, except…

# A Fateful Church Fete—John Meets Paul

St. Peter's Parish Church in Woolton isn't far from the Menlove Avenue home where John grew up. On Saturday, July 6 1957, its annual garden fete (basically just an outdoor party, rhymes with "fate") took place in the field behind the church, and several hundred people attended to see the crowning of the local Rose Queen, accompanied by a parade of kids in fancy dress, boy scouts, girl guides, and youth club members. Throughout the afternoon, musical entertainment was provided by the Band of the Cheshire Yeomanry as well as "the popular Quarry Men Skiffle Group," for whom the engagement had been secured by Pete Shotton's mother.

The lineup on that sunny summer afternoon featured John on guitar and vocals, Pete on washboard, Eric Griffiths on guitar, Len Garry on bass, Rod Davis on banjo, and Colin Hanton on drums—and in the audience were a couple of interested observers. One was Aunt Mimi, who had apparently been unaware of the band's existence until she heard their sound blasting through the refreshment tent as she sipped her tea. Looking out to the field to see where all the noise was coming from, she saw a group on stage, including John and "that Shotton" (as she would warmly refer to him).

John and she had argued that morning over his *Teddy boy* appearance, and now, as he saw his aunt approaching, he started to ad-lib the words to the song that he was singing: "Mimi's coming… Oh-oh, Mimi's coming down the path…"

In the Quarry Men repertoire that day were songs such as Elvis' "Baby, Let's Play House"; the traditional Liverpool number "Maggie May," which had recently been popularized by The Vipers Skiffle Group; Lonnie Donegan's "Cumberland Gap," "Railroad Bill," and

**Say the Word**
Teddy boy is the description applied in Britain to male rockers who sport Elvis-style greased-back hair and side-burns, together with long Edwardian (or "Teddy") drape jackets, tight pants, and crepe-soled shoes.

"Putting On The Style"; and The Del-Vikings' "Come Go With Me." Incredibly, an amateur recording of two of those July 6, 1957 peformances—"Baby, Let's Play House" and "Putting On The Style"—has recently surfaced.

John's rendition of "Come Go With Me" particularly caught the attention of another notable member of the audience on that fateful afternoon: one Paul McCartney. Standing next to his friend Ivan Vaughan, Paul was intrigued by the way John substituted the song's barely decipherable second line, "Please don't send me 'way beyond the sea," with the more bluesy—if hardly credible—"Down, down, down to the penitentiary." Paul also couldn't help noticing that the few chords that John was playing looked a little strange. They were, in fact, the banjo chords that Julia had taught him. Paul was blown away by the charismatic, 16-year-old Teddy boy and leader of the group, but he must have also been aware that he was a more accomplished guitarist, and this played no small part in the events that followed.

Having already tried his hand at the piano and his mouth at the trumpet, Paul had focused on the guitar after going to a Lonnie Donegan concert at the Liverpool Empire the previous November. Now, as Ivan Vaughan introduced him to The Quarry Men while they set up for the evening dance inside the church hall, Paul picked up a guitar and displayed his virtuosity. He played one of John's favorite hits of the moment, Eddie Cochran's "Twenty Flight Rock," and impressed everyone not only with his performance, but also the fact that he actually knew all the words! John was lousy at memorizing lyrics, and grateful when Paul wrote down those to "Twenty Flight Rock" and Gene Vincent's "Be-Bop-A-Lula." However, his gratitude turned to pure (if concealed) admiration when Paul showed him and Eric Griffiths another trick he had up his sleeve: He knew how to tune a guitar! And to think they had actually been paying a guy to do this for them!

Quit while you're on top—always sound advice, and that's exactly what Paul did. He walked out of the church hall that evening and left John Winston Lennon dazzled but confused. After all, what should he do? Improve the band but threaten his own supremacy by recruiting someone who was, at the very least, his equal in the talent department? Or should he just hang onto his unrivaled leadership?

A couple of weeks later, Pete Shotton happened to meet Paul while cycling in Woolton. There and then he asked him on behalf of John and the group if he'd like to join. After weighing his options and giving it some serious thought (all of a few seconds), Paul said that he would. However, although he began rehearsing regularly with The Quarry Men from July onwards, he didn't make his concert debut with them for another three months. At the New Clubmoor Hall in Liverpool on October 18, 1957, Paul played lead guitar on stage for the first and only time. Thereafter, he was relegated

**I Want to Tell You**

"John and I walked home alone, and John said to me, 'What do you think of him?' I said, 'I like him,' and he said, 'What about asking him to join the band then?' So I said, 'Well, if he wants to, it's okay with me.' Okay with *me*! Lucky you, Paul!"

—Pete Shotton, 1984

to rhythm, and the reason? Well, he totally blew his long-awaited solo, during a rendition of "Guitar Boogie." Clearly, a case of first-night nerves!

# Play "Raunchy" for Me—And George Makes Three

Soon after Paul joined The Quarry Men, things began to change. For one thing, the professional bookings became more frequent and a little more prestigious (even if one of the venues was a slaughterhouse!). For another, the demise of skiffle just happened to coincide with the departure of several band members.

## Do You Want to Know a Secret?

During the late 1950s, John's Aunt Mimi appears to have had a mistaken impression of her unruly nephew. For instance, when she first met Paul, a polite boy in whom the only sign of "rebelliousness" was the fact that he sported an Elvis hairdo (and a neatly trimmed one, at that), she immediately passed him off as a bad influence on John(!) Meanwhile, Paul paled in comparison to George, the working-class kid who wore bright clothes, flashy shoes, and talked with a thick Scouse accent. "You always go for the low types, don't you, John?" Mimi groaned, without realizing that this kind of disapproval gave him good reason to adopt the opposite point of view.

The Quarry Men now comprised John, Paul, Eric Griffiths, Len Garry, and Colin Hanton, with John "Duff" Lowe sometimes sitting in on piano. Then, on February 6, 1958, they encountered a 14-year-old school friend of Paul's at a gig they played in the suburb of Garston. His name was George Harrison.

To 18-year-old John, George was little more than "a kid," but afterwards, while they were taking a ride on the top deck of a late-night bus, his eyes were drawn towards the flashy guitar that George had "coincidentally" brought along with him. Egged on by Paul, John asked George to play "Raunchy," an instrumental that he was adept at playing on the bass strings. He did, and after that Lennon would constantly tease his gaunt-looking admirer by saying, "Come on, George. Give us 'Raunchy'!" No matter where they were, he knew George would oblige.

George was not the most natural of musicians, but he worked hard at his craft. He and his brother Peter had taken up the guitar at about the same time, and

**I Want to Tell You**

"I couldn't be bothered with [George] when he first came around. He used to follow me around like a bloody kid... It took me years to come around to him, to start considering him as an equal or anything."

—John Lennon, *Rolling Stone* magazine, 1970

together they had formed a skiffle group named The Rebels. Their only gig was at the British Legion Club near their home in Speke, yet on the bus journeys to and from school each day George became more friendly with Paul because of their shared passion for the guitar. They even practiced together in the bathroom of the Harrison home, and that's precisely what The Quarry Men began to do soon afterwards.

George's hero-worship of John irritated the chief Quarry Man. Nevertheless, the kid did have a great guitar, undoubted technical ability, and a convenient place to rehearse. Soon his persistence paid off. Eric Griffiths was unceremoniously bumped from the lineup, and George Harrison took his place.

# Johnny and the Moondogs

Sometime in the spring or summer of 1958, John, Paul, George, Colin Hanton, and John Lowe made what could loosely be described as the first-ever Beatles recordings. I say "loosely," because obviously two of these participants were soon to play no further part in the group's musical ventures, and besides, they were still named The Quarry Men. However, three of the Fab Four were now firmly in place, and they would form the nucleus of the band we've known for all these years.

Turning up at the home studio of an old Liverpudlian named Percy Phillips, the five young guys parted with a small amount of money in return for the privilege of taping two songs: Buddy Holly's "That'll Be The Day" and a Harrison-McCartney composition entitled "In Spite Of All The Danger." John sang lead on both recordings, which were then transferred to a two-sided shellac disc. Percy Phillips wiped the tape, but John Lowe held onto the disc, and in 1981 he sold it to Paul McCartney for a tidy sum. Fourteen years later the two cuts would be included on the CD set, *The Beatles Anthology 1*.

So, even though he hadn't written either song, John Lennon still asserted himself as the head honcho and took care of the lead vocals. That practice didn't last for long, and neither did the Quarry Men careers of Messrs. Lowe and Hanton. Len Garry had already vacated the bass player's position thanks to a bout with meningitis, and John Lowe was never a full-time member anyway. Colin Hanton, on the other hand, may not have been Liverpool's greatest drummer, but he did have an expensive kit to offer, so he lasted until early 1959. Then a drunken row after a gig ensured that he wouldn't see John, Paul, or George ever again.

As it happens, there was more than enough reason for the odd grizzly mood and bad-tempered outburst. Paul's induction into the band had been followed by a relative burst of concert activity, but then things appear to have gone down the tubes for much of 1958 and 1959.

The lads' diaries weren't exactly full of bookings, but John and Paul may have used theirs to scribble the words to the glut of songs they were now writing. Among them were titles like "I Lost My Little Girl," "Thinking Of Linking," "Years Roll Along," "Too Bad About Sorrows," "Just Fun," "Keep Looking That Way," and "That's My Woman," as well as some others you may have heard of: "Love Me Do," "Hello Little Girl," "The One After 909," and "When I'm Sixty-Four."

So, as you can see, times may have been lean but these guys were no slackers. In late 1958 they failed an audition at the Manchester studios of ABC Television, and, as things virtually ground to a halt over the next few months, even George Harrison started to find other musical outlets. One was The Les Stewart Quartet. On August 29, 1959, a row with the group's bass player, Ken Brown, led Stewart to pull the plug on an engagement, and so Brown asked George if he knew anyone who could help out. The gig was for the opening night of a new venue named the Casbah Coffee Club, located in the basement of a house owned by Mona Best (more on her in the next chapter). George's suggestion? How about teaming up with that modestly talented duo of Lennon and McCartney?

**With a Little Help**
Most of the songs John and Paul wrote during the earliest years of their partnership were never recorded, so don't bother trying to seek out many of the titles that you'll read or hear about. However, one song you *can* listen to is Paul's first-ever composition, "I Lost My Little Girl," which, in updated form, appears on his 1991 solo album, *Unplugged (The Official Bootleg)*.

Ken Brown went along with the idea, and for the next six weeks, the resurrected Quarry Men not only had a bass guitarist but, with the weekly Casbah bookings, a regular venue in which to play. Then Ken fouled things up by having another row, this time with his new and soon-to-be-former band mates. The cause of all the unhappiness was Brown's "audacity" in accepting his share of the fee from Mrs. Best, when he had a cold one night and was too ill to perform. Talk about all being friends together—Paul was having none of it. No play, no pay! Ken dug his heels in. He was keeping his portion of the generous £3 ($8) fee, and that was that. And so it turned out to be for Ken Brown, short-lived member of The Quarry Men.

Ah well, it was back to the Fab Threesome of John, Paul, and George, and, for a brief time, a change of name and an upturn in their fortunes. (Which wasn't difficult, being that they were at rock-bottom.) Under the moniker of Johnny and the Moondogs, the trio took another shot at auditioning for the TV talent show, *Discoveries*, hosted by "Mr. Star-Maker," Caroll Levis. More than two years before they had been an outstanding flop, but in October of 1959, without a drummer or a bass player, they managed to get through three qualifying rounds at Liverpool's Empire Theatre and make it to the grand final. (When asked why there wasn't a drummer they'd respond, "The rhythm's in the guitars!")

**Say the Word**
Clapometer is the name commonly given to the sound-sensitive device used to measure audience applause during a talent contest. The higher the volume of clapping, the further the clapometer pointer moves up the scale.

That was all well and good, but when they turned up for the final in Manchester on November 15, John, for some reason, didn't even have a guitar. The hasty solution was for Johnny to stand center-stage with his arms draped around the shoulders of his strumming, harmonizing Moondogs. Since George is right-handed and Paul left-handed, their guitar necks pointed outwards, so the visual effect was pretty good.

They performed a couple of Buddy Holly numbers, "Think It Over" and "Rave On," but then unfortunately had to catch the last train home before being judged by the all-important *clapometer*.

Still, just before their departure a solution was at least found to Johnny's lack of a musical instrument. As Paul put it in 1995, "I believe that day some unfortunate person in that theater was relieved of his guitar."

# You Know My Name... Well, Maybe Not— Naming the Band

The Black Jacks, The Quarry Men, Johnny and the Moondogs—how many names, you may well ask, did those guys actually go through before they arrived at The Beatles? Well, the answer is quite a few.

I've already documented the progression from Black Jacks to Moondogs in this chapter, but now, at the risk of getting slightly ahead of myself in terms of the story, I'll give you the whole shebang: the names, the relevant periods, and, where necessary, the reasoning. All right? Here goes...

➤ The Black Jacks: March 1957.

➤ The Quarry Men: March 1957—October 1959.

➤ Johnny and the Moondogs: October—November 1959.

➤ The Nerk Twins: April 23 & 24, 1960.

During an Easter break in the south of England, John and Paul stayed and worked at the pub of Paul's cousin, Elizabeth Robbins, and her husband Mike. In return for serving behind the bar at the Fox and Hounds in Caversham, Berkshire, Lennon and McCartney were very generously allowed to perform live. (Imagine that—"If you work for us, we'll *allow* you to give a couple of free performances!") Still, John and Paul were so desperate for any kind of musical outlet that they sat on stools, played acoustic guitars, and sang without microphones. It was Mike Robbins who named them The Nerk Twins. Those were the days...

➤ Early May 1960: The Beatals.

It's unclear whether John Lennon or his friend Stuart Sutcliffe (who, by this time, had joined the band as its inept bass player) concocted this name—they possibly did so together. Either way, both Paul and George recall meeting them at their flat in Gambier

Terrace and being told that they had just come up with a great new name for the group. Basically, it was a play on that of Buddy Holly's band, The Crickets; another variety of insect, with the added bonus of misspelling the word so that it contained "Beat." From this point on, for the next few months, they toyed around with variations of the same name until settling on you-know-what.

## Do You Want to Know a Secret?

The July 6–21, 1961 edition of Liverpudlian pop-music paper, *Mersey Beat*, featured a piece of nonsense prose by John Lennon entitled, "Being a Short Diversion on the Dubious Origins of Beatles." In it he stated that his band's name "came in a vision—a man appeared on a flaming pie and said unto them 'From this day on you are Beatles with an A'." Paul, George, and Ringo were going to allude to this in the *Beatles Anthology* documentary as an example of John's humor. However, according to a 1995 Paul interview, Yoko objected, stating, "If it's okay for Paul to dream 'Yesterday' then it's okay for John to have a vision."

Paul had the last laugh. He named his 1997 album *Flaming Pie*.

➤ May 10—early June, 1960: The Silver Beetles.

While readying themselves for an audition to back singer Billy Fury (who you'll read all about in the next fab chapter), the would-be Beatals were informed in no uncertain terms by a member of another local band that their name was "ridiculous." This was Brian Cassar, of Cass and the Cassanovas, who went on to suggest that they call themselves something a little more logical… like Long John and the Silver Beetles. (As in Long John Silver, get it?) Well, the Long John part never made it as far as the audition, and The Silver Beetles didn't succeed in backing Billy Fury, but they did secure a small tour of Scotland behind the lesser-known Johnny Gentle, and for that sortie into the big time they went all out.

Paul chose the stage name of Paul Ramon because he thought it was "very exotic" and "French-sounding"; George transformed himself into Carl Harrison as a tribute to his American rockabilly idol, Carl Perkins; and Stuart Sutcliffe became Stuart de Staël in acknowledgment of Russian painter, Nicholas de Staël. As for John, he later insisted that he always retained his own name, but Paul has since contradicted this by asserting that, for the duration of the Scottish tour, he was definitely known as Long John. Oh well. Just put it down to the fantasies of youth.

➤ May 14, 1960: The Silver Beats.

We jump backwards here to a single Liverpool engagement, and a sort of aberration in the middle of being Silver Beetles. They just weren't sure about that name, were they?

*The Aintree Institute, where The Beatles made 31 appearances from January 1961 to January of 1962. A favorite pastime of some charming patrons here was to throw chairs at the band.*
©Richard Buskin

➤ Early/mid-June 1960: The Beatles.

Aha! Could this have been inspired by the identical name of one of the gangs in the 1954 Marlon Brando/Lee Marvin biker movie, *The Wild One*? Who knows? In any case, don't break out the champagne just yet...

➤ Mid-June—early July 1960: The Silver Beetles.

One step forward, two back.

➤ Early July—early August 1960: The Silver Beatles.

Okay, okay... That's good... Now come on... Just one more little adjustment...

➤ August 16, 1960—eternity: The Beatles.

We're there at last! Now that wasn't *so* difficult was it?

### Do You Want to Know a Secret?

On July 6, 1997, exactly 40 years to the day after John and Paul first met at the St. Peter's Parrish Church garden fete in Woolton, all of the original members of The Quarry Men (except John, of course) gathered there for a reunion concert. Pete Shotton, Eric Griffith, Len Garry, Rod Davis, and Colin Hanton reprised their original roles, and were somewhat surprised by the response that their get-together inspired. Paul McCartney sent a fax message of support to the event organizer, while John's widow, Yoko Ono, relayed her message by phone. If that wasn't recognition enough, there were also personally signed congratulations from British Prime Minister Tony Blair and the Queen!

# The Least You Need to Know

➤ John and Paul met for the first time at a fete at St. Peter's Parish Church in Woolton on July 6, 1957.

➤ John invited Paul to join The Quarry Men after weighing whether or not Paul's talent would threaten his leadership role in the group.

➤ George Harrison was introduced to John through Paul, and "auditioned" by playing the song "Raunchy."

➤ John and Paul honed their skills as songwriters when the band wasn't getting much work.

➤ The band chopped and changed names many times before becoming The Beatles.

# Too Much Monkey Business

1960 really marked a turning point for The Beatles. Not only did they settle on a permanent band name, but, after an uneventful start, they also began to secure more worthwhile bookings. They undertook their first tour; started to build a local following; made their initial, arduous but exciting trip to Hamburg (in what was then West Germany); and topped things off on their return to Liverpool by experiencing their first real taste of fan mania.

More than anything, as 1960 wore on, The Beatles began to get the feeling that, just maybe, they could make a living doing all of this. Sure, there had been problems fleshing out the lineup, but by the year's end they had at last found someone who was willing and able to back them full-time on the drums, as well as a man who was prepared to kick-start their career.

Anyway, before we get to that, let's begin by taking a look at what our boys were doing (or, more to the point, *not* doing) in terms of their studies and "sensible" employment. It was the dawn of an exciting new decade, but to have foreseen that these dead-end kids were going to have any sort of impact on it you'd have had to be a psychic… or a complete idiot.

## Studies and Not-So-Steady Jobs

Back in 1957, the writing had clearly been on the wall for John Lennon in terms of his career prospects. Aunt Mimi had done her best, overseeing her nephew's studies at home and trying to pull him back into line when he misbehaved at nearby Quarry Bank High School. Then along came Elvis Presley, and it was all over.

Entered for nine *GCE O-levels*, John failed the lot, including art, which was his best subject. Still, in the fall of 1957, his impressive portfolio of drawings did gain him entry to Liverpool College of Art, and immediately he stood out… for all of the wrong reasons. Here, among all of these arty young intellectuals in their casual coats and chunky sweaters, was a greasy-haired Teddy boy wearing a pale blue drape jacket, tight black "drainpipe" jeans, lilac shirt, bootlace tie, and crepe-soled shoes. Not a sight for sore eyes, and his behavior in class was likely to cause sore ears. Basically, John had expected to be given free rein to express himself with pencil and paintbrush, but when he discovered that he had to take courses in geometry, architecture, object drawing, and lettering, he just gave up and generally fooled around in class.

Eventually, having observed the bohemian lifestyle of fellow students Stuart Sutcliffe and Rod Murray, John decided that he wanted to move out of "Mendips." Stu and Rod shared a run-down room in a large Georgian house on Gambier Terrace, near the college. John fancied moving in with them, not only because they shared a love of art and poetry, but also because this would enable him to spend more time with his girlfriend, Cynthia, and as little as possible listening to Mimi's persistent nagging. "I feel like a baby living at home," he told his aunt, before charmingly adding, "Anyhow, I can't stand your food!"

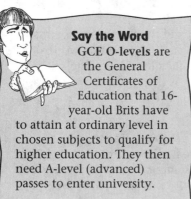

**Say the Word**

GCE O-levels are the General Certificates of Education that 16-year-old Brits have to attain at ordinary level in chosen subjects to qualify for higher education. They then need A-level (advanced) passes to enter university.

Fine—he could go. And go he did, with his full college grant. Four weeks later, he was broke and starving. The money that was supposed to last three months had all been spent, the Gambier Terrace flat was a shambles, and by the middle of winter, John, Stu, and Rod reportedly had to burn furniture in the middle of the room to keep warm.

Occasionally, when his hunger got the better of him, John would turn up on Mimi's doorstep and she would oblige with a meal. She would also plead with him to give up the guitar and concentrate on his drawing, but all to no avail. "I'll be okay," he would say. "I don't need the bits of paper to tell me where I'm going."

*The house at 3 Gambier Terrace, in which John shared a room with Stu Sutcliffe and Rod Murray, and where they slept on mattresses surrounded by paints, clothes, and garbage.*
©Richard Buskin

Where he was going was Scotland, for which he cut class in May of 1960 in order to tour with The Silver Beetles. Soon afterwards, having ended his course and failed his lettering exams, he felt free to do as he liked.

**I Want to Tell You**

"The guitar's alright as a hobby, John, but you'll never make a living out of it."

—Aunt Mimi, c.1958

Paul's teen education consisted of a somewhat similar story to John's—plenty of promise to begin with before petering out at the end. There, however, the similarity ends. Paul was always far more studious and conscientious than John. He was fairly well behaved, and certainly didn't present his teachers with a rebellious problem. However, you also have to remember that he was nearly two years younger than his Lennonish friend, and his own education was interrupted even earlier when things began to get interesting for The Beatles.

Paul did manage to pass enough O-levels at the Liverpool Institute to carry on and prepare for his A-levels in English and Art. However, he didn't exactly over-extend himself in that regard. In the spring of 1960 he should have been deep in revision for the forthcoming exams. Instead, he was packing his bags for Scotland, having somehow convinced his vigilant but kindly father, Jim, that—now get this—the break would help his chances by giving his brain a rest!

After Scotland, after A-levels, the plan was still on for Paul to go to teacher training college. (Isn't that a beauty? Talk about "what might have been"!) However, the Hamburg trip was looming, and for P McC the offer was just too good to pass up. Once again his persuasive powers did the trick on his father, who reasoned that it would be good for his son to get this whole business "out of his system." Then he could settle down and go to college. Yeah, right!

Meanwhile, what about George? Well, here we're *really* beginning to slide down the academic scale (as we head towards Ringo). George, like John, ended up with zip O-levels. George, unlike John, quit all forms of studying right there and then. (In fact, he had basically quit them long before.) That was in 1959, when The Quarry Men/Johnny and the Moondogs were going through a particularly lean period.

For several months George just played his guitar whenever and wherever the opportunity arose, and got by with some financial assistance from his hard-working dad. Eventually, however, due to a combination of pressure from his father and his own admitted embarrassment, George tried to get a job at the Liverpool Corporation. He failed the test. Then he went to the Youth Employment Centre and was told about a job as a window dresser at Blackler's, the Liverpool department store. When he arrived there that job had already gone, so he was taken on as an apprentice electrician instead. And there he remained... until that tour of Scotland came up with The Silver Beetles.

Which brings us to Ringo, whose education had been decimated by illness, and whose first job at age 16 was as a messenger boy for British Rail. That could have been a nice, steady vocation—not too demanding, regular wage increases, two weeks vacation each year. But Ritchie was disgruntled. His lowly status didn't qualify him for a proper uniform, so he walked out after six weeks. (Or perhaps he took the train.)

Disappointed with life around the tracks, young Mr. Starkey next tried his luck traveling across the water. This was on a Mersey River ferry boat making regular trips between Liverpool and New Brighton, featuring Ritchie as a barman. Unfortunately, it appears that he became a little confused as to whether he should be serving the drinks or *consuming* them, and, after some drunken revelry, he was fired.

Still, Ritchie wasn't disheartened, and soon, thanks to the intervention of his stepfather, Harry Graves, he was set up with what could have been another steady job for life. This was as an apprentice fitter at Hunt's engineering firm, which is where, as I've previously mentioned, the future Beatle joined forces with fellow apprentice, Eddie Miles, to form The Eddie Clayton Skiffle Group.

That still leaves us in about 1957, but I've decided not to tell you any more about Ringo until Chapter 11. That may seem mean, but believe me, there's method to my madness.

# Stuart Sutcliffe: The Fifth Beatle

Several people have been referred to as "the fifth Beatle," from manager, Brian Epstein, and ex-drummer, Pete Best, to record producer, George Martin. Famous New York disc jockey Murray the K latched onto the group when they first visited the States in 1964 and anointed himself "the fifth Beatle," apparently hoping some of the "silver" would rub off on him.

In truth, of course, John, Paul, George, and Ringo were the only Beatles who shook the world, but there had been a time when the group featured a five-man lineup by choice. (At least *John Lennon's* choice.) This consisted of George on lead guitar, John and Paul on rhythm, Pete Best and a variety of others on drums, and Stuart Sutcliffe on bass. Stu was John's closest friend at Art College, and if anyone could justifiably be called "the fifth Beatle," Stu was the one.

Born to Scottish parents in Edinburgh in 1940, Stuart Fergusson Victor Sutcliffe had moved to Liverpool with his family as a toddler, and from an early age displayed a precocious, unconventional talent for art. Subsequently, he was accepted into Liverpool College of Art before he had even reached the normal age of admittance.

In early 1959, the quiet, thoughtful, slender Sutcliffe ran into John Winston Lennon, and although the two may have appeared to be polar opposites, in truth they were spiritual soulmates. Each had a passion for art and literature, especially the stream-of-consciousness writings by then-popular "beat" poets such as Kerouac and Ferlinghetti, which expressed their need to break free from life's constrictions.

> **With a Little Help**
> If you want to gain more insight into Stu Sutcliffe's involvement with The Beatles, rent the 1994 film, *Backbeat*. Although some facts are a little inaccurate, this is generally a realistic account of Stuart's adventures with the group, his friendship with John Lennon, and his untimely death. Among all of the Beatle-related biopics, it's one of the best.

In John, Stuart saw the literate, witty, extrovert character that he admired but could never be; in Stuart, with his arty, tight-fitting clothes, swept-back hair, dark glasses, and general air of mystery, John saw the understated qualities that he himself admired but could never aspire to. At the same time, he also recognized a vulnerability and a sensitivity that he could identify with, as well as a deep-rooted knowledge of art and literature that fascinated him.

The whole idea of playing in a rock and roll band appealed to Stu. He had no innate musical ability, but the image was the thing; it would give even greater resonance to his status as an artist. John evidently agreed. If he was the band's hard-edged rocker and Paul its handsome, romantic type, then Stu could be its James Dean: sensitive, wounded, a "man of mystery."

In November 1959 and January 1960, the second biennial John Moores Exhibition took place at Liverpool's celebrated Walker Art Gallery. A painting submitted by Stu was among the few selected to hang there, and it made such an impression on Moores himself that, once the exhibition was over, he bought it for £65 (about $160).

Now, according to John, Paul, and George, what better way to use this hard-earned cash than to spend it on a bass guitar? Stu was quickly persuaded; instead of purchasing art materials he invested in a Hofner President bass and joined the group. The basic skills of playing were beyond him, but he looked great, and whenever he felt that he was in danger of being exposed on stage, he'd just turn his back to the audience!

Stu skipped college to go with The Silver Beetles on their tour of Scotland, and he was with them when they made the first trip to Hamburg. Girls in the audience would swoon when he stepped up to the microphone to croon the Elvis Presley ballad, "Love Me Tender," and among them was a local photographer by the name of Astrid Kirchherr. When The Beatles returned to Liverpool towards the end of 1960, Stuart remained in Hamburg with Astrid. He stayed until February and then was back in Hamburg the following month, before The Beatles arrived there to commence their second round of German concerts. By now his membership in the group was basically over. He'd occasionally join them on stage and was always around to see them perform, but, with the other members' merciless criticism of his playing (especially Paul's), his own lack of musical interest, and his all-consuming love for Astrid, his attentions lay elsewhere.

**With a Little Help**

If you want to hear Stuart Sutcliffe playing bass alongside John, Paul, and George, listen to the rough recordings of "Hallelujah, I Love Her So," "You'll Be Mine," and "Cayenne," on *The Beatles Anthology 1* CD set. Taped during a rehearsal at Paul's Liverpool home in the spring or early summer of 1960, this is the only session to have survived from Stu's time with the group.

As I've already mentioned, Stu was the first Beatle to have his hair styled into a "moptop" by Astrid. Unfortunately, he also, according to legend, received a crushing kick to the head from a local thug outside a Liverpool venue sometime in 1960. Whether this was the cause of his blinding headaches is not clear, but they steadily grew worse, and on April 10,

1962, he collapsed in the Hamburg apartment that he and Astrid shared. He had suffered a brain hemorrhage. Stu died in her arms as an ambulance sped them to a nearby hospital. He was 21.

Unaware of the tragedy, The Beatles arrived for their third stint in Hamburg the very next day. Astrid met them at the airport and they were devastated by the news, yet the show had to go on. On April 13 Stuart's mother, Millie Sutcliffe, arrived in Hamburg to formally identify her son and take his body back to Liverpool. That night The Beatles opened at the soon-to-be legendary Star-Club.

# Failed Auditions: Part I

At the end of the rooftop concert that provides the finale to the Beatles documentary movie, *Let It Be*, John wryly expresses his thanks to the makeshift audience and a hope that the group has "passed the audition." This seemingly blasé comment, however, may have been a little more pointed than most people realized, for, over the years, The Beatles had their fair share of auditions, and their fair share of failures.

A few of these were documented in Chapter 8 and there are a bunch to follow, but among the most notable of their early try-outs was one that took place at the Wyvern Social Club in Liverpool on May 10, 1960. This was owned by Welsh-born businessman, Allan Williams, who had recently teamed up with top British impresario, Larry Parnes, to promote an all-star concert in Liverpool. Parnes had been impressed by some of the local musical talent, and he was now interested in auditioning groups that could back his own stable of touring artists.

Thanks to Larry, these singers had been re-christened with turbulent-sounding stage names such as Billy Fury, Tommy Steele, Duffy Power, Marty Wilde, Georgie Fame, Lance Fortune, Vince Eager, Nelson Keene, and Dickie Pride. Fury, a native Liverpudlian whose real name was Ronald Wycherley, was about to embark on a nationwide tour, and so he was the one most desperately in need of a band. Williams set up the auditions and invited many of Liverpool's top beat groups, including Derry and the Seniors, Cass and the Cassanovas, and Gerry and the Pacemakers. The newly re-named Silver Beetles turned up as well, decked out in matching black shirts and pants, and white-top shoes. The only problem—they didn't have a drummer.

Tommy Moore, who had recently been fulfilling this role for the group, still hadn't arrived when The Silver Beetles began their 10-minute spot. Johnny Hutchinson of the Cassanovas was persuaded to sit in with them until Moore showed up half way through, but although the boys gave it their all, this wasn't quite enough.

According to the recollections of Allan Williams, Billy Fury loved The Silver Beetles, but Larry Parnes wasn't fooled by Stu Sutcliffe turning his back to them while fumbling around on his guitar. They could tour if they were four, but not with Stu. John, Paul, and George flatly refused. This story, however, was later refuted by Parnes. He stated that his main problem was with 36-year-old Tommy Moore, who arrived late and looked positively old in comparison to his four young colleagues.

Either way, no backing group was found for Billy Fury on that occasion. However, The Silver Beetles were awarded the opportunity to tour Scotland behind one of Parnes' lesser known artists, Johnny Gentle. Now, considering that the guys could have been asked to support an artist with a name like Fury, Steele, Power, or Wilde, the limp moniker of Gentle came as a profound disappointment. So, for that matter, did the tour.

Each Silver Beetle was paid £18 (about $45) per week and part expenses for the seven-engagement, nine-day jaunt, but their money soon ran out. They were starving, their clothes were tattered, and they were freezing cold, cooped up in a battered van as they zig-zagged around Scotland's northeast coast. When they got home they were broke and fed up.

So much for the notion of rock and roll being glamorous.

# The Man Who Gave it All Away: Allan Williams

Allan Richard Williams may have been, by his own admission, only a small cog in the giant wheel of The Beatles' career, yet the role that he did play was an absolutely vital one.

Aside from securing the band gigs around Liverpool, Williams was also the man who took them to Hamburg. There, among other things, they became seasoned stage performers, had their hair styled into the soon-to-be famous "moptop," and made a recording that would eventually bring them to the attention of manager Brian Epstein. Had The Beatles never visited Hamburg, there's no telling how their fortunes would have fared. For that reason alone, they should be extremely grateful to Allan Williams. Basically, here's what happened…

## Bumping 'n' Grinding

Not that the entrepreneurial Williams assisted The Beatles for purely charitable reasons. After all, why should he? He was running a small Liverpool coffee bar named the Jacaranda when he first set eyes on them, sitting at a corner table sharing a Coke or a *jam butty*. When things got really desperate, they agreed to redecorate the Jac's bathrooms for some free meals, but after Williams found the band a drummer in the shape of Tommy Moore, and they went on the Scottish tour, he began to take them more seriously.

> **Say the Word**
> **Jam butty** is the Liverpool slang term for a bread, butter, and jam sandwich, which is what The Silver Beetles sometimes used to subsist on when concerts were few and money was hard to come by.

Through his company, Jacaranda Enterprises, he started to book them into venues on either side of the River Mersey. Also, in return for a very generous Coca-Cola and plate of baked beans on toast, they'd play in the basement venue of the Jacaranda when the resident Royal Caribbean Steel Band had the night off. Nevertheless, Allan Williams was also responsible for what could be viewed as the nadir of the band's career.

In the early summer of 1960, Williams engaged them to play at the New Cabaret Artistes, yet another venue he had recently opened. The fact that the NCA was an illegal *strip* club meant that, in the eyes of the breathless customers, the group's performance could never match that of the "artiste" they were backing. Her name was Janice, a class act who insisted on exhibiting her talents to live music, not crackling records.

The again-renamed Silver Beatles were, by now, drummerless once more, but with three guitars and a bass piled onto the tiny stage, they gave Janice what she'd asked for. Well, almost. She had provided them with sheet music to works by Beethoven and Khachaturian, but they couldn't read notation. Instead they strummed their way through "Summertime," "Begin The Beguine," "Harry Lime (*Third Man* Theme)," "Moonglow And The Theme From *Picnic*," "September Song," and—you'll love this—"It's A Long Way To Tipperary." Their payment was £2 (about $5) per night, and they played for a week. What a pity no one filmed the performance!

Williams promised that things would get better. After all, what else could he say? However, not even he could have foreseen what his own enterprise and some incredible luck would soon achieve.

## Playing For Hamburgers

One night Allan Williams discovered that his Royal Caribbean Steel Band had been secretly lured away to a club in Hamburg. Some of the band's members subsequently contacted Williams, told him about the exciting German nightlife, and suggested that he visit there with some other groups.

*Allan Williams, The Beatles' first manager-cum-booking agent, who was responsible for taking the band on their first trip to Hamburg.*
©Richard Buskin

The tireless businessman's response was to make a recording of several local bands, including The Silver Beatles, and then take this to Hamburg where he met with one Bruno Koschmider. The owner of a club named the Kaiserkeller, Koschmider was impressed by Allan's boast that he managed some of "the greatest rock bands in the world," yet he was less than enthused when he heard the tape. Somewhere along the journey from Liverpool this had become demagnetized, and the audible result was noisy gibberish.

Williams returned home with egg on his face, only to be confronted by another of his acts, Derry and the Seniors. They had quit their jobs when Larry Parnes had promised them work backing some of his singers. Now Parnes had canceled his plans and the band was ready to kill. In desperation, Williams drove them all to London, and the Two I's Coffee Bar, where acts such as Tommy Steele had been discovered. Allan knew the manager there and persuaded him to let Derry and the boys perform. Meanwhile, who should be there but Bruno Koschmider! Do the words "incredible" and "coincidence" come to mind?

Despite the useless tape that Williams had taken to Hamburg, Koschmider had been impressed by the Welshman's outlandish boasts. Maybe he should pay a visit to England... London, England. Now he was watching a performance by Derry and the Seniors, and he liked them. There and then he signed the band to play at the Kaiserkeller.

Soon after the Seniors started appearing at his club, Koschmider wrote to Williams, informing him that he was about to open a second venue, the Indra, where he would like to engage another of Allan's terrific groups. After approaching several local outfits and finding them unwilling or unavailable, Williams eventually offered the booking to The Silver Beatles, provided that they could come up with a drummer. This they did.

### Do You Want to Know a Secret?

In November 1961, shortly after seeing The Beatles for the first time at the Cavern Club, Brian Epstein got it into his head that maybe he could manage the band. Relatives, friends, and business associates all tried to dissuade him; after all, he was a complete novice in this field. Still, he began to seek the advice of people "in the know," and one of these was Allan Williams, who Epstein sought out at yet another of Williams' clubs, the Blue Angel. "What should I do?" inquired Brian. "Don't touch 'em with a f—g bargepole," was the memorable reply. Epstein ignored the advice, and Williams was left to eat his heart out.

Allan Williams, his wife, brother-in-law, business partner, and an interpreter all accompanied the newly renamed Beatles to Hamburg, arriving there on August 17, 1960. From that point on the group would never look back, and neither would they honor their verbal agreement with their manager-cum-booking agent. After negotiating the terms of their club contract just prior to their second Hamburg visit in early 1961, the band members decided that Williams no longer deserved his commission. He threatened to sue—and probably would have won—but he didn't bother. Fourteen years later Allan Williams was the co-author of the highly entertaining memoir, *The Man Who Gave the Beatles Away.*

# The Search for a Drummer

Okay, so now we arrive at the real problem-spot for the early Beatles (or whatever their name was at a given moment): finding someone to put behind the skins. After all, you needed money to own a full kit, and in Liverpool those days that wasn't always easy to come by. Which is why Colin Hanton, for all of his technical shortcomings, was still a handy chap to have around. When a drunken squabble resulted in his departure, John, Paul, and George probably assumed that they could "find more where he came from," but soon realized that they couldn't.

Hanton had been a founding member of The Quarry Men, and, as such, he was basically in it for the long haul. Several of those who succeeded him, however, had a different attitude. Tommy Moore was brought on board by Allan Williams, who heard about him sitting in with various bands at a club run by local concert promoter, Sam Leach. Moore had little in common with his fellow Silver Beetles, but he needed the money, which was one of the reasons why he was so fed up after returning virtually penniless from the Scottish tour.

Another factor had been a crash involving the van in which they were traveling, resulting in Tommy suffering from a concussion and the loss of several front teeth. Dragged out of hospital to carry on with the tour, he then found himself constantly on the receiving end of John's malicious humor. As he himself put it, by the end of the tour he'd had "a bellyful of Lennon," and soon after that he was an ex-Silver Beetle with a job at the Garston bottle works.

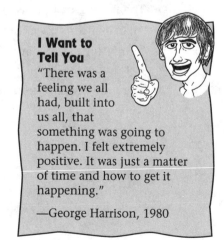

**I Want to Tell You**

"There was a feeling we all had, built into us all, that something was going to happen. I felt extremely positive. It was just a matter of time and how to get it happening."

—George Harrison, 1980

One evening, John, Paul, George, and Stu tried to persuade Tommy to climb down from his forklift and help them out on a gig that had already been booked. He flatly refused, which meant that they were now in a sticky situation. Then, just to make matters worse, Lennon's loose tongue sprang to life and things got even stickier.

You see, the band still had Tommy's kit. Therefore, when they took to the stage that night, John decided that it would be wise to tell the audience about their predicament. Fair enough. Then, half-jokingly, he asked if any drummers present would like to help out.

This was at the Grosvenor Ballroom in Liscard, a venue notorious for its naked violence and vicious thugs. One such individual, a hefty Teddy boy named Ronnie, immediately took Lennon up on his offer and seated himself behind the kit, where he proceeded to thrash away at the drums like a mad gorilla. Only Allan Williams' hasty intervention in response to John's frantic phone call ensured that the band got out with their lives, as well as their equipment.

Not surprisingly, John didn't bother to ask if anyone cared to drum with them when they played at the New Cabaret Artistes strip club. Soon afterwards, however, they did manage to recruit an excellent drummer named Norman Chapman. He played with the group for a few weeks before being among the last young Brits to be conscripted into the Army.

Which brings us back to August, and Allan Williams' offer to send The Silver Beatles to Hamburg... if they would just find themselves a drummer! The only gigs that they'd been able to secure without one were the regular Saturday night bloodfests at the aforementioned Grosvenor Ballroom. That was until August 6, when residents' complaints about all of the hooliganism forced the local council to cancel that week's "swing session." With nothing better to do, John, Paul, George, and Stu turned up at the Casbah Coffee Club run by Mona Best, and there they saw her handsome 18-year-old son, Pete, playing drums with a band named The Blackjacks.

The Silver Beatles were interested to hear that The Blackjacks were on the verge of disbanding, and that Pete Best, having recently left Liverpool Collegiate Grammar School with several GCE exam passes, was looking for a full-time career as a professional drummer. Equally fascinating to them was his gorgeous new kit. After a quick audition, Pete was offered the chance to join them in Hamburg. He was on his way.

## The Least You Need to Know

➤ The Beatles were neither good students nor good laborers (outside of music, that is).

➤ The Beatles' first professional tour, in Scotland, was a profound disappointment.

➤ Allan Williams played a vital role during the band's early development.

➤ John, Paul, George, and Stu were reduced to backing a stripper before their first trip to Hamburg.

➤ The Beatles went through a series of drummers until they found Pete Best.

# Leather and Liquor— Live in Hamburg

The first major turning point in The Beatles' career occurred in Hamburg, in what was then West Germany. Before the first trip, the band had no permanent drummer, and was basically a ramshackle collection of part-time musicians who had little idea about how to perform on stage. The Hamburg experience changed all that.

For one thing, the incessant nightly routine of playing very long hours before demanding audiences ensured that The Beatles evolved into a tight-knit musical unit. They had to expand their repertoire and perform the songs over and over again. As a result, they now not only knew the parts that they were playing, but they were also able to refine, innovate, and craft the sound that would one day rock the world.

At the same time, playing in nightclubs where the patrons' expectations appeared to rise along with their blood alcohol level, our heroes really had to put on a show. Standing like statues while performing limp renditions of other people's songs just wouldn't cut it in front of these crowds. No, for them the Liverpool lads had to jump around and belt out rock numbers like "Long Tall Sally" and "Sweet Little Sixteen" in a style that was light years away from their tame 1958 recording of "That'll Be The Day" (on *The Beatles Anthology 1*).

Between August 1960 and December 1962, The Beatles made five trips to Hamburg and performed more than 800 hours on stage. During that time they also found plenty to do away from the clubs, being situated, as they were, smack in the middle of the city's red-light district. You see, Hamburg was where "the boys" grew up in more ways than one, and if that line doesn't tempt you to read on, nothing will…

# Up and Down the Reeperbahn

Loud night-clubs, oceans of booze, brawling sailors, gaudy women, gangsters, transvestites, pimps, and prostitutes… ah yes, Hamburg's St. Pauli neighborhood was quite a place to be back in the early 1960s.

*Allan Williams, wife Beryl, business partner Lord Woodbine, Stu Sutcliffe, Paul, George, and Pete Best, pose in front of a prophetic war memorial in Arnhem, Holland, en route to Hamburg on August 16, 1960.*
©Hulton Getty

Like Liverpool, Hamburg is a seaport, populated with its fair share of no-nonsense, hard-nosed individuals, and during the Second World War both cities endured heavy bombing. The major similarities end there, however. Basically, John, Paul, George, Stu, and Pete had never seen anything like the sights that greeted them on August 17, 1960, when their van rumbled down the Reeperbahn and made its way to the Grosse Freiheit. Sure, they may have taken trips to the English seaside resort of Blackpool to look at the Disney-like illuminations, but now, late at night, they were attracted by lights of another kind: flashing neon ones, with signs boasting about the entertainment—musical and otherwise—that the numerous bars and clubs had to offer.

High-heeled shoes, fishnet stockings, scanty panties, and a leather *bustier* appeared to be *de rigueur* clothing among many of the women (and several of the men) parading their wares, both on the street and in the shop windows. Okay, so Disneyland may be "the happiest place on earth," but hey, if you were in your late-teens, where would you rather be? For the not-yet-Fab Five there could be little doubt; this place was cooking, and they couldn't wait to get out of the van and into those clubs.

Nevertheless, The Beatles had arrived so late at night that the Indra Club, where they would be playing, was closed. They therefore searched for the owner at another of his venues, the Kaiserkeller, where they ran into the resident Liverpool band, Derry and the Seniors. With the exception of singer Derry Wilkie, these were the guys who—led by sax player Howie Casey—had sent a letter to Allan Williams a short time before, moaning that he would ruin the scene for everyone if he sent over "that bum group The Beatles." As you'd expect, Howie and Co. were none too happy to now see those bums on their turf. The bums moved on, back to the Indra.

## Do You Want to Know a Secret?

You know that old saying about being careful how you treat people on the way up, because you never know if you'll need them on the way down? Well, Howie Casey is a case in point. Howie, of course, once dismissed The Beatles as a "bum group." Dear, oh dear! Thirteen years later, one fifth of that bum group was employing Howie as a backing musician. In 1973 the burly saxophone player appeared on Paul McCartney and Wings' *Band On The Run* album, and then accompanied the group on their 1975/76 world tour and 1979 British tour. That same year, he also played on the *Back To The Egg* album. Er, what did you say, Howie?

An altogether smaller and pokier venue than the comparatively plush Kaiserkeller, the Indra at least provided John, Paul, George, Stu, and Pete with somewhere to bed down for the night. To that end, they stretched out on the club's red leather bench seats. It got worse the next day, when club owner Bruno Koschmider led them to their full-time sleeping quarters: a decrepit little room behind the flimsy screen of a flea-pit cinema around the corner. Named the Bambi Filmkunsttheater (careful how you pronounce it!), and known as the Bambi Kino, this Koschmider-owned joint specialized in old American Westerns. Its filthy "bathroom" was where The Beatles were told they could wash, and they probably debated which would be more hygienic to bathe themselves in—the sink or the toilet.

At least they didn't have to worry about taking girls back there. After all, their usual acquaintances—an assortment of strippers and other career women—invariably had their own accommodations arranged. So, here was the social setup: the Gretel and Alphons or

**I Want to Tell You**

"What with playing, drinking, and birds, how could we find time to sleep?"

—John Lennon on life in Hamburg

Willi's Bar when they fancied a few dozen beers; the Reeperbahn or Grosse Freiheit for some early morning "action"; and then all down to the British Seamen's Mission at around noon for steak, eggs, and fries, or some refreshing bowls of *Cornflakes mit milch*. The place they saw the least of was the Bambi Kino, and who could blame them? Not only was it a hell-hole, but they often only had an hour or two to crash there.

Later on, when The Beatles played at the Top Ten Club, they slept in bunk beds in the overhead attic—not exactly the Ritz, but at least they were moving *up!*

## Band on the Run

The Beatles' time at the Indra was short-lived, and so, for that matter, was the Indra. To start with, this tawdry strip club–turned–music venue was hardly suited to live bands. It was poorly lit, had a tiny stage, and was shabbily decorated. Consequently, few people turned up to dance to the sounds of some unknown Liverpudlians, and when the group did try to enliven things by cranking up the volume, the old woman in the upstairs apartment complained to the police. Obviously she preferred the sound of grinding dancers and groaning patrons. Precisely 48 days after opening the Indra, Bruno Koschmider closed it down.

**I Should Have Known Better**

Tony Sheridan was not the real name of the talented singer/guitarist who befriended The Beatles in Hamburg. Actually, it was Anthony Esmond Sheridan McGinnity—a mouthful to use on stage. Having made several records and TV appearances in the UK, Sheridan was held in high esteem by The Beatles. His backing band, The Jets, were from London.

This turned out to be a decent break for The Beatles. On October 4, Koschmider moved them into the Kaiserkeller to alternate with one of Liverpool's top bands, Rory Storm and the Hurricanes, featuring a certain Ringo Starr on drums. Things went well there, and on October 16 their contract was extended until December 31. Then trouble raised its ugly head in the form of yet another new club and, for Koschmider at least, some unwanted competition.

The name of the new venue was the Top Ten, and its owner, Peter Eckhorn, struck an immediate low-blow against the Kaiserkeller by luring away its chief bouncer, Horst Fascher. With hard-drinking thugs regularly visiting the St. Pauli district, a good bouncer was a prized possession, and Bruno Koschmider was not a happy man. Imagine his fury, therefore, when he learned that his newly beloved Beatles had committed the ultimate treachery: They had been moonlighting at the Top Ten, jamming on stage with the resident singer/guitarist, Tony Sheridan! This was in direct contravention of the clause in their contract, stipulating that they couldn't play anywhere within a 25-mile radius without his permission. The Beatles were given a month's notice. Then things went from bad to worse.

The band apparently didn't know that in West Germany there was a curfew, preventing anyone under the age of 18 from even being in a club after midnight. Well, George was just 17, and not only frequenting the night spots well into the wee small hours of the morning, but also working in them. Somehow the authorities learned about this, and on November 21 The Beatles' lead guitarist was deported back to Liverpool.

As if that wasn't enough, Paul and Pete then fell foul of the law as well. Together with John and Stu, Pete Eckhorn had offered them the room above the Top Ten—infinitely better than the rotten old Bambi Kino. Since they were already on the outs with Bruno Koschmider, they really didn't care what he thought; and, just to prove the point, Messrs. McCartney and Best indulged in an innocent—yet untimely—prank. As they were leaving the Bambi with packed bags, they stuck a rubber condom (unused) on one of the walls, set fire to it, and watched as it made a small, black scorch mark. No big deal, yet word of the incident immediately reached the vengeful ears of Koschmider, and Paul and Pete were thrown behind bars for "attempting to set fire to the Bambi."

After a night in the slammer, both Beatles were temporarily released, only to be re-arrested several hours later and informed that they were being deported on the midnight flight to London. The next morning, December 1, they were on a train from London's Euston Street station to Lime Street in Liverpool, and nine days later a dejected John arrived home, too. Only Stu remained behind in Germany, to be with his new love, Astrid Kirchherr.

This whole debacle could have been a major setback to the group, but instead they turned adversity to their advantage and capitalized locally on their Hamburg stage experience. (You'll find details of this in Chapter 11, but don't skip ahead!) Furthermore, subject to the lifting of their deportation bans (and without Allan Williams' knowledge), The Beatles had already negotiated a one-month booking at the Top Ten Club for the following April. So, things weren't all that bad after all.

## Mach Shau! The Hamburg Clubs

John, Paul, George, Stu, and Pete were each paid 210 DM ($43) per week for performing at the Indra. This included stretches of four and a half hours between 8 p.m. and 2 a.m. every night during the week, six hours on Saturdays, between 7 p.m. and 3 a.m., and another six on Sundays, between 5 p.m. and 1:30 a.m. Little reward for a heavy workload, which, as I've already told you, was matched by a lack of audience enthusiasm. (Or just a plain lack of audience.)

## Do You Want to Know a Secret?

If you're planning a trip to Hamburg and wish to visit the sites of the venues where The Beatles played, you really won't have very far to walk between them. Here are the addresses:

The Indra, 34 Grosse Freiheit

The Kaiserkeller, 36 Grosse Freiheit

The Top Ten Club, 136 Reeperbahn

The Star-Club, 39 Grosse Freiheit (Now demolished and rebuilt.)

Things were considerably different at the Kaiserkeller. A basement venue with unusual nautical decor, this afforded The Beatles one of the largest stages they had ever performed on, even though they didn't know how to make use of it. That was until October 10, their seventh night there, when Allan Williams, making a return visit to Hamburg, decided that he'd had enough of watching his proteges stand around like store-window dummies. "Make a show, boys!" he urged them, and when Koschmider and his customers heard this, they decided to follow suit. "Mach shau!" they would shout in their best broken-English. This was all the encouragement they needed—especially John Lennon.

Every one of them, with the exception of Pete Best, started jumping around on-stage like crazy men, wiggling their legs in best Elvis fashion, and even limping like the unfortunately crippled Gene Vincent. The audiences loved it. Night after night there would be cries of "mach shau!" and The Beatles wouldn't let them down—but for Lennon the contortions weren't quite enough. Determined to dent German pride, he took to performing *Sieg Heil* salutes, goose-stepping around the stage, and screaming at everybody that they were "f—king Nazis." While some patrons clearly objected, others continued to gulp their beer and scream "mach shau!" Fair enough. If it was "shau" they wanted, then "shau" they'd get. Another night, Herr Lennon would turn up on stage in a pair of bathing trunks with a toilet seat around his neck, shouting, "I'm wearing this because that's what this club is: S—t!"

### Say the Word
**Prellies** was the nickname applied to Preludin, the small stimulant pills—or "uppers"—that The Beatles consumed in Hamburg to help them maintain their level of energy during the long hours performing on stage.

Of course, Koschmider wasn't exactly enchanted by all of the pleasantries, but somehow or other the routine brought an increasing number of locals in to see and hear The Beatles. These patrons would often not only buy drinks for themselves, but also pay for a crate or two of beer to send up onto the stage for the group to enjoy. Which was all very well, save for the fact that, except for Pete Best, The Beatles were taking stimulant pills known as Prellies. After washing these down with loads of free alcohol, John, Paul, George, and Stu would be practically reeling.

The stage at the Kaiserkeller may have been large, but it was also rotten, and a competition soon developed between The Beatles and Rory Storm and the Hurricanes to see who could demolish it first. Rory won the bet, courtesy of a leap and heavy landing during a rendition of "Blue Suede Shoes." Bruno Koschmider was seething and docked the costs from Rory's pay packet, but he was also aware of The Beatles' role in the vandalism and, when they defected to the Top Ten, that was the last straw.

Like the Indra and many other venues in and around St. Pauli, the Top Ten had also been a strip joint in a previous incarnation. Situated in the Hippodrome, the building had until recently been home to a circus, where naked girls rode on horses and did the splits on the high trapeze. It was located on the main drag, the Reeperbahn, where The Beatles had always wanted to play, and it was large enough to accommodate huge crowds. Nevertheless, the contract that they negotiated without Allan Williams' knowledge still earned them a meager salary—35 DM ($8) per man per day—in return for a brutal schedule: from 7 p.m. to 2 a.m. during the week, and 7 p.m. to 3 a.m. on weekends, with a 15-minute break each hour.

By the time The Beatles took to the Top Ten stage in their tight black leather pants and jackets on March 27, 1961, George Harrison was old enough to stay out after midnight, the deportation bans had been lifted, and Stu Sutcliffe had left the group. Looking like a quartet of teenage Gene Vincents, they would remain there, through a twice-extended contract, until July 2, clocking a staggering 535 hours on stage and returning to Liverpool with newly fashioned "moptop" hairstyles. That was it for Hamburg in 1961, but The Beatles would outdo themselves with three separate stints there the following year. None would be at the Top Ten.

In November 1961, Brian Epstein started managing the band, and part of his guarantee to them, aside from securing a recording contract, was to ensure that they played better venues for higher fees. (I'll tell you more about this later on.) Accordingly, when Pete Eckhorn arrived in Liverpool in December to sign acts for the forthcoming year, his generous offer to nearly double The Beatles' weekly salary to 450 DM ($100) per man was turned down by Brian. He wanted 500 DM ($112) each, but still agreed to consider Eckhorn's proposal.

Then, in late January of 1962, Horst Fascher, the former bouncer at the Kaiserkeller who had defected to the Top Ten, also arrived in Liverpool. (Clearly, the soon-to-be-Fab Four were already turning it into a

**With a Little Help**
To sample how The Beatles took liberties with their German audiences, listen to *The Beatles 1962 Recordings* (featuring sleeve notes by Yours Truly), which captures the band at the Star-Club. You'll hear "Shimmy Shimmy" turn into "Sh—ty Sh—ty"; "Your Feet's Too Big" evolve into "Your Feet's Too F——n' Big"; and Paul introducing "Besame Mucho" as "a special request for Hitler; a cha-cha-cha cha-cha-cha for Hitler."

pretty popular place.) He had recently quit Eckhorn's venue in order to manage a huge new Hamburg rock establishment, the Twist Club, which was scheduled to open in the spring. The owner, Manfred Weissleder, had dispatched Fascher to Liverpool to sign up what he considered to be the best possible opening-night act: The Beatles.

Brian Epstein duly got the 500 DM per man that he had been looking for, and his clients were booked for a seven-week engagement, from April 13 to May 31. Their subsequent trip to Hamburg was done in style. John, Paul, and Pete flew there on April 11—George, who was unwell, flew out with Brian Epstein on the 12th—and it was when they arrived that they learned of Stu Sutcliffe's death the previous day. In the meantime, the Twist Club had been renamed the Star-Club, and The Beatles were a major attraction there, even sharing the bill with Gene Vincent for a couple of weeks.

When The Beatles returned for a two-week engagement on November 1, it was with the prized recording contract under their belts, a certain Starr sitting behind the drum kit, and yet another increased weekly salary of 600 DM ($135) per band member. This time they shared the bill with Little Richard. Then, for their last visit, from December 18–31, their weekly pay packet would rise to 750 DM ($170) per man, meaning that in just over a year, thanks to their greater musicianship, increased following, and the invaluable help of Brian Epstein, they had managed to triple their Hamburg fee. Yet, by then that hardly mattered anymore. They were on their way to the top, and long hours on stage were about to become a thing of the past.

# The Hamburg Recordings

During the course of their five Hamburg stints The Beatles made several recordings, some amateur, others professional, and the first of these actually captured a 1960 performance by John, Paul, George, Ringo...and Wally.

It was on Sunday, October 15, just under two years before Ringo joined the group, that he filled in for Pete Best when the others all entered a small studio, named the Akustik, to cut a song. Ringo was there as a member of Rory Storm and the Hurricanes, and, while he sat behind the drums, The Beatles' lineup that day was also augmented by the Hurricanes' bass player, Walter Eymond (known as Wally, although his stage name was Lou Walters). The fruits of their efforts were nine 78-rpm discs, featuring the group's rendition of George Gershwin's "Summertime" on one side, and an ad for leather handbags and shoes on the other. Perhaps it was intended for release. Either way, only one of the discs is reputed to have survived, and if anyone out there has it, I'm prepared to trade my 1963 Beatles mug and a free copy of this book.

The Beatles' first professional recording took place during the group's second trip to Hamburg. At that point, in addition to their own performances at the Top Ten Club, they were also backing Tony Sheridan there. Word of this successful union with The Beatles reached the ears of Bert Kaempfert, the German composer, producer, and orchestra leader, who had recently topped the American charts with the instrumental, "Wonderland By Night." Kaempfert subsequently visited the Top Ten and a buzz went around; play well and it may result in a recording contract. Sheridan was already signed to the Polydor label, and when Kaempfert heard The Beatles' energetic performances, they were invited to his office and promptly signed to record for him as an independent producer. The results would be assigned to Polydor.

Expectations were running high on June 22, when two taxis transported the band and their equipment to the studio. This, however, turned out to be no more than a screened-off stage inside the main hall of a school, and the guys' disappointment was compounded when they realized that they were only there to back Tony Sheridan. This they did on five numbers (without Stu Sutcliffe, who was just an observer): the standards, "My Bonnie Lies Over The Ocean" and "When The Saints Go Marching In"; Sheridan's own "Why (Can't You Love Me Again)"; the Hank Snow country song, "Nobody's Child"; and Jimmy Reed's "Take Out Some Insurance On Me, Baby." Once this was completed, the four Beatles then recorded a couple of numbers on their own: the old Eddie Cantor hit, "Ain't She Sweet," treated to a rock arrangement and a distinctively raw-edged Lennon lead vocal, and a Harrison/Lennon instrumental composition, which they initially considered naming "Beatle Bop." This was eventually titled "Cry For A Shadow," a send-up of Cliff Richard's backing group, The Shadows, who were then enjoying chart success of their own with a string (excuse the pun) of guitar-based instrumentals.

In August 1961, Polydor issued a single featuring "My Bonnie" coupled with "The Saints" (as they were trendily titled), and credited the recordings to Tony Sheridan & The Beat Brothers. This was because the label execs felt that Beatles sounded uncomfortably similar to "peedles," a German slang word for penis. Regardless, the record reached number five on the local charts and sold about 100,000 copies in the process. Back in Liverpool it would also serve to bring The Beatles to the attention of Brian Epstein.

The following year, when Epstein was trying to attain a full-fledged British recording deal for his clients, he asked Bert Kaempfert if he would release them from his own contract. Kaempfert agreed to this, as long as he could still have the opportunity to once again

**I Should Have Known Better**

Discount any stories that you read or hear about The Beatles having recorded the songs "Fever" and "September Song," along with "Summertime," in a small Hamburg studio on October 15, 1960. The first two were indeed recorded, but by members of Rory Storm and the Hurricanes without the lead man himself. Only "Summertime" featured the participation of John, Paul, and George.

**I Should Have Known Better**

While all of the tracks that John, Paul, George, and Pete are known to have recorded for Bert Kaempfert have been released in one form or another, beware of others that are consistently and incorrectly credited to Tony Sheridan and The Beatles: "Let's Dance," "Ya Ya," "What'd I Say," "Ruby Baby," and "Skinny Minny." Tony Sheridan is indeed featured on all of these, but his backing band definitely is not The Beatles.

**I Should Have Known Better**

On the recording of The Beatles' live performance at the Star-Club in Hamburg, two of the tracks, "Be-Bop-A-Lula" and "Hallelujah I Love Her So," feature a vocalist who sounds similar to Paul. In truth, however, the man taking center stage was neither Paul, John, George, or Ringo—but former bouncer turned manager, Horst Fascher!

record them himself when they returned to Hamburg in April. Consequently, between the 23rd and 27th of that month, at an unspecified venue, The Beatles again backed Tony Sheridan, this time on "Sweet Georgia Brown" and, most probably, "Swanee River." The only doubt about the second track centers around the saxophone part, but this was probably overdubbed by a session musician at a later date.

Still, while all of the aforementioned Hamburg recordings were made with decent equipment, in many ways the most interesting one is that which boasts by far the poorest audio quality. The reason? It just happens to capture The Beatles' last-ever performance at the Star-Club, and as such it's a priceless piece of history. Never again would the band play gigs of this duration and with such a diverse selection of material—from Lennon-McCartney originals and rock and roll standards to curios such as "Falling In Love Again (Can't Help It)" and "I Remember You." Within a few months they would be treating their fans to just tightly formatted half-hour concerts.

Given how The Beatles' image is now inexorably tied to the mass screaming and adulation, it's fascinating to hear the informality of a Star-Club show. The audience talks while the band plays, bottles and glasses can be heard to clink, and John and Paul engage in casual banter with the customers and club staff. It's New Year's Eve 1962 and The Beatles are clearly tired, yet there is still an energy to some of the performances that's hard to ignore. It's pretty clear why they were already held in such high regard both in Hamburg and their own home town.

The Beatles were captured on a portable Grundig recorder by Ted Taylor, the hefty leader of Liverpool group Kingsize Taylor and the Dominoes, who were also playing a residency at the Star-Club. The tape was reportedly offered to Brian Epstein during the mid-1960s, but at that time, with the ability to make much better recordings of the band's then-current concerts, he turned it down. The Beatles would regret that decision.

In 1977 the original mono master was transferred to 16-track, cleaned up, and, against the Fab Four's wishes, released to the general public as a double album. It has since been re-issued on several occasions.

By their fifth and final Hamburg stint, The Beatles had a recording contract and were poised for the big time. They no longer needed to play the grueling hours and were thankful to move on, yet in many ways their Hamburg days represented a golden period for them, both in a personal and a professional sense. They could never go back, but they would never forget.

# The Least You Need to Know

➤ While in Hamburg, Germany, The Beatles played the Top Ten Club, the Indra, the Kaiserkeller, and the Star-Club.

➤ The Beatles faced abysmal living conditions in Hamburg and led a raunchy lifestyle.

➤ Deportation from Germany didn't hinder their career.

➤ The Beatles honed their live act from the long sessions in Hamburg and repeat visits.

➤ Several Beatles recordings survive from that era.

# Chapter 11

# From a Keller to a Cellar

**In This Chapter**

➤ Liverpool's reaction to The Beatles following their first Hamburg trip

➤ Ringo's pre-Beatle musical ventures

➤ How the band prospered in a tiny (now legendary) local venue

As you saw in the last chapter, The Beatles made giant strides in their musicianship when they were in Germany. They also learned how to make an impression on their audiences—not always the *best* kind of impression, but a lasting one nonetheless.

Well, in this chapter I'll describe how they utilized what they learned in Hamburg back home in Liverpool, and enjoyed local success as a result. I'll then burst the band's bubble by telling you about a pretty disastrous early attempt to attract attention in the south of England, before bringing you up to date on Ringo's musical activities prior to joining The Beatles. Lastly, I'll tell you about the most legendary Fab Four venue of them all: The Cavern Club in Liverpool, where The Beatles were heroes to adoring fans who would faithfully line up during lunch hours or in the evenings to see and hear "the boys" playing in a musty basement.

Are memories really made of this?

# Fun in Litherland: The First Rumblings of Beatlemania

When The Silver Beatles last played in Liverpool prior to their first Hamburg trip, they were a pretty desperate bunch. The only weekly gigs they had were at the violent Grosvenor Ballroom, where they faced heavy competition from other local bands and were largely considered something of a joke. A bad joke. In fact, things were so desperate that, when the group had no one to fill in for them, Paul would play the drums. Then they went to Hamburg with Pete Best… and when they returned in mid-December 1960, it was a different story.

For one thing they were now renamed The Beatles; for another, the fact that they had just returned from performing overseas appeared to stir up interest on the home front. Never mind that three of the band members had actually been deported; they pretty much kept that to themselves, re-grouped, and immediately capitalized on some new bookings. One of these engagements proved to be a turning point.

*Litherland Town Hall. It was during a concert here, on December 27, 1960, that The Beatles had their first taste of fan mania.*
©Richard Buskin

The Beatles were added to the bill of a December 27 gig at the Town Hall Ballroom in Litherland, a suburb of northern Liverpool. Since they had only played in that area once before, few people there had even heard of the group, and so when the locals saw them billed as "Direct from Hamburg," they naturally assumed that they were German! That night, Beatlemania was born.

As Paul commenced the set by belting out the opening lines to Little Richard's "Long Tall Sally," the effect was instantaneous. The large crowd rushed to the front of the stage and just went crazy, almost mesmerized by the musicians who, just a few months before, would have largely been ignored while they played. Normally, The Beatles were used to a lot of idle chatter while they sang their little hearts out; suddenly they were faced with a horde of kids either shaking their heads furiously to the beat or standing there goggle-eyed.

The band must have been bewildered by all of this, but among the many lessons The Beatles learned during more than 500 hours on stage in Hamburg was how to pounce on the moment. If the customers were ready to rock, they'd give them every reason to, jumping around to a solid, well-rehearsed repertoire of songs that would blast their ears and blow their minds.

In one fell swoop, The Beatles shut the door forever on playing for baked beans on toast or backing a stripper with "It's A Long Way To Tipperary." From now on, the fees improved and, with increasing regularity, the fans went wild. The promoter of the Litherland gig, Brian Kelly, immediately booked the band for no less than 35 engagements during the next two and a half months. In the process, they became Merseyside's number-one rock attraction.

# Oh, Mr. Bass Man

Playing bass guitar with The Beatles at the Litherland Town Hall concert was one Chas Newby. Staying behind in Hamburg, Stu Sutcliffe was evidently far more interested in pursuing his art career and his relationship with Astrid Kirchherr than in remaining a Beatle. John and Paul had constantly mocked Stu's lack of musical ability, and Paul had pressured him—sometimes not too subtly—to quit the group. Now the job was up for grabs, and with ex-Quarry Men bassist Ken Brown down in London (and out of favor), Pete Best thought of Chas Newby, who had played rhythm guitar in his former band, The Blackjacks.

Chas was on a Christmas break from college when he was asked to join The Beatles, and, after borrowing a bass guitar and the obligatory leather jacket, he made his debut with them at the Casbah Coffee Club on December 17, 1960. Thereafter, the lineup of John, Paul, George, Chas, and Pete (it sounds quite good, doesn't it?) gave performances at the Grosvenor Ballroom on Christmas Eve, Litherland Town Hall on the 27th, and again at the Casbah on New Year's Eve. Then Chas went back to college and was never heard of again.

At that point, John Lennon evidently recognized that the main core of the group was sufficient, as long as one of the three guitarists would take over on bass. The only problem was that he wasn't interested in switching from rhythm and George didn't want to give up the lead. Paul was another matter. Since flunking his lead solo during his debut as a Quarry Man just over three years before, he had doubled on rhythm guitar while also dabbling on piano and, when the need arose, drums as well. Now, with no one else willing to assume the role of Beatle bass man, here was an opportunity to carve out his own instrumental niche. He went for it.

Initially, Paul borrowed Stu's giant Hofner President 500/5 bass, which apparently boasted strings that had been snipped from an accommodating piano. Being left-handed, he played this upside down, and initially even tucked the guitar lead into his pocket instead of the amplifier just in case his shortcomings would be audible. (Hey, at least it was more convincing than turning his back on the audience!) However, as I've told you earlier, Paul was by far the most adept all-round musician in The Beatles. It wasn't long before he could plug that lead into the amp without hesitation, at which point he invested in a left-handed violin-shaped Hofner 500/1.

Paul bought the Hofner during the course of The Beatles' stint at Hamburg's Top Ten Club in 1961, and he would later acquire another model with differently arranged pickups. Today, along with a Fender bass, Paul still plays the Hofner in concert; having established himself as one of rock's premier bassists, the "Beatle bass guitar" is the instrument with which he is most closely associated.

# Going South: Alone in Aldershot

Okay, a few paragraphs ago I stated that, in the wake of the Litherland Town Hall gig, "with increasing regularity, the fans went wild." Now, I didn't say that they would *always* go wild, did I? No. And the reason for my caution? Well, let's jump forward a year to the night of December 9, 1961, and the occasion of The Beatles' first-ever live performance in the south of England.

Liverpool promoter Sam Leach bravely decided to venture there by booking five consecutive Saturday nights at the Palais Ballroom in Aldershot, a town 37 miles south-west of London. Then he invited some of the top pop impresarios to see his grandly titled "Battle of the Bands," in which he would pit a rock outfit from Merseyside against a combo from London. A fine idea in principle, but in reality, Sam was wide of the mark.

**I Want to Tell You**

"What we generated was fantastic, when we played straight rock, and there was nobody to touch us in Britain. As soon as we made it, we made it, but the edges were knocked off."

—John Lennon, *Rolling Stone* magazine, 1970

The most appropriate aspect to the whole "battle" notion was the fact that Aldershot is the site of one of Britain's largest military bases. Aside from its army connections and a perennially struggling soccer team, Aldershot had nothing. The music biz bigwigs were hardly going to travel there. (It was enough trouble getting them to leave their offices and go anywhere without the lure of free food and drink.) Why Leach didn't book his battles in London was anyone's guess, but Aldershot's Palais Ballroom was his chosen venue and the first "Battle of the Bands" featured The Beatles "versus" the totally unknown London group, Ivor Jay and the Jay-walkers.

Which brings us to the next problem. The "Big Beat Session," as it was headlined on posters, wasn't properly advertised. According to Leach, he placed an ad in the local *Aldershot News*, but, unbeknownst to him, the paper apparently wouldn't accept his check, as he was not a regular customer. Furthermore, he hadn't supplied them with his address or phone number, so they couldn't contact him. The ad didn't appear.

The Beatles did appear, though, having traveled all day down from Liverpool. When they realized that they faced playing to a completely empty house, they undertook a lightning tour of the town's pubs and coffee bars, informing everyone that there was "a dance going on at the Palais tonight," and that they could get in for free! Now, can you imagine that? There you are, knocking back a pint of beer or sipping a cup of Brazilian blend on a cold Saturday night, when who should pop their heads around the door but John Lennon, Paul McCartney, and George Harrison, asking if you'd like to come and hear them play—*for free!* Within a few years, girls would be hiding out in hotel air-conditioning shafts just to get a glimpse of them! This, however, was December of 1961, the place was Aldershot, and only 18 people took them up on their offer.

That's right, folks. A grand total of 18 adventurous Saturday nighters were there to witness The Beatles' first-ever show "down south," and a show is what they got. Professional to the last, John, Paul, George, and Pete gave their audience the full works, and the patrons responded by spreading out across the ballroom floor and dancing to their heart's content without fear of bumping into anyone. No rushing the stage, no wild scenes, just a nice, sedate, cozy get-together.

Afterwards, with the place cleared of the thronging masses, The Beatles broke open the beer bottles and started kicking bingo balls around the huge floor. Aldershot didn't take kindly to that kind of out-and-out hooliganism. The police arrived and ordered the Liverpudlians to leave their pleasant town. They did, and headed for the brighter lights of London.

As for the battle between The Beatles and Ivor Jay's outfit, there are no surviving score-cards to indicate who won. However, perhaps it was the Jaywalkers who got the nod, as it was they who were back at the Palais Ballroom the following week for "Battle of the Bands II," fending off the challenge from Rory Storm and the Hurricanes. Two hundred and ten paying customers attended that event, after an ad did actually appear in the local paper. Then Sam Leach decided that he'd had enough of Aldershot, and the three remaining battles were canceled.

# Ringo's Roots: Clayton Skiffle and the Raving Texans

There's one other mildly interesting footnote to the whole "Battle of the Bands" fiasco, and that concerns the fact that, for the second of those star-spangled events, the drummer with Ivor Jay and the Jaywalkers had to cross sticks with one Ringo Starr. That's right, Ringo wasn't yet a Beatle, but his and The Beatles' paths were regularly crossing.

As I mentioned earlier, young Mr. Starkey's first musical venture was with The Eddie Clayton Skiffle Group, who played around the same kind of small Liverpool venues as The Quarry Men. I also told you that when a band was in need of a drummer, anyone who

**Say the Word**
**Winkle-pickers**
were the long,
pointy shoes that
were considered
extremely hip
during the late 1950s and
early 60s. A winkle is a small,
edible sea snail which,
presumably, could almost be
pierced by the shoes' pointed
toes!

owned a shiny new kit was often a prime candidate, even without an abundance of percussive skill. Well, Ritchie was fortunate in that his grandfather lent him £50 ($120)—a considerable sum in those days—to purchase a brand-new set of drums, and in 1959 he subsequently joined a band led by vocalist Alan Caldwell.

Caldwell's five-piece group went from Al Caldwell's Texans to The Raving Texans, Al Storm and the Hurricanes, Jett Storm and the Hurricanes, and, finally, Rory Storm and the Hurricanes. At the turn of the 1960s, the Hurricanes were Liverpool's top rock band—not The Beatles—and "Rory," with his blonde bouffant hairdo and flamboyant stage movements, was Merseyside's number one attraction.

Another marked difference was the Hurricane's dress code—the scruffy jeans and leather look was not for them. Instead they would deck themselves out in sharp-looking suits— Rory, perhaps, in powder blue, and the others in hot pink—along with white and black *winkle-pickers*.

"Ritchie" first drummed with the group on March 25, 1959 and joined on a permanent basis that November. His fellow band members started calling him "Rings" because he wore so many, and then amended this to Ringo as, in line with his taste for country & western music, it made him sound like a character in a cowboy film. Starkey was abbreviated to Starr, so that the spot in each show when Ringo took care of the vocals or a drum solo could be billed as "Starr Time."

In May 1960 Rory Storm and the Hurricanes were booked for an entire summer season at Butlin's holiday camp in the Welsh town of Pwllheli. (And if you can pronounce that correctly, you deserve a medal.) Then, in November, they joined The Beatles at the Kaiserkeller in Hamburg, during which time John, Paul, George and Ringo—along with Walter Eymond—made their first amateur recording together. The four men found that they all got along, and, on occasions when Pete Best wasn't feeling well or didn't turn up for a gig, Ringo would sit in with them. For their part, John, Paul, and George were quite impressed by the diminutive drummer—not only did his beard and moustache make him look "sophisticated," but they also knew that back in Liverpool he drove a flashy Ford Zephyr Zodiac. What a guy!

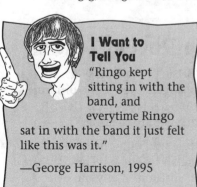

**I Want to
Tell You**
"Ringo kept
sitting in with the
band, and
everytime Ringo
sat in with the band it just felt
like this was it."
—George Harrison, 1995

Ringo continued playing with the Hurricanes, but, as they became locked into an unvarying routine—gigs around Liverpool, summer seasons at Butlin's—he grew restless. In October 1961 he actually wrote to the chamber of commerce in Houston, Texas, with a view to emigrating to the USA, but then lost interest when he realized how much red tape he'd have to deal with. In December he returned to Hamburg. This trip, however, was not made with the

Hurricanes, whom he had just quit. Instead he was backing Tony Sheridan as part of the house band at the Top Ten Club, and he stayed there until March 1962, when Sheridan's argumentative nature encouraged him to re-join Rory and the boys on a French working holiday.

There was also another summer season coming up at Butlin's, this time in Skegness, and it would be there that Ringo's life would be changed forever by a single phone call. However, this is my book, and I've decided that he isn't going to join The Beatles just yet. So, for now, say "bye, bye" to Ringo, and "see you later in Chapter 13…"

# Sweat and Grime: Let's Go Down The Cavern!

If one concert site has become synonymous with The Beatles, it's The Cavern Club, the dingy Mathew Street basement venue located 18 steps below a former fruit and vegetable warehouse, in a run-down city-center back street of Liverpool.

The Cavern is where The Beatles took up residency, where they truly bonded with a hard-core following of die-hard fans, where the adoring girls in the front rows would go out of their way to look their best for their heroes, where Brian Epstein had his initial glimpse of them, and where the group's legend officially started. It was also at The Cavern that TV cameras captured The Beatles for the first time. Yet the place itself was little more than a hole in the ground.

With bare brick walls and stone floors, the venue was something of a death trap. There was no ventilation—the electrical system would have failed the most basic safety inspection, and in the event of a fire the means of escape would have been desperate to say the least. With an off-the-scale humidity factor, sweat would quite literally drip down the walls, producing not only a foul atmosphere but also a threat to the on-stage musicians.

"Either the amps would pack up or there would be a complete power cut," recalled Keef Hartley, a former drummer with Rory Storm and the Hurricanes, John Mayall's Bluesbreakers, and his own Keef Hartley Band, when I interviewed him in 1981. "If this happened, John would immediately jump up onto the piano and go into his routine; 'Here we have Paul McCartney, in a string bag, no arms, no legs…' It was completely unrehearsed, but at the same time it was 'instant Lennon,' with that sick, sick humor of his! That gave The Beatles a tremendous advantage over all of the other bands, and I'm sure that people who went regularly to The Cavern were almost more entertained by that than by the live music."

**With a Little Help**
To sample a little of The Cavern atmosphere, search out *Mersey Beat 62-64*, a 1973 double album on United Artists, featuring club performances by bands such as Rory Storm and the Hurricanes, The Big 3, and Faron's Flamingos. Then there's *Recorded Live at The Cavern*, a 1985 release on the See For Miles label, which showcases Lee Curtis and the All-Stars, Beryl Marsden, The Dennisons, and The Big 3.

Indeed, the intimate setup at The Cavern provided John with ample opportunity to sharpen his cynical, razor-like wit, while Paul made eyes at the girls, the girls made eyes at Pete, and George kept his eyes on his fingers during the guitar solos. The audience, seated on wooden chairs or standing crammed together, were only a couple feet away from the tiny wooden stage, which itself was just a few feet above the floor. Positioned at the end of a central archway, this was lit by several plain white 60-watt bulbs, while in an adjoining archway there was just about enough room to dance. The third main archway, over on the other side, was where the money was taken. Meanwhile, the rest of the club, with its various interconnecting tunnels and Bambi Kino-type "bathroom" facilities, was largely in the dark.

Still, it should be pointed out that, while The Cavern made for a somewhat dodgy rock venue, it had originally been designed (for want of a better word) as a typical late-1950s jazz cellar. Named after Le Caveau Français Jazz Club in Paris, it had opened in January 1957 and immediately began attracting an assortment of name artists and unknowns. Among the latter, believe it or not, was The Quarry Men! Given skiffle's jazz roots, John and his cronies managed to secure a gig there on the night of August 7, 1957, after Paul had agreed to join the group, but before he was able to make his debut.

The McCartney-less Quarry Men took The Cavern stage and kicked things off with an acceptable rendition of "Come Go With Me" (no doubt "down, down, down to the penitentiary"). So far, so good—polite applause and approving smiles. Then Lennon launched into Elvis Presley's "Hound Dog" and "Blue Suede Shoes" and the smiles began to disappear. Club owner Alan Sytner was outraged. He sent a note up to the stage, and the message was brief yet straight to the point: "Cut out the bloody rock!"

That was that until February 9, 1961, when The Beatles made their debut there during a lunchtime session. By then, Alan Sytner's accountant, Ray McFall, had bought the club, and, with the trad jazz (traditional/Dixieland) boom having peaked in Britain, he began to acknowledge the beat groups' impact on the city and recognize the potential income. As a result, some of them were allowed to perform, much to the regular clientele's annoyance, during the intermission.

Just after the disastrous end to The Beatles' first Hamburg trip, Pete Best's mother, Mona, had telephoned McFall and told him about "my son's group," which had been playing at, among other places, her own Casbah Coffee Club. Then The Cavern's resident deejay, Bob Wooler, had weighed in by singing the band's praises, having already seen and heard them at a number of local dances where he had been the emcee. McFall took the bait and The Beatles were in, at an initial fee of £5 ($12) for a lunchtime session and £15 ($37) for a nighttime one. Yet, in the beginning, they still didn't meet with the approval of the ever-present jazz and blues aficionados. This in spite of such efforts as introducing "a song by Leadbelly" before launching straight into Little Richard's "Long Tall Sally"!

*The Beatles '64: Conquering the world.*    © *Hulton Getty*

*Quarry Bank Grammar School, where John Lennon wreaked havoc during the mid-1950s.*
*© Richard Buskin*

*Liverpool College of Art, which John Lennon and Stu Sutcliffe both attended, stands next door to The Liverpool Institute (now LIPA), where Paul and George ended their*

*George Martin, the man who signed The Beatles to Parlophone and then played such a big part producing their recordings.* © *Richard Buskin*

*Abbey Road Studio 2, where The Beatles made most of their classic recordings. George Martin and the engineers would sit in the upstairs control room.* © *Richard Buskin*

*The Apple office building at 3 Savile Row, the London HQ of The Beatles' business empire. It was on the roof here that the group gave its final live performance.*   © *Richard Buskin*

*Beatlefest: Responsible for the world's largest mail order catalogue and the most popular fan conventions.* © *Beatlefest*

*The Cavern Walks Shopping Centre in Mathew Street, Liverpool, incorporating a Beatles Information Centre and a replica of the original Cavern Club.*    © *Richard Buskin*

*June 23, 1982: Paul, Ringo, and George Martin reunite to tape a video for Paul's single, "Take It Away."*　　© *Richard Buskin*

*A "mock-up" of the cover of The Beatles'* Sgt. Pepper's Lonely Hearts Club Band *album, at Rock Circus in Central London.*　　© *Rock Circus*

*The Strawberry Fields section of New York City's Central Park, commemorating the life and work of John Lennon. It was opened by his wife, Yoko Ono, and sons Julian and Sean on October 9, 1985.* © *Richard Buskin*

*October 1977: Your author in his Beatle-mad youth—with (at left) a fellow*

Eventually, the jazzies could see that their haunt was a lost cause and they moved out, to be replaced by the rock and roll brigade. And so, every lunch time and evening, Bob Wooler, a genial man with an in-depth knowledge of the Liverpool beat scene, would kick things off by smoothly announcing, "Hi, all you Cavern-dwellers, welcome to the *best* of cellars."

As for The Beatles, he introduced them on nearly 300 separate occasions. He and the adoring fans saw the band evolve from scruffy leather boys who smoked, drank, and turned their backs on stage, to disciplined, smart-suited chart-toppers who were rapidly taking the nation by storm.

Whereas the exhausting stints in Hamburg helped shape The Beatles as stage performers, The Cavern Club provided the band with a devoted fan-base whose word of mouth would eventually spread around the world. In return, its connection with the band invested The Cavern with a legendary status, although, typically, it was only after the club's demise that its status was fully appreciated.

**I Should Have Known Better**

When it was clear that The Beatles' August 3, 1963 appearance at The Cavern would be their last, deejay Bob Wooler checked through the club diaries and counted the band's total number of appearances there. The figure that he came up with was 292, yet this is now impossible to ratify as the diaries themselves were subsequently destroyed and several gigs remain undocumented.

Once The Beatles departed Liverpool and dragged many other "Merseybeat" groups along with them, things went into rapid decline. The energy, heart, and soul appeared to vanish from the local scene, and, on February 28, 1966, The Cavern was closed with debts of £10,000 ($24,000). It eventually re-opened, only to be closed down a second and final time in June 1973, when it was demolished to make way for—now hear this—an underground railway air vent!

Not until 1984 would there be a worthy tribute constructed on the site. This would be The Cavern Walks Shopping Centre, an indoor mall that resulted from the global attention focused on Liverpool and its "favorite sons" in the wake of John Lennon's death, which revived local interest in the city's "favorite sons." Underneath the assortment of stores, bars, and dining areas, there is a near-perfect—although more health- and safety-conscious—replica of the cellar club, positioned just a few feet away from the original and even boasting some of its old bricks. This has attracted not only live bands, but also other Beatles-related stores and "museums" to Mathew Street.

So, at least the tourists now have something worthwhile to visit. Yet for those who can still recall visiting The Cavern during its glory years, nothing, no matter how clean and modern it is, can replace the look, the feel, the vibe, or indeed the *smell* of the real thing.

*For more than 10 years this plastic sign and modest tribute opposite the deserted Cavern site were Liverpool's only homage to The Beatles. The angel at right was added after John's murder.*
©Richard Buskin

# The Least You Need to Know

➤ The Beatles had their first taste of fan mania at Litherland Town Hall on December 27, 1960.

➤ Paul started playing the bass because no one else in the group wanted to play it.

➤ Ringo Starr of Rory Storm and the Hurricanes crossed paths with The Beatles numerous times before joining.

➤ The Cavern Club, a dark, dank, smelly venue, is where The Beatles played hundreds of performances—and where their legend officially began.

# Part 3
# A Taste of Honey—The Rise of The Beatles

*Okay, we're almost there. In this part of the book, having served their apprenticeship the hard way, The Beatles finally get their act together and reap unimaginable rewards. However, they don't reach that light at the end of the tunnel without some invaluable assistance, a few lucky breaks, several disappointments, and a lone casualty.*

*Fortune smiles on our heroes in the form of two men who, although totally inexperienced in the field of rock and roll, have the artistic vision and priceless ability to turn raw material into rare treasure. At that point events start to accelerate and we are headed for the stars…or at least John, Paul, George, and Ringo are. They have to say some fast goodbyes while rapidly leaving their old world behind. As for us—well, we're just looking up and observing.*

# Baby You're a Rich Man: That Posh Mr. Epstein

Brian Epstein's role in The Beatles' success cannot be overestimated.

Without a doubt, John, Paul, George, and Pete were already making a name for themselves in both Liverpool and Hamburg before Brian ever appeared on the scene. However, given their general lack of discipline and organizational skills, those cities may well have remained the only places to hear of them. As they were presenting themselves, The Beatles were in no way marketable on a national basis, let alone international. Brian almost immediately solved that problem, and, by way of a strong vision and sheer determination, he helped fulfill his clients' wishes beyond their wildest dreams.

On that basis I think you'll agree that Brian, or "Eppy," as they used to call him, deserves his own chapter, in which I'll fill you in on his background, his first encounters with The Beatles, his talents, and his initial foray into the world of rock and roll management.

After all, if The Beatles were diamonds in the rough, Brian was the man who made them glitter. (And if that isn't a corny line, then I don't know what is.)

# Beautiful Dreamer: The Man and His Aspirations

Brian Samuel Epstein was born in a private Liverpool maternity hospital on September 19, 1934. His parents, Harry and Queenie, lived in a five-bedroom house in Childwall, one of the city's smartest suburbs, as befitting their very comfortable middle-class lifestyle. There was a maid on hand to help around the home, and, when a second son, Clive, was born in 1935, a nanny as well.

Harry, together with his father, Isaac, ran a popular and very prosperous furniture store, as well as an adjacent shop selling sheet music, gramophones, and radios. Known as NEMS (for North End Music Stores), this name would one day loom large in The Beatles' legend. Brian enjoyed a privileged childhood, yet his performance at some of Merseyside's best private schools was no better—and often worse—than that of his future charges. Classified as a "problem child" by some of his teachers, he basically hated academia and didn't get along with his fellow pupils, some of whom taunted him for being Jewish. Harry and Queenie paid huge sums to send their eldest son to no less than eight different establishments, but the results were invariably the same; he hated the schools and the schools were none too keen on him.

**I Should Have Known Better**

When The Beatles performed "Little Queenie" in concert during their early years, they weren't paying tribute to Brian Epstein's mother. They were just covering a favorite Chuck Berry record from 1959. Queenie's real name was Malka, which is the Hebrew word for queen. She and Harry also lived on Queen's Drive. Yet there is no record of her ever having jived on-stage to the band's rendition of "Little Queenie."

Not that Brian was a bully or troublemaker. Rather, he was overly sensitive, with a love for the finer things in life: the theater, painting, ballet, and classical music. In fact, his performances in school plays finally won him plaudits from teachers and pupils alike, and during the final stages of his formal education he actually came top of his class in art and design—which led to his first flight of fancy. Quitting school with no qualifications at age 15, Brian announced that he was going to London to become a dress designer. Harry Epstein nearly had a fit.

Here was a respectable Jewish family in the North of England, with a son and heir who had been sent to the best schools that money could buy, and now, with nothing to show for all of the investment, what had he decided to do? Design dresses! Harry was hearing none of it, and neither, for that matter, would he listen to Brian's next big idea, to study art. This was all wishy-washy nonsense as far as Harry was concerned, and no way for a young man to be thinking. What if the relatives were to find out? They quickly installed him in I. Epstein & Sons as a furniture salesman and hoped for the best.

In September 1950, shortly after his 16th birthday, Brian started work in the family business and immediately showed he was up to the task. A woman came in to buy a mirror and walked out with a dining room table. (Okay, she probably had it delivered.) With his smooth demeanor, sophisticated voice, and quiet charm, Brian was a natural born salesman. But he didn't manage to charm old Isaac for too long.

Organized and efficient, Brian displayed a flair for the unusual when it came to dressing the store's windows. He arranged dining room chairs with their backs to the street because he felt they looked "more natural" that way, at which point Grandpa Epstein decided that it would be more natural if his grandson took his flair elsewhere. Brian did just that and became an apprentice with the Times Furnishing Company for six months, during which time he again he excelled at selling and window-dressing. Soon afterwards, he was drafted for National Service in the Army. (And guess where he received his basic training? Here's a clue: 18 people at a Saturday-night gig... that's right—Aldershot!)

> **I Want to Tell You**
>
> "When Epstein said, 'You're going to be bigger than Elvis, you know,' we thought, 'Well, how big do you have to be? I mean, I doubt that.' That seemed outrageous, yet he did have the right attitude."
>
> —George Harrison, *I Me Mine*, 1980

However, instead of being selected as officer material, Brian was assigned a clerical position and posted to London. Before long an innocent mistake resulted in him being charged for impersonating an officer. He was confined to barracks, and put under medical and psychiatric supervision. Then, less than half-way through his two-year military stint, he was discharged on "medical grounds."

Back in Liverpool Brian reverted to wearing expensive, dapper clothes and returned to the family business, although this time around Harry put him in charge of running the new record department at NEMS. Brian's organizational skills and love for classical music proved to be a sure-fire recipe for success, yet shop life didn't fulfill his artistic aspirations and secretly he yearned to enter the theater. On the advice of an actor friend he auditioned for London's Royal Academy of Dramatic Art. To his astonishment he was accepted. Once again, Harry and Queenie were more than a little disappointed, but Brian was now 21 and they could no longer stand in his way.

He went to RADA and, although not especially endowed with acting talent, did fairly well there. At the same time, just as in Liverpool, Brian never felt that he really fit in with the people around him. For Brian Epstein was gay, and, with homosexuality still being illegal in England, this basically meant that he had to lead a double life. The dapper sophisticate of the day pursued activities by night that, back then, could have resulted in a jail term. Furthermore, Brian also had to live with the fear that, if his family ever found out, he might be excommunicated. Due to this way of thinking, Brian and millions of other gay people were prey to blackmailers and extortionists. A decade later, worldwide fame would only increase his fear of being "outed."

After just over a year at RADA, Brian returned to Liverpool to run another small furniture outlet that his family had recently opened. Shortly thereafter, with the electrical business continuing to expand, he moved to a new NEMS store in the center of Liverpool, taking charge of the record department while younger brother, Clive, looked after the household appliances division. Then, the following year, 1959, saw the launch of a much vaster NEMS store in the city center business district of Whitechapel.

### Do You Want to Know a Secret?

For many years there have been strong rumors that Brian Epstein used his position within NEMS to hype The Beatles' first British single, "Love Me Do." A week after its release on October 5, 1962, the record charted at 49. For the next two and a half months, it weaved its way upwards very slowly and not so surely, dropping down on a couple of occasions, before peaking at 17 on December 27. The word around Liverpool, and within the record industry, was that Brian himself had bought 10,000 copies of "Love Me Do," the vast majority of which remained stockpiled at NEMS. Epstein always denied this, but certain business associates have asserted otherwise.

With sales departments, stock rooms, and offices spread over four floors of a good-sized building, this branch of NEMS was able to offer "The Finest Record Selection in the North." The classical discs were on the ground floor, pop was in the basement, and Brian devised a system whereby colored strings attached to cardboard folders informed him as to which records were in stock and which needed re-ordering. In fact, he made it a company policy to never turn away customer requests without exploring every means of locating a rare disc. Well, within a short time *that* little idea would pay off in a way that neither he or anyone else could have possibly foreseen.

## Brief Encounters

There is some dispute as to how Brian Epstein first heard about The Beatles. According to Epstein's own account, Stuart Sutcliffe had sent several copies of the Tony Sheridan/Beatles record, "My Bonnie," from Hamburg to Liverpool, and on a Saturday night in August 1961 George Harrison handed one of these to Cavern deejay Bob Wooler. Since Wooler MC'd shows all over Merseyside, he was able to play the record to a fairly wide local audience, encouraging people to ask for the disc at record stores in the hope that it would be officially imported.

So it was that 18-year-old Raymond Jones, from the Liverpool suburb of Huyton, walked into NEMS in Whitechapel at 3:00 in the afternoon of Saturday, October 28, 1961, and asked the manager for a copy of "My Bonnie." Brian was puzzled, as he'd apparently never heard of either the record or The Beatles, but, true to his policy, he promised Jones that he would try to locate the disc for him. When the store re-opened on Monday morning two girls also asked for "My Bonnie," and now, with his curiosity piqued, Brian set about calling specialist record importers. None of them had heard of the disc either, so he next turned to Bill Harry, the editor of local pop paper *Mersey Beat*. Brian learned that, far from being German, The Beatles were a Liverpudlian group who regularly performed at a club named The Cavern, which was located just around the corner from NEMS.

**With a Little Help**
To read Brian's own account of his early years managing The Beatles and other Liverpool acts, look for his 1964 autobiography, *A Cellarful of Noise*, published by Doubleday in the U.S. and Souvenir Press in the UK. John occasionally referred to it as "A Cellarful of Boys." The cutting Lennon humor could turn even more offensive. When Brian had originally asked The Beatles to suggest a title, John's response was "Queer Jew."

Now, there are several problems with this version of events. First, you may remember that, due to record company fears about Beatles sounding similar to the German slang word for penis, "My Bonnie" was credited to Tony Sheridan & The Beat Brothers. (The label amended until January 1962, and then at Brian Epstein's own instigation.) Bob Wooler would have read this on the record label, and so there would have been no point in him advising people to ask retailers for a record by The Beatles. Secondly, Bill Harry himself has asserted that, since *Mersey Beat*'s launch just four months earlier, NEMS had been one of the paper's main outlets, selling 12-dozen copies of the second issue, which featured the front-page headline, "Beatles Sign Recording Contract!" This was accompanied by a photo of the band and an article about their deal with Bert Kaempfert.

Furthermore, starting with the third issue, Brian had actually been reviewing the latest record releases in the paper. So, even though he may not have been overly interested in rock music, the chances of him ignoring the other articles—including one entitled "Well Now—Dig This!" by Bob Wooler, in which the knowledgeable disc jockey celebrated The Beatles' talents a good two years before anyone else—have to be slim to none. Besides, NEMS had also been selling concert tickets featuring The Beatles' name.

All of this gives you some idea of how personal recollections often fly in the face of undeniable facts. Whatever the truth of the matter, there is no doubt that on November 9, 1961, Brian Epstein's curiosity resulted in his unexpected presence at a Beatles lunchtime session at The Cavern. When Bob Wooler announced that the manager of NEMS was there, all heads turned to see a suave man in a pin-striped suit with a briefcase under his arm, looking decidedly out of place in the dank atmosphere of this musty cellar. Then The Beatles took the stage, and Brian was mesmerized.

**Say the Word**
"I was immediately struck by their music, their beat, and their sense of humor and even afterwards, when I met them, I was struck again by their personal charm."

—Brian Epstein, in a 1963 BBC Television documentary

*Brian Epstein, the suave, sophisticated businessman whose ingenuity, dedication, and love for The Beatles made all of their dreams come true.* ©Paul Fender

Now, whether or not this was actually due to Brian *fancying* one or more of The Beatles—as has been alleged by various authors—is open to conjecture. What is known, however, is that, when Brian made his way to the club's band room after the show, George Harrison's "personal charm" manifested itself in the form of a sarcastic, "What brings Mr. Epstein here?" Brian's typical reaction would have been to blush, but he explained that he was searching for the group's recording of "My Bonnie," and, after having heard it courtesy of Bob Wooler, he left.

Brian would return, though. This man who loved the classical arts and knew very little about pop music was, for reasons best known (or perhaps even unknown) to him, completely smitten with The Beatles, and throughout the rest of November he attended a number of their gigs at The Cavern. Soon a thought began to germinate inside his head: Maybe, just maybe, he could somehow take these scruffy rockers under his wing and give them some professional guidance.

## Being for the Benefit of The Beatles

Okay, so we've now taken a brief look at Brian's fascination with The Beatles, but, from their perspective, what was there to see in him? Well, quite a lot, actually.

For one thing, even though Brian was clearly from a completely different social class compared to the kind of circles that they mixed in, the band would have immediately recognized the benefit of being associated with somebody who appeared to be more like "one of them"—the entertainment industry bigwigs who they'd have to impress to obtain a prized recording contract, TV appearances, and so on.

John, Paul, George, and Pete were more than aware of the gulf between themselves, with their leather gear and Liverpudlian accents, and the men in suits in flashy offices down in London. Indeed, they realized that Brian could build a much-needed bridge between themselves and those seemingly out-of-reach execs. In short, he would give them class. Even though he was still only 27, Brian Epstein looked and sounded just like one of those power-brokers—who would normally never venture anywhere near Liverpool, let alone a dump like The Cavern. Hence George's inquiry as to what "Mr. Epstein" would be doing there.

When it emerged that he was actually interested in The Beatles and wanted to assist them in achieving their goals, their natural cynicism began to be replaced by curiosity and interest. Brian was professional in his approach, sincere in his attitude, and, unlike many of the small-time opportunists they'd associated with, intent on developing their *long-term* prospects. What did they have to lose?

Besides, Brian drove a brand-new Ford Zephyr Zodiac! Ringo Starr was the only other guy they knew who owned one, and his wasn't in the same immaculate shape as Brian's. No, there could be little doubt. This man was impressive.

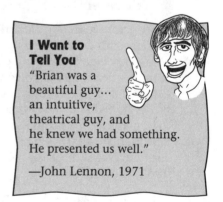

**I Want to Tell You**

"Brian was a beautiful guy... an intuitive, theatrical guy, and he knew we had something. He presented us well."

—John Lennon, 1971

## The Rookie Manager

Each time Brian visited The Cavern Club to watch The Beatles perform during November 1961, he would also hang around to say a few words to them and, in a roundabout way,

### I Should Have Known Better

Before Brian Epstein came onto the scene, The Beatles did have someone taking care of their bookings for them: their drummer, Pete Best, whose mother, Mona, also helped secure the band some of its gigs. Furthermore, the Casbah Coffee Club, located in the basement of the Best family home, served as a rehearsal venue and retreat for the group before and after many shows.

find out where else they were playing and for how much. Soon, he began asking his record company and retail contacts in London about the artist/manager relationship, and he even visited Allan Williams at the Blue Angel Club to ask what he thought about handling The Beatles. Williams, as you may recall, stated that he "wouldn't touch them with a f—king barge-pole," and while others were perhaps not quite so explicit in their advice, they were equally negative. What did Brian know about managing a band or even the pop music business in general? And why would he want to get involved with a bunch of unprofessional layabouts in the first place?

Brian was not going to be dissuaded that easily. He at least wanted to have a formal meeting with John, Paul, George, and Pete, and form some opinions of his own. He therefore invited them to come to his office at 4:30 in the afternoon of December 3, and they accepted. Paul, however, was cautious of Brian's possible involvement in the band's affairs, and he conveyed this by being the only one to not turn up on time. Even disc jockey Bob Wooler was there as The Beatles' friend and adviser. Brian, always punctual himself, was less than impressed by Paul's no-show, and his impatience turned to angry frustration after George had telephoned the McCartney home and discovered that P McC had just got out of bed and into the bath. "He's going to be very late," fumed Brian, to which George retorted, "Yes, but he'll be very clean!"

When Paul eventually did arrive, all six men went to a local bar to discuss business. Brian expressed his desire to manage the group, but The Beatles, while not rejecting his proposal, were not yet ready to commit. Another meeting was set for Wednesday, December 6. In the meantime, Brian consulted the Epstein family attorney and next-door neighbor, E. Rex Makin, asking for advice on the type of contract that should be drawn up. Makin, however, had known Harry and Queenie's eldest son all his life, and he made it clear that, to him at least, this whole pop-management idea sounded like another in the long line of fanciful plans that young Epstein invariably lost interest in. If Brian was looking for encouragement, he wasn't about to find it in Liverpool or on the phone to London. He'd have to go it alone.

On Wednesday the 6th he made his pitch to The Beatles. He would arrange all of their concert bookings and ensure that they were better organized, in better venues, and in many more areas of England than just Merseyside. (He didn't mention Aldershot.) Consequently, from now on the minimum performance fee would be £15 ($37), except for Cavern lunchtime sessions where he would settle for doubling their present payment to £10 ($24). The Beatles listened and were fairly receptive. Brian, however, was saving the best for last: He would work on Bert Kaempfert to have the band released from its

West German recording contract, and then utilize his contacts within the industry to secure a proper deal with a major British record company.

This was heady stuff coming from a man with no previous pop experience. Besides, what did he expect in return? The answer was a pretty hefty 25% of the group's gross weekly income. Certainly, if the band was going to make the money that they were all hoping for, then this manager would be *quids in*. The Beatles looked at each other. Paul asked if being managed would interfere with the kind of music that they played. Brian assured him that it wouldn't. Again The Beatles looked at each other, and by now, though

> **Say the Word**
> **Quids in** is a British expression for making a profit, derived from a **quid**, which is a slang term for one pound sterling (£1) in British currency. This word can also be applied to a lump of chewing tobacco.

trying to retain an air of cool professionalism, Brian must have been breaking into a hot sweat. John, however, quickly took charge of the situation. "Right then, Brian, manage us," he said. "Where's the contract? I'll sign it."

At this point Brian's hot sweat probably turned cold, because he didn't actually have a contract. The problem was, when he had looked at the typical agreement artists and managers entered into, he had found it totally weighted in favor of the manager. The artist was a virtual slave to exploitation, and Brian, whose inherent sense of fairness characterized all of his business dealings until the end of his life, was not about to be a party to that. He would have the standard contract modified accordingly.

On Sunday, December 10, there was yet another meeting, this time at the Casbah Coffee Club. John, Paul, George, and Pete agreed to the amended contract in principal, but they didn't sign it until January 24, 1962, when they went to the NEMS office after a lunch-time session at The Cavern. Brian's assistant, Alistair Taylor, witnessed and countersigned all of the signatures, including Brian's, even though the new manager didn't actually put pen to paper. The reason for this isn't altogether clear--perhaps Brian was being canny about tying himself into an agreement with these wayward rock and rollers who hadn't yet proved their reliability. Or maybe he just didn't want to commit them before having proven himself. Whatever his motives, he eventually signed about nine months later. In the meantime, he was, to all intents and purposes, The Beatles' official manager.

So, Brian had, in the space of about two and a half months, gotten what he wanted. Now it was a case of whether he could achieve what The Beatles wanted. Some of the parents were not too sure. Harry and Queenie, of course, were disturbed to hear that their young man would once again be distracted from his duties within the family business. John's Aunt Mimi, on the other hand, had other concerns. "It's all right for you," she said to Brian. "If all this group business just turns out to be a flash in the pan, it won't matter. It's just a hobby to you. But what happens to *them*?"

She needn't have worried.

# The Least You Need to Know

➤ Brian Epstein, The Beatles' manager, was not a successful student or soldier, but he had a certain flair for salesmanship and an intuitive theatrical sense.

➤ To this day, Brian's reasons for becoming interested in the group are not altogether clear.

➤ The Beatles realized that Brian had certain invaluable qualities as a business representative and as an advisor on how they presented themselves.

➤ All of Brian's relatives, friends, and associates thought that the venture was doomed to failure.

# Chapter 13

# Moptop Hair and Mohair Suits: The Road to Success

After their years of struggling, of playing to indifferent audiences in venues for lousy money, The Beatles finally turn the corner in this chapter.

Within less than a year of taking over as the group's manager, Brian Epstein came through on every single one of his promises. Initially, however, it looked as if he would fall at the final and biggest hurdle: the much sought-after recording contract. None of the major London companies were interested in signing the group, and The Beatles themselves began to lose faith in what Eppy could achieve. Yet he persevered, and the subsequent results were hardly disappointing.

Except, that is, for Pete Best. John, Paul, and George made some shifty maneuvers to oust their faithful drummer just as Success came knocking on their door. Pete was shell-shocked, his fans were furious, but, at the midnight hour, Ringo became a Beatle and the Fab Four took a bow.

# Failed Auditions: Part II

In the early morning hours of New Year's Day, 1962, The Beatles crammed themselves into an old van alongside their equipment, and, with Neil Aspinall at the wheel, embarked on the long journey down to London. Their destination was the studio of Decca Records, where they were to perform a recording audition that Brian Epstein had attained for them with the help of a London-based pop journalist named Tony Barrow.

Thanks to Barrow's efforts, the previous month Decca's Head of *A&R*, Dick Rowe, had sent his young assistant Mike Smith to see and hear The Beatles play in The Cavern. Smith was duly impressed, but he wasn't prepared to sign them to a contract until his boss had the chance to hear them for himself. Hence the band's New Year's Day trip down to London.

The Beatles reached their destination at around 11 a.m. and were met there by Brian, who had traveled down by train. Mike Smith would be supervising the audition, but he had been at an all-night New Year's Eve party and didn't show up on time. Brian was miffed. Then, when Smith finally did appear, he recommended that John, Paul, and George should discard their own battered amplifiers in favor of the studio's more up-market and better-condition equipment. They agreed, but The Beatles may well have felt uneasy about making yet another concession.

You see, although Brian had only just reassured them that he would play no part in their musical decisions, he made strong recommendations as to the songs that he thought would be most suitable for the Decca audition. Feeling a little out of their depth, and in light of the fact that Brian had secured this recording test, they deferred to his "better judgment." They wouldn't do *that* again.

In an attempt to display The Beatles' versatility, Brian had proposed an eclectic set that encompassed several musical styles: Lennon-McCartney originals such as "Like Dreamers Do," "Hello Little Girl," and "Love Of The Loved"; pop ballads such as "Till There Was You"; country & western ditties such as "Sure To Fall (In Love With You)"; R&B numbers such as "Searchin'"; and old standards given the "comic" treatment, such as "Three Cool Cats" and "The Sheik Of Araby." In all, there were 15 songs and plenty of variety, yet no cohesion.

**Say the Word**
A&R is the abbreviation for "artistes and repertoire," the record company department that auditions and signs an act, selects the producer, assigns the recording budget, and decides what material is fit for release.

The Beatles plugged their guitar leads into unfamiliar amps and went for it, but they were being prevented from doing what they did best: no-holds-barred rock and roll. "Money (That's What I Want)" was the only exception. Brian had most probably perused the pop charts, noted how tame the hit records were, and deduced that hard rock music was a thing of the past. He failed to realize, however, that it would be a thing of the future.

## Do You Want to Know a Secret?

Having composed separately or together for the past five years, John and Paul had reportedly amassed no less than a hundred of their own songs by The Beatles' Decca audition on January 1, 1962. At that time it was rare for acts to be so self-sufficient, and the band therefore hoped to impress Decca by performing three Lennon-McCartney originals. Nevertheless, after signing to EMI, they never recorded those same numbers. Instead, Cilla Black would release "Love Of The Loved" in 1963; fellow Liverpudlians, The Fourmost, would do likewise with "Hello Little Girl" that same year; and a Birmingham band, The Applejacks, would follow suit with "Like Dreamers Do" in 1964.

After two hours, during which time they hadn't been able to re-record or overdub any extra parts, The Beatles were rushed out of the studio to make way for another band that Mike Smith was auditioning: Brian Poole and the Tremeloes. John, Paul, George, and Pete would have to wait for Decca's decision. Smith, however, had seem impressed, and so they were quietly confident. They returned to Liverpool and a string of gigs at The Cavern.

On January 4 the band's confidence received a boost when a local pop paper, *Mersey Beat*, published its first-ever popularity poll. The Beatles had been clear winners in the group category, fending off tough competition from other Liverpool bands, such as Gerry and the Pacemakers, The Remo Four, Rory Storm and the Hurricanes, and Johnny Sandon and the Searchers.

Capitalizing on that success, Brian sent an application to the BBC six days later for The Beatles to perform a radio audition. This was duly approved, and on February 12 the band was put through its paces by producer Peter Pilbeam at Broadcasting House in Manchester. Pilbeam didn't like Paul's renditions of "Like Dreamers Do" and "Till There Was You," but he was impressed by John's vocalizing on "Memphis, Tennessee" and "Hello Little Girl." Noting that the group leaned more towards country & western than rock and roll (thanks, Brian), he nevertheless gave The Beatles the thumbs-up and booked them for their first-ever radio appearance. This would be on *Teenager's Turn—Here We Go*, to be recorded on March 7 and broadcast the next day.

In the meantime, there was an unexpected setback: In early February, Decca rejected The Beatles and opted to sign Brian Poole and the Tremeloes instead! Brian was fuming. How could the company turn down his boys after Mike Smith had seen them play twice and been so enthusiastic? The main reason offered—that "guitar groups are on the way out"—was totally unacceptable. He was going to London!

Once there, he met with Decca's A&R chief, Dick Rowe, and the company's sales manager, Sidney Arthur Beecher-Stevens. Brian gave them the whole pitch on The Beatles'

141

**I Want to Tell You**

"The Beatles won't go, Mr. Epstein. We know these things. You have a good record business in Liverpool. Why not stick to that?"

—Dick Rowe, Decca Records' Head of A&R, February 1962

talents and then some. Still, the executives weren't interested, and Brian was now outraged. "You must be out of your minds," he exclaimed as his voice rose several octaves. "These boys are going to explode. I am completely confident that one day they will be bigger than Elvis Presley!" The execs probably smiled facetiously and thought, "Yeah, right!" (Or, "Hardly, my dear fellow!" After all, they were English.)

Now, who do you think was closer to the mark? In truth, the line that Decca fed Brian about guitar groups being "on the way out" was almost certainly just record company malarkey. After all, Brian Poole and the Tremeloes were hardly a jazz combo. They were a beat group like The Beatles, but in Mike Smith's eyes they had one distinct advantage; they were from Barking in Essex, close to London, and a couple hundred miles south of Liverpool. That would make them far easier and—more to the point—cheaper to work with. Dick Rowe had only permitted the inexperienced Smith to sign one of the bands that he auditioned. He therefore went for Brian Poole and the Tremeloes. (And what a great decision *that* was! Dick Rowe would later sign The Rolling Stones thanks to a tip-off by George Harrison, yet a series of bad maneuvers by Decca Records would eventually result in the company's demise.)

Horribly disillusioned, Brian now had to contend with criticisms from The Beatles (especially John), to the effect that he had messed up their big chance. After all, hadn't he been Mr. Know-It-All when it came to deciding what songs to perform at the audition? Maybe now he had some other great suggestions! As it happened, he didn't.

While still in London, and with the pair of reel-to-reel recordings from the Decca disaster in his briefcase, Brian decided to visit the few major British record labels that hadn't yet rejected The Beatles. (In those days there weren't many labels to start with.) At both Pye and Oriole he made his pitch and played the tapes, but in both cases the response was the same: a two-letter word beginning with "N" and ending with "O." Brian knew that he had very few cards left in his hand.

## Smartening Up for Better Bookings

A few months into 1962, The Beatles appeared to be a very different group from the one Brian had first laid eyes on just several months earlier. No longer were they late for gigs; and, when they were on-stage, they performed the music, related to their audience, and cut out the smoking, eating, and talking among themselves. Brian had made things very clear: If The Beatles wanted a prosperous future, it really was a case of shape up or ship out.

Having always loved the theater, Brian knew a thing or two about presentation. From now on, The Beatles would conform to carefully pre-arranged sets of about an hour's duration. As for the song-lists, the musicianship, the presentation—everything had to be tight. Those grubby leather outfits would have to go, too, along with the scruffy T-shirts, jeans, and sneakers.

John Lennon would later say that, unlike Paul, he and George hated the idea of wearing suits, but in reality it appears that all four group members were more than happy to go along with Brian's directive. The disheveled look had got them nowhere. Maybe the smart one would help do the trick.

On March 7, 1962, The Beatles walked onto the stage of the Playhouse Theatre in Manchester for their radio debut on *Teenager's Turn—Here We Go*, wearing dark gray mohair suits with pencil-thin lapels, button-down shirts, and knitted ties—all obtained from Beno Dorm, "The Master Tailor For Impeccable Hand-Made Clothes," located in the Liverpool suburb of Birkenhead. This was the sharp, early '60s look for young guys in the West. From now on The Beatles would be fashion leaders, not followers.

> **I Want to Tell You**
>
> "It was a bit sort of old-hat anyway, all wearing leather gear, and we decided we didn't want to look sort of ridiculous... More often than not too many people would laugh. It was just stupid. We didn't want to appear as a gang of idiots."
>
> —Paul McCartney, 1963

Meanwhile, around the time "the boys" were changing into more natty clothes, Brian also saw to another significant switch: the move away from tatty "jive halls" such as the Aintree Institute and Hambleton Hall (where, for some reason, there would be a fight whenever the band played "Hully Gully") to more sedate, respectable, and up-market concert venues. This was a hallmark of the Epstein touch, and it became evident almost immediately after he took over the managerial reins. Theaters, ballrooms, and colleges were now the norm, not just around Merseyside, but up and down the entire country, and The Beatles soon became used to performing shorter sets for more money.

This was even the case with regard to their stints at the new Star-Club in Hamburg. Now, if only Brian could deliver on his promise to secure a decent recording contract...

# Congratulations Boys: The EMI Signing

Having nearly exhausted the list of major British record companies, Brian turned up at the massive HMV record store on London's Oxford Street on February 8, 1962. He went in to renew his acquaintance with yet another industry contact, Bob Boast, and, of course, to play him some of the Decca audition recordings. Boast couldn't help, but he did tell Brian that it might be worthwhile utilizing the services of the small HMV studio located within the same building—they could transfer the tapes onto 78 rpm discs, and these would look quite professional when presented to whatever record companies were still out there. Brian agreed.

*Looking smart and loving it—George, Paul, Ringo, Brian, and John, arriving at London Airport after the first North American tour. September 21, 1964.*
© Hulton Getty

Jim Foy cut the discs that day, and, when he remarked that The Beatles demo sounded very good, Brian proudly pointed out that some of the songs were actually written by members of the group. Foy asked if these had been published. They hadn't. He therefore put in a call to Sid Colman, the general manager of Ardmore and Beechwood, one of EMI's publishing companies. (HMV is also a subsidiary of EMI.)

Coming down from the top floor of the HMV building, Colman liked what he heard and, back in his office, offered to publish John and Paul's songs. Brian was more interested in a recording deal. Colman understood, and immediately phoned Judy Lockhart-Smith, the secretary (and future wife) of George Martin, head of A&R for EMI's smallest label, Parlophone. The reason Colman didn't first contact the A&R people at EMI's other, more prestigious labels, HMV and Columbia, was probably because they had already turned Brian down by mail prior to the Decca audition, having listened to "My Bonnie."

A meeting between Martin and Epstein was subsequently arranged for on February 13. When the scheduled hour arrived, Eppy sat down in Martin's office and, before playing him the Decca recordings (on shiny new discs, no less), went into his *spiel* about how massive the band was on Merseyside. Okay, now for the big moment. Martin listened to the recordings, and, although a little underwhelmed by what he heard, still felt that there was "something interesting" to the band's sound. That feeling would change many lives, including his own, but in the short term it led George Martin to conclude that maybe he should meet The Beatles face to face. Brian was encouraged, but George turned out to be apathetic. Nearly three months passed before Sid Colman, eager to sign Lennon and McCartney to a publishing deal, pushed him into meeting their manager a second time.

By then, with The Beatles having embarked on their third Hamburg jaunt, Brian was back in London to see if he could make any headway with the remaining record companies. One of these was Philips, who Colman was thinking of introducing him to should Parlophone's A&R chief pass up the opportunity. He didn't. At 11:30 on the morning of Wednesday, May 9, George Martin met Brian Epstein at the EMI Studios in Abbey Road, St. John's Wood, and decided to take the plunge... in the shallow end. He would arrange to have a recording contract drawn up for Brian to sign. However, the all-important EMI signature wouldn't be added unless he approved of what he saw and heard when the band performed in the studio on June 6.

Brian was ecstatic. He ran around the corner to a post office on Wellington Road, telephoned Harry and Queenie, and then rattled off a couple of telegrams. The first of these was addressed to The Beatles in Hamburg: "Congratulations boys. EMI request recording session. Please rehearse new material." The second, sent to Bill Harry at *Mersey Beat*, stated: "Have secured contract for Beatles to recorded [sic] for EMI on Parlaphone [sic] label. 1st recording date set for June 6th."

> **With a Little Help**
> Just two of the four songs that John, Paul, George, and Pete recorded during their first (and, for Pete, last) EMI recording session have survived the years. These are "Besame Mucho," which resurfaced in 1991, and "Love Me Do" (complete with an unusual tempo change), which was rediscovered in 1994. Both appear on the retrospective 1995 album, *The Beatles Anthology 1.*

In his excitement, Brian had, of course, jumped the gun. Perhaps he hadn't grasped the fact that the June 6 session was to be an audition as well as a recording date. Or maybe, figuring that this would be an all-or-nothing opportunity (both for himself and for the group), he decided to conceal the whole truth and take his chances.

On June 2, 1962, The Beatles returned from Hamburg, and four days later found themselves in EMI's Studio 2 for the first time, expecting to record a debut single that would be released in July. Out of the many songs that they performed for George Martin's assistant Ron Richards that day, four were recorded: the old Latin-American number, "Besame Mucho," and three Lennon-McCartney compositions, "Love Me Do," "PS I Love You," and "Ask Me Why." It was only when balance engineer Norman Smith particularly liked the sound of "Love Me Do" that the tape operator, Chris Neal, persuaded George Martin to leave his sandwich behind in the canteen and join everyone else in the studio.

# Not the Best of Exits... And Ringo Makes Four

According to Paul McCartney, he, John, and George had started to become "a little bit dissatisfied" with Pete Best when comparing him to other drummers in Hamburg. According to George, Pete would sometimes fail to turn up for gigs and the band would have to turn to Ringo Starr. And according to many of the Liverpudlians who knew and watched The Beatles during 1961 and 1962, John, Paul, and George were basically jealous of the fact that handsome Pete was the most popular member of the group, especially among

**I Should Have Known Better**

Pete Best was actually not born in Britain. His father, John Best, a well-known Liverpool boxing promoter, was posted to India as an Army physical training instructor during World War II. There he met and married Mona, who had been born in India to English parents, and on November 24, 1941, in Madras, Randolph Peter Best entered the world. The family moved to England in December 1945.

the female fans. Mix all of these recollections together and you may just find the truth in there somewhere.

You see, the same "mean, moody, magnificence" that undeniably excited the girls was also one of the factors that set Pete apart from the other Beatles. All of them, even George, had brash, devil-may-care personalities, but not Pete. He was shy and introverted. He was the only one not to take Prellies in order to stay awake during the long Hamburg nights. He was also the sole Beatle to resist having his brushed-back hair re-styled into a moptop. So, on the one hand he was the loner of the group, and on the other he was its biggest attraction.

With hindsight it's clear that, without Pete's knowledge, his colleagues had been thinking of ousting him for quite some time. It was in early 1962 that they started to exclude him from the group's affairs—he was the last to discover that the band had failed the Decca audition, because the others supposedly "didn't want to upset" him. Then, in mid-June, Joe Flannery, manager of a Liverpool group named Lee Curtis and the All-Stars, asked, "When are you going to join us, Pete?" Best didn't know what he meant, and Flannery replied that he must have "jumped the gun," while mumbling that what he'd been hearing around town was perhaps just a rumor!

A few days later, Pete questioned Brian Epstein about this "rumor" and was assured that there were absolutely no plans to replace him in The Beatles. However, while from Pete's perspective things continued as normal, the ax was about to fall and Brian knew it. By highlighting Best's lack of ability, George Martin had simply added fuel to the flames. No one even told Pete that EMI had signed The Beatles.

Personally, John, Paul, and George obviously didn't feel that they had much in common with their drummer. Musically, they no longer needed him. They were now Liverpool's hottest band and they would have little difficulty recruiting a more competent percussionist. Still, what was unforgivable was the timing of their decision and the manner in which they chose to have him dismissed. I say "have him dismissed" because they never had the good grace to confront Pete themselves. Instead, they left that task to their hapless manager.

After salvaging the band from its drummer-less Silver Beetles days, struggling through all of the disappointments, and even taking care of many of the bookings, Pete Best played with The Beatles for the last time on Wednesday, August 15. It was a nighttime Cavern gig, and afterwards, as John was leaving, Pete called out that, as usual, he and Neil Aspinall would come to fetch him in the van the following evening before setting off for a concert in Chester. John told him not to bother. He had "other arrangements." Then

Brian approached Pete and said that he would like to meet him at his NEMS office at 10:00 the next morning.

When Pete arrived at NEMS, Brian appeared nervous. He made a lot of small talk but avoided talking about business. Pete was waiting for him to get to the point. Brian eventually did: "The boys want you out and Ringo in," he announced. A bomb exploded inside Pete's head. What was the reason? "They don't think you're a good enough drummer, Pete." It had taken them two years to come to that decision. "And George Martin doesn't think you're a good enough drummer." Right. What about Ringo? Did he know about this yet? Oh yes, the fellow musician who Pete had hung out with in Hamburg and entertained in his own home had already agreed to join.

**I Want to Tell You**

"Never to my face, during my two years as a Beatle, did one of them declare that my drumming was not up to standard.... Right to the end we were still drinking together and seemingly the best of friends."

—Pete Best, *Beatle! The Pete Best Story*, Plexus, 1985

So there it was, signed, sealed, and delivered. Yet Brian, having at last got this worrying issue off his chest, now had the incredible cheek to ask for one last favor: As Ringo couldn't join until Saturday, would Pete play at the two preceding gigs? (How's *that* for nerve!) In his befuddled state of mind, Pete actually agreed, but, after trying to drown his sorrows in a few pints of beer, he came to his senses and changed his mind. Brian and

The Beatles were surprised and disappointed when Pete never turned up at Chester, but they got by that night and the next after quickly drafting Johnny Hutchinson. He was the drummer with The Big Three who, just over three years earlier, had fulfilled the same task for The Silver Beetles at the Larry Parnes audition.

On the morning of August 15, in the middle of a summer season with Rory Storm and the Hurricanes at Butlin's holiday camp in Skegness, Ringo had received a phone call from Brian asking him to join The Beatles. He would be paid a weekly wage of £25 ($62). Ringo immediately accepted, but, out of a sense of loyalty to Rory, decided that it would be fair to give him a whole three days to find a replacement. His first official appearance as a Beatle, therefore, took place at a Horticultural Society Dance(!) in Chester on Saturday, August 18, 1962. No doubt, a splendid time was had by all, but the following night it was a very different story down in The Cavern.

**I Should Have Known Better**

It's been reported that, during Ringo's first Cavern gig as a Beatle, George got a black eye from an irate Pete Best fan. George claims he was butted in the face as he left the dressing room—and later was hit by a double-decker bus! His eye injury isn't visible in the film of the group at The Cavern on August 22, yet it is evident in photos at EMI on September 4. George probably received it in late August or early September.

**With a Little Bit of Help**

For a sample of how some Beatles fans supported Pete Best after his dismissal from the group, watch the film of the band performing "Some Other Guy" at The Cavern just four days after Ringo joined. This is included in the first installment of the *Beatles Anthology* TV documentary. At the end of the song, along with the cheers and applause, you'll hear "We want Pete!"

Word of Pete Best's sacking had spread like wildfire among The Beatles' followers, and many of them now turned up looking for a confrontation. As a result, Brian needed a bodyguard to walk down Mathew Street and his nice new car was vandalized. Protesters shouted, "Pete forever, Ringo never!" "Pete is best!" and "We want Pete!" Meanwhile, Ringo's supporters were having none of it, and fists started to fly both inside and outside the club. It took quite a few weeks before things settled down.

As for Pete Best—well, life carried on, but, as you might imagine, it wasn't easy. Not only did The Beatles manage to pour a ton of salt into his wound by becoming the biggest showbiz phenomenon of the 20th century, but he also had to watch this happen while he himself failed to make any impact whatsoever. It has to be said that, while the way in which The Beatles got rid of Pete was deplorable, their musical reasons were fairly justified—listen to his performances on many of the recordings that he made with the band and it's evident that Ringo was a much better drummer.

Resounding failure led Pete to quit the music business altogether in 1968 and totally shun the media spotlight. Then, in 1978, he accepted the invitation of TV host and producer, Dick Clark, to talk about his Beatle days on U.S. television, and the following year he also acted as Technical Adviser on Clark's TV movie, *Birth of the Beatles*. Since then, Pete has appeared at numerous Beatlefests and conventions, and has even co-written his memoirs (with Patrick Doncaster and, most recently, Bill Harry).

Many key players in The Beatles' story died young. Pete Best is a survivor, and in 1995 he at last earned some royalties from his work with the band. Ten of the 19 musical tracks on *The Beatles Anthology 1* consist of recordings that they made together for Bert Kaempfert in Hamburg, and for Decca and EMI in London. Still, some things never change—on the album cover, a central portrait of the leather-clad Beatles features Pete's head torn off to reveal Ringo's face underneath...

# The Least You Need to Know

➤ The Beatles felt that Brian Epstein spoiled their chance to gain a record deal with Decca by advising them on what songs to play.

➤ At the time, the band members were more than happy to trade in their leather gear for sharp suits and polish their stage presentation.

➤ The Beatles' first EMI recording session was also an audition.

➤ The dismissal of Pete Best may have been the right decision, but it was handled terribly.

➤ Despite some painful years, Pete Best has emerged a survivor.

# Chapter 14

# Hitman For Hire: George Martin

> **In This Chapter**
>
> ➤ The Beatle producer's non–rock and roll background
>
> ➤ How George worked together with the band
>
> ➤ What George and the engineers contributed to the group's recordings

George Martin may not have been overly enthused when he first heard The Beatles perform, but he was soon converted. From the time he worked with them on their first EMI single in 1962 to their final recordings in 1970, he was completely dedicated to what the band did in the studio. (Even if, towards the end, he was not always fully involved.)

The producer's role in recording changed quite dramatically during those years, and I'll look at that in this chapter. I'll also explain why George and The Beatles hit it off, and how they collaborated in the studio. After all, working alongside engineers Norman Smith and Geoff Emerick, George certainly contributed to the sounds the band made and the arrangements they played.

## Anything but Pop

George Martin's assistant, Ron Richards, initially took charge of The Beatles' first EMI recording session/artist audition on June 6, 1962, simply because he knew a lot more about rock and roll than Parlophone's chief producer and head of A&R.

Having studied piano and learned to play the oboe at the London Guildhall School of Music, George had carved out a career for himself in light orchestral music and comedy records since joining EMI back in 1950. At that time he had been assistant to Parlophone's then head of A&R, Oscar Preuss; when Preuss retired in 1955, George, at 29, became the youngest A&R head of any major British record label. (That same year, EMI bought out the American company Capitol Records.)

In the grand scheme of things, Parlophone was something of a joke within the EMI empire. This was largely due to the fact that its client roster didn't boast the kind of mainstream artists that were signed to the company's bigger, more prestigious labels, Columbia and HMV. Columbia's Head of A&R, Norrie Paramour, had, for instance, discovered and nurtured Britain's biggest pop discovery to date, Cliff Richard and the Shadows.

In the late 1950s, Cliff was Britain's main "answer to Elvis," and his biggest rival in teen popularity was a cockney singer by the name of Tommy Steele. George Martin had auditioned Tommy but turned him down, opting instead to sign up his backing band, The Vipers Skiffle Group. Not a great decision—basically, this was George's own small-scale version of Decca signing Brian Poole and the Tremeloes. (And Decca actually signed Tommy Steele.)

Parlophone did eventually add hit artists Adam Faith and Shane Fenton to its roster, but rock and roll really wasn't George's bag. He left that to Ron Richards while he concentrated on producing the solo comedy records of Goons member Peter Sellers; the live recordings of comic team Flanders & Swann; and an album of the ground-breaking comedy show, *Beyond the Fringe*, featuring the talents of Cambridge University undergraduates Dudley Moore, Peter Cook, Jonathan Miller, and Alan Bennett. There were also the middle-of-the-road musical talents of Matt Monro and The Temperance Seven, so all in all, even though Parlophone's small budgets were in proportion to its chart successes, George Martin was kept pretty busy. Then along came The Beatles.

His initial lack of involvement at the June 6 audition/recording session probably indicates that, once again, he was ready to hand over the rock and roll reins to Ron Richards. So, considering that neither George nor Richards were exactly stunned by the band's performance that day, why did the head of A&R then actively take on the producer's role himself? Well, there may have been a couple of reasons. For one thing, George Martin's intuition could have identified The Beatles as a possible means by which to diversify both his own career and the offerings of his label. More than that, however, it was almost certainly their endearing personalities—at least those of John, Paul, and George—that eventually reeled him in.

When the 7–10 p.m. session was over, George and recording engineer Norman Smith spoke to The Beatles about the workings of the recording studio and the inadequacies of the band's amplifiers. John, Paul, George, and Pete just sat around in the control room, listening but not reacting, and once he finished lecturing them, George said, "Look, I've laid into you for quite a time. You haven't responded. Is there anything you don't like?"

The Beatles looked at each other with blank expressions, until George Harrison finally broke the ice by responding, "Yeah, I don't like your tie!"

*On April 5, 1963, The Beatles receive their first-ever silver disc from producer George Martin, for selling 250,000 copies of their "Please Please Me" single.*
© Hulton Getty

The deadpan line immediately struck a chord with George Martin, who The Beatles admired for having worked with one of their beloved Goons. The joking continued for another 20 minutes or so, and, when they all left Studio 2 that night, there was more than a hint of mutual admiration between the two parties. Now George had to decide—who should he focus on as the group's leader? After all, so many bands had one—Cliff Richard and the Shadows, Shane Fenton and the Fentones, Peter Jay and the Jay Walkers. Fortunately, Pete Best's below-par performance and downbeat personality excluded him from the reckoning, otherwise wouldn't *that* have been a classic choice?

As things turned out, none of the four got the nod. The Beatles each had personal traits and abilities that appeared to complement one another, he decided, and they should be presented to the public as a balanced unit.

## Well, Look Chaps

The Beatles, now with Ringo as their drummer, returned to the EMI Studios in Abbey Road on September 4, 1962, to record their new single. Again, Ron Richards initially took charge, rehearsing the band in the afternoon. George Martin took over for the evening session, recording take after take of a song written by Mitch Murray. Entitled "How Do You Do It," George thought it would be ideal as The Beatles' first A-side, and had mailed them the demo, featuring a lead vocal by Barry Mason and backing by an unknown London group named The Dave Clark Five. The Fab Four rearranged the song and committed it to tape on September 4, yet they weren't keen about releasing someone else's material, and the so-so results reflected that.

John and Paul wanted only their own compositions to be released as singles, yet they came to this session with hardly any studio experience and no chart success. Therefore, on the pointed advice of their manager, Brian Epstein, they followed the wishes of the man in charge, George Martin. In this respect they wouldn't do so again.

George soon took heed of their protests and agreed to give their own material a chance. That proved to be a wise decision. Throughout The Beatles' career, all of their singles, both A-sides and B-sides, would feature the compositions of only Messrs. Lennon, McCartney, and Harrison. They would cover other people's songs on most of their early albums, but "How Do You Do It" was not among them. Instead, it would be passed on to fellow Merseysiders, Gerry and the Pacemakers, who would record The Beatles' arrangement and take the single to the top of the British charts. At the same time, impressed by the Lennon-McCartney compositions that he'd already heard, music publisher Dick James set up a meeting with Brian Epstein and eventually signed a deal to publish their songs.

So, round one in the creative decisions arena went to The Beatles. This would soon become the trend, to the point where George Martin would eventually make suggestions rather than issue directives. For now, however, he still had his hands on the wheel. The Beatles recorded more than 15 takes of "Love Me Do" on September 4, and none of them were deemed satisfactory. Furthermore, the producer and—according to Ron Richards—Paul McCartney were not too impressed with the drumming technique of Ringo, who, on discovering that he only had two hands with which to play several percussion instruments, at one point resorted to hitting the hi-hat with a maraca instead of a drumstick.

**I Should Have Known Better**

Don't believe rumors about non-Beatles—including George Martin!—drumming on the Fab Four's records. Apart from the September 11, 1962, session that utilized session man Andy White and three recordings on which Paul assumed the role in 1968 and '69, Ringo was The Beatles' drummer *par excellence* from start to finish.

When The Beatles returned to Abbey Road seven days later they discovered that George Martin's assistant, Ron Richards, was taking no chances. He'd booked a session drummer named Andy White. Ringo feared the worst—perhaps they were about to "do a Pete Best" on him!

While Andy White took care of the beat, Ringo was given a tambourine for "Love Me Do" and some maracas to shake on "PS I Love You." Still, when these two tracks were released as The Beatles' first single on October 5, 1962, the version of "Love Me Do" actually *did* feature Ringo. To add some confusion, the *Please Please Me* LP released in March 1963 included the version of "Love Me Do" with Andy White. This was also used for later pressings of the single, coupled with White's drumming, of course, on "PS I Love You." Oh, the indignity of it all for poor Ringo!

In hindsight, it seems clear that the Andy White episode was really just an insurance measure. In the days when four songs were expected to be recorded within three hours, The Beatles had gone through two three-hour sessions and still hadn't nailed down their first single. (Whoa!) Ron Richards obviously wanted to ensure that the third session would achieve the right results, and so he brought in Andy White because he knew he would be reliable. Now, it isn't clear whether Richards and George Martin were impressed by Ringo's maraca and tambourine-shaking, or if they just recognized that White didn't do anything that Ringo couldn't. Either way, Ringo was there to stay as The Beatles' full-time drummer, both on stage and in the studio. Not quite so permanent, however, was the whole studio routine.

When The Beatles first entered the EMI Studios in 1962, they, their producer, and the recording engineers were still expected to wear shirts and ties. The technical staff walked around in white coats, the equipment that they oversaw had to be used according to the strict guidelines that they laid down, and there were just three sessions per day: from 10 a.m.–1 p.m., 2:30–5:30 p.m., and 7–10 p.m. Within a few years The Beatles changed all that—with the exception of the Abbey Road technicians, who didn't discard their beloved white coats until the early 1970s.

During the *Rubber Soul* sessions in late 1965, the group started booking sessions that lasted well into the morning hours. Given the success of these clients, EMI wasn't about to stand in the way of more hit records, so the scheduling arrangement became freer and easier… as did the amount of time (and therefore money) allotted to recording. Instead of a few hours, it invariably became days, weeks, and even months.

As The Beatles and other Liverpudlian acts that he signed in their wake began to take off, Parlophone's head of A&R distanced himself from the company's business affairs to concentrate more on studio work. As a result, in the landmark year of 1963, the singles that he was credited with producing spent 37 weeks at the top of the British charts. EMI couldn't believe its luck—and neither could George Martin when he compared his meager salary to the fortune that he was helping the

**With a Little Help**

During the early 1960s, most recording studios still belonged to the major record companies, who would book only their own artists. Eventually, however, independent studios started appearing, and the record company facilities had to attract outside clients to compete.

**I Want to Tell You**

"George had done no rock and roll and we'd never been in the studio, so we did a lot of learning together. He had a great musical background, so he could suggest things… We'd say, 'We want to go "ooh" and "eeh-eeh,"' and he'd say, 'Well, look chaps, I thought of this, this afternoon'… We'd say, 'Oh, great! Put it on here!' We grew together, so it's hard to say who did what. He taught us a lot and I'm sure we taught him a lot by our primitive musical ability."

—John Lennon, BBC-TV, 1975

company to amass. In 1965 he quit and, along with some industry colleagues, formed his own enterprise, Associated Independent Recordings. A production deal was subsequently struck between AIR and EMI, and George Martin therefore continued to produce The Beatles.

In a broad sense, "producing" amounted to arranging the songs, introducing innovative ideas, inciting the right performances, and judging which were best. Yet, this was truly a collaborative effort—almost right from the start, the group had a major say in the creative process.

In a nutshell, George Martin went from being The Beatles' musical director to the man who fleshed out and helped them realize many of their own ideas. He was the man who advised them to speed up "Please Please Me" from a Roy Orbison-type ballad to a more commercial up-tempo number; the man who thought it would be better to commence "Can't Buy Me Love" with the chorus; the man who orchestrated the "pop" songs, "Yesterday" and "Eleanor Rigby"; the man who lent that classical touch to "In My Life" by playing the Elizabethan piano solo; the man who fed John Lennon's vocal through the rotating speaker of a Hammond organ on "Tomorrow Never Knows," in order to fulfill his wish to sound like "a Dalai Lama singing from the highest mountain top"; and on and on.

George Martin's contribution to The Beatles' artistic development and end product was immense, yet not immeasurable. After all, he can quite easily point to each of the songs that he produced for the group and say, "That's what I did!"

# George and Norman

Over the years several recording engineers worked alongside George Martin on the Beatles sessions, but only two men assumed the role on a consistent basis: Norman Smith and Geoff Emerick. By pure coincidence they each worked on roughly the same number of projects, and the eras in which they did so relate to the two most easily identifiable periods of The Beatles' career: For Smith it was the Beatlemania years, when the band recorded songs that could be performed in concert; for Emerick it was the studio years, when live performance was no longer a consideration.

Norman Smith engineered nearly all of The Beatles' recordings until the end of 1965, often referred to as "Normal" by John, Paul, George, and Ringo. Having balanced the sound on the band's successful June 6, 1962 audition, he was assigned the task for almost every session thereafter. That was the EMI custom back then. As for the equipment that Norman had to work with—well, it wasn't exactly sophisticated, even by early 1960s standards.

The facility already had *four-track* tape machines by the time The Beatles entered Abbey Road, yet the group was not able to take advantage of them until they had recorded their first two albums, *Please Please Me* and *With The Beatles*. On October 17, 1963 they taped

"I Want To Hold Your Hand," and this was the first time that they made use of the four-track. This in turn would enable them to, say, record the basic instrumental rhythm and then add vocals later on.

Norman Smith also had a small bag of tricks whenever certain effects were desired or required. Among them were…

➤ **Echo**, achieved naturally in a reverberant room, or artificially with a vibrating plate.

➤ **Double-tracking**, whereby lead vocals, for instance, are recorded more than once onto the same track to fatten the sound.

> **Say the Word**
> **Four-track** refers to the number of individual tape tracks onto which voices and instruments can be recorded. By being on a separate track, the sound and volume of just that particular voice or instrument can be adjusted.

➤ **Compression**, which narrows the dynamic range.

➤ **Limiting**, which curbs the higher frequencies.

➤ **Equalization**, which alters the sound by way of changing the frequency response.

Still, Norman's job was more straightforward than that of engineers today, when it's not uncommon to make 72- and 96-track recordings utilizing all sorts of sound effects.

During the years when Norman Smith engineered The Beatles' records, the group took no active interest in the mixing sessions—when all of the sounds would be properly balanced, certain takes spliced together, and some performances either faded or edited out. Instead, George Martin would simply oversee these sessions, with Norman adjusting the sound levels and tones at the mixing console, and an assistant operating the tape machine. The producer usually also decided on the running order of songs on each album.

Of course, that soon changed, but "Normal" wasn't around to witness it. Having joined the EMI Studios staff in 1959, he was promoted to producer in the company's A&R department in February 1966. This was largely due to the gap left when George Martin, Ron Richards, and another colleague, John Burgess, quit EMI the previous August to form their own production setup, AIR, along with Decca's Peter Sullivan. In January 1967, Norman Smith got the opportunity to produce an unknown London group named The Pink Floyd. He took his chance and that turned out to be a fairly wise decision. Then, in 1972, he crossed over to the other side of the studio and actually enjoyed short-lived popularity as a recording artist. His single, "Oh, Babe, What Would You Say?" topped the *Cashbox* singles chart in America. Which all goes to show that, for some people at least, there *was* life after The Beatles.

# George and Geoff

When Norman Smith moved up, so did Geoff Emerick. Just 20 years old when he was offered the job as The Beatles' recording engineer, Geoff had already operated the tape

**I Want to Tell You**

"It was a great working combination, just incredible. In fact, everyone used to think it was a little bit odd, because of the way we'd virtually go through a session without saying two words to each other."

—Geoff Emerick on his studio partnership with George Martin

machine on a few of their sessions going back to 1963. Now here he was in April 1966, sitting alongside George Martin and working on a John Lennon composition entitled "Mark I." This would eventually be re-titled "Tomorrow Never Knows," and, with its tape loops, artificial double tracking, processed vocals, and backwards guitar solos, it was without doubt the most revolutionary Beatles track to date. Talk about a baptism by fire!

Still, Geoff was more than equal to the task. He was young, bright, talented, eager to experiment, and unconcerned by those white-coated technicians warning, "You can't do that with this piece of equipment," or "That just won't work!"

George Martin wasn't exactly slow off the mark either when it came to innovating sounds and transforming the offbeat ideas of Messrs. Lennon, McCartney, Harrison, and Starr into musical reality. So, the die was cast: The innate musical talents of The Beatles merged with the incomparable team of Martin and Emerick. Great things were bound to happen.

Sometimes George and Geoff would come up with a terrific idea only to be thwarted by a niggling little problem—the piece of equipment they needed hadn't been invented yet. In that case they could turn to Ken Townsend and his technical staff, who would either tamper with the existing studio gear or come up with some new device to satisfy the demands of artists, producer, and engineer. In fact, some of Ken's innovations have been incorporated into several of today's recording studio devices.

For his part, Geoff Emerick's inventiveness can be heard on The Beatles' post-1965 recordings, not only in the form of the multitude of special effects, but also the difference in the actual sound of their own instruments. For example, just listen to the thump of Ringo's bass drum on tracks such as "Tomorrow Never Knows" and "Sgt. Pepper's Lonely Hearts Club Band." Thanks to how Geoff positioned the microphones—up close and inside the drum—and then processed the sound, there is a real boom. Today, this isn't unusual, but back in the mid-1960s, when the bass drum was recorded just as part of the overall beat, it was pretty revolutionary. But then, so were a lot of the things that were going on in Abbey Road's Studio 2 at that time.

"Everything—vocals and instruments—was doctored in some way on *Sgt. Pepper*," Geoff Emerick told me in a 1987 interview. "The technical approach up until that time had roughly been that you can't do it, because on paper it looked horrendous…. Things we were doing at the time of *Pepper* were horrendous, and would never have been allowed by EMI 18 months prior. We were driving the equipment to its limit."

The tape echo employed on John's voice on "A Day In The Life," the fading up and down of the orchestra on that same track, the intricate recording of Indian instruments on

George's "Within You Without You," the up-front sound of Paul's bass guitar—all of these attributes and more earned Geoff a Grammy Award for his engineering work on *Sgt. Pepper*.

## Do You Want to Know a Secret?

Until the mid-1960s, most recording engineers were employed by record companies and studios. Very few of them were independent, and they were rarely credited on album sleeves. Only the producers earned that distinction. Accordingly, Norman Smith's name doesn't appear on the original British Beatles records he engineered; Geoff Emerick's does, if only twice, in the form of a "thanks" on the *White Album* (where his name is misspelled as "Jeff Emerick") and *Abbey Road*. Geoff is credited as engineer on the relevant CD releases, yet EMI still omitted Norman Smith from the albums up to and including *Rubber Soul*.

Still, although he was only in his early twenties and working with the world's most famous rock and roll band, Geoff had a mind of his own and a clear idea as to how people should work together in the studio. Therefore, when tensions began to flare among The Beatles during the *White Album* sessions, Geoff Emerick walked out. That was in July 1968, and he didn't return for the troubled *Let It Be* sessions the following year. (From early 1968 to early 1970, different people engineered on Beatles recording sessions, including Phil McDonald and Glyn Johns.)

Precisely 12 months after his departure, Geoff re-joined The Beatles, quitting EMI to run Apple Studios, located in the basement of the group's Central London office building. A week later, he became the first-ever engineer to work at EMI Studios in a freelance capacity, when he joined the sessions for The Beatles' *Abbey Road* album.

That turned out to be the band's swansong, but not the end of the story as far as either George Martin or Geoff Emerick were concerned. Both have continued to work with Paul McCartney over the years, and Geoff even engineered the two new Beatles recordings that were released respectively in 1995 and 1996: "Free As A Bird" and "Real Love."

### I Want to Tell You

"When you get as rich and famous as The Beatles, everyone thinks you're fantastic. You are, of course, and everybody tells you so. A lot of people don't mean to be sycophants but they are, and they wouldn't dream of saying anything untoward. There aren't very many people who are able to say to the emperor, 'You aren't wearing any clothes, Jim,' but that's one thing I've always been able to do."

—George Martin to the author, 1987

# The Least You Need to Know

➤ George Martin had little knowledge of rock music and initially had Ron Richards work with The Beatles on the first recording session.

➤ The band and their producer learned a great deal from each other in the studio.

➤ EMI's recording engineers and technical staff worked wonders with unsophisticated equipment.

➤ Engineers Norman Smith (1962–1965) and Geoff Emerick (1966–1969) worked in two distinct periods of The Beatles' music.

# Her Majesty's a Pretty Nice Girl: Changing Audiences

## In This Chapter

➤ The Beatles' final Star-Club concert

➤ Their farewell gig at The Cavern

➤ How one TV show helped spread Beatlemania around Britain

➤ How quickly the Fab Four won over the aristocracy

As you've already seen, The Beatles walked a long and sometimes tortuous road before they achieved any measure of success. However, once they arrived at their destination, things changed very rapidly—indicated by the new venues they played.

In this chapter the key words are "stark contrast," and never were these more appropriate to a period of The Beatles' career than the 12 months from December 1962 to November 1963. In that time the band went from playing in a Liverpool basement club to the London Palladium, and performing for audiences ranging from late-night beer-swillers to royal rockers. (Well, almost. They did reportedly nod their heads... politely.)

A quartet of concerts perfectly symbolized the Fab Four's sudden rise to prominence, so let's now join the group in saying some fast hellos and quick goodbyes.

# Last of the Long Nights—Auf Wiedersehn, Hamburg

When The Beatles left for their fifth and final trip to Hamburg on December 18, 1962, "Love Me Do" was a Top-20 hit on the British charts, and they were in the middle of numerous radio and TV appearances. The last thing the band wanted to do was face another grueling stint in Germany, but they had already been contracted to do so. They took to the Star-Club stage the night they arrived, embarking on yet another 42 hours of performances in two weeks.

One concession that the venue made was to allow The Beatles to have all of Christmas Day off. Nevertheless, on New Year's Eve they were back onstage for their last Star-Club performance, and, as you've already learned, Ted "Kingsize" Taylor was there with his portable Grundig tape recorder to capture part of the show. The recording, which lasts just over 70 minutes and has numerous edits, comprises one of the two sets the band performed that night, and its 30 numbers provide a snapshot of The Beatles at *the* vital turning point in their career.

> **With a Little Help**
> On certain releases of The Beatles' last-ever performance at the Star-Club is a rendition of "Hully Gully," complete with saxophone that is definitely *not* by our heroes. However, one song that features them and has been edited out of official releases is "Red Hot," a portion of which can be heard in the first installment of the *Beatles Anthology* video documentary.

The songs include just two Lennon-McCartney originals, "I Saw Her Standing There" and "Ask Me Why," both of which they soon recorded for their first album. Interestingly, the two sides of the group's then-current and, thus far only single, "Love Me Do"/"PS I Love You," are not included. (Perhaps they were in the other set.) Of the remaining numbers, nine were eventually recorded and released on Beatles albums, while the others—an eclectic mixture of rock and roll oldies, rearranged music-hall numbers, contemporary pop hits, and past and present romantic ballads—would all disappear from their stage repertoire within a year.

> **Say the Word**
> Package tours during the 1950s and '60s were concerts with several popular acts all playing on the same bill performing their hits, with the more successful artists playing the longer sets.

By then, the Fab Four would be headlining *package tours* in which they only had around half an hour to perform a selection of their own current recordings. No longer would they play sets boasting either the variety or duration of those at the Star-Club, and, while that may have been a relief to them, it was certainly a loss to their future fans.

# The Best of Cellars—Goodbye, Cavern

On February 19, 1963, when Bob Wooler (who you'll remember was The Cavern Club DJ) informed the audience that The Beatles' second single, "Please Please Me," had just reached the top of the UK's *New Musical Express* chart, there was almost complete silence. Proud yet possessive of "their boys," the hometown fans realized that success would result in John, Paul, George, and Ringo moving out of The Cavern and away from Liverpool. Many of them even resisted buying the record to avert that possibility, yet they were battling the inevitable. (Some of them probably knew this when they started to form a line for tickets a whole two days beforehand.)

During the next few months The Beatles' follow-up single, "From Me To You," would top the UK charts for seven weeks; their debut album, *Please Please Me*, would also hit the Number One spot; and a non-stop series of nationwide concert, radio, and TV appearances would turn them into the new sensations of the British pop scene. At the same time, while groups such as Gerry and the Pacemakers, Billy J. Kramer and the Dakotas, and The Searchers joined Liverpool's invasion of the "hit parade," The Beatles started to attract blanket coverage in both the local and national press. On August 1 they even became the sole subject of a new magazine entitled *The Beatles Monthly Book*. A couple of days later, the inevitable finally happened: The group gave its last performance at The Cavern Club.

The venue that had helped shape and nurture The Beatles wasn't able to accommodate the number of people who now wanted to see them play. Nor could it pay the kind of appearance fees that Brian Epstein was now commanding for them. Nearly 300 Cavern appearances earlier they had been paid £5 ($12). Now the club shelled out a record £300 ($720) for what was only their second Cavern gig in the past five and a half months. The tickets had gone on sale at precisely 1:30 on July 21, and by 2:00 they were all gone. So, for that matter, were the chances of The Beatles ever returning.

*The life-sized bronze statues of The Beatles that stand inside Cavern Walks, close to the site of the original club.*
©Richard Buskin

Brian Epstein reportedly assured Bob Wooler that, one day, the Fab Four would be back, yet that day never came. In many ways, it was a shame. The Cavern may not have been as attractive as the venues The Beatles would perform in from now on, but its intimate atmosphere was virtually irreplaceable. After all, at least people could *see* and *hear* them playing there!

# In Everyone's Home—Sunday Night at the London Palladium

On October 13, 1963, much of Britain (well, over a quarter of its population) got to see what all the fuss was about when The Beatles topped the bill on *Val Parnell's Sunday Night at the London Palladium*. Produced by Associated TeleVision, Britain's top-rated entertainment show was broadcast live across the nation from 8:25pm to 9:25pm and attracted an estimated 15 million viewers—not a record-breaking statistic, but pretty significant nonetheless.

One of many variety shows that were extremely popular during television's earlier years, *Sunday Night at the London Palladium* offered British viewers the same diverse assortment of acts their American counterparts watched on *The Ed Sullivan Show*—jugglers, dancers, acrobats, ventriloquists, comedians, singers, you name it. The host was all-round entertainer, Bruce Forsyth, and members of the public even took to the stage each week to compete in a game called "Beat the Clock."

On October 13, 1963, however, it was The Beatles who almost everyone tuned in to see, and, judging by the crowds outside the famous old theater, *turned out* to see as well. Pictures of the crowds blocking Argyll Street in Central London were splashed across the next day's newspapers, as were reports of how "fab" and gorgeous The Beatles were. Certainly, John, Paul, George, and Ringo had made the most of their big opportunity.

**I Should Have Known Better**

Dispelling an oft-circulated rumor, the term "Beatlemania" was definitely *not* coined in British newspapers the day after the Fab Four's October 13, 1963 appearance on *Sunday Night at the London Palladium*. It first appeared in a *Daily Mirror* article on Saturday, November 2, in which a concert report, photos of screaming fans, and a "Beatlemania!" headline helped illustrate how "the with-it bug bites so hard"...

Normally, the headlining act didn't appear until the end of the show, but, on this particular occasion, the decision was taken to wind up the screaming teens by providing them with a brief glimpse of their idols right at the start. Bruce Forsyth set the bait by teasing, "If you want to see them again, they'll be back in 42 minutes..." That allowed the kids to go off and have a Coke while American R&B singer Brook Benton and British singer/comedian Des O'Connor did their thing.

Then the big moment arrived. Forsyth strung things out as long as he could, counting down "5-4-3-2-1" while the squealing members of the audience were practically beside themselves with excitement—especially when The Beatles appeared and launched straight into "From Me To You." The result was instant hysteria—not just inside the Palladium, but in living rooms all across Britain. Allan Williams, watching at home, suddenly regretted not patching things up with the band he took to Hamburg just over three years earlier.

The Beatles stormed their way through "I'll Get You" and their latest chart sensation, "She Loves You." When Paul tried to announce their last number, John shouted at the screaming girls to "Shut up!" Paul then encouraged members of the audience to clap their hands and stamp their feet, and, as usual, John responded by clapping and stamping like a spastic cripple. These days, political correctness would prohibit such "clowning around." Back then the audience just laughed and clapped.

"Twist And Shout" was the final song. The performers and their host all followed with the traditional show-closing routine of standing on a revolving stage and waving to the folks in the theater and at home. Twelve minutes was all it took to slay the Great British public.

For many, this kind of appearance would be an all-time career high. For The Beatles it was just another step up the ladder.

# By Royal Command

Just two days after the Palladium appearance, it was announced that The Beatles had accepted an invitation to perform at the 1963 Royal Command Performance. It would take place at Central London's Prince of Wales Theatre on Monday, November 4, and be broadcast on network TV on Sunday, November 10.

Basically a lengthy, up-scale variety show, this annual charity gala always boasts an international lineup of stars—as well as the attendance of certain residents of Buckingham Palace, or their immediate relatives. In 1963, Queen Elizabeth II had prior engagements, so she and Prince Philip were replaced in the Royal Box by the Queen Mother and Princess Margaret.

Now, while the Royals never pay, *and* they get the best seats in the house, it is considered an honor to perform in their presence. In 1963, The Beatles' fellow honorees included Marlene Dietrich, Buddy Greco, and those singing puppet-pigs, Pinky and Perky. In all, there were 19 acts and the Fab Four were the seventh on-stage, yet at this point in 1963, with British Beatlemania in high gear, there was little doubt that they would steal the show.

**I Should Have Known Better**

Even though it was the Queen Mother and Princess Margaret at the 1963 Royal Command Performance, Paul McCartney has asserted in interviews over the years that they actually played for the Queen. This only goes to show that memories are often no match for hard facts, and, while famous figures may resent being contradicted, there *is* a need for historical accuracy.

As at their Palladium gig, The Beatles kicked off "From Me To You" just before the curtains opened. Their playing was tight, their moptops looked perfect, and Paul's nervousness manifested itself in the form of a blunt "Good evening. How are you? All right?" You would have thought he was at The Cavern rather than the Prince of Wales, yet it was just this kind of unpretentious, down-to-earth attitude that personified The Beatles, and it quickly disarmed the assembled glitterati.

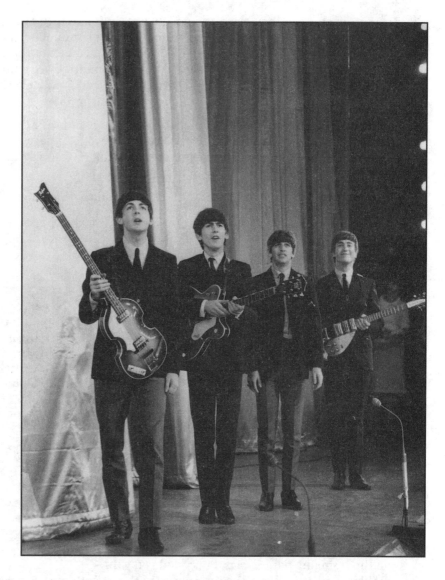

*...ractice their ... e VIPs during rehearsals for the Royal Command Performance.*
©Hulton Getty

After a lively rendition of the band's biggest hit to date, "She Loves You," Paul again amused the audience (this time intentionally) when introducing "Till There Was You." Pointing out that it was from the show, *The Music Man*, he alluded to the ample figure of another artist by explaining that the song had been "recorded by our favorite American group, Sophie Tucker." (Unlike The Beatles' pre-1963 stage repartee, all of the jokes were now clearly well-rehearsed.) Once more, there was polite laughter, and Paul nervously crooned "Till There Was You" while nodding his head furiously from side to side.

So far, so good. However, John Winston Lennon hadn't said his piece yet, and anyone who knew John would have been waiting in trepidation to hear what little gem would be coming out of *his* mouth. They didn't have to wait long.

Peering out at the staid, stuffy audience, he ventured, "For our last number I'd like to ask your help. Would the people in the cheaper seats clap your hands…" There was mild, almost nervous chuckling, as if the aristocrats were monitoring reaction up in the Royal Box, unsure of where this joke was heading. "…and the rest of you, if you'll just rattle your jewelry."

> ### I Want to Tell You
>
> "They loved them—Yeah, Yeah, Yeah!"
>
> —*Daily Mirror* headline, the morning after the 1963 Royal Variety Show

A couple of hundred years before, Lennon may well have had his head chopped off for that quip. On November 4, 1963, however, it just confirmed the "lovable, cheeky impudence" of the Fab Four. Laughter and applause rang out around the theater, and the usually sedate audience started clapping along when The Beatles launched full-tilt into "Twist And Shout." The House of Windsor had never seen anything like it.

> ### Do You Want to Know a Secret?
>
> Towards the end of The Beatles' appearance at the 1963 Royal Command Performance, John Lennon's request for people in the more expensive seats to "rattle their jewelry" was greeted with laughter and applause. However, Brian Epstein was probably clapping with sweaty hands. In the dressing room beforehand, Brian had almost been reduced to tears when John threatened to grab the attention of the assembled socialites, debutantes, and royals in a slightly more pointed way. "I'll just tell 'em to rattle their *fookin'* jewelry," he had promised. Still, Brian needn't have worried. John knew this wasn't Hamburg, and that, for now at least, it would be wise to remain "adorable."

The newspapers had a field day, blaring the word "Beatlemania" all over their front and center pages with regard to the reportedly favorable royal reaction. Consequently, the general public could hardly wait to see the cause of all the excitement. When the show aired on TV the following Sunday, nearly 40 percent of the population tuned in to watch, while many of the three million people who still didn't have television sets listened to the BBC Radio highlights.

As for The Beatles themselves—well, having rapidly scaled the heights in their home country, they would soon be looking to conquer foreign shores. They were obviously glad to get the royal show under their belts, yet to them it represented an experience rather than a real move forward.

Every year after 1963 The Beatles would secretly be invited to make another appearance at the Royal Command Performance. Every year they would decline.

## The Least You Need to Know

➤ The length and variety of The Beatles' Hamburg shows soon became a thing of the past.

➤ The Beatles' appearance on *Val Parnell's Sunday Night at the London Palladium* brought the group national attention at all age levels.

➤ The Cavern Club fans were sad when their heroes achieved national success: They knew they'd lost them.

➤ As more people were able to see The Beatles perform, more were won over.

➤ The Fab Four charmed the aristocracy with their personalities as well as their music.

# Part 4
# To the Toppermost of the Poppermost

*"When they were depressed or we were all depressed,"* John Lennon once recalled with regard to The Beatles, *"thinking that the group was going nowhere, and this is a shitty deal and we're in a shitty dressing room, I'd say, 'Where are we going, fellas?' And they'd go, 'To the top, Johnny,' in pseudo-American voices. And I'd say, 'Where is that, fellas?' and they'd say, 'To the toppermost of the poppermost!' And I'd say, 'Right!' Then we'd all sort of cheer up."*

*Well, in this part of your* Complete Idiot's Guide, *that ambition turns into reality. The Fab Four become international superstars of the stage, television, radio, and the silver screen, before growing sick of all the pressure and deciding to kick back for a while. We'll take a look at their public careers and private lives, and then, just to give you some sense of the incredible decade with which The Beatles will always be associated, I'll run through some of the burning issues of those turbulent years.*

*If you can remember the '60s, then you probably weren't there!*

# Chapter 16

# Scene and Heard: Radio Days and TV Times

---

**In This Chapter**

➤ The Beatles' BBC Radio appearances

➤ Their live and animated TV adventures

➤ The inside track on the band's promotional videos

➤ How the Fab Four were portrayed in the press

---

Several million people attended The Beatles' live concert performances over the years. However, during the 1960s, several billion others had to make do with watching the group on TV, listening to them on the radio, and reading about them in the press. Until the end of 1966, John, Paul, George, and Ringo were hardly slackers about touring, but if it hadn't been for the electronic image and the written word, most people wouldn't have had a clue as to what they were really like.

In this chapter I'll tell you about the band's radio and TV performances, how they chose to present themselves, and how others chose to portray them. The Beatles were very much children of the modern media age, and while they took full advantage of every means they could to publicize themselves, they were exploited by the same people who helped promote them. It was, in essence, a truly symbiotic relationship.

# The Beatles at the Beeb

In January 1962, Brian Epstein wrote to the Variety Department at the Manchester headquarters of *the Beeb,* asking if The Beatles could audition for *Teenager's Turn—Here We Go.* As you now know, that was one audition that they did pass, and from March 1962 until March 1963 they appeared five times on the show (entitled just *Here We Go* from October 1962). Unfortunately, no quality recordings exist of The Beatles' 1962 BBC radio broadcasts, or of their Luxembourg debut in October of that year on *The Friday Spectacular.*

In 1963 the BBC then helped spread the band's name at home and, eventually, abroad. To start with, on January 26, the Fab Four made their first of 10 appearances on *Saturday Club,* the Beeb's premiere pop show. This two-hour show could attract an audience of around 10 million people—double that figure during the second half-hour, when the company's General Overseas Service (now known as the World Service) also broadcast the proceedings to Africa, the Middle East, the Far East, Southeast Asia, Australasia, and parts of Europe.

**Say the Word**
The Beeb is an affectionate nickname given to the BBC, or, as it is fully titled, the British Broadcasting Corporation. Because of its age and stature it is also sometimes referred to as "Auntie."

**I Want to Tell You**
"We have here four young fellas who, since they emerged from the trackless interior of Merseyside a mere matter of months ago, have been laying 'em in the aisles all over the Isles, from Land's End to John O'Groats. So, mind your backs, wacks, for it's the earth-shaking sounds of The Beatles!"

—*Steppin' Out* host Diz Disley, June 3, 1963

After both "Please Please Me" and "From Me To You" topped the British charts (the latter in the spring of 1963), not only did The Beatles' BBC radio appearances dramatically increase, so did the number of shows willing to feature them: *The Talent Spot, Here We Go, Saturday Club, Easy Beat, Pop Inn, Parade Of The Pops, Non Stop Pop, Side By Side, Steppin' Out, The Beat Show, The Public Ear, On The Scene,* and *Swinging Sound '63.*

*Swinging Sound '63* captured a live performance at London's Royal Albert Hall. Otherwise, while a few shows were taped at Manchester's Playhouse Theatre, the majority were recorded at London venues—yet another Playhouse Theatre, Aeolian Hall, the BBC's own Broadcasting House, Piccadilly Studios, Maida Vale Studios, and Paris Studio (on Regent Street, nowhere near the Eiffel Tower).

For the most part, the band had only a few hours to record several songs. The BBC's tape machines were mono, so everything had to be performed live, with no opportunity to overdub any of the voices or instruments. The most strenuous sessions took place on July 16, 1963, when 17 songs were taped for three separate broadcasts, and on September 3, when 18 were recorded for another three broadcasts.

Both of these sessions were for *Pop Go The Beatles*, the band's own half-hour show that ran for 15 weeks in the summer of 1963. Since they had so little time to rehearse, it's hardly surprising that many of the songs they performed were culled from their stage repertoire. During the 15 episodes, they ran through 56 different numbers, 25 of which were never released on any albums or singles. Many were classics by rock pioneers like Chuck Berry, Carl Perkins, Elvis Presley, and Little Richard, as well as unusual numbers such as Marino Marini's "The Honeymoon Song." Lee Peters hosted the first four shows and was promptly named "Pee Liters" by The Beatles. Thereafter, "Pee" was replaced by Rodney Burke.

When the last edition of *Pop Go The Beatles* was broadcast in late September, the band's fourth single, "She Loves You," was firmly in pole position on the British charts, and John, Paul, George, and Ringo were on the verge of becoming household names. They no longer needed to rush all over the place to capitalize on radio's publicity value, and Brian Epstein—perhaps also trying to avoid over-exposure—even began canceling BBC contracts. As a result, whereas the first nine months of 1963 saw them performing on 34 BBC radio shows, from October 1963 to June of 1965 they only played on 15.

The corporation that had, only a short time earlier, auditioned The Beatles, now found itself begging them to make return appearances. Brian agreed to several more appearances on *Saturday Club*, on a new late-night show named *Top Gear*, and also for some "holiday specials" entitled *From Us To You*. In addition, they sometimes recorded messages for overseas radio stations, and, when they were touring abroad, they agreed to incessant interviews, as well as to the occasional broadcast of their concerts.

The end of radio performing came with a BBC special broadcast on June 7, 1965 ("Whit Monday" in England) and unimaginatively called *The Beatles (Invite You To Take A Ticket To Ride)*.

Thereafter, the Beeb and other radio stations would have to make do with interviews, usually with individual group members.

On March 7, 1982, the BBC's Radio 1 network celebrated the 20th anniversary of the Fab Four's first broadcast with a two-hour show entitled *The Beatles at the Beeb*. This contained songs and chit-chat that had been unheard since the original 1960s transmissions.

Now stories began to circulate about a legitimate album of these recordings being issued. The problem was, who had the right to authorize such a release? The BBC, who owned the tapes? EMI, who had an exclusive record deal with the group during the years when the BBC sessions took place? Or Apple Corps, The Beatles' own company, which always appears to have first and last say about such matters? Negotiations among all three parties were long and protracted, but in 1994 a two-CD set on the Apple label, under exclusive license to EMI Records, and by arrangement with BBC Enterprises, was finally released.

## Do You Want to Know a Secret?

While the BBC still owns the rights to all the radio appearances The Beatles made on its network during the 1960s, it no longer has all of the recordings. Some were either lost over the years, or even, before The Beatles became famous, recorded over with other material! (Why waste expensive tape?) However, while research was being conducted for *The Beatles at the Beeb* and *Live at the BBC* projects, certain recordings did resurface, courtesy of listeners who had taped them (illegally) when they were originally broadcast. That's why a few of the released songs "do not represent the usual fidelity of studio recordings."

Entitled *Live at the BBC*, the CD features 56 songs digitally re-mastered and compiled by George Martin. Interspersing the songs with chat and banter, this package revives memories of an era when music was the message and innocence still reigned.

# Beatles on the Box

TV sets were already in most Western homes by the early 1960s. Indeed, they were almost a part of the family. Television's cultural impact was enormous, so it was only natural that The Beatles quickly developed a close relationship with "the box." Let's take a look at The Beatles' TV exploits—both live and animated—and see how, as with radio, they used the medium as their career progressed.

## Early Fabs in the Flesh

Although The Beatles performed in front of TV cameras for the first time during a Cavern lunchtime gig on August 22, 1962, this didn't turn out to be their first TV appearance.

The cameras were there as a result of fans writing to Manchester-based Granada Television, and the results were supposed to end up on a local show called *Know The North*. John, Paul, George, and the recently installed Ringo performed two numbers, "Some Other Guy" and "Kansas City"/"Hey-Hey-Hey-Hey!" but the sound was less than satisfactory and the broadcast was canceled. The footage didn't turn up on TV until November 6, 1963, when Granada aired "Some Other Guy" on *Scene At 6.30*. The film has been widely shown ever since, complete with silent "cut-away" shots, which are all that remain of the band's performance of "Kansas City."

### Do You Want to Know a Secret?

Acetate discs of "Some Other Guy," recorded by Granada TV, were pressed at the instigation of Brian Epstein and distributed from his NEMS store. However, these featured a different version than what accompanied the footage, proving that The Beatles performed it more than once for the cameras. On September 5, the Granada crew returned to The Cavern and made further sound recordings of The Beatles performing "Some Other Guy" and "Kansas City." Five 7-inch acetates of these recordings were pressed, and in 1993 Apple bought one of them for £15,000 ($22,000) at auction. Consequently, a snippet of "Kansas City" appears in the first installment of the *Beatles Anthology* video documentary.

In the meantime, The Beatles did appear on TV in 1962, on a variety of local networks spanning several parts of Britain. The very first show was *People And Places*, broadcast live on October 17 from Granada's Manchester studios to the north and north-west of England. Once again, the group performed "Some Other Guy" (it's interesting that this band favorite was never recorded for an album) and "Love Me Do." Then, on October 29, they taped a return appearance for broadcast on November 2, singing "Love Me Do" and "A Taste Of Honey."

The Beatles next appeared on *Discs a Gogo* (set in "the gayest coffee bar in town") broadcast in Wales and the west of England, followed by *Tuesday Rendezvous* in the London area, *Roundup* in Scotland, and then the top-rated *Thank Your Lucky Stars* across the nation. Independent Television (ITV) was responsible for these aforementioned broadcasts, but BBC TV soon got in on the act and, between them, these two networks ensured that 1963 was a hectic year for the Fab Four.

Among the many shows to feature them were: *At Large*, *The 625 Show*, *Scene At 6.30*, *Pops and Lenny*, *Juke Box Jury*, *Day by Day*, *Big Night Out*, *This Week*, *South Today*, *Ready, Steady, Go!*, *Late Scene Extra*, and the ludicrously titled *Move Over, Dad*. Then there were the landmark *Sunday Night at the London Palladium* and *The Royal Command Show* performances, which focused on the Liverpudlian music craze that was sweeping the nation. In fact, by the end of 1963, the BBC was increasingly being referred to as The "Beatles Broadcasting Corporation"!

## Small Screens, Big Screams

The British were no longer the only people who could turn their TV dials to a Beatle broadcast. In October, when John, Paul, George, and Ringo undertook their first foreign

**I Should Have Known Better**

In interviews Paul McCartney has repeatedly asserted that, having vowed not to visit America until they had a number-one record there, The Beatles only agreed to do so after "I Want To Hold Your Hand" topped the *Cashbox* chart in January 1964. This, however, is refuted by the fact that, the previous November, Brian Epstein had already signed the deal for them to appear on *The Ed Sullivan Show*.

tour—a week-long jaunt around Sweden—they taped a performance on the pop show *Drop In* (broadcast on November 3). Then, on October 31, they returned to the UK and wild scenes of Beatlemania at London Airport—witnessed by, of all people, a certain Ed Sullivan. This was the man whose Sunday night variety show had become a TV institution in the U.S., promoting the talents of too many stars to mention, and, in 1956 and 1957, helping the young Elvis Presley take the nation by storm. Now here Ed was in 1963, watching normally sedate British teens screaming themselves into a frenzy. It set him thinking...

In early November, while Brian Epstein and Billy J. Kramer (one of several artists Brian was by now managing) were in New York on a promotional visit, Ed met with the young manager and talked terms. Brian demanded that The Beatles, then unknown in the U.S., be given prominent billing on Sullivan's Sunday night extravaganza. That sounded completely ridiculous to the stone-faced host, but he hadn't yet heard what Epstein was willing to do in return. Probably not realizing that a top act would normally command a fee of $7,500 for one of Ed's broadcasts, he stated that he would accept $10,000 in return for The Beatles making *three* appearances! Ed generously agreed, and offered to pick up the tab for the group's air fare and hotel stay. It's pretty clear which man gave up more, yet neither of them ended up regretting a thing.

Before The Beatles ever made it to New York, a clip of them singing "She Loves You" from the *Mersey Sound* documentary was aired on *The Jack Paar Show* on January 4, 1964. The next morning, *New York Times* critic Jack Gould commented, "It would not seem quite so likely that the accompanying fever known as Beatlemania will also be successfully exported. On this side of the Atlantic it is dated stuff." Right on!

Cut to February 7, and The Beatles' arrival on U.S. soil, prompting a media frenzy unlike anything ever seen in America. Then, a couple of days later, the Fab Four appeared live on *The Ed Sullivan Show* and all hell broke loose.

During the afternoon of that historic day, The Beatles actually taped what would be their third Sullivan appearance, to be broadcast a couple of weeks later, after they had returned to the UK. The group performed "Twist And Shout," "Please Please Me," and "I Want To Hold Your Hand," after Ed stated, with the utmost feeling, "All of us on the show are so darned sorry, and sincerely sorry, that this is the third—and thus our last—current show with The Beatles, because these youngsters from Liverpool, England, and their conduct over here, not only as fine professional singers but as a group of fine youngsters, will leave an imprint on everyone over here who's met them..."

The third audience, so to speak, was shipped out of CBS' Studio 50 in midtown Manhattan and replaced by the "first audience," comprising the lucky 728 people who had somehow managed to get tickets. The show went on air live at 8:00 that night, and an estimated 73 million people in more than 23 million homes tuned in to see The Beatles confirm all of the pre-publicity hype. This smashed the U.S. TV-viewing record, and for the next hour not one car hubcap was reported stolen in all of New York. (Now that *was* a record!)

If the October 13, 1963 broadcast of *Val Parnell's Sunday Night At The London Palladium* helped spread Beatlemania across Britain, the February 9, 1964 edition of *The Ed Sullivan Show* rewrote the history books.

*February 16, 1964: CBS cameras capture The Beatles and their audience during the band's second live appearance on* The Ed Sullivan Show, *at the Deauville Hotel in Miami.*
© Hulton Getty

At the same time, American film producers Albert and David Maysles, with funding from Britain's Granada Television, were filming much of what The Beatles said and did on their first U.S. visit. This included scenes at Kennedy Airport, inside their Plaza Hotel suite, at a Central Park photo shoot, inside their limo, out on the town, on the train to Washington, D.C., and in Miami, where, on February 16, they made their second live *Ed Sullivan Show* appearance, watched this time by a mere 70 million people.

The resultant 36-minute documentary was screened in the UK on February 12, 1964, while a 45-minute version aired in the U.S. on November 13. (In 1991, an 83-minute video was released. Entitled *The Beatles: The First U.S. Visit*, this also included footage from the Sullivan shows and the band's first American concert, in Washington, D.C.)

**With a Little Help**
To glimpse Beatlemania at its peak, try to find these 1964 shows from around the globe: the first *Ed Sullivan Show* (U.S.); *Around The Beatles* (UK), which features the group performing and acting in a Shakespeare spoof; *The Beatles In Nederland* (Holland), featuring the band and temporary drummer, Jimmy Nicol, performing and being interviewed; and *The Beatles Sing For Shell* (Australia), 22 minutes of a Melbourne concert.

The Beatles performed on *The Ed Sullivan Show* for a fourth (and last) time on August 14, 1965. The next evening, they played their legendary concert at Shea Stadium in New York. To tie in with that momentous occasion, the group was filmed behind the scenes and on stage, as more than 55,000 delirious fans went wild. *The Beatles At Shea Stadium* captured Beatlemania at its peak, and it was given its world premiere on BBC1 on March 1, 1966. British TV broadcasts were still only black and white, but American viewers were able to view the documentary in glorious color… later. ABC didn't screen the film until January 10, 1967.

Between 1964 and 1966, TV viewers in Australia, France, Britain, Germany, and Japan all saw local concert performances by the Fab Four. At around the same time the touring stopped, however, so did the live television appearances. The next-to-last of these took place on BBC1's *Top Of The Pops* on June 16, 1966, with The Beatles miming to "Paperback Writer" and "Rain." It was the group's only live contribution to the Beeb's premiere pop show, yet in 1971, as part of the corporation's ridiculous "waste not, want not" policy, this film was scrapped. An irreplaceable piece of history was destroyed, and all for the price of a length of tape.

Fortunately, more respect has been accorded to The Beatles' very last live television appearance. It wasn't announced as such at the time—no one, including The Beatles, was aware of it—but, since it did turn out to be an end of sorts, the size of the audience was certainly fitting. People in North and Central America, Britain, Europe, North Africa, Australia, and Japan all watched a live broadcast of the BBC's *Our World* show on June 25 or 26, 1967 (depending on their location). In Britain, it was Sunday evening, and The Beatles, George Martin, a 13-piece orchestra, and assorted family and friends were all assembled inside EMI's Studio One on Abbey Road.

Selected as Britain's representatives for this first-ever TV link across five continents, The Beatles were asked to compose and perform a song especially for the occasion. Their only instruction was to keep the lyrics simple, so people from all nations could understand them. John's response was "All You Need Is Love," an anthem for the "summer of love." Decked out in beads and bells, and assisted by friends including musicians Mick Jagger, Keith Richard, Marianne Faithfull, Keith Moon, Graham Nash, and Eric Clapton, the Fab Four relayed their message to the world. Thankfully, this time it wasn't lost to future generations. A 16mm black-and-white print of the full *Our World* broadcast was deposited with the United Nations. In 1995, the *Beatles Anthology* TV series unveiled a computer-colorized version of the "All You Need Is Love" performance.

## Cartoon Characters

In September 1965, while The Beatles were taking a well-earned break following their second U.S. concert tour, their dwindling live performances on American television were suddenly supplemented by the appearance of some cartoon doubles.

Entitled simply *The Beatles*, the 52-part series had been in the works since late 1964, when U.S.-based King Features Syndicate secured the TV animation rights to the Fab Four. Half of the episodes were made in Britain, and the others were put together by independent teams of Canadian and Australian animators, working from Peter Sander's character models that specified how the characters should look, move, and behave.

Taking a month to create, each half-hour episode contained at least two songs by the real-life Beatles. Their speaking voices, however, were not quite as original, with American actor Paul Frees supplying those of John and George, and British actor/comedian Lance Percival filling in for Paul and Ringo.

Sophisticated it wasn't, but this was 1965; Beatlemania was still at its peak, and the fans couldn't get enough of their fab idols. *The Beatles* cartoon shot straight to the top of the U.S. television ratings and remained there throughout its first season... aside, that is, from a brief period of shame, when the World Series pushed it into second place!

## Fab Video Promos (Pre-MTV!)

While they were taping the television special *The Music Of Lennon & McCartney* in November of 1965, The Beatles first thought of producing and video-taping their own promotional clips to accompany the release of their songs.

The show featured a variety of artists performing some of John and Paul's compositions, while The Beatles themselves plugged their new single by miming to "Day Tripper" and "We Can Work It Out." Before the show aired in Britain in mid-December, the group decided to do more of the same in the form of some formally conceived pop videos.

By distributing their own promotional videos to TV stations, they avoided the hassle of filming separate appearances for the UK and U.S. markets. This way, everyone could be included in one fell swoop.

**I Want to Tell You**

"Make it 3,000 miles long and 2,000 miles wide—the size of the States."

—Sponsor's directive to supervising director Jack Stokes, regarding the appeal of cartoon series *The Beatles*

**I Should Have Known Better**

Although The Beatles released "I Feel Fine" as a single in November 1964, the video in which they mime to the song—with George singing into a punch-ball and Ringo riding an exercise bike—was actually shot a full year later. A second video, in which The Beatles eat fish and chips, was not sold to TV because Brian Epstein was reportedly unhappy with the result.

On November 24 and 25, 1965, The Beatles mimed their way through 10 separate black-and-white clips for five songs: three versions of "We Can Work It Out," three for "Day Tripper," one each for "Help!" and "Ticket To Ride," and two for "I Feel Fine."

On May 19 and 20, 1966, The Beatles went before the cameras once again to promote a new single, "Paperback Writer"/"Rain." There were mimed performances in color for exclusive broadcast on *The Ed Sullivan Show*, as well as separate black-and-white versions (two of "Paperback Writer," one of "Rain") for the UK and elsewhere. The following day, John, Paul, George, and Ringo were filmed in the 18th-century gardens of Chiswick (pronounced "Chisick") House in West London, for color promos of both songs.

The Chiswick House clips differed in that The Beatles only partially mimed the songs. Breaking with the tradition of "performing" the numbers, at some points they were filmed walking, relaxing, and being themselves while the music continued. Their next set of promotional clips, for "Strawberry Fields Forever" and "Penny Lane," went even farther. Shot in color in late January and early February 1967 at outdoor locations in London and nearby Kent, these were the most elaborate promo clips The Beatles ever made, interpreting the music with abstract visual images and pioneering the rock videos we see on MTV today.

*November 10, 1967: Ringo, John, and Paul dance a manic version of "The Twist" for one of the films shot at Brian Epstein's Saville Theatre in London, to promote "Hello Goodbye."* © Hulton Getty

Thereafter, things regressed a little. A promo film for "A Day In The Life" never made it onto TV screens when the song itself was banned. In November 1967, Paul directed a number of clips featuring The Beatles once again miming to a song—in this case, "Hello Goodbye." Unfortunately, Britain's Musician's Union had already instigated a miming ban on all TV appearances by singers and musicians, so these clips couldn't be screened in the UK either.

In March 1968, the promo for the song "Lady Madonna" comprised footage of The Beatles recording in the studio (even though they were actually recording "Hey Bulldog"). Interesting enough, but this still couldn't hold a candle to the promos shot on September 4 of the same year. These were for both sides of the group's landmark single, "Hey Jude"/"Revolution," and they did full justice to the great songs that they were publicizing.

Two color clips were shot for each number, and in all of them The Beatles were captured "in performance." And what performances they were! For "Revolution" they were on-stage (at Twickenham Film Studios) and completely dynamic, with John belting out the lead vocal while George and Paul supported him with well-rehearsed "shooby-doo-ah's." For "Hey Jude," on the other hand, the seated band members were backed by a 36-piece orchestra and surrounded by an audience of 300.

To fool Britain's Musician's Union into thinking that no miming had taken place, The Beatles did sing live for these promos. The music had been pre-recorded. Still, the ruse worked, and the "Hey Jude" clip had its world premiere on British TV's *Frost On Sunday* on September 8, 1968.

## Do You Want to Know a Secret?

David Frost was as deceptive as The Beatles about the "Hey Jude" promo. Present at Twickenham Film Studios on September 4, the *Frost On Sunday* host was taped watching the Fab Four perform his show's theme (composed, incidentally, by George Martin). "Magnificent! A perfect rendition!" he exclaimed, before announcing, "Ladies and gentlemen, there you see the greatest tea-room orchestra in the world. It's my pleasure to introduce now, in their first live appearance for goodness knows how long in front of an audience... The Beatles." "Hey Jude" followed, and Brit viewers thought the band was performing live in the London Weekend Television studios. But you know better, don't you?

In 1969 and 1970, clips of The Beatles performing during the *Let It Be* sessions were utilized for the "Let It Be" single and, in part, "The Ballad Of John And Yoko." But the group's November 1969 promo, shot to coincide with the release of "Something," clearly spelled the end. The Beatles and their wives are all seen strolling around outdoors, yet at no time are John, Paul, George, and Ringo ever in the same shot. John and Yoko are filmed outside their home in Ascot, Paul and Linda are on their Scottish farm, George and Pattie are at their home in Esher, and Ringo and Maureen are in the garden of their house in Elstead.

No longer could—or would—The Beatles make a joint effort to promote their work. They were nearing the end of the road.

# Have You Heard the News?

In the beginning The Beatles could do almost no wrong according to the British press. I say "almost" because their first national headline—"Beatle in brawl"—happened to be about John getting drunk and beating up Cavern deejay, Bob Wooler, at Paul's 21st birthday party in Liverpool. That made the back page of the June 21, 1963 edition of *The Daily Mirror*. Soon afterwards, however, the newspaper coined the term "Beatlemania" and became one of the group's chief advocates.

Throughout 1963 there were continuous reports in all the papers about screaming, sobbing, fainting fans all over the British Isles. Intellectuals wrote about The Beatles' artistic endeavors, psychologists gave their opinions as to the fans' reaction, and every two-bit reporter attempted to drum up a new piece of Fab Four gossip. No publication, it seemed, considered itself above discussing anything relating to John, Paul, George, and Ringo.

"An examination of the heart of the nation at this moment would find the name 'Beatles' upon it," concluded London's *Evening Standard* in an article headlined "Why Do We Love Them So Much?" Meanwhile, in *The Times* of London, music critic William Mann referred to the "chains of pandiatonic clusters" in "This Boy," and "an Aeolian cadence—the chord progression which ends Mahler's 'Song Of The Earth'" in "Not A Second Time." Lennon and McCartney, according to Mann, were "the outstanding English composers of 1963."

Daily papers, weekly papers, monthly magazines—almost everything the Fab Four said and did was reported in the press during the Beatlemania years. When John's entire acceptance speech at an April, 1964 *Foyle's* literary luncheon honoring *In His Own Write* amounted to, "Thank you. It's been a pleasure," the papers immediately transformed the quote into the more Beatle-like "Thank you. You've got a lucky face." (*The Daily Mirror* ran the headline, "I Wanna Hold My Tongue!") And when, in August of 1964, an irascible George threw his drink at a photographer during a visit to the Whisky-A-Go-Go nightclub in Los Angeles, the victim's picture of this incident was published in newspapers across America. Some of them even ran a doctored version of the shot, in which droplets of George's drink had clearly been drawn on in order to enhance the effect.

**Say the Word**
Foyle's in London is one of the world's most famous bookstores and, back in the mid-1960s, it also purported to be the largest.

Perhaps the most amusing articles were those in which certain so-called "experts" attempted to analyze the effect The Beatles had on their teenage fans. In British weekly newspaper *The News of the World*, a psychologist asserted that, "The girls are subconsciously preparing for motherhood. Their frenzied screams are a rehearsal for that moment." In the U.S., the *Seattle Daily News* had a Dr. Bernard Saibel blaming adults for "allowing the children a mad, erotic world of their own," while the *New York Post* described an episode in which two "teenage blondes" perched themselves on the 22nd floor ledge of New York City's

Americana Hotel and demanded to see Paul McCartney. After the police grabbed them, doctors at the nearby Roosevelt Hospital diagnosed their behavior as "acute situation reaction." According to the *Post*—well the entire incident had simply been a case of attempted "Beatlecide"!

To press editors (including the *Philadelphia Daily News'* very own "Beatle Editor") the message was clear—Beatle-related stories and photos helped sell papers. Therefore, run the reports about George's influenza and Ringo's tonsil operation, and try to ensure that the source of all the profit doesn't run dry. To that end, avoid criticizing the group. It wouldn't make any sense... for now.

> **I Want to Tell You**
>
> "The Beatles are whacky. They wear their hair like a mop—but it's WASHED, it's super clean. So is their fresh young act. They don't have to rely on off-colour jokes about homos for their fun."
>
> —*The Daily Mirror*, 1963

Later on I'll tell you about some of The Beatles' more negative media experiences, but suffice it to say that, once John, Paul, George, and Ringo had been placed on a pedestal, the only thing left to do was to knock them back off. That's one of reporters' favorite and most malevolent games; build them up, knock them down. However, this too would run its course—The Beatles, it soon became clear, were not a passing fad.

Today they are legendary, and, as such, worthy of everyone's respect. The word "Beatles" is like a magnet to millions of people, so why not use it... in a headline, an article, a photo caption? After all, it still sells papers.

# The Least You Need to Know

➤ The Beatles received tremendous radio exposure in England on the BBC, known as the Beeb; 56 previously unreleased songs and 13 pieces of chat and interviews were issued on CD in 1994 as *Live at the BBC*.

➤ The Beatles made a number of TV appearances in England on ITV and BBC.

➤ The Beatles' appearances on "The Ed Sullivan Show" caused a media frenzy in New York, and drew record ratings.

➤ They were pioneers in the field of rock videos.

➤ The press gained mileage out of any Beatle-related topic.

# Beatlemania: You Make Me Wanna Shout!

The Beatles weren't the first people in the 20th century to be the cause of widespread hysteria or the subject of mass adulation. Elvis Presley, for one, had already experienced that. However, the phenomenon that came to be known as Beatlemania was truly special because it was *global*. In recent history, no one person or group of individuals has been adored on the scale that John, Paul, George, and Ringo were in the mid 1960s.

John later likened the whole experience to standing in the eye of the hurricane while the rest of the world went completely crazy—Beatle-crazy. Indeed, for the masses, Beatlemania was an almost entirely positive experience, but for the main men themselves, what started out as wild fun soon turned into something of a nightmare. Privacy was almost non-existent, safety was a major concern, and freedom was a thing of the past. With wealth and success under their belts, the Fab Four once again yearned for the simpler things in life.

You have to have your own memories of Beatlemania to really know what it was like—but you can still learn a few things and then use your imagination. In this chapter I'll put you in the picture by describing how the fan worship exploded around the world between 1963 and 1966, and how this in turn affected our heroes.

# 1963—That Was The Year That Was

It seems fairly appropriate that the suffix "mania" is used to indicate an extreme enthusiasm for something, or even a form of madness. Consider this: The Reverend Ronald Gibbons of the Trinity Methodist Church in Basildon, Essex, publicly asked The Beatles to record "Oh Come All Ye Faithful, Yeah, Yeah, Yeah" to help boost his Christmas congregation. Or how about a bakery in northern England that sold "Beatle cakes" for the very generous "party price" of five shillings (then equivalent to about 12 cents). If those didn't keep you happy, you could also chew on some "Ringo Roll" or plan on watching a ballet entitled *Mods and Rockers* featuring the music of Lennon and McCartney.

This was Beatlemania in 1963 Britain. Still, the national newspapers didn't really pick up on the craze until late-spring, when The Beatles undertook their third nationwide tour of the year. The first, in early February, had the band at the bottom of a six-act bill topped by 16-year-old singer Helen Shapiro. Five days after that tour ended, a second one commenced. American artists Tommy Roe and Chris Montez were supposed to top the bill, but fan reaction during the first concert convinced the promoter to have the Fab Four close the show.

Much the same happened during the third tour, which ran from May 18 to June 9. Roy Orbison was the original headliner, but he couldn't compete with the exploding popularity of John, Paul, George, and Ringo. Every time they walked on stage and launched into their 25-minute set, the girls would become hysterical, alternately screaming and stuffing handkerchiefs into their mouths, sobbing, clawing at themselves, and throwing jelly babies at the band. (The result of George having divulged in an interview that he liked them!) Some even wet themselves in all the excitement. Meanwhile, the numerous male members of the audience would just watch the manic proceedings and try (often in vain) to listen to the music.

In the wake of The Beatles' success, numerous other Merseyside acts managed to crash onto the British pop charts during the next few months, including Gerry and the Pacemakers, Billy J. Kramer with the Dakotas, Cilla Black, The Searchers, The Fourmost, The Swinging Bluegenes, and The Merseybeats. Some of them recorded Lennon-McCartney compositions, many of them were managed by Brian Epstein, and, during 1963, three of them spent a combined 45 weeks in the top ten. The Beatles outdid that, enjoying their own 40 weeks in the top ten. At the end of 1963, *Record Retailer* estimated that, during the past 12 months, the Brits had spent £6.25 million (about $15 million) on Beatles records alone.

## Do You Want to Know a Secret?

During the latter part of 1963, the catchy "yeah, yeah, yeah," refrain in "She Loves You" became a common sight and sound, in print and on the radio. In fact, when Paul's father, Jim, first heard the new composition he suggested that it would be far more proper to sing, "Yes, yes, yes." He was a caring guy, but thankfully he didn't write the songs!

After the Fab Four's televised October appearance on *Sunday Night at the London Palladium,* the media really caught on and all hell broke loose. Following a highly successful tour of Sweden, the group returned to London Airport on October 31 and a reception they didn't expect. Braving heavy rain, several thousand enthusiastic fans showed up and screamed so loud they drowned out the noise of the jet engines. The press bombarded the four young men the moment they descended the aircraft steps.

Completely astonished, The Beatles initially assumed that the welcome was intended for a dignitary or head of state. Wrong! The "airport receptions," with Beatles songs being broadcast over London Airport's public address system, would hereafter be a tradition whenever the band departed for—and returned from—foreign shores.

## Do You Want to Know a Secret?

On November 16, 1963—the same day Clark's Grammar School in Guildford, Surrey, became the first to send boys home for sporting Beatle haircuts—the three American networks sent teams to England to film the Fab Four. During a concert at the Winter Gardens Theatre in Bournemouth, Hampshire, ABC, CBS, and NBC cameras captured part of The Beatles' performance and the fans' hysterical reaction. While his rival reporters were full of praise for Britain's new pop heroes, CBS's Alexander Kendrick was less than complimentary, referring to The Beatles' "non-music" and their "dish-mop hairstyles." At least he got the "mop" part right!

As bedlam ensued at these arrivals and departures, the police had the unenviable task of keeping matters under control. Unfortunately, they didn't always succeed. In Carlisle, for instance, 600 fans waited 36 hours for the box office to open. When it did, the sudden surge of bodies propelled some people through store windows and nine of them ended up in hospital. In Newcastle-upon-Tyne, an estimated 10,000 fans "went wild in a fantastic stampede" (according to *The Daily Mirror*) while they waited to buy tickets. Apparently, one girl lost her jeans amidst the excitement (or at least that's what she told her parents),

**I Want to Tell You**

"Lookit, I thought I was supposed to be getting a change of scenery, and so far I've been in a train and a room, and a car and a room, and a room and a room."

—Wilfred Brambell, as Paul's grandfather, in *A Hard Day's Night*

while 120 others had to receive first aid and seven were treated for shock. Such scenes were repeated around the country.

The next tour, kicking off on November 1, consisted of two shows per night in 34 towns across Britain. For The Beatles—who now sometimes resorted to wearing disguises when venturing out in public, and whose family homes were constantly under siege—concert work presented a mind-numbing routine: arriving in a town, being smuggled into a theater, performing a show (or often two) where the screaming was so loud that the band could hardly hear themselves play, and then being hustled back out of the theater and into a waiting van for a high-speed escape to a nearby hotel.

This was "normality" for The Beatles during those frantic final months of 1963. So, imagine how they must have felt when a Labour Party Member of Parliament stood up in Britain's House of Commons and demanded that, to save on unnecessary public costs, there should be no further police protection for The Beatles. Loose talk like that costs politicians votes!

# 1964—12 Months That Shook the World

If 1963 was the year of Beatlemania in Britain, 1964 was when the "with-it bug" went global. While the French took their time making up their minds about The Beatles, every place else the Fab Four visited took them to their hearts in a big way. This was great news not only for John, Paul, George, and Ringo, but also for the host of other British artists who suddenly found themselves in demand—first at home, then overseas.

Let's take a look at how those foreign visits panned out in 1964.

## Les Français? Pouf!

After completing the 16-night, 30-performance run of "The Beatles' Christmas Show" at the Astoria Cinema in North London and making a return appearance on *Val Parnell's Sunday Night at the London Palladium*, The Beatles set off for a three-week engagement in Paris. John, Paul, and George arrived on January 14, while Ringo, trapped by fog in Liverpool, followed with Neil Aspinall the next day. This initial delay turned out to be an ominous sign, as did the fact that The Beatles could walk down Paris' main thoroughfare, Les Champs Elysées, without being crowded.

Still, after giving what even they considered to be a below-par performance at the Cinéma Cyrano in Versailles, the Fab Four embarked on 18 days at Paris' Olympia Theatre, during which they played two—and sometimes three—shows a night. The premiere, on January 16, proved to be a profound disappointment. For one thing, the audience comprised not teenage fans, but mostly Parisian socialites in full evening dress. It was like being back at the Royal Command performance, except that this crowd wasn't nearly as friendly. The French appeared to be largely unimpressed by *Les Beatles*, and, for their part, *Les Beatles* were less than impressed with the Olympia's facilities.

Before the show, attempts by the group's press officer, Brian Sommerville, to keep reporters and photographers out of the band's dressing room resulted in a violent scuffle. Then, when The Beatles' amplification equipment broke down on three separate occasions during their performance, George Harrison openly complained of sabotage. The traditionally fragile Anglo-French relations were teetering on the brink.

The next day, the critic for the popular evening paper, *France-Soir*, dismissed the moptops as "delinquents" and "has-beens," while the famous Parisian department store, Les Galaries Lafayette, canceled plans to fill one of its main windows with Beatles merchandise. Not that the group really cared—after returning to their suite at the George V Hotel the previous night, news came that "I Want To Hold Your Hand" was topping the *Cash Box* singles chart in America.

John, Paul, George, and Ringo played their way through the rest of their three-week Paris engagement, facing audiences that often appeared to be more interested in the sexy pouting of local *chanteuse* Sylvie Vartan and Texas-born Trini Lopez singing "If I Had A Hammer." The French got a second chance about 18 months later, at which point they fell in line with the rest of the Beatle-mad planet. For now, however, The Beatles had their minds on bigger things in the U.S.

# Around the World

1964 was quite a year. After their brief, triumphant initial visit to the U.S. (which I covered in the last chapter), the longest rest The Beatles had during those hectic 12 months was four weeks in May. Then they were off on a 25-day world tour, commencing in Denmark on June 4. The day before, Ringo had collapsed during a photo session and was rushed to a hospital suffering from tonsillitis and pharyngitis. George wanted to cancel the tour, but was persuaded by Brian Epstein and George Martin that this couldn't be done. Instead, a temporary replacement for Ringo would have to be found.

Enter Jimmy Nicol, a relatively unknown session drummer who, it was correctly assumed, wouldn't be perceived by anyone as a permanent fixture within The Beatles. Nicol played with his own group, The Shubdubs, and had also backed artists such as Georgie Fame and Brian Epstein-protegé Tommy Quickly. Now, just hours after Ringo's collapse, 24-year-old Jimmy found himself at EMI's Abbey Road studios, rehearsing six numbers with the world's greatest supergroup. Then he went home to pack his bags in preparation for the following day's flight to Denmark. Talk about instant stardom!

Beatlemania followed the band wherever they appeared, not only at the concert venues in Denmark, the Netherlands, and Hong Kong, but also when their plane touched down for refueling. At all hours, in even the remotest of places, there would inevitably be hordes of screaming fans trying to catch a glimpse of their idols. This was fine, except for those inconvenient occasions when The Beatles were expected to reciprocate. Take the band's arrival at Mascot International Airport in Sydney, Australia on June 11, when they were cajoled into parading in an open-top truck in a torrential rainstorm while the crowd was packed safely into the sheltered airport enclosures. Guess who got drenched?

### Do You Want to Know a Secret?

After Ringo rejoined The Beatles in Australia, Jimmy Nicol returned to London and almost immediate obscurity. He later claimed that a falling-out with Brian Epstein led to his being "blacklisted" in the music business: Despite his status as a former Beatle, Nicol found it difficult to gain employment. His Fab Four stint earned him £500 ($1,200) and a gold wrist-watch inscribed "From The Beatles and Brian Epstein to Jimmy—with appreciation and gratitude"; however, less than a year later, Nicol filed for bankruptcy. His son, Howie, was the sound recordist on the *Beatles Anthology* documentary series.

### I Want to Tell You

"I hope to have enough money to go into a business of my own by the time we do flop. It may be next week, it may be two or three years, but I think we'll be in the business...for at least another four years."

—George Harrison, August 1963

Ringo rejoined The Beatles in Australia, where their reception was even *more* manic than it had been in America back in February. In Adelaide, an estimated 300,000 people gathered outside the hotel where the group was staying, while in Melbourne the crowd numbered a mere 250,000!

As if the hordes of fans alone weren't enough, death threats against the band were now becoming an uncomfortable part of the Beatlemania package. Prior to a flight from Auckland, New Zealand to nearby Dunedin, someone anonymously—and, as it turned out, falsely—claimed to have planted a "germ bomb" on board the plane. Similar instances would occur during the American tour, and while no one actually was hurt, the collective feelings of anxiety were becoming unbearable.

## The Beatles Are Coming!

I've already told you about the Fab Four's activities during their first trip to the States in February of 1964—their Kennedy Airport reception, the landmark appearances on *The Ed Sullivan Show*, their first U.S. concerts, and so on. Now we'll discuss all the hype and fan reactions surrounding that visit, as well as the tour that followed a few months later.

Due to coincidence of the very best kind, The Beatles' 1963 albums and singles were storming the American charts when the group arrived in New York on February 7, 1964.

As you know (if you haven't been skipping pages), Brian Epstein had arranged the trip the previous November. By then, Capitol Records had at last been persuaded by its parent company, EMI, to release "I Want To Hold Your Hand." Coupled with the fact that the small, independent labels, Tollie, Swan, and Vee Jay, were pushing the group's other discs, there was no shortage of Beatles material for Americans to purchase.

At first there was little interest, but when "I Want To Hold Your Hand" started getting airplay on U.S. radio stations, the single sold by the bucket-load— remember, 10,000 copies per hour in New York City alone. The sound was so fresh, so different, so exciting—just what the doctor ordered to counter the mass depression over President Kennedy's assassination a few weeks earlier.

> **I Should Have Known Better**
> The Beatles' first visit to the United States in February 1964 is often incorrectly referred to as their first American tour. In addition to their appearances on *The Ed Sullivan Show*, the group only performed two concerts, in New York City and Washington, D.C. The first proper nationwide tour was during August and September.

The kids couldn't wait to see who was responsible for this new music. Capitol Records embarked on a crash publicity program to stir excitement, distributing five million posters and car bumper stickers announcing "The Beatles Are Coming!" This same message was played repeatedly by disc jockeys, who, as the big day approached, also informed their listeners that "The Beatles will be touching down this Friday at 1:20 Beatle-time!"

In classrooms across the country on that memorable day, Beatles-obsessed pupils started counting down as the magic moment finally arrived. Others cut class to listen to the up-to-the-minute radio reports concerning the band's visit. In New York, about 3,000 screaming Beatlemaniacs appeared at Kennedy Airport to greet Pan Am flight 101. Needless to say, John, Paul, George, and Ringo were all over the nation's TV screens that evening.

From that moment on, the U.S. was totally besotted with The Beatles. Everything they said or did seemed to be of major importance, as was anything or anyone connected to them or in possession of a British accent. Today The Beatles—tomorrow The Rolling Stones, The Dave Clark Five, The Kinks, The Animals, Gerry and the Pacemakers, Dusty Springfield, Petula Clark, and Herman's Hermits. The charts were swamped, and the sudden tidal wave was quickly dubbed "the British Invasion."

> **I Want to Tell You**
> "The Beatles— they're a passing phase; symptoms of the uncertainty of the times and the confusion about us."
> —Dr. Billy Graham, 1964

Of course, none of those bands had the same initial impact as The Beatles. Half a ton of Beatle Wigs and 24,000 rolls of Beatle wallpaper were flown in from Britain to meet the huge demand for all things Fab. Back in the UK, George Harrison received 52 sacks of mail containing around 15,000 cards on his 21st birthday, together with four large hampers packed with gifts. In March, the release of the single "Can't Buy Me Love" was preceded by advance orders of 2.1 million copies in the U.S. (with another million in Britain). And in *Billboard* magazine's "Hot 100" singles listing for April 4, Beatles records stood at numbers 1, 2, 3, 4, 5, 31, 41, 46, 58, 65, 68, and 79! I kid you not!

Now, aside from this being the only occasion when one act has held the first five positions, those records were also on *four different* labels:

1. "Can't Buy Me Love" (Capitol)
2. "Twist And Shout" (Tollie)
3. "She Loves You" (Swan)
4. "I Want To Hold Your Hand" (Capitol)
5. "Please Please Me" (Vee Jay)

Can you imagine *anyone* matching that achievement today? In short, what took place in the U.S. (as well as in Britain) during 1964 was a musical and cultural revolution, not just a quick craze that would fizzle and fade.

The Beatles were going to be a major force for some time, and if this needed confirming, the proof was evident when the band undertook its first full-fledged American tour during August and September. The tour consisted of 32 shows in 24 cities within 34 days, and now the car/concert/car/hotel routine was extended to airplane/limousine/press conference/meeting with dignitaries/concert/limo/hotel. John, Paul, George, and Ringo saw little of the cities they were in. Sometimes they didn't even know *which* city they were in. All they knew was that they were making a lot of money, and they saw rampaging fans everywhere they went. Aside from traveling to and from the concert venues, and to and from the airports, they certainly couldn't leave their hotels.

The Beatles' check-out from the hotel wasn't always the end of the story. In Kansas City, for instance, the manager of the Muehlebach sold the 16 sheets and 8 pillow cases from The Beatles' suite to a pair of Chicago businessmen for $750. Of course, in order to remain authentic, the linen couldn't be washed; it was cut into three-inch squares, mounted on a card, and sold at a bargain $10 a piece! Much the same fate was accorded the towels with which The Beatles wiped their faces after leaving the stage of the Hollywood Bowl.

By the summer of 1964, no commodity was too outrageous for eagle-eyed American "entrepreneurs": bottled "Beatle Breath," "Beatle Bathwater," and even used shaving foam were among the many items that exploited fans were lured into purchasing. Beatlemania had gone over the top.

*August 23, 1964: The Beatles, and their reflected images, in concert at the prestigious Hollywood Bowl.*
©Hulton Getty

# 1965–1966—"Like Monkeys in a Zoo"

The last "official" Beatlemania years, so to speak, were 1965 and 1966, when the band was still touring. This was a case of "more of the same," save for the unprecedented 1965 Shea Stadium gig in New York, and visits to previously uncharted territories such as Italy, Spain, Japan, and the Philippines.

### Do You Want to Know a Secret?

On August 27, 1965, during The Beatles' second American tour, a historic meeting took place between the Fab Four and their idol, Elvis Presley, at the King's home in Beverly Hills. Both sides were apprehensive and The Beatles were disappointed by how the once-hard rocker had "gone Hollywood." When Elvis disclosed that his latest film had been shot in under three weeks, John quipped that, while they were all together for the evening, maybe they should make a classic! The five men spent the evening chatting, listening to records, and, according to John, jamming. Paul, George, and Ringo now refute this last fact, but it can certainly be said that a lasting friendship never developed.

The Fab Four were still the biggest showbiz attraction on the planet, yet during 1965 and even more so during 1966 it became clear that Beatlemania was starting to lose steam. The fans still turned up to greet the band at airports, but now they numbered in the hundreds rather than the thousands. And whereas in 1964 there had been the occasional concert venue that didn't sell out, this became more common in 1965 and almost the norm in 1966.

### I Want to Tell You

"Your own space, man, it's so important. That's why we were doomed, because we didn't have any. It is like monkeys in a zoo. They die. You know, everything needs to be left alone."

—George Harrison, 1980

At the same time, the hoax death threats increased, as did the unintentional terrorization by fans. A notable example of this took place in Houston, Texas, on August 19, 1965. It was 2:00 a.m., yet 5,000 screaming kids were present for The Beatles' arrival. As the plane taxied to a halt, the hysterical crowd broke through the airport barriers and police cordons. Within seconds people were thronging around the plane, underneath it, and even on top of the wings, looking through the windows; meanwhile, the Fab Four were trapped inside. Forty minutes passed before they were able to jump into a service truck from a nine-foot-high emergency exit at the rear of the plane.

Representatives for Lloyd's of London, who had insured each Beatle for $5.5 million against personal injury, would have been panic-stricken if they'd witnessed scenes like this. Imagine, therefore, what it was like to be one of The Beatles.

Just under three weeks after arriving back from America, the Fab Four embarked on their first UK tour of 1964, comprising 54 shows in 25 cities within 33 days. All of this, and they also found time to make studio recordings, as well as TV and radio appearances, before launching themselves into "Another Beatles Christmas Show" at London's Hammersmith Odeon—38 shows over the course of 20 nights during December and January. The Beatles never attempted to repeat this kind of schedule.

With ample money and more fame than they'd ever dreamed of, The Beatles were fast becoming fed up with not only the incessant tours, but also everything to do with Beatlemania. They had no privacy and no freedom, they feared for their own safety, and, what with all of the screaming at their concerts, they were also regressing as musicians. No wonder their main enjoyment was now only found at home or in the recording studio.

# The Least You Need to Know

➤ Britain went Beatle-crazy during the final months of 1963.

➤ The Beatles' first trip to the U.S. only consisted of appearances on *The Ed Sullivan Show* and performances in New York and Washington, D.C.; the first national tour took place a few months later, in August and September 1964.

➤ The French didn't initially take to the Fab Four.

➤ Beatlemania resulted in a virtual mass-hysteria: screaming fans, over-the-top merchandising, and The Beatles' domination of the charts and radio airplay.

➤ The pressures of Beatlemania soon began to bear down on the group.

# Act Naturally: The Big-Screen Beatles

The Beatles not only revolutionized the twin worlds of pop music and pop culture in the 1960s, but also, thanks to their own personalities and the combined talents of some of the people with whom they worked, they also changed the whole nature of pop *movies*.

Make no mistake about it: The Fab Four were musicians, not actors. Yet, given the opportunity to deliver their lines on the big screen, they certainly didn't fluff them. Let's catch up on those efforts, as well as the other celluloid projects that they were—or intended to be—involved with.

# A Hard Day's Night: "The Citizen Kane of Juke Box Musicals"

To state it plainly, *A Hard Day's Night* is a classic film and one of *the* great screen musicals. However, The Beatles' big-screen debut was originally envisioned as a "cheapo-quickie"

**I Want to Tell You**

"We'd made it clear to Brian that we weren't interested in being stuck in one of those typical 'nobody understands our music' plots, where the local dignitaries are trying to ban something as terrible as the Saturday night hop."

—John Lennon

project to exploit the band's image. In the summer of 1963, United Artists signed a three-picture deal with Brian Epstein, and, since The Beatles' recording contract with EMI didn't cover movie soundtracks, they figured this would be lucrative. UA's head, Bud Ornstein, allocated the black-and-white film a £200,000 ($500,000) budget and commissioned independent producer Walter Shenson to put everything together by mid-1964, when the Fabs might also be big news in America. Any later than that, and they may already be on the way down(!).

Shenson hired British-based American Richard Lester to direct the picture, and this was his first good move. Like George Martin, Dick had a Goon connection: He had directed a number of British TV shows featuring their talents, as well as an 11-minute home movie, *The Running, Jumping And Standing Still Film*, with Peter Sellers and Spike Milligan, which had been nominated for an Academy Award. This, together with the fact that Lester had also helmed a 1961 teen pic named *It's Trad, Dad!* (*Ring-a-Ding Rhythm* in the U.S.) featuring a performance by Gene Vincent, immediately enhanced his standing with The Beatles.

Meanwhile, at the end of October 1963, Liverpudlian playwright Alun Owen, best known in Britain for perceptive TV productions such as *No Trams On Lime Street*, was brought aboard to write the Fab Four's screenplay. His directive from Walter Shenson was to clearly delineate each of their personalities, while also capturing their youthful energy and anarchic humor. On November 7, 8, and 9, 1963, Owen joined the group in Ireland and in London and observed their characters, their mannerisms, the way they interacted with one another, and, just as importantly, their hectic lifestyle. Then he went to work, and the result was a fictionalized, documentary-style account of one day in The Beatles' life.

Centering around the adventures of John, Paul, George, and Ringo traveling down to London to film a TV show, Alun Owen's screenplay managed to capture The Beatles' claustrophobic, goldfish-bowl existence, while conveying the general feeling of good fun and mayhem that surrounded them. Indeed, the finished picture often gives the impression that they are just improvising in front of the cameras, whereas in fact every line was tightly scripted.

With a Royal Premiere scheduled for July 6, 1964, John and Paul wrote many of the film's new songs during The Beatles' January and February trips to France and the U.S. Then, on their return from America, the band had just four days to record nine tracks: "Can't Buy Me Love," "You Can't Do That," "And I Love Her," "I Should Have Known Better," "Tell Me Why," "If I Fell," "I'm Happy Just To Dance With You," "I Call Your Name," and Little Richard's "Long Tall Sally." Dick Lester declined the last two, while a segment featuring "You Can't Do That" was filmed and then cut from the finished picture. The title track wasn't written and recorded until the movie was near completion.

### Do You Want to Know a Secret?

During the early stages of shooting, The Beatles' first movie didn't have a name. Proposed titles were: *Beatlemania* and *The Beatles Film*; George suggested *It's a Daft, Daft, Daft, Daft World*; and Paul chipped in with *Oh! What A Lovely Wart*. All were rejected. Then, after one particularly long filming session, when someone commented on what a hard day it had been, Ringo innocently amended it to "a hard day's night." He may well have seen this phrase in the "Sad Michael" story of John's book, *In His Own Write*, but it didn't matter. Everyone loved Ringo's catchy title, and John and Paul subsequently wrote the song.

The Beatles saw the shooting script for the first time on February 29, filming began two days later, and ended on April 24. After the non-soundtrack songs were recorded in early June, *A Hard Day's Night* ended up being the first Beatles album ever to consist 100% of Lennon-McCartney songs.

In the end, The Beatles really enjoyed their first excursion into the movies, and it shows. Each of them are immensely likable, delivering their lines with a mixture of charm and innocence, and they also manage to shine in their solo scenes. (Except Paul, since he doesn't have a solo. He shot a lengthy scene in which he chats to an actress, but the director thought it was awkwardly scripted and decided to edit it out.) John may have later dismissed Alun Owen's characterizations of them as being phony, but The Beatles were forever identified with these onscreen characters.

Dick Lester's quick-fire pacing enhances The Beatles' performances and infuses the picture with an infectious energy. So do break-with-reality segments such as one in which The Beatles are seen inside a train and then running and cycling alongside it. At the same time, the madcap visual style of some of the musical sequences are precursors to today's MTV-style pop videos. Indeed, the *entire film* was inspirational—and you only have to watch an episode of *The Monkees* to recognize *that*!

### Do You Want to Know a Secret?

Believe it or not, when some of United Artists' American executives saw the final cut, they pressed Dick Lester to wipe The Beatles' voices from the soundtrack and replace them with the "clearer" mid-Atlantic tones of professional actors. Lester, who thankfully refused, was furious, and, when they heard about it, so were The Beatles!

The film's World Premiere, in the presence of Princess Margaret (who was fast becoming The Beatles' biggest Royal fan), took place at the London Pavilion in Piccadilly Circus on July 6, 1964. Outside, 200 policeman tried to contend with 20,000 hysterical fans. Then, for the picture's "Northern Premiere," which took place in Liverpool four days later, more than 200,000 people lined The Beatles' 10-mile route from the airport to the city center, where they were also honored with a civic reception at the Town Hall.

Meanwhile, the critics were nearly falling over themselves in their efforts to praise the film and its stars. In America, alluding to Orson Welles' cinematic masterpiece, *The Village Voice* proclaimed *A Hard Day's Night* to be "The *Citizen Kane* of juke box musicals." In England *The Daily Express* described it as "gorgeous fun! It's a mad, mad, mad, mad film, man. Nothing like it since the Goons on radio and the Marx Brothers in the thirties. Delightfully loony. Palpitating cinema."

*A Hard Day's Night* wasn't nominated for an Academy Award, and neither were its actors or its director. Scriptwriter Alun Owen was, but lost out to the authors of *Father Goose*. In the music category, *Mary Poppins* scooped the honors, with "Chim-Chim Cher-ee" being voted "Best Song." Still, The Beatles' fans didn't seem to mind. In fact, they screamed so loudly when their heroes appeared onscreen that they couldn't hear the music anyway!

*A Hard Day's Night* earned $5.8 million during the first six weeks of its release. Not a bad return on a £200,000 ($500,000) investment.

# Help!

Whereas *A Hard Day's Night* is an all-time classic, The Beatles' second movie, *Help!*, is of its time and doesn't stand up as well today.

Like its predecessor, *Help!* was produced by Walter Shenson, directed by Richard Lester, and starred John, Paul, George, and Ringo playing themselves. As in *A Hard Day's Night,* Victor Spinetti again appeared in one of the supporting roles; John and Paul (and this time George) again wrote the songs without reading the script; and, as with their previous big-screen project, the film again had no title. (Originally it was referred to simply as *Beatles 2*, before being named *Eight Arms to Hold You*. That, however, didn't make for an easy song title, so Lester then came up with *Help!*) There, however, the similarities with *A Hard Day's Night* end.

Now that the Fab Four had fully established themselves, UA was prepared to more than double the budget to £500,000 ($1.2 million), assign an 11-week shooting schedule (February 23 to May 12, 1965), and have the proceedings filmed in glorious Technicolor. With a directive to come up with a comedy adventure rather than a comic "documentary," Marc Behm—whose previous credits included the original storyline for the Cary Grant/Audrey Hepburn movie, *Charade*—began work on the script. Then Charles Wood, who that year also co-wrote the screenplay for Dick Lester's film *The Knack, and How to Get It* was brought in to revise Behm's efforts.

*While George smiles pretty for the camera, Dick Lester and Brian Epstein chat at the world premiere of Lester's film* The Knack, and How to Get It *(1965).*
©Hulton Getty

The result was a lightweight, comic-strip adventure about the bungled attempts of followers of a Middle-Eastern sect to get hold of a sacred, sacrificial ring that has attached itself to one of Ringo's fingers; if the sad-eyed drummer can't remove it, he'll become the cult's next sacrifice. The Beatles themselves fancied filming in some foreign locales, so scenes taking place in the Bahamas and Austria were promptly incorporated into the flimsy storyline.

Basically, The Beatles were no longer as enamored with the whole process of movie-making as they had been the previous year. Instead of waiting around on the set for hours at a time in order for the crew to set up a single shot, they could be elsewhere—writing songs, recording in the studio, or even just relaxing. They had fun making *Help!*, but often this was achieved by smoking pot to alleviate the boredom. This, in turn, meant that their concentration wasn't quite 100%, and you can tell by the finished product. Compare The Beatles' alert appearance in *A Hard Day's Night* with their more laid-back persona in *Help!* and you'll see what I mean.

**I Want to Tell You**

"*Help!* was a drag because we didn't know what was happening … we were on pot by then and all the best stuff is on the cutting-room floor, with us breaking up and falling all over the place."

—John Lennon, *Rolling Stone* magazine, 1970

Still, *Help!* turned out to be a colorful, mildly amusing film with great songs. It did good business at the box office and was, for the most part, greeted warmly by critics. However, there could also be no denying that it was somewhat disappointing in comparison to *A Hard Day's Night.*

# Yellow Submarine (or "The Best Film They Never Made")

In 1966, Al Brodax, who had produced 39 episodes of the King Features TV cartoon *The Beatles*, began pitching Brian Epstein about the possibility of making a full-length animated feature about the Fabs for cinema release. When it became clear that, if released by UA, this would fulfill the group's three-picture deal with the company, Brian agreed, and Lee Minoff was commissioned to write an original story based upon one of The Beatles' hit songs. He chose "Yellow Submarine."

Brodax and Minoff, together with Erich Segal and Jack Mendelsohn, wrote the screenplay in which those enemies of happiness, color, and music, The Blue Meanies, launch a merciless attack on the fun-loving but defenseless inhabitants of Pepperland. Eventually, The Beatles come to the rescue, after making a long and harrowing journey from Liverpool in a Yellow Submarine. They fight off the invaders, and everyone lives happily, colorfully, and musically ever after.

German graphic artist, Heinz Edelmann, created the varied and imaginative cast of characters, including Max the Blue Meanie, the Snapping Turtle Turks, the Apple Bonkers, the Flying Glove, the Count Down Clown, orchestra leader Old Fred, and Jeremy the Boob (the "Nowhere Man"). A team of 40 animators and 140 technical artists then adapted Edelmann's original sketches into around half a million cells (the individual animated frames that together make up an animated work), following the directives of George Dunning—who had previously directed the Beatles TV cartoons—to create a collage of 1960s pop art and hallucinatory psychedelia.

Disney this was not, even though when they were first consulted about the project, The Beatles themselves envisaged a far-out yet Disney-esque picture. The King Features team didn't agree and, thereafter, the Fab Four had absolutely no involvement in the conception and production processes. Indeed, the UA execs even got the mid-Atlantic "Beatle" voices that they had always desired, courtesy of professional actors.

As for the deluge of one-liners that they had to speak, these attempt—but largely fail—to match up to the sharp and witty humor of *A Hard Day's Night*. Visually, however, the film is a treat, chock-full of splendidly bizarre sight gags that, in those days at least, only animation could achieve. And then, of course, there is the music, combining four new or previously unissued songs—"Hey Bulldog," "Only A Northern Song," "It's All Too Much," and "All Together Now"—with numerous other Beatles hits largely from their psychedelic period. These four originals, together with the title track and "All You Need Is Love," made up side one of the *Yellow Submarine* album (released in January of 1969), while the second side consisted of George Martin's orchestral film score.

In January 1968, possibly to fulfill contractual obligations, or perhaps just to give the impression that they were actually involved with the project, The Beatles filmed a short cameo appearance that was inserted just before the end of *Yellow Submarine*. All four attended the film's world premiere at the London Pavilion on July 17 of that year, where there were Beatlemania-type scenes reminiscent of 1964 and 1965, with a massive crowd bringing the Central London traffic to a standstill.

Even though it initially did disappointing business in the UK and didn't even get a general release, *Yellow Submarine* was applauded by the critics, and today, as an encapsulation of late-1960s sensibilities, it's loved by old and young alike. As one reviewer commented, it is "the best film The Beatles never made."

**With a Little Help**

The "Hey Bulldog" segment of *Yellow Submarine* was omitted from the American version of the animated feature. Therefore, if you want to see this sequence, you'll have to view the unedited print that was released to cinemas in the UK and has since been transmitted on British television. Check it out—after all, it's the only song that was written specifically for the movie.

# Let It Be

The *Yellow Submarine* premiere was the last occasion on which all four Beatles attended an opening night together. None of them turned up for *Let It Be*. They were past caring.

In Chapter 23, I'll tell you about the problems that plagued the recording sessions, but suffice it to say that the finished movie doesn't disguise them. Apart from one notable instance, in which George tells Paul, "I'll play whatever you want me to play, or I won't play at all if you don't want me to play," we don't actually see The Beatles arguing. However, you only have to note their listless appearance, laid-back attitude, and generally lackluster standard of musicianship to realize that this is a band disintegrating before your very eyes.

Throughout much of 1968, enthusiasm had been waning within the world's greatest supergroup. Only Paul still seemed to have any motivation to keep things moving along, and so, in an attempt to turn things around, he suggested that The Beatles should return to the way they were before fame and fortune took over. This amounted to a live performance. The other three (especially George and John) weren't overly keen about this, but they half-heartedly went along with an idea to perform an eight-song, one-hour

**With a Little Help**

There are plenty of illegal bootleg sound recordings from the *Let It Be* sessions, some with several of the group's arguments intact. However, to see pristine quality outtakes from the film, watch the last installment of the *Beatles Anthology* documentary series. Among other things, this includes previously unseen footage of "Get Back" being rehearsed in the studio and The Beatles discussing their upcoming rooftop performance.

show in front of an audience for a live or video-taped television broadcast. The big question, however, was where to stage it. After all, this was the late '60s, and so the setting just *had* to be exotic or, at the very least, unusual!

After a few ideas—a disused flour mill, a ship, a stage in the middle of the Sahara Desert, a Roman amphitheater in North Africa—were tossed out, Denis O'Dell (appointed to produce the TV show) suggested that the band should get started by rehearsing for the big occasion… whatever that might be.

O'Dell would be producing the Peter Sellers/Ringo Starr movie *The Magic Christian*, at Twickenham Film Studios from early February 1969. The Beatles therefore accepted his advice to rehearse there, and allowed themselves to be filmed for a possible "at work" TV documentary that could tie in with the live performance. The director was Michael Lindsay-Hogg. However, as soon as John, Paul, George, and Ringo assembled at Twickenham on January 2 and the cameras started to roll, there was trouble in the air.

Everything was captured on 16mm film: George and Paul bickering; Ringo looking totally bored; and John virtually tuning out while paying constant attention to his ever-present girlfriend, Yoko Ono. On January 10, George, frustrated at what he considered to be John and Paul's uncaring, condescending attitude towards his musicianship, quit the band. Several days later he returned, but on the proviso that the idea of a live performance be abandoned and, instead, The Beatles just concentrate on making an album. The TV show idea went out the window, and the cameras and the not-feeling-Fab Four switched location to their new Apple recording studio for the purpose of producing an "at-work" feature film. The title? *Get Back*.

At George's invitation, keyboard player Billy Preston sat in with The Beatles during the recording sessions, and the atmosphere lightened a little. Then, towards the end of January, someone came up with the idea of the group giving an unannounced live performance on the Apple rooftop. They could do this during the lunch hour and provide free entertainment for the people working in Central London. This garnered general approval, and, despite some last-minute hesitations, the performance went ahead as planned on Thursday, January 30. It was The Beatles' last live appearance together, and it therefore provides a fitting end to the motion picture that was eventually given the more wistful title, *Let It Be*.

**I Want to Tell You**

"I thought it would be good to go out, the sh—ty version, because it would break The Beatles, you know, it would break the myth… 'This is what we are like with our trousers off, so would you please end the game now.' But that didn't happen."

—John Lennon, *Rolling Stone* magazine, 1970

After much wrangling within the group, and the necessary heavy editing of the film itself, *Let It Be* made it onto the big screen in May 1970, and at the following year's Academy Awards ceremony The Beatles finally got their Oscar—*Let It Be* won for Best Original Song Score. By then, however, the band was already history.

Today, *Let It Be* serves as an invaluable document of The Beatles falling out of love with one another. The original concept was to show them at work and at play, yet their purposes would have been better suited had the cameras started rolling about 18 months earlier. By 1969 the game was basically over. The work was haphazard and even the "play" was largely strained. Nevertheless, the movie still contains some fine moments, most notably towards the end of the film when, having rehearsed numerous songs half to death, The Beatles perform a few of them properly both in the studio and on the roof.

This leads us to the inevitable conclusion: When they put their personal problems to one side and got on with the job of making music, the Fab Four were still unbeatable.

# Aborted Projects

Okay, so now, among other things, you know about the feature films The Beatles made. But what about the ones that they didn't? No, I don't mean *Gone With the Wind* or *The Ten Commandments*, but the scripts they were offered and turned down. Here's a rundown of the half dozen aborted projects.

## The Yellow Teddybears

In 1963, before *A Hard Day's Night,* The Beatles were offered a cameo role in a low-budget, British exploitation flick called *The Yellow Teddybears* (aka *Gutter Girls* and *The Thrill Seekers*). Richard Hartford-Davis was producer/director of this turkey, which was about a bunch of teenage girls who would wear a teddy bear pin on their blouses to boast to the world that they had slept with a guy. The Beatles turned this down because they were told they'd either have to perform songs written by someone else, or have their songs copyrighted by the film's production company. In the end, the music was written and performed by a singer/guitarist named Malcolm Mitchell.

## A Talent for Loving

In early 1965, around when *Help!* was going into production, it was announced that The Beatles' third movie would be a gun-totin' Western entitled *A Talent For Loving*. It would start shooting the following year and be based on a true-life, 1,400-mile horse race that took place between the Rio Grande and Mexico City in 1871. The winner's prize was a wealthy and glamorous girl.

Richard Condon, who was adapting the script from his own novel, envisioned The Beatles as a bunch of pioneering Liverpudlians who had traveled west. For reasons that were never made perfectly clear, however, The Beatles withdrew from the project. *A Talent For Loving* was released in 1969, with leads Richard Widmark, Topol, Caesar Romero, and Genevieve Page.

## Lord of the Rings

During the mid-1960s, John Lennon thought it would be a good idea for The Beatles to purchase the rights to J.R.R. Tolkien's epic fantasy novel *The Lord of the Rings*, casting himself in the most attention-getting role! For those familiar with the book, John wanted the part of Gollum, while Paul would play Frodo Baggins, George would portray Gandalf, and Ringo would be Sam Merryweather.

Needless to say, this idea didn't appeal to the others, and so when the rights to the book weren't even attainable, the project was conveniently forgotten.

## The Three Musketeers

*The Three Musketeers* had already been filmed in 1935, 1939, and 1948 when The Beatles considered starring in another remake of Alexander Dumas' classic novel. Done properly, this actually could have been a good vehicle for them, yet the Fabs ultimately felt they just weren't suited to the characters of the Musketeers and D'Artagnan.

It isn't clear who suggested this idea or who would have directed the film, yet it's interesting to note that when *The Three Musketeers* next reached the big screen in 1974, Dick Lester was at the helm. He also directed *The Four Musketeers* (1974) and *Return of the Musketeers* (1989).

## Shades of a Personality

By 1966, producer Walter Shenson was desperately searching for a Beatles movie vehicle that would mark a significant departure from *A Hard Day's Night* and *Help!* At the end of the year, Shenson announced that Owen Holder was working on a script for what was initially being referred to as "Beatles 3." By June 1967 this had evolved into *Shades of a Personality*, to be shot in Malaga, Spain, and directed by the award-winning maker of *Blow-Up*, Michelangelo Antonioni. The story would concern a man (John) who suffers from a three-way split personality. Each of these personalities (portrayed by Paul, George, and Ringo) would emerge in separate sub-plots.

An interesting idea, but with the release of the *Sgt. Pepper* album, The Beatles were soon moving on to new projects, one of which was the *Magical Mystery Tour* TV movie (which I'll also be telling you about in Chapter 23). *Shades of a Personality* was quickly dropped from the schedule.

## Up Against It

In January 1967, while the script for *Shades of a Personality* was still in development, Walter Shenson also approached English playwright Joe Orton (*Loot*) about writing a screenplay for The Beatles. Orton's darkly humorous writing style appealed to The Beatles. Walter Shenson therefore paid him an advance of £5,000 ($12,000) to come up with something.

Unbeknownst to Walter Shenson and the Fab Four, Orton adapted one of his early novels, *The Silver Bucket*, and added in elements of another that would later be published as *Head To Toe*. The result was *Up Against It*, and, to quote an entry in Orton's own diary, "with its political assassination, guerrilla warfare, and transvestitism, it might have been designed with The Beatles in mind!"

Orton completed the script for *Up Against It* in late February. In early April he received it back from Brian Epstein's office without even an explanation. On August 9, 1967, 18 days before Brian's death, Joe Orton was murdered at home by his lover, Kenneth Halliwell. He was just 34.

As you can see, the most notable film projects The Beatles rejected ranged from the inane to the insane, the enticing to the unexciting. Beyond that there's no way of knowing how any of them would have turned out, but one thing's for certain: They would have been hard-pressed to match—let alone improve on—*A Hard Day's Night*.

# The Least You Need to Know

➤ The Beatles' first two movies, *A Hard Day's Night* and *Help!*, met with worldwide acclaim.

➤ The Beatles had difficulty finding a suitable third follow-up film, and turned several projects down.

➤ The Fab Four had very little involvement with the animated feature *Yellow Submarine*, which even today is still enjoyed by adults and kids alike.

➤ *Let It Be* captured the band's disintegration, but won the Academy Award for Best Song Score.

# Hop Off the Bus: An End to Touring

As the saying goes, all good things must come to an end, and after giving more than 1,400 live performances in just nine years, The Beatles finally quit the concert scene in 1966. What had once been fun-filled events in which the band and the fans shared in a mutual love for the music had by now turned into what John Lennon described as "bloody tribal rites."

Often playing in huge outdoor stadiums, John, Paul, George, and Ringo were no longer in close contact with their audiences, who had come to scream at their idols instead of listen to them sing and play anyway. Sometimes the noise was so loud that The Beatles would simply stop playing and mime. Nobody noticed, so why bother? Not surprisingly, the Fab Four's performances began to sound tired and lackluster. Their obvious boredom was increased by the fact that, in those days of relatively primitive concert equipment, they weren't able to reproduce on stage the revolutionary new sounds that they were creating in the studio. In 1966 they never performed any of the numbers on their then-current *Revolver* album.

If The Beatles were now seriously considering withdrawing from the live scene, their minds were made up by several unsavory incidents that took place during their final tours. Let's now take a look at some of the highlights—and low-lights—of that tumultuous year.

# May Day in the UK

At the start of 1966, The Beatles enjoyed their longest period of relaxation since their Quarry Men days—a full three months. Wow! Wasn't that something! At the start of April, they entered the studio to commence work on what would become their *Revolver* album, after which they were scheduled to tour West Germany, Japan, and the Philippines in late June and early July; North America in August; and then Britain towards the end of the year. At least, that had been the plan announced back in February. However, after events during the summer, the British tour was shelved and their homeland fans had to make do with their memories and just one live performance in the UK that year.

On Sunday, May 1, the *New Musical Express* Annual Poll-Winners' All-Star Concert was staged in front of 10,000 fans at London's Empire Pool (now renamed Wembley Arena). And what a lineup there was—The Beatles, The Rolling Stones, The Spencer Davis Group, The Who, The Yardbirds, Herman's Hermits, Roy Orbison, Cliff Richard, The Small Faces, Sounds Incorporated, Dusty Springfield, and The Walker Brothers. No big deal—just some of the most popular acts of the time!

Still, there always have to be some spoil-sports, don't there? Just prior to this occasion, the executives of Britain's ABC Television network—which was videotaping the event—and the managers of both The Beatles and The Rolling Stones failed to come to terms over the broadcast contract, and, as a result, the cameras were switched off during both of those bands' performances. That's right, folks—the Fabs' last British concert was never filmed!

**I Want to Tell You**

"I reckon we could send out four waxwork dummies of ourselves and that would satisfy the crowds. Beatles concerts are nothing to do with music any more."

—John Lennon, 1966

Not that there was a great amount to see—just five songs in 15 minutes: "I Feel Fine," "Nowhere Man," "Day Tripper," "If I Needed Someone," and "I'm Down." Then the cameras were switched on again to capture The Beatles receiving their poll-awards, as well as John being handed an individual award.

The first day of the fifth month is known as May Day, and it's celebrated as an international holiday in honor of workers. Accordingly, it's a pity that The Beatles' work wasn't properly celebrated by ABC Television on this notable occasion.

# Hamburg: Full Circle

Although Hamburg played such a big part in helping to shape The Beatles as concert artists, the group never actually played there—or anywhere in West Germany—during 1963, 1964, or 1965. Perhaps they figured that, having performed for around 800 hours on Hamburg club stages, the people there had had more than enough chance to see them. Still, by 1966 it seemed only fair that they should return to the country where they had enjoyed early success. Also, being that their concert career was almost at an end, it was appropriate that they should perform for a last time (or two) in Hamburg itself, even if they had outgrown the Star-Club long ago.

*June 24, 1966: The Beatles kick off a short tour of West Germany, sponsored by* Bravo *magazine, with a performance at the Circus-Krone-Bau in Munich.*
©Hulton Getty

After concert appearances in Munich and Essen on June 24 and 25, The Beatles arrived by train in Hamburg on the morning of the 26th. There to greet them at the city's central station—as well as backstage before the group's two shows—were a number of familiar faces from the past, including Astrid Kirchherr, who so long ago fashioned their famous moptop hairdos; Bert Kaempfert, who produced the group's first professional recordings; and Bettina Derlien, the generously proportioned Star-Club barmaid who had been a particular favorite of John.

The 5,600-capacity Ernst Merck Halle was the chosen venue for The Beatles' latest—and, as it turned out, last—Hamburg concerts, and this time around there would be no all-night performances, no cries of *"mach shau,"* no crates of beer being passed onto the stage, and no insulting comments made about the Nazis by Herr Lennon. Instead, at each show the all-seated, all-screaming audience was treated to a straightforward 30-minute performance consisting of just 11 songs and a few pre-rehearsed comments.

Afterwards, for old times' sake, John and Paul somehow managed to take a late-night stroll down the Reeperbahn, visiting some of the clubs and bars that they had once frequented, and looking up various former friends and acquaintances. Some were still there, others weren't, yet Hamburg hadn't changed nearly as much as The Beatles since they'd last set foot in the city on January 1, 1963.

Within a few short months it would change again.

# Sayonara Japan

It was during The Beatles' only visit to Japan that things started to go wrong, commencing a cycle of events that would put an end concert tours once and for all.

The group left London for Tokyo on June 27, but when a typhoon was forecast to be approaching, their plane had to touch down in Anchorage, Alaska. Needless to say, several hundred Alaskan Beatlemaniacs immediately crawled out of the woodwork and surrounded the group's hotel until the Fab Four resumed their trip to Tokyo. They arrived on June 29 at 3:40 a.m. and were soon greeted by a storm that had been brewing in Japan for several days—a storm of protest.

**With a Little Help**

You can see how The Beatles performed in Tokyo by watching the recordings that exist of two of their concerts at the Nippon Budokan Hall. These were videotaped in color by Nippon Television (NTV) on June 30 and July 1, 1966, and can be distinguished by the group's clothes; they wear dark suits in the first performance, and light striped ones during the second.

Tokyo promoter Tatsuji Nagashima had booked The Beatles to perform five shows in three days at the city's Nippon Budokan Hall, an octagonal venue that catered to traditional martial arts events. By some it was considered far too sacred to host Western rock and roll concerts, and there were violent demonstrations outside the building both before and after The Beatles' appearances. (And for what purpose? The Budokan has since been used to host numerous rock concerts, but The Beatles, of course, were the first.)

Thirty-five thousand security men were on hand to "control" the disturbances, while at each concert the 10,000 fans were closely watched by 3,000 policemen. Anyone who stood was ordered to sit down. Consequently, while there was enthusiastic applause in between numbers, the audiences sat quietly and listened while the band played, which perhaps wasn't all that wise considering the level to which the Fab Four's live musicianship had now slipped. During the usual scream-fests they couldn't hear themselves sing or play, resulting in some off-key, out-of-time performances, and that's how things remained in Japan, even if nobody appeared to notice.

Meanwhile, when they weren't at the Budokan, The Beatles were forced by the local security forces to stay at the Tokyo Hilton Hotel. There, in their 18th-floor suites, heavily protected by armed guards, John, Paul, George, and Ringo were visited by assorted sales people with all kinds of goods to offer—cameras, radios, clothes, you name it.

While this proved to be profitable entertainment (for the merchandisers, that is), The Beatles were virtually trapped. When they tried to escape, they were caught by the police and returned briskly to their rooms. John subsequently did manage to slip by them, but the security force's response was to threaten to withdraw its protection of the group. Among other things, this would have meant no more 70 mph escorted motorcades to and from the Budokan. (And, as anyone in traffic-filled Tokyo will tell you, a 70 mph car trip is a treat to be savored!)

If our heroes thought their Japanese visit was less than fun, they would soon look upon it as a lighthearted pleasure trip by comparison to their sojourn in the Philippines.

# The Thriller in Manilla

Remember Filipino dictator Ferdinand Marcos and his wife Imelda? He ruled his country under a brutal regime before being chased out of his palace during the 1980s. She was his extravagant sidekick, who became famous for having literally thousands of pairs of shoes (the better to run away in).

Ferdinand and Imelda were at the height of their power when The Beatles arrived in Manila on July 3, 1966, prior to giving two concerts there the next day. *The Manilla Sunday Times* ran an article stating that the President, his wife, and their three children had been invited as guests of honor at the concerts, and that beforehand—at 11 a.m. the next morning—The Beatles would be paying a courtesy call on the First Lady at Malacañang Palace. At least, that's what Imelda had apparently been told.

In fact, on the schedule drawn up by local promoter Ramon Ramos Jr., the palace visit was originally scheduled for 3:00, but since the first show was due to start at 4:00, The Beatles rejected this idea. Ramos, however, had committed himself, and the last thing he wanted to do was offend Mrs. Marcos. Therefore, when 11:00 a.m. was suggested, he left matters there, assuming that the Fab Four would naturally do what was expected of them.

The Fab Four, unfortunately, weren't aware of the new arrangement, so when a palace official came to collect them the following morning, they were fast asleep and Brian Epstein refused to wake them. He would have been better off putting up with The Beatles' grumpy response than trying to deal with the national outrage that ensued. The group performed its two concerts that day, and the next morning, all hell broke loose.

*The Manilla Times* ran an article headlined "Imelda Stood Up," in which it reported that The Beatles had

**I Should Have Known Better**

In numerous books it has been reported that, when The Beatles played in the Philippines, they did so before an audience of 80,000 (or 100,000) people. Wrong! They did perform to a *total* of 80,000, but this was for two shows; the first, in the afternoon of July 4, 1966, attracted 30,000 people; and the evening concert drew another 50,000.

"snubbed" the First Lady and her three children, not to mention 400 Marcos family friends. A photo showed Imelda "waiting in vain." For his part, Ramon Ramos expressed his own outrage by refusing to hand over the group's substantial share of the concert receipts, while the British Embassy and The Beatles themselves received bomb and death threats. Brian Epstein tried to intervene by having a camera crew visit the band's hotel and videotape a statement that he had written with press officer Tony Barrow, explaining how The Beatles had no knowledge of the rearranged rendezvous with Imelda. It was transmitted later that evening but, wouldn't you know it, at the precise moment that the statement commenced, a surge of static just happened to obliterate the message on TV sets nationwide. Broadcast technicians did manage to correct the problem... just as the statement finished.

The following day a Filipino tax commissioner insisted that The Beatles couldn't leave the country unless they paid income tax on the concert revenue that they hadn't even received! (Now *that's* novel. Not even the IRS has come up with that one yet.) The inevitable row ensued, but Brian Epstein realized that it might be worth biting the bullet just to make a safe getaway. He filed a bond for just under £7,000 (about $17,000), but this in no way guaranteed the safety of either his clients or himself.

For one thing, the security forces who'd been protecting The Beatles had now been withdrawn, and the band members and their entourage were subsequently kicked and punched as they departed the hotel. Much the same happened when they arrived at Manilla International Airport, in addition to the terminal manager also ordering that power to the escalators be shut off, forcing the group to haul their luggage up several flights of stairs. Then, when they reached the second floor, a mob of 200 Filipinos set upon them. Remarkably, The Beatles emerged unscathed, yet Brian Epstein was injured, Mal Evans was knocked to the floor and kicked in the ribs, and the band's chauffeur, Alf Bicknell, suffered a fractured rib and damage to his spine.

As if all of this wasn't enough, John, Paul, George, Ringo, and their party all had to sprint, bags in hand, across the tarmac to their airplane, only to then be told that Mal Evans and Tony Barrow had to return to the terminal. Big Mal, fearing the worst, was almost in tears and asked his fellow travelers to tell his wife that he loved her. Yet, back inside the airport, he and Barrow were simply informed that The Beatles' plane still wasn't permitted to take off. Somehow there was no record of the group arriving in the first place, therefore they were now technically "illegal immigrants" (don't you love this story?!), and they couldn't leave either!

It took three quarters of an hour to sort out the necessary paperwork before the plane—with all of its passengers aboard—at last took off. Then, and only then, did President Marcos issue a press statement, acknowledging that in no way had The Beatles intended to slight Imelda or his government. A timely gesture!

# Half an Hour in the Park

The Beatles' troubles on their final U.S. tour began before they'd even arrived in America.

In Chapter 22 I'll describe how John Lennon caused an uproar in parts of the U.S. when, in a London newspaper interview, he predicted Christianity's demise and asserted that, in 1966, The Beatles attracted more attention than Jesus Christ. Suffice it to say, the ensuing bad publicity cast a shadow over the first part of the tour, culminating in an anonymous phone call on August 19 promising that one or more of the band would be assassinated during either of their two shows in Memphis later that day. When a firecracker subsequently exploded mid-way through the evening concert, The Beatles immediately looked at each other to see who had been shot.

> **I Want to Tell You**
>
> "We're going to have a couple of weeks to recuperate before we go and get beaten up by the Americans."
>
> —George Harrison, on arriving back in London after the Philippines trip

Of course, none of them had, but the following night the Fab Four were equally scared when they were due to take to the open-air stage of Cincinnati's Crosley Field during a torrential rainstorm. The promoter had failed to cover the stage with a canopy, and so, while 35,000 fans sat inside the stadium waiting to see their idols, the musicians feared almost certain electrocution if they were to plug in their instruments or handle the microphones. Petrified, Paul threw up backstage, but at the last minute the show was canceled and re-scheduled for the following day.

And so the tour wound on unhappily for The Beatles, until the cold and windy night of Monday, August 29, 1966, when, at 9:27, they took to a concert stage for the very last time. The setting was San Francisco's Candlestick Park, and the stage itself—positioned at second base far away from the 25,000 fans—was elevated five feet above the ground inside a six-foot metal fence, and surrounded by 200 policemen. The Cavern Club this was not.

The Beatles played until precisely 10:00, closing the show nostalgically for the only time on the tour with "Long Tall Sally" instead of "I'm Down." Then they departed in an armored car. They all knew that this was the end. John had carried a camera up on stage and taken photos of himself (at arm's length) and the other group members between songs. Meanwhile, Paul had asked press officer Tony Barrow to make a cassette recording of their performance, and Barrow had obliged. However, since "auto reverse" wasn't yet available, the 30-minute-per-side-tape didn't capture "Long Tall Sally."

"Well, that's it," George Harrison commented dryly as The Beatles' plane left San Francisco that night. "I'm not a Beatle any more."

# The Least You Need to Know

➤ The Beatles' final British concert was in London on May 1, 1966; ironically, the TV cameras were turned off during their performance.

➤ The Beatles visited some old friends and haunts during their return to Hamburg.

➤ Protests in Japan were nothing compared to the horrors of their Philippines trip.

➤ The Beatles' last-ever concert was at San Francisco's Candlestick Park on August 29, 1966.

# Chapter 20

# When I Get Home: Life Away From the Road

## In This Chapter

➤ How The Beatles occupied themselves immediately after they quit touring

➤ Brian Epstein's difficulty adapting to a less active role

For more years than they cared to remember, The Beatles had worked their socks off. The packed schedule and incessant globetrotting meant that they'd hardly had time to stop, think, and take stock of their situation. Once the band quit touring, all of that changed. Money was no longer a concern and neither was publicity, so the Fab Four could now devote their creative energies to working in the recording studio. The only problem was figuring out what to do in their spare time.

In this chapter you'll learn about the recreational activities with which John, Paul, George, and Ringo occupied themselves during the last quarter of 1966, prior to reentering the recording studio—*individual* activities, which encouraged habitual press speculation about the group splitting up. You'll also learn about the quandary that Brian Epstein found himself in: Although he had numerous clients and various business interests, The Beatles were still the center of his universe. With no concert tours to arrange, his overall role was greatly diminished. Clearly, major changes loomed.

# John: Floating Downstream

The Beatles returned to the UK from their last concert tour in the U.S. on August 31, 1966, and five days later John was off to Celle in West Germany to film a role opposite Michael Crawford in *How I Won the War*, a movie produced and directed by a name that should be familiar by now: Dick Lester.

In this anti-war black comedy adapted from a novel and set during World War II, John played Private Gripweed, a role for which he had his hair cut into a "short-back-and-sides" and donned circular National Health "granny glasses." After two weeks of filming in Celle, the entire company then moved on to Carboneras in Spain. There John was joined by his British chauffeur who drove him to the set in his Rolls Royce each morning, and then back each evening to the villa in Almeria that John and wife Cynthia were sharing with Michael Crawford and his family.

By November 7 the filming was completed and the Lennons returned to England. (The movie garnered hostile reviews and did mediocre business.) Two days later, John attended a private preview of a London art exhibition entitled "Unfinished Paintings and Objects." The artist was Yoko Ono, and I'll tell you more about this first meeting—as well as John and Yoko's subsequent adventures—in Chapters 22 and 24. During the last months of 1966, John visited a number of art events, while being chased by publishers to write a follow-up to his best-selling books, *In His Own Write* and *A Spaniard In The Works*.

---

**I Should Have Known Better**

It's often reported that the first instance of John wearing his trademark circular "granny glasses" was in the movie *How I Won the War*. This isn't true. *Help!* contains a scene in which the Fab Four all wear disguises; John adopts the round glasses, a false beard, and a moustache.

---

*"Kenwood," the mock-Tudor house that John and Cynthia bought for £20,000 ($48,000) in July 1964, and where they lived until their marriage collapsed four years later.*
©Richard Buskin

Other than that, prior to The Beatles' return to the recording studio on November 24, he whiled away the hours at home. There, in Weybridge, Surrey, just southwest of London, John would drift for days on end—reading, watching TV, or just staring out of windows, hardly uttering a word to Cynthia or their three-year-old son Julian. He would disappear into his small home studio and write songs or make private recordings. Intense introspection was consuming an increasing amount of his time—and *he* was consuming increasing amounts of the hallucinogenic drug LSD, which he and George had been introduced to the previous year. (There'll be more about this in…yes, Chapter 22!)

Basically, John was subconsciously waiting for "the next big thing" to happen. He just didn't have a clue what it would be. Meanwhile, on November 27, shortly after The Beatles began recording "Strawberry Fields Forever," John filmed a brief appearance for an episode of the BBC2 TV comedy series *Not Only…But Also*, starring Peter Cooke and Dudley Moore. In the sketch he played the part of Dan, a doorman at a trendy London nightclub, garbed in fancy clothes and granny glasses. Clearly, the new image was here to stay.

> **I Want to Tell You**
>
> "I was always waiting for a reason to get out of The Beatles from the day I filmed *How I Won the War*. I just didn't have the guts to do it. The seed was planted when The Beatles stopped touring and I couldn't deal with not being onstage. But I was too frightened to step out of the palace."
>
> —John Lennon, *Newsweek* magazine, 1980

## Paul: Semi-Attached in Swinging London

Of all The Beatles, Paul enjoyed live performance the most. However, as the last American tour wore on, even he became convinced that the time had come to quit the road, and so, on returning to London, he assumed the role of the young man-about-town.

While John, George, and Ringo were all married and living in cozy suburbia, Paul had purchased a luxurious property in St. John's Wood, around the corner from the EMI Studios in Abbey Road and only a few minutes from the capital's bustling West End district. Having always been interested in the theater, he now attended more productions than ever, accompanied by his actress-girlfriend, Jane Asher, or watching her on the stage. This, however, comprised only a small part of his social calendar.

"People are saying things and painting things and writing things that are great," he told London's *Evening Standard* newspaper with regard to the city's thriving cultural scene. "I must *know* what people are doing."

Which is what he set out to do, mingling with actors, musicians, artists, journalists, film directors, and various young movers and shakers hanging out in "Swinging London." Later John and Yoko Ono became synonymous with the *avant-garde* art scene in both London and New York, but in 1966, while John was still living the seemingly quiet life in

Weybridge, Paul was very involved in *avant-garde* activities, making his own home movies and even recording a tape of electronic noises that, in January of 1967, would be utilized at the "Carnival of Light" at London's Roundhouse Theatre.

But don't get the idea that everything Paul did when The Beatles quit touring was geared towards the unusual. He composed the music for a British film starring Hayley Mills and Hywell Bennett entitled *The Family Way*, and during November he spent a couple of weeks on a safari vacation in Kenya with Jane Asher. Life was exciting, if, for the first time in years, somewhat unfocused.

# George: In Search of Eastern Promise

While Paul was the Beatle most in love with live performances and contact with the fans, George was the one who hated intrusions on his private life and made the strongest case for stopping the concert tours.

Having succeeded, at just 23 years old he was the only Beatle with a strong sense of the direction he wanted to take in his life: Eastward, towards India, whose music, culture, and philosophy he was increasingly embracing in an effort to escape from the stifling pressures of Beatlemania, not to mention the oppressive dominance of John and Paul in the recording studio. George, like John, was taking LSD to "expand the consciousness," and he'd at last spotted a way to carve out his own artistic niche by introducing entirely new instruments and arrangements to Beatles recordings.

George's fascination with the sitar originated during the 1965 filming of *Help!*, when he heard it utilized for an Easternized rendition of the song "A Hard Day's Night." This was performed for comedic effect, but the sound of the long-necked stringed instrument grabbed his attention. Soon thereafter, George purchased a sitar and introduced it to Western pop music in John's song, "Norwegian Wood (This Bird Has Flown)." The following year, George met Ravi Shankar at a dinner party in London, where he immediately took the Indian sitar virtuoso up on his offer to give lessons at Harrison's home in Esher, Surrey.

### Do You Want to Know a Secret?

When George Harrison and Ravi Shankar first met, George explained how he had recently written a song, "Love You To," entirely on sitar. Shankar had to admit that he wasn't familiar with George or The Beatles, yet he wasn't the only one to show his cultural naiveté. The next day, while Ravi was teaching George sitar scales, the telephone rang. George put the instrument down and stepped across it, and the sitarist whacked the guitarist on the leg. "Don't ever do that," exclaimed Ravi. "You must show respect for the instrument!" In India, George soon learned, music is considered close to God.

During a brief stop-off in India after The Beatle's horrific trip to the Philippines, George bought a more expensive sitar, and in September 1966 he and Pattie traveled to India, checking in at the Taj Mahal Hotel in Bombay under the alias of Mr. and Mrs. Sam Wells. Their cover was soon blown, however; after holding a press conference in which they stated that they had come to India to study yoga and the sitar, as well as to relax, they moved on to Kashmir. For the next four and a half weeks, George immersed himself in learning to play the sitar under Ravi Shankar's guidance, while also conversing with assorted students and holy men—although not the Maharishi Mahesh Yogi, who The Beatles would first encounter the following year.

A few days after returning to Britain, George turned up at London Airport to once again greet Ravi Shankar. This time, however, the Indian was wearing Western clothes while George was garbed in Eastern attire. The cultural intermingling of popular music was well underway.

## Ringo: The Suburban Squire

Of all The Beatles' post-touring schedules in 1966, Ringo's was by far the most straightforward. He opted to stay with wife Maureen and son Zak at "Sunny Heights," their home in Weybridge, Surrey, located nearby to the Lennons' "Kenwood."

The spacious house was set in beautiful, landscaped gardens and boasted a billiard table, a slot machine, six TV sets, and its own movie projector—all very state-of-the-art for the mid-1960s, and a huge contrast to the Dingle, the rough Liverpool neighborhood where Ringo had grown up. He had worked hard for his success and now he was enjoying it.

In early October, Ringo and Maureen flew to Spain to spend a few days with John and Cynthia during the filming of *How I Won the War.* John never really took to the painfully slow process of moviemaking, yet during the next few years The Beatles' drummer made a concerted effort to become a Starr of the silver screen.

## Brian: Nowhere Man

At 31, Brian Epstein was one of the world's most successful show-business impresarios. His company, NEMS Enterprises, had made the transition from the Merseybeat boom to managing acts such as Cream, The Bee Gees, and The Moody Blues, while also retaining clients such as Cilla Black and, of course, The Beatles. In 1965 Brian had purchased the lease on the Saville Theatre in London's West End in order to stage ballet, opera, and rock concerts that he himself promoted, and recently he'd even indulged his artistic aspirations by directing a play, producing a record, and part-funding a few feature films. London's

**I Want to Tell You**

"What am I going to do now? Shall I go back to school and learn something new?"

—Brian Epstein, immediately after The Beatles' last-ever concert, August 29, 1966

*Financial Times* estimated his personal wealth to be in the region of £7 million ($17 million). Yet none of this made him happy.

The Beatles were the sole reason Brian wasn't still running a record store back in Liverpool, and they remained the chief love of his life. All of his other acts and activities were simply distractions—only John, Paul, George, and Ringo could truly inspire him, fulfill at least some of his dreams, and make him feel special. Between November 1961 and August 1966, Brian had negotiated The Beatles' recording contract; remodeled their appearance; arranged their concert, TV, and radio appearances; fielded suggestions for prospective movie projects; and generally dealt with any problems that came their way.

However, after The Beatles quit the road, with radio and TV appearances mostly a thing of the past, Brian's workload relating to the group went way down. So did his influence on them, as the Fab Four began to take more and more charge of their own affairs. In previous years Brian had felt that they really needed him. Now he knew that they no longer did, and, coupled with his steady stream of doomed love affairs, this was a source of severe depression. In late 1966, Brian overdosed on sleeping pills in what appeared to be a failed suicide attempt. Around that time, in November, he also had to dismiss a newspaper report that two of The Beatles had approached Allen Klein to manage the band once Epstein's contract expired in October 1967.

Klein, a New Yorker with a reputation for profitably renegotiating record deals for artists such as The Rolling Stones, had recently been quoted as saying that if he were to handle The Beatles, he could turn them into "modern Marx Brothers." Brian asserted that the rumor about an imminent takeover by Klein was "ridiculous," but perhaps he knew better. (Allen Klein enters the story for real in Chapter 24.)

For one thing, it was increasingly clear that, while The Beatles still regarded Brian with affection, they were excluding him more and more from their professional decisions. Sensing this, Brian sometimes attempted to reassert some influence, even if his methods didn't always conform to established guidelines.

Ever since the group signed with EMI, he'd basically left all musical considerations to them and their producer. But one night in 1966, during a recording session at Abbey Road, Brian crossed this line and suffered the consequences. Standing alongside George Martin in the control room, he switched on the studio intercom after John Lennon finished singing a particular song and commented that he didn't think the vocal was "quite right." John's response was immediate and devastating: "You stick to your percentages, Brian," he snarled. "We'll look after the music!"

For Brian Epstein, the writing was clearly on the wall.

# The Least You Need to Know

➤ After the group stopped touring, John began to contemplate life without The Beatles.

➤ Paul was initially more involved in the avant-garde world than John.

➤ One of George's main inspirations came from Indian music, culture, and religion.

➤ Ringo was happy just to stay at home.

➤ Brian Epstein grew depressed and desperate once he saw his role diminishing.

# Chapter 21

# Those Swinging Sixties

## In This Chapter

➤ The Cold War tensions between East and West

➤ Exciting times and rising living standards

➤ Racial disharmony, social conflicts, and the explosion of rebellious youth

➤ A trio of assassinations that changed the face of the decade

The 1960s are often looked back upon as some of the best years of the 20th century; years of fun, excitement, hope, prosperity, discovery, and advancement. And they were, as long as you weren't fighting in a war, living in a ghetto, suffering racial discrimination, or experiencing the down-side of the burgeoning culture of drugs and violence. It's all a matter of your perspective, and therefore, while a term such as "the swinging Sixties" makes for good nostalgia, those who were alive at the time have mixed memories.

Still, the multi-faceted nature of this undeniably action-packed decade—fun-filled and miserable, peaceful and violent—provided a backdrop to The Beatles' success and influence, and so it's both informative and interesting to have a basic knowledge of the major social and political events. If you lived it, so be it; after all, this is a *Complete Idiot's Guide,* and I'm not going to make any rash assumptions…

# Cold War Blues

Given that 70 percent of Americans thought that Russia was trying to rule the world, Cold War fever was obviously rampant during the early 1960s. There wasn't as much of a rush on bomb shelters as there had been during the previous decade, but as tensions mounted between East and West, American schoolchildren and TV viewers were still being instructed that, in the event of a nuclear attack, citizens should assume the duck-and-cover position. Now, wasn't *that* great advice? Can you imagine—your city, town, or village is being razed to the ground, but by crouching down, shutting your eyes, and putting your arms over your head you should be perfectly safe!

Actually, there was good cause for people to panic, for, during John F. Kennedy's brief presidency, two notable "incidents" placed the world on the brink of a nuclear show-down. The first was the 1961 Bay of Pigs fiasco, in which a CIA-trained-and-equipped force of 1,400 Cuban exiles attempted to overthrow Fidel Castro's regime. President Kennedy denied American involvement in the force's landing at the Bay of Pigs, but the Soviets knew better and vowed to back Castro militarily. In the end it didn't matter. The invasion failed within three days, producing a severe dent in America's pride.

The following year, there was a second and more serious *contretemps* between the USA and the USSR. On October 22, JFK informed the American public—and the world—that the Soviet Union was constructing offensive nuclear missile bases in Cuba. The rockets could easily reach not only the United States but also many other countries in the Western hemisphere. American air, land, and sea forces were deployed to block the transportation of arms from the Sovet Union to Cuba, while the President warned that the firing of any missiles would be viewed as a declaration of war. For nearly a week the Soviet buildup continued and the world held its breath, until the Russian leader, Nikita Khrushchev, agreed to halt construction, and dismantle and remove the rockets in return for an American guarantee to stay out of Cuba.

Today, the Bay of Pigs fiasco and the Cuban Missile Crisis seem like figments of history, but at the time, people in both East and West really did fear that the world could be coming to an end. This concern was reflected in movies such as *Dr. Strangelove (or How I Learned to Stop Worrying and Love the Bomb)* and *Fail Safe*. Yet, having stared into the abyss and contemplated the consequences, the two superpowers now drew their fingers back from the nuclear buttons and started to shadow-box with each other in altogether different ways.

One of these was to take opposing sides in other nations' conflicts without actually fighting face-to-face. (Convenient in theory, unpleasant in practice.) The Vietnam War and the 1967 "Six-Day War" between the Arabs and the Israelis were prime examples of this. And then there was the space race, in which the quest to put a human being on the moon turned into a battle for supremacy between America and the Soviet Union.

**I Want to Tell You**

"The Beatles are my new secret weapon."

—Sir Alec Douglas-Home, British Prime Minister, 1964

Looking back from a 1990s vantage point, when peace has thankfully broken out between East and West, the whole Cold War conflict is seen for what it really was—costly, unnecessary, and pointless. Yet, back in the 1960s, it claimed many lives and cast a pall over countless others, so it's little wonder that those fun-loving moptops—as well as the later, peace-preaching Beatles—were so wholeheartedly embraced as a welcome relief from the doom, gloom, and misery.

# Fly Me to the Moon: A Time of Hope

For many, the 1960s represented a period of tremendous optimism; a time when, thanks to scientific and technological advances, anything seemed possible. It was a time when people got excited about daredevils attempting to set land-, sea-, and air-speed records, and computers were still largely a novelty in sci-fi films (with plenty of flashing lights, of course). Great things were promised, but not too much was taken for granted. Only by the end of the decade, when the Americans managed to land a manned spacecraft on the moon, did people start to grow blasé.

Another reason for optimism was the general rise in living standards. Beginning in the 1950s, Britain was enjoying almost full employment; West Germany and Japan were on the road to full economic recovery; France was attempting to lead the way in Europe; and, at the start of the decade, the real income of the average American was more than a third higher than just 15 years earlier. With this extra money came a greater choice of goods to buy, and many people were able to enjoy unsurpassed material comforts.

In America, this often amounted to a comfortable home with all of the modern amenities, as well as two cars parked on the driveway. This was the "affluent society," and with the improved mobility came a rapid exodus of families and industries from city centers out to the suburbs. It was, however, a trend still mainly confined to white people, resulting in an even greater division of the so-called "two nations"—one white and one black—that had taken root in America long before.

Eventually, a decade that had opened so brightly began to wind down on a bitter note. The hopeful image of nearly half a million youngsters congregating at the Woodstock music festival seemed to be canceled out by the violence of anti-war, anti-establishment riots; a series of key political assassinations; and the senseless Tate/La Bianco murders by the Charles Manson gang.

To many it seemed to be a case of abusing too much of a good thing.

# Riots, Protests, and the Youth Revolution

The 1960s were a decade notable for social reform, violent unrest, and relaxed standards for lifestyles, behavior, and recreation. The push for equal rights for racial and gender minorities, increased self-awareness of a historically large group of young people, new forms of music and chemical stimulation, and a war around which unprecedented protest spiraled, all converged to create a climate of chaos, experimentation, and upheaval.

## We Shall Overcome

In America, this centered largely around the black Civil Rights movement that had started to pick up steam during the 1950s. By the early '60s, desegregation was still a hot topic, with the Universities of Mississippi and Alabama both attracting international attention for their steadfast refusal to admit black students. In the case of Mississippi, the U.S. Justice Department and U.S. Marshals had to be called in to enforce federal law, while in Alabama it took the National Guard to prevent Governor George Wallace from personally blocking the path of two black students who were trying to register.

Dr. Martin Luther King Jr. was a leading light among those who sought to attain racial equality by way of peaceful protests. On August 28, 1963, more than 200,000 people gathered in front of the Lincoln Memorial in Washington, D.C., to hear him deliver his now-historic "I Have a Dream" speech, in which he demanded equality not only for black Americans but for "all of God's children." Nevertheless, the Civil Rights movement provoked expectations among black citizens that extended far beyond the inferior housing, education, and employment opportunities that they were still experiencing by the mid-1960s. Many began to lose faith in Dr. King's pacifist approach and instead began to turn their attention to the "black power" demands of Stokely Carmichael, as well as radical organizations such as the Nation of Islam and the Black Panther Party.

**I Want to Tell You**

"We never play to segregated audiences and we're not going to start now. I'd rather lose our appearance money."

—John Lennon prior to The Beatles' appearance at the Jacksonville Gator Bowl, Florida on September 11, 1964

The Panthers demanded the release of all black prisoners, together with the redistribution of property and wealth from whites to blacks. They also urged the black community to arm itself in order to "off the pigs"—a term for killing white policeman—and this simply added fuel to the flames that were already burning in ghettos across America. A case in point was the Watts area of Los Angeles, where, in August 1965, 35 deaths and $200 million worth of damage resulted from an uprising among the residents.

For the most part, however, the "black power" movement had more cultural impact than political, and, during the second half of the 1960s, "black is beautiful" became a popular catchphrase among people who were no longer trying to "act white" to be accepted. Instead of straightening their hair, black people now opted for a more natural look, while wearing African-style clothing and promoting their own style of pop music. On TV, actors such as Bill Cosby and Diahann Carroll portrayed characters that were far less stereotypical than the shuffling, smiling servants of previous decades.

# By the Time We Got to Woodstock

At the same time, moral attitudes were changing, long-held values were being questioned, and the old order was being challenged by the voice of youth. This manifested itself in several ways. For one, there was the music itself, which evolved from simple boy-loves-girl, boy-loses-girl pop ditties into songs with a message... whatever that message might be.

During the mid-1960s Bob Dylan led the way, taking the revolutionary step of plugging his folk guitar into an electric amplifier in order to reach a wider youth audience. Despite heavy criticism from his old "folky" fans, Dylan's protest songs—dealing with issues such as social injustice and a counterculture populated by drug peddlers and homeless young-sters—burst onto the pop charts. In a turbulent decade, music became a means of mass communication, whether The Beatles were singing "All You Need Is Love" or Country Joe and the Fish were attacking America's involvement in the Vietnam War with "I Feel Like I'm Fixin' To Die Rag."

Huge pop music festivals such as Monterey (1967) and Woodstock (1969) were the natural result of a youth movement that was pushing for peace, love, and unity. However, the chaos of The Rolling Stones' Altamont Festival on December 6, 1969, culminating during the Stones' performance in the fatal stabbing by Hell's Angels of an 18-year-old black spectator, Meredith Hunter, was also symbolic of pacifist optimism (or naivete) going badly awry as the 1960s wound to a close.

A sure sign of this was evident in the violent protests that exploded on university cam-puses around the United States and Western Europe. In May 1968, students across France took to the streets to vent their anger against what they considered to be an archaic, inadequate university system, as well as the national government. Pitched battles were fought with the police, cars were burned, and gasoline bombs were thrown, and when teachers and workers decided to join in the action, the country was brought to a virtual standstill. For a time it looked as if there would be civil war, until the usual promises of reforms managed to calm everyone down.

In America, where students were largely against their nation's involvement in the Viet-nam War, there was further violence on university campuses such as Kent State and Berkeley, and the famous 1967 march on the Pentagon. The following year, plenty of blood was also spilled in front of the American Embassy in London's Grosvenor Square when anti-Vietnam protestors clashed with the police.

> **Say the Word**
> Bag, in the context of "It's not my *bag*, man," means "It's just not my thing." This was a popular term in the late 1960s, when John Lennon and Yoko Ono even formed a company called Bag Productions.

Basically, the young rebels of the 1950s and early '60s had been superseded by political radicals, while rockers and beatniks had given way to flower children, college politicos, and a counter-culture of freaks, hippies, and yippies. Psyche-delic music, mind-bending drugs, and conflicting messages of peace, love, and bloody insurrection were more their *bag*, and who should be right there at the forefront of all these intertwining movements, pastimes, and activities but The Beatles!

The Fab Four were were among the chief influences of an era when all of the youthful challenges to traditional law and order were accompanied by more liberal attitudes towards sexual freedom. Courtesy of John Lennon, "All You Need Is Love" and "Give Peace A Chance" were virtual anthems for a generation, while "make love, not war," was another popular late-1960s slogan, thanks largely to a contraceptive pill that had more of a widespread social impact than the LSD tablets that enabled people to "turn on, tune in, and drop out."

However, perhaps the biggest threat to the long-established status quo was the onset of the women's liberation movement. No longer content just to stay at home and raise babies, many more females went out and got jobs. At the same time, while men grew their hair long, wore bright clothes, and some of them openly proclaimed their homosexuality, radical women burned their bras and put on pants.

# The Assassins' Bullets: Robert, Martin, and John

As I've already mentioned, the killing of President John F. Kennedy on November 22, 1963 had a devastating effect on America and was a profound shock to the rest of the world. A youthful man with promises of reform had been snatched away from the millions of people who he had instilled with hope, and after his slaying it was almost as if those same people had to grow up and face some harsh realities.

Still, JFK's death wasn't the end of the dream as far as those involved in the Civil Rights movement were concerned. While militant organizations such as the Black Panthers advocated the use of force to achieve their ends, those who sought a more peaceful solution to the racial strife and Vietnam conflict were still able to look towards luminaries such as Dr. Martin Luther King and, for a brief time, Senator Robert Kennedy.

Having served as Attorney General under his older brother's presidency, Robert Kennedy represented renewed hope to millions the world over when he entered the presidential race in 1968. Within just a few months, however, that hope would be extinguished.

On April 4, Dr. King was gunned down while standing on a motel balcony in Memphis, Tennessee. Riots immediately exploded in black neighborhoods across America, and one of the leading figures to make a well-heard plea for calmness was Bobby Kennedy. Then, on June 5, Kennedy himself was fatally shot while campaigning in Los Angeles.

The previous day, in London, John Lennon had recorded the vocal to "Revolution 1," in which he expressed doubt about whether he should be counted "out/in" when talking about destruction. It seemed about time that people made up their minds.

*The rocking president: John Fitzgerald Kennedy in the Oval Office at the White House.*
©Hulton Getty

# The Least You Need to Know

➤ During the early 1960s, there was widespread fear that the world might be coming to an end, especially with the Cold War in progress.

➤ Race riots, peace protests, and women's-lib rallies were evidence of the major social unrest taking place in America in the 1960s.

➤ The assassinations of President Kennedy, Robert Kennedy, and Dr. Martin Luther King had widespread ramifications in America and around the world.

# Part 5
# Upsetting the Apple Cart

*Oh well, you can't have a book full of good news I suppose, and I'm afraid that, in this part of your* Complete Idiot's Guide, *there really isn't that much to celebrate… unless you're a fiend for controversy! If that's the case, you'll love what's coming up!*

*What we're dealing with here are the episodes that garnered The Beatles less than lavish praise. (Okay, so they actually got heavily criticized. I was just trying to be diplomatic.) Then there are the setbacks they experienced, both personally and professionally, before we get to that point in the story that shall live in infamy for all time with Beatle People—the group's split and the acrimony that followed. Lastly, even though this book's main focus is on The Beatles, I'll also give you a brief run down on each of their solo careers.*

*So, are you sitting comfortably? Okay, here comes the gossip…*

# Chapter 22

# Bad Boys (You Can't Do That)

## In This Chapter

➤ Controversy over royal rewards!

➤ Uproar over tasteless album cover!

➤ Outrage over a blasphemous remark!

➤ Shock over Beatles drug scandals!

➤ Gasps over naked escapades!

Yeah, yeah, yeah, you've seen them all before; those sensational headlines for all of the wrong reasons. Well, The Beatles didn't get off scot-free. Sure, during the Beatlemania years it was pretty much all good news (*almost*), but then, when the tide turned, those waves of bad press came crashing down on more than one occasion.

Not that our Fab heroes didn't sometimes court controversy by way of their unconventional words and actions. They did as they pleased and faced the consequences. At other times, those consequences were both unjustified and unexpected. Still, every good story needs its fair share of ups and downs—it would be boring otherwise. So, let's get *down and dirty*!

# Rocking with the Royals

As I told you earlier, when Beatlemania was at its height during the mid-1960s, there was seemingly no one, including royalty, who considered themselves above being associated with the world's most famous musical quartet. However, when the Queen actually rewarded the Beatles' "services to British industry" with Membership of the Most Excellent Order of the British Empire, some people thought that things were going too far. They protested, and four years later they would feel that their stance had been justified. Here's why...

## Day-Trip to the Palace: Receiving the MBEs

It was on the night of June 11, 1965 that the world learned about The Beatles being awarded MBEs by Queen Elizabeth II. John, Paul, George, and Ringo had known about the honor for some time, but had to remain silent until the news embargo was lifted. This didn't prove to be difficult for them.

Reaction among the group members had been mixed. John especially didn't have much regard for the whole concept of royalty, and he would later admit to having had reservations about accepting the honor in the first place. Nevertheless, in 1965 Brian Epstein was still able to exert some measure of influence over the band, and so John was soon persuaded to toe the line and "do the right thing."

Others weren't so compliant. Certain military figures and heroes objected to The Beatles receiving MBEs, asserting that this cheapened the honor, and several of them even returned their medals to Buckingham Palace as a protest. One such character was Hector Dupuis, a member of the Canadian House of Commons, who complained that he'd been placed on the "same level as vulgar nincompoops!" Now, that wasn't a very dignified way to refer to The Beatles, and so George suggested, "If Dupuis doesn't want the medal, he had better give it to us. Then we can give it to our manager, Brian Epstein. MBE really stands for 'Mr. Brian Epstein.'"

**I Want to Tell You**

"I can't believe it. I thought you had to drive tanks and win wars."

—John Lennon, on being awarded an MBE by the Queen, June 1965

After the investiture took place in the Great Throne Room of Buckingham Palace on October 26, 1965, Paul asserted that the Queen had been "just like a mum to us." As for what to do with the awards, he said that this would be "what you normally do with medals. Put them in a box." John actually gave his to Aunt Mimi, who placed it proudly on top of her television set. It wouldn't remain there for very long, however.

## From Me to You: John Returns His MBE

Okay, so now it's late 1969. Brian Epstein's no longer around, The Beatles have all but officially disbanded, and John and Yoko have been attracting widespread attention and notoriety for many—if not all—of the wrong reasons (more of which a little later). For now, let's just say that, having done one outrageous thing after another, none of the Ono-Lennons' activities surprised anyone anymore.

For instance, on November 25, John returned his MBE to the Queen, his chauffeur, Les Anthony, having delivered it to Buckingham Palace along with a letter: "Your Majesty, I am returning this MBE in protest against Britain's involvement in the Nigeria-Biafra thing, against our support of America in Vietnam, and against 'Cold Turkey' slipping down the charts. With love, John Lennon of Bag."

A copy was also sent to Prime Minister Harold Wilson. Reaction was predictably hostile. The same people who had condemned The Beatles being awarded MBEs in the first place were now pointing out how right they had been all along. Such an honor should never have been bestowed on a bunch of irresponsible young upstarts. Still, they would say that, wouldn't they?

## Butchers Undercover

On March 25, 1966, The Beatles had their photos taken at a London studio by Robert Whittaker. For some they wore light turtleneck sweaters and dark jackets; these would serve as that year's official publicity shots of the group. For others, they donned white butcher's smocks and posed gleefully with decapitated dolls and chunks of raw, bloody meat. Their motivation for this still isn't clear, yet The Beatles attempted to get away with using one of these macabre photos for ads in the UK for the "Paperback Writer" single, and for the cover of their new album release in the United States, *Yesterday And Today*. For a short time, they did.

Album sleeves for *Yesterday And Today* were printed and, in early June, promotional copies of the record

**I Should Have Known Better**
Even though John took great satisfaction in returning his MBE to the Queen, British law still ensured that he didn't have things all his own way. Recipients of royal awards certainly have the right to send back their medals, yet they can't actually renounce the honor itself. To the end of his life, therefore, the "controversial Beatle" technically remained John Winston Ono Lennon MBE.

**With a Little Help**
If you have trouble deciphering the words to the backing vocals on the song "Paperback Writer," that's because John and George are singing the title of the French nursery rhyme, "Frere Jacques," over and over again. For that matter, listen to Paul and George's backing on "Girl" and you'll hear them sing "tit-tit-tit..." while lead vocalist John contributes a spot of heavy breathing!

were sent out to deejays and reviewers. At the same time, billboards and posters adorned with the "Butcher" photo started appearing all over America, before between 6,000 to 60,000 copies of the album (as you can tell, estimates vary wildly) were issued to the stores. Public reaction was swift and largely negative, and Capitol Records announced that it was immediately withdrawing and replacing the original album sleeve.

*Yesterday And Today*, slightly retitled as *"Yesterday"...and Today*, was subsequently released to the American public with a bland cover photo of The Beatles posing in and around an empty trunk. They looked bored and miserable, and who could blame them? In some cases, the record had been placed inside a brand new sleeve, but then there were also countless others that had the new photo simply pasted over the old one. Capitol, the company that had been raking in *millions* during the past couple of years thanks to The Beatles, wanted to save a few thousand dollars.

Of course, it didn't take the eagle-eyed fans long to spot the sleeves with the pasted-on covers, or to work out that, by carefully applying a little steam, said cover could be peeled off to reveal the "real" shot underneath. Capitol could have saved themselves a lot of time and effort...as well as several thousand more dollars!

# Bigger Than Jesus

Boy oh boy, what a year 1966 was for the Fab Four. Not only did they have to contend with the horrors of their final concert tours and the flak over the "Butcher" cover, but then there was the furor in the United States caused by an innocent remark that John had made regarding religion.

On March 4, John gave an in-depth interview to journalist and friend Maureen Cleave for publication in the London *Evening Standard*. In the interview, John described his domestic life and his interests in art and reading, while also taking the opportunity to express a few opinions on money, politics, and religion. Having read extensively about the latter subject, John noted the dwindling role of the church within modern society, as well as people's increasing preference for material rather than spiritual possessions.

"Christianity will go," he predicted. "It will vanish and shrink. I needn't argue about that; I'm right and I will be proved right. We're more popular than Jesus now; I don't know which will go first—rock 'n' roll or Christianity. Jesus was all right but his disciples were thick and ordinary. It's them twisting it that ruins it for me."

Now, this wasn't sacrilegious stuff. If anything, John was condemning the fact that more people were flocking to Beatles concerts than to their local churches. However, when the American teen magazine *Datebook* picked up on the quote on July 29, it totally distorted what John had said. A banner headline paraphrased him as having said that The Beatles were *greater* than Jesus, not bigger, and the result was that he was quickly denounced by a number of holier-than-thou conservatives in the American "Bible-belt" regions.

Led by Birmingham, Alabama's WAQY, 22 radio stations banned the broadcasting of Beatles music on the airwaves (some of them conveniently ignoring the fact that they hadn't ever played them in the first place). At the same time, for the benefit of the press and TV cameras, public "Beatles bonfires" were organized in order to burn records, books, and merchandise relating to the group. Meanwhile, the Ku Klux Klan boasted that they would somehow disrupt the band's upcoming American tour.

Brian Epstein could see things were getting out of hand, and so on August 6, 1966, he held a press conference in New York, to explain the true meaning of John's remarks. Still, the zealots weren't satisfied; they wanted to hear what that "devil-worshipping Beatle" now had to say for himself. On August 11 they found out, when John and his bandmates faced the press at Chicago's Astor Towers Hotel, prior to kicking off their tour. "You know, I'm not saying that we're better or greater, or comparing us with Jesus Christ as a person or God as a thing, or whatever it is. I just said what I said and it was wrong, or was taken wrong, and now it's all this…" Thus sayeth the beleaguered Beatle—as well as "sorry." Thereafter the tour proceeded pretty much as planned.

## Do You Want to Know a Secret?

During the controversy, John wasn't completely without the help of some "divine intervention." Radio station KLUE in Longview, Texas, organized a public "Beatles bonfire" for Friday, August 13, 1966, yet the very next morning the station was wiped off the air when a lightning bolt struck its transmission tower, knocking the news director unconscious.

# Day Trippers

Lysergic acid diethylamide is a powerful hallucinogenic drug that had a major influence on the rock generation of the mid to late 1960s. The music community actually started to experiment with it seriously back in 1965, when non-medical use of "acid" or LSD—as it is more commonly known—hadn't yet been outlawed.

Many acts of the day "dropped acid" as a means of artistic experimentation and "expanding the consciousness." These ranged from The Byrds to The Beach Boys, and The Jefferson Airplane to The Rolling Stones. The Beatles' first experience with LSD took place when someone covertly dropped it into John and George's drinks at a London dinner party. In the past all of the Fab Four had partaken in swallowing "uppers" such as Preludin and smoking pot, but LSD was initially too much of a step into the unknown for either Paul or Ringo. They resisted while Messrs. Lennon and Harrison began swallowing the little pills willingly and frequently. Soon it would have a marked influence on their music, most notably on John's songwriting.

## I Should Have Known Better

Don't believe rumors about the title of The Beatles' song "Lucy In The Sky With Diamonds" standing for "LSD." Its author, John Lennon, always denied any drug connection. Simply, his four-year-old son, Julian, returned from school with his colorful painting of a classmate named Lucy. When asked what it was, Julian answered, "Lucy in the sky with diamonds."

**With a Little Help**

Look for the scene in *A Hard Day's Night* that contains a drug reference. It occurs in the train sequence, shortly after The Beatles' road manager, Norm, enters their carriage for the first time and starts issuing directives. "Are you listening to me, Lennon?" he asks, while John sniffs the top of a Coca-Cola bottle. (Coke/cocaine—get it?)

Numbers such as "Tomorrow Never Knows," with its quasi-religious, drug-induced lyrics, and "A Day In The Life," in which the orchestral crescendos serve as a musical representation of the mind-swirling effects of "tripping out," were composed in direct response to John's experiences with LSD. So were numerous other tracks on both the *Revolver* and *Sgt. Pepper* albums. "She Said, She Said," for instance, evolved out of an acid trip that John had at a Hollywood party. Actor Peter Fonda had also taken the drug, and he kept approaching John and murmuring, "Hey, man, I know what it's like to be dead!"

Eventually, Paul and Ringo were tempted to experiment with LSD themselves—John later opined that the opening line to "Got To Get You Into My Life" on the *Revolver* album alluded to Paul's first trip. On May 20, 1967, just under a week before the release of *Sgt. Pepper*, the BBC placed a TV and radio ban on "A Day In The Life," explaining that it could encourage drug-taking. Several U.S. stations followed suit. Then, soon afterwards, Paul commented in an interview with *Life* magazine that LSD had "opened my eyes," before stating that "we only use one-tenth of our brains. Just think what we'd accomplish if we could tap that hidden part."

Britain's *Daily Mail* responded by calling Paul "an irresponsible idiot," and much the same was implied by a TV reporter when Paul admitted to his use of LSD during an interview intended for a news broadcast. Since The Beatles' young fans imitated their idols in oh-so-many ways—from their appearance to their actions and opinions—didn't the band have a moral duty to act responsibly and set the right example? Paul immediately pointed out that the interview needn't be broadcast. "It's you who've got responsibility not to spread this," he said. "If you'll shut up about it, I will!"

Of course, the interview *did* make it onto British TV screens, on June 19, 1967, and it was seen around the world shortly thereafter. Uproar and condemnation ensued. Then, on July 24, all four Beatles, as well as Brian Epstein, appeared to confirm their stance on drug-taking when they signed a petition that appeared in the London *Times* newspaper, calling for the legalization of marijuana.

As things turned out, all of this gave John, Paul, George, and Ringo added credibility in the eyes of many of their fans. For them they truly lived up to their unofficial title of "leaders of a generation." However, from the perspective of numerous other people in their teens and early-twenties, not to mention the majority of parents, things could never be the same again.

The four men at the center of the storm, meanwhile, were only too glad to dispense with a glossy image that they considered to be both outdated and, more to the point, out of sync with who they truly were.

# Busted! It's Pilcher of the Yard!

Sgt. Pilcher had been building up to this moment for quite some time. Donovan had been the first British pop star to be busted for drugs, and he'd been followed by a number of other acts, including Mick Jagger, Keith Richard, and Brian Jones of The Rolling Stones. At the top of the pecking order, however, were The Beatles, and so on October 18, 1968, Sgt. Pilcher made his move.

Just a few months after having separated from his wife, Cynthia, John was staying with his girlfriend Yoko Ono at 34 Montagu Square in Central London, in an apartment loaned to them by Ringo. John and Yoko were in bed when Pilcher arrived with his men and a posse of sniffer dogs, threatening to break the door down if they weren't permitted immediate entry to search the premises. John stalled while he contacted his lawyer, and as a result he and Yoko were immediately charged with obstructing the police in execution of a search warrant.

Having received a tip-off from *Daily Mirror* journalist Don Short that Scotland Yard might pay him a visit, John had tidied up the apartment. Yet, that still didn't prevent the police from "finding" some cannabis stored in a trunk. John would later insist that he'd been set up, but in the meantime he was concerned that, as Yoko wasn't a British citizen, she could face deportation. Therefore, when the case came to court on November 28, John himself pleaded guilty to possession of cannabis resin, while he and Yoko were found not guilty of the obstruction charge.

For his trouble John was fined £150 with 20 guineas' costs (about $410 dollars; guineas were old currency). Yet the overall cost would prove to be far greater when the drug charge would be utilized by the U.S. government to try to deport him during the 1970s. (I'll tell you more about that in Chapter 25.)

Okay, so that was one Beatle down, three to go. On March 12, 1969, the day that Paul married Linda Eastman, Sgt. Pilcher was at it again, although Paul wasn't the Fab he had in his sights. Instead it was George, who was sitting in one of the offices at Apple when he received a phone call from wife, Pattie, informing him that Pilcher and his men were swarming all over the Harrison home in Esher, Surrey. After talking things over with Neil Aspinall, George decided it was best to reveal where he kept his drugs. He therefore told Pattie to inform the cops that there was a small amount of marijuana in a box on top of the mantelpiece in the living room. By that time, however, Pilcher and Co. had managed to "find" a much larger stash of the drug inside a boot in George's closet!

On March 31, George and Pattie were each found guilty of cannabis possession, and both were fined £250 with 10 guineas' costs (about $625). Ringo never fell afoul of the law in the same way, yet Paul and Linda's turn would certainly come—several times—after The Beatles split.

*March 31, 1969: Happy Pattie and serious George leave Esher and Walton Magistrates Court after being convicted and fined for possession of cannabis.*
©Hulton Getty

### Do You Want to Know a Secret?

Sgt. Pilcher, who had a long and successful career with the drug squad, was nabbed himself not long after busting John and George. For what, you ask? Perjury—for which he received a four-year prison sentence.

# Bare Assets: Yoko and the Walrus

It was on November 29, 1968, the day after John had been convicted and fined for possessing cannabis, that his and Yoko's album, *Two Virgins*, hit the stores. And what an album it was. First, however, let me recount how the couple's relationship took off.

As you may recall, the two first set eyes on one another in November 1966, when John attended a preview of Yoko's avant-garde art exhibition, *Unfinished Paintings and Objects*, at London's Indica Gallery. John, who had thought he was heading to an "artsy-fartsy orgy," instead discovered an offbeat concept of art that had him mesmerized.

Seven years older than John, Yoko Ono was in the middle of her second marriage and had a daughter named Kyoko when the two of them met. The daughter of the president of the Bank of Tokyo in New York, Yoko had rejected her family's wealthy lifestyle in favor of becoming an avant-garde artist. During the mid 1960s, she had moved to London and gained notoriety for covering one of the lion statues in Trafalgar Square in huge white sheets. Then there was her film that focused on 365 naked bottoms.

*6 Mason's Yard in London's West End, former site of the Indica Gallery where John and Yoko first met on November 9, 1966.*
©Richard Buskin

Still, for all of the apparent excitement, John wouldn't hook up with Yoko until 18 months after they first met. During that time, Yoko kept pursuing him, turning up at places where John and Cyn visited, and inching her way into his thoughts by mailing him cryptically "humorous" messages such as "Breathe," "Dance," or "Watch all the lights until dawn." All of this appealed to John's sense of the absurd, and eventually her persistence paid off. When Cynthia went with friends on a vacation to Greece in May of 1968, John invited Yoko over to his Weybridge home.

There they retired to his small studio, where the Beatle played the progressive artist some experimental tapes that he'd recorded, consisting of various sound effects and electronic noises. Yoko was impressed. Why not make some recordings themselves? This they did, squawking, screeching, and "passing wind" in both directions to the occasional accompaniment of a piano and slowed-down tape effects. To quote John: "It was midnight when we started *Two Virgins*, it was dawn when we finished, and then we made love at dawn. It was very beautiful."

For John and Yoko, certainly, but not for Cynthia, who returned from Greece to find the "virgins" having virtually set up home together in *her* house. She and Julian promptly moved out, and the Lennons' divorce became final on November 8, a couple of weeks before Yoko suffered a miscarriage.

If Cynthia tried to come to terms with what had happened, the press wasn't yet prepared to. There was outrage when John and Yoko started appearing together, planting acorns

**I Want to
Tell You**

"'What are they
doing? This
Japanese witch
has made him crazy and he's
gone bananas!' But all she did
was take the bananas part of
me out of the closet more,
that had been inhibited by
the other part. It was a
complete relief to meet
somebody else who was as far
out as I was."

—John Lennon, December 8,
1980, in an RKO Radio
interview

"for peace," attending the first night of the National
Theatre's staging of part of John's book, *In His Own Write*, or
hosting their first joint art exhibition, *You Are Here*. While
newspapers and magazines made fun of them (not least by
way of crude racial slurs aimed at Yoko), people who saw
them would shout out "Chink!" (ingenious, since she wasn't
Chinese) and "Where's your wife?"

Still, the appearances that John and Yoko made in public
were nothing compared to the ones that they made on the
album sleeve of *Unfinished Music No.1: Two Virgins* (to give
the record its full title). There they stood, on the front cover,
facing a remote-controlled camera in all of their naked glory,
while on the back they could be seen equally bare from
behind. Now, this would be completely outrageous even by
today's standards, so just try to imagine the reaction in
1968! Let's just say that, in late-November, old ladies were
hardly passing out from the effects of the summer heat.

And what did the other Beatles think of all this? On the
cover of *Two Virgins*, underneath the full-frontal nude shot
of John and Yoko, Paul McCartney was quoted as saying: "When two great saints meet it
is a humbling experience." In private, however, there wasn't such a rich endorsement,
George reportedly complaining to John, "You realize that, when you show *your* cock, it's
like all of us showing our cocks!"

EMI pressed *Two Virgins* but refused to distribute it, with company Chairman Sir Joseph
Lockwood advising John and Yoko that a naked Paul would have made a prettier sight
on the cover! In the UK, Track Records therefore took care of distribution, enclosing the
album in a plain brown wrapper, while a label named Tetragrammaton did the same in
the U.S. Nevertheless, 30,000 copies never made it out of a Newark warehouse, having
been confiscated by police in New Jersey.

And all for what? Simply because John and Yoko wanted to "make a statement," or,
more like it, test the boundaries of public tolerance. If the reaction was anything to go
by, they'd certainly managed to do that, yet this was by no means the end of their
buffoonery.

## The Least You Need to Know

➤ After reluctantly accepting his MBE, John could hardly wait to return it.

➤ By recalling the *Yesterday And Today* sleeve and pasting a new photo over it, Capitol
Records inadvertently turned the "Butcher cover" into a collectible.

➤ John's statements about Jesus Christ were taken out of context and misinterpreted,
getting him into a lot of hot water.

➤ The Beatles' use of drugs made for some remarkable music, but landed them in trouble with the public and the police, and even led to the banning of some Beatles songs.

➤ John and Yoko's *Two Virgins* album, which featured nude photos of the couple on the front and back covers, caused a public uproar.

# Chapter 23

# THE BEATLES

# Something to Get Hung About: Cracking Up

## In This Chapter

➤ The tragic demise of The Beatles' manager

➤ The wild rumors over Paul's supposed death

➤ The troubled TV film that The Beatles wrote, produced, directed, and starred in

➤ The band's endorsement and then denouncement of the Maharishi Mahesh Yogi

➤ The discord that finally split the group

Artistically, The Beatles were strong right until the end, producing what many believe are some of their finest recordings during the latter part of their career. In numerous other ways, however, the years 1967 to 1969 represented troubled times for the band, both personally and professionally.

The seeds of their downfall were sown with the tragic early death of Brian Epstein, their adoring manager who had done so much to establish The Beatles as the world's foremost supergroup. Things started to go awry from that point on; once they slipped off the tracks, with no one to take hold of the wheel they really couldn't find their way back home.

# A Death in the Family: Brian Epstein

At the age of 32, Brian Epstein was, along with Elvis Presley's manager Colonel Tom Parker, the world's most successful pop impresario. In 1967 he was also the most envied, with a client roster that included The Beatles; a theater on Central London's Shaftesbury Avenue; a Georgian house in the capital's exclusive Belgravia neighborhood; and a spacious country home at Kingsley Hill in Sussex. Yet, he still wasn't a happy man.

Devoid of non-stop work relating to The Beatles, Brian's days now seemed empty, while his nights were often consumed with trips around the London casinos, drinking brandy, and suffering muggings and extortion threats as a result of his frequently dangerous sexual encounters. Sleeping pills were necessary to help him rest from the early morning until late afternoon, and Brian also used them in a second suicide attempt at the beginning of 1967. He went to clinics several times to "dry out," but the thought that The Beatles might look to someone else when their management contract expired in October kept coming back to haunt him.

In mid-August, following the death of Harry Epstein at age 63 from a heart attack, Brian's mother Queenie came to stay with him for 10 days at his Belgravia home. During that visit Brian got his act together and conformed to a healthy routine.

**Say the Word**
Transcendental Meditation is an abstract technique of meditation and relaxation based on the Hindu practice of yoga, in which the person practicing it is reunited with the universal spirit. It is also referred to as TM.

Queenie returned to Liverpool on Thursday, August 24, and that night The Beatles, together with Pattie, Maureen, Jane Asher, and Paul's brother Mike, attended a lecture on *Transcendental Meditation* that was being given by the Maharishi Mahesh Yogi at the Hilton Hotel on London's Park Lane. Enticed by a philosophy that promised them "inner peace" and "spiritual regeneration," The Beatles immediately agreed to follow the Maharishi to Bangor, North Wales, the next day, where he would be conducting a weekend seminar on TM. Brian was invited to go along, but, this being the start of a holiday weekend in Britain, he'd already made plans to entertain some people at Kingsley Hill in Sussex. He said that he might join them in Wales later on.

At Kingsley Hill, however, things didn't turn out as planned for Brian. Several of the guests he'd invited couldn't make it, so he ended up spending Friday night eating dinner with just a couple of old business friends, Peter Brown and Geoffrey Ellis.

At around 10:00, Brian announced that he was driving to London and would return the next morning, but he didn't actually phone Peter Brown until around 5:00 Saturday afternoon. He'd been sleeping all day at his Chapel Street home and still felt drowsy. He therefore agreed to travel back to Sussex by train and would call just before he left. That call, however, never came. By late morning Sunday, August 27, with Brian still not having emerged from his bedroom, the butler and his wife became worried. Brian's assistant,

Joanne Newfield, was alerted, as was a doctor, and both rushed to the house. At around 2:00, the butler and the doctor broke the bedroom door down and discovered Brian lying on his side in bed. He was dead.

*The Yogi Bearers: Paul, Jane Asher, Pattie Harrison, Mike McCartney, Ringo, Maureen Starkey, George, and John (seated) pay full attention to the Maharishi at the London Hilton.*
©Hulton Getty

In Bangor, Paul McCartney answered the telephone to hear the shocking news, and, after fielding news reporters' questions, he and his colleagues immediately returned to London. None of them attended Brian's funeral in Liverpool on August 29—that was strictly a family affair—yet they did later go to a memorial service at the New London Synagogue. This was around the corner from the recording studios in Abbey Road where, thanks to Brian, The Beatles had auditioned for EMI just over five years earlier.

An inquest into Brian's death concluded that he had died accidentally due to the cumulative effects of the sedative Carbitrol and alcohol. There have since been countless rumors about his death being a suicide, and Beatles' biographer Philip Norman even implied that Brian may have been the victim of a "hit," set up by enemies in the business world. Whatever the truth, John Lennon understood full well the state they were

> **I Want to Tell You**
>
> "[I had] the feeling that anybody has when somebody close to them dies. There is a sort of little hysterical, sort of 'Hee, hee, I'm glad it's not me,'...and the other feeling is 'What? What the f—k?' You know, 'What can I do?'"
>
> —John Lennon, on his reaction to Brian Epstein's death, *Rolling Stone* magazine, 1970.

in without a manager. "I knew that we were in trouble then," he told *Rolling Stone*'s Jann Wenner in 1970. "I didn't really have any misconceptions about our ability to do anything other than play music, and I was scared. I thought, 'We've f—kin' had it.'"

# Who Buried Paul?

It's one thing to mourn the death of someone near, dear, or just admired and beloved. However, it's always advisable to ensure that the person is actually deceased before breaking out the Kleenex and delivering the eulogy!

Take James Paul McCartney. In October 1969, the release of *Abbey Road* and Paul's foray out of the public spotlight for several weeks fueled an idiotic rumor that he'd been killed and replaced by a look-alike. This was started by one Russ Gibbs, program coordinator for radio station WKNR-FM in Detroit, who claimed to have received a phone call informing him of Paul's death, while stating that there were vital "clues" on the *Abbey Road* album cover to prove it:

➤ On the front, as they walk along a zebra-crossing, George is dressed as a "gravedigger"; Ringo like an "undertaker"; and John like a "minister." Paul is garbed in a "burial suit," walking out of step with the other Beatles, and barefoot—he is, after all, a corpse!

➤ On the left-hand side of the road, a Volkswagen Beetle bears the license plate "LMW 281F," relating to the "fact" that Paul would have been "28 IF" he had still been alive. (In reality, he would have been 27, but never mind!)

➤ On the back cover, a crack in the word "Beatles" signifies a fracture in the band itself.

Politically, at least, this last point was correct, but can you honestly imagine The Beatles deciding to reveal their "big secret" by way of such ridiculous hints?

Clearly, some people did, especially in America, where the rumor spread like wildfire and "investigators" were soon finding a whole host of other "clues" that had supposedly been dropped during the previous three years:

➤ According to their "research," the real Paul had been replaced by an actor named either William Campbell or Billy Shears, who had undergone plastic surgery in order to effect a perfect likeness. Thus the introduction of Billy Shears at the end of the opening track on *Sgt. Pepper*.

➤ The cause of his death (blowing his mind out in a car) is revealed in a line from the song "A Day In The Life." (In reality, it refers to the fatal road accident of Guinness heir, Tara Browne, in December 1966.)

➤ At the end of "Strawberry Fields Forever," John's faint "cranberry sauce" quip was construed as "I buried Paul."

➤ On the *White Album* song, "Glass Onion," the line "the walrus was Paul" again symbolizes death, just as the character of the Walrus does in the Lewis Carrol story, *The Walrus and the Carpenter*.

➤ On the run-out groove to the vinyl *Sgt. Pepper* album, there's also a quick burst of randomly spoken gibberish. When some fans spun the record backwards, they thought they could hear the message, "Turn me on, dead man."

➤ If you held the British *Magical Mystery Tour* EP cover up to a mirror, you could see a telephone number which, when dialed, would connect you to Paul in the Hereafter! As it turned out, the number belonged to a journalist from Britain's *Guardian* newspaper, who was none too pleased when a glut of early morning calls started coming his way from across the Atlantic!

Then there are "clues" on the *Sgt. Pepper* album cover itself:

➤ Four dark-suited wax dummies of The Beatles look mournfully at a "grave" bearing a flower wreath shaped like a bass guitar (and a left-handed one at that!).

➤ Above the head of the real Paul (or is it Billy Shears?) a raised hand "signifies death."

➤ On the back cover, a group photo features only "Billy" facing away from the camera, as his "plastic surgery" has not yet been perfected(!)

➤ Meanwhile, the gatefold sleeve's central picture shows "Billy" sporting an arm-patch bearing the letters "OPD," supposedly standing for "Officially Pronounced Dead." (It was, in fact, the badge of the Ontario Police Department.)

As for the main man himself? When tracked down by representatives of *Life* magazine to his farm on the Mull of Kintyre in northwest Scotland, the real Paul McCartney asserted, "The rumors of my death have been greatly exaggerated. However, if I was dead I'm sure I'd be the last to know."

Perhaps, but there again, if it was Billy Shears who was responsible for conceiving The Beatles' first TV movie…

# Tragical Mystery Tour

On September 1, 1967, just five days after Brian Epstein's death, The Beatles all met at Paul's house in St. John's Wood to discuss their future. Among their immediate decisions was to press ahead with the *Magical Mystery Tour* TV film, which had been formulated several months earlier but then put on hold during the summer.

Paul came up with the basic concept on a flight from Los Angeles to London on April 11. It was inspired by *The Electric Kool-Aid Acid Test*, writer Tom Wolfe's account of an LSD-drenched bus journey that a hippie troupe called Ken Kesey's Merry Pranksters had made through California in 1965. Macca devised a plan for The Beatles to hire their own bus and set off on a mystery tour around the English countryside, while a film crew captured whatever magic occurred along the way. After all, there was bound to be plenty of magic, wasn't there?

Paul drew a circle on some paper and divided it into segments containing some of the main "plot devices"; these would involve some "midgets," a "fat lady," a "lunch" scene, and so on. "He came and showed me what his idea was," John later recalled. "He said, 'Well, here's the segment, you write a little piece for that.' And I thought, 'F—kin' Ada, I've never made a film! What's he mean, write a script?'"

With the benefit of 20/20 hindsight, it's easy to see where things went wrong. Having succeeded at practically everything they'd attempted—and basking in the glory of their *Sgt. Pepper* album and latest smash-hit single, "All You Need Is Love"—The Beatles were seemingly infallible. Consequently, they didn't see the need to act in a slick movie that was devised for them by a bunch of professionals. No, they would approach *Magical Mystery Tour* as they now did everything else, flying by the seat of their pants. To this end they would write, produce, direct, and supervise the editing of the movie, in addition to starring in it, of course, and composing all of the songs.

John, Paul, George, and Ringo apparently overlooked several key things, however. To start with, while they had turned in charming performances in *Help!* and, especially, *A Hard Day's Night*, they'd had a lot to thank Walter Shenson for in terms of the production values, not to mention Dick Lester for his skills overseeing the direction, camerawork, and editing. None of the Fabs were exactly accomplished actors, yet their experience in this field was gargantuan compared to what they knew about scriptwriting, directing, and editing.

**With a Little Help**
Can you spot the cameo appearances in *Magical Mystery Tour*? Look for Mal Evans, Neil Aspinall, Mike McCartney (then known as Mike McGear), Spencer Davis (of The Spencer Davis Group), and The Bonzo Dog Doo-Dah Band. This last act perform "Death Cab For Cutie" behind stripper Jan Carson, in an amusing scene shot at The Raymond Revuebar in London's Soho.

Then there was the job of production. In The Beatles' case this amounted to hiring a small film crew, a tour bus, and a cast of actors, relatives, and friends, while assigning one week to shooting around Devon and Cornwall in southwest England; another for interior scenes at Shepperton Studios; and a third week for the editing. After that they could all go off to India and spend some time with the Maharishi. It couldn't be simpler!

Well, that at least was the theory. On Monday, September 11, The Beatles set the enterprise in motion, and the result was an administrative (as well as artistic) nightmare.

The multi-colored *Magical Mystery Tour* bus was still being hastily decorated when most of its passengers gathered at the starting point in Central London. It eventually arrived two hours late. Hotel bookings were also only made at the last minute, and so Neil Aspinall was landed with the unenviable task of making accommodations for 43 people who were often choosy about who they wanted to share a room with. On the first full day of filming, the bus driver decided to take an unconventional route to avoid traffic and managed to get the large vehicle wedged on a narrow bridge, blocking cars in both directions. While the cameras rolled, tempers flared—especially John's—and the driver had to reverse the bus for half a mile before the situation was resolved. Little magic was to be found anywhere on the trip.

While Paul conceded in 1967 that *Magical Mystery Tour* perhaps wasn't ideal Christmas entertainment, he has recently revised that opinion by asserting, "it's quite a little classic for its time." Yet, even though it's true that the film—with its sporadic moments of inspirational, *Monty Python*-esque humor—comes off somewhat better today than it did 30 years ago, it still stands as little more than what it always was: a confused, self-satisfying home movie with several moments of Beatles' magic.

> **I Want to Tell You**
>
> "We went out to make a film and nobody had the vaguest idea of what it was all about. What we should have been filming, if anything, was all the confusion, because that was the *real* mystery tour."
>
> —Beatles assistant, Neil Aspinall

# In the Court of Sexy Sadie

Although much delayed, The Beatles' Indian summer came early in 1968, John, Cynthia, George, and Pattie all arriving there on February 16th, with Paul, Jane, Ringo, and Maureen following four days later.

The twin objectives were peace and meditation, and Rishikesh was the destination where, high amidst the Himalayas, the Maharishi Mahesh Yogi had his private compound. This boasted, among its many amenities, a number of fully furnished guest bungalows, offering modern comforts to The Beatles and their companions. Unsure about a vegetarian curry diet, Ringo and Maureen had brought a suitcase full of canned Heinz baked beans with them from London. For the Starkeys, however, these didn't do the trick, and neither did the daily regime of chanting *mantras*, meditating, and mass prayer. On March 1, just 12 days after arriving, the couple departed Rishikesh, with Ringo likening the compound to Butlin's, the holiday camp where he had played summer seasons with Rory Storm and the Hurricanes back in the early 1960s. The other Beatles, meanwhile, decided to stick it out, at one point engaging in a private competition to see who could meditate the longest(!).

Still, no one could quite compete with Mia Farrow's sister, who, according to John, "seemed to go slightly balmy, meditating too long, and couldn't come out of the little hut that we were livin' in…" The result was John's composition, "Dear Prudence," which was one of many songs that The Beatles wrote for *The White Album* while they were in India.

Meanwhile, not content with just a search for internal peace, John and Paul were also looking to the Maharishi for an answer to life, the universe, and

>
>
> **Say the Word**
> A **mantra** is a Hindu or Buddhist devotional incantation. In 1969, the "Hare Krishna Mantra," performed by the Radha Krishna Temple and produced by George Harrison, was a hit in the pop charts.

everything. Nothing was forthcoming in that regard, even when John managed to charm his way onto the Yogi's helicopter and survey the ashram from the air.

On March 26, Paul and Jane decided that they'd had enough and returned to England. John and George stayed on, until a nasty rumor started to form around their teacher. The word around the compound was that the Holy Man had attempted to grab hold of Mia Farrow and enlighten more than just her spirit. Now, whether or not that was true, the damage had been done.

When even George started to have doubts about the Yogi's credibility, John became convinced. He announced to Cynthia that they should pack their bags and get ready to leave. Then he led the way into the principal bungalow and informed the Maharishi about this. The pint-sized guru, no longer giggling, asked John why they wanted to depart so suddenly. "Well, if you're so cosmic, you'll know why," came the Lennonish response. Reportedly, the Maharishi couldn't figure that one out. From John and George's viewpoint, however, the game was now up and they were on their way, although not before John quickly penned "Sexy Sadie," a barely disguised attack on the Yogi.

On April 12, 1968, John, Cynthia, George, and Pattie arrived back in London. On May 14, John then publicly denounced "Sadie" on NBC-TV's *The Tonight Show*. George would continue to pursue his interest in Indian culture and the Hindu faith, but, as far as The Beatles and the Maharishi Mahesh Yogi were concerned, all bets were off.

# White Mischief and Trouble Getting Back

It's pretty clear that The Beatles started to lose their sense of direction after Brian Epstein's death, yet it was during recording sessions for the *White Album* that all-out disharmony between the group members first reared its ugly head.

The failure of the *Magical Mystery Tour* movie had been a definite career low-point; it was a sign to the public that the Fab Four couldn't actually walk on water, and an undermining of The Beatles' normally rock-solid confidence in relying on each other's artistic judgment. Their convictions were further called into question when the Maharishi, who they'd originally looked upon as some sort of personal messiah, turned out to be—in their eyes, at least—little more than a charlatan. Bitterness began to set in, and then, just at the moment when band unity was of paramount importance, a divisive influence entered onto the scene and, more importantly, into the studio.

Up until now, The Beatles' work inside Abbey Road had largely been the domain of John, Paul, George, and Ringo, together with George Martin and the technical staff. Wives and girlfriends might very occasionally visit during a session, but nothing more. From May 31, 1968 onwards, however, Yoko Ono attended virtually every Beatles recording session that John participated in, sitting by his side, whispering secretively in his ear, openly making suggestions and criticisms with regard to the music, performing herself when she or John so desired, and generally making her presence known.

Paul, George, and Ringo were ill at ease, to say the least. They resented the fact that the couple were totally inseparable—even when they went to the bathroom—and that they could no longer glean an opinion from John without his new partner adding her 10 cents' worth.

Yoko, meanwhile, was encouraging John to explore his most wayward and avant-garde artistic ideas, and when it became clear that the other Beatles were not receptive to them or to Yoko's participation in group affairs, this meant the beginning of the end. You see, although John had started the band and, in the early days, acted as its leader, his colleagues had since invested far too much of their own time and talents to be coerced into activities that didn't interest them.

> **With a Little Help**
> Yoko's influence on John's work can be heard throughout The Beatles' *White Album*. Aside from the sound-collage "Revolution 9," she sings sporadically on "The Continuing Story Of Bungalow Bill," has her name translated into English as "ocean-child" in "Julia," and is referred to in "Everybody's Got Something To Hide Except For Me And My Monkey" (the British press having likened her to a chimpanzee).

Realizing this, John began to dedicate more of his energy to pursuits with Yoko, and this kind of self-absorption soon proved to be catching.

Many but not all of the basic rhythm tracks for the 30 numbers on the *White Album* involved the participation of the four group members. However, the overdubbing of extra instrumental and vocal parts would usually be carried out by the composer of each song. Therefore, instead of pooling their talents in the creative process, The Beatles—especially John and Paul—were now only taking an interest in their own work and simply utilizing the other Beatles as a backing band. In many cases this attitude caused resentment, leading to friction within the once-cohesive band unit, frayed tempers, and, ultimately, high tension and heated arguments.

Feeling totally unappreciated for his own steadfast contributions, the normally easygoing Ringo actually quit The Beatles on August 22. News of this was kept from the press and public while John, Paul, and George continued with the troubled *White Album* sessions. After a couple of weeks Ringo was cajoled into returning and by mid-October the recordings were finally completed, yet the damage had been done. The double-set *The Beatles* was yet another magnificent body of work, complemented by the concurrent single "Hey Jude," but the group itself was in trouble and all four men knew it.

Paul remained the only one who appeared to have the will to try to keep things moving along. Aside from Yoko's presence and Brian's absence, Paul noted that the two main differences from the good old days were that the band was no longer performing live, and that it was also taking an eternity to record its songs. Therefore, he reasoned, it might pay for he and his fellow Fabs to dispense with the over-complicated approach to recording, spending weeks and months adding extra parts, and instead just rehearse their numbers

**I Want to Tell You**

"If the new Beatles soundtrack album *Let It Be* is to be their last then it will stand as a cheapskate epitaph, a cardboard tombstone, a sad and tatty end to a musical fusion which wiped clean and drew again the face of pop music."

—Alan Smith, *New Musical Express*, 1970

as a unit and then record them in a few takes without overdubs. Furthermore, while touring was out, they should at least return to giving live performances.

The result, as I already described to you in Chapter 18, was the *Get Back* project, which, when eventually unveiled to the public in the form of a film, an album, and even a book, was renamed *Let It Be*. (A text-and-photo book originally accompanied the album in an over-priced boxed set.) However, the tensions that had characterized the *White Album* sessions immediately resurfaced and, this time around, their disruptive influence was clearly evident in the end products. As captured on film, The Beatles were no longer able to click consistently as a band.

With George Martin wiping his hands of the project, producer/engineer Glyn Johns was given the unenviable task of compiling the *Get Back* album. He made two attempts. By sticking to the directive of not adding any extra instrumentation or sound effects to the recordings, he produced results that not even The Beatles at their most carefree would dare release. They therefore went back into the studio with George Martin at the helm, got their collective act together, and recorded one final, polished (and absolutely classic) album, *Abbey Road*.

Still, with too much money tied up in *Get Back* to shelve it, legendary producer Phil Spector was called in to try to "tidy up" the recordings. He did so by editing the material and, most notably on "The Long And Winding Road," adding an orchestra and female choir. This last act was too much for Paul McCartney to bear, and he attempted to have the strings and voices removed just prior to the (now-retitled) *Let It Be* album's release. He was too late, however, and subsequently went public in expressing his annoyance at Spector's intrusive over-production of his material.

Nevertheless, if only The Beatles had applied themselves with more discipline in the first place, none of this would have come to pass.

## The Least You Need to Know

➤ Brian Epstein's death on August 27, 1967 set The Beatles toward the skids.

➤ Despite some outlandish rumors and falsely identified "clues," Paul McCartney is *not* dead!

➤ The *Magical Mystery Tour* TV movie was the band's first artistic failure.

➤ The Beatles' faith in the Maharishi Mahesh Yogi was short-lived.

➤ Yoko's unnerving presence caused tension in the recording studio and a rift in the band itself.

# Coming Down Fast: The Curtain Falls

Well, this is it—the chapter in which The Beatles dissolve amidst bitter arguments and legal action. Considering how much John, Paul, George, and Ringo had achieved together during the previous seven years, not to mention their undeniable love and admiration for one another, the manner in which they ended their collaboration was unfortunate to say the least. Yet, given the strength of their personalities as well as their diverging interests, in many ways this was inevitable. The Beatles' breakup was like a bad divorce, with all of the accompanying pain and bitterness.

Still, before I bring you to that point, I'll set the scene by describing the Fabs' late-'60s pursuits both inside and outside of the band, including their joint business activities that served as a prelude to disaster.

# Life with the Ono-Lennons

In Chapter 22 I told you about John and Yoko's naked portraits of themselves as *Two Virgins*, their drug-related run-in with the law, and their general alienation of many of those people who had once held "the cynical Beatle" in high esteem. Well, in 1969 the couple truly gave free rein to their expression, involving themselves in all forms of outlandish activities that attracted ridicule on a global scale.

Towards the end of the January *Get Back* sessions, Yoko's divorce from her second husband, Anthony Cox, became final, paving the way for she and John to marry. They did so on the British-governed isle of Gibraltar on March 20, before flying on to Paris and then Amsterdam where, on March 25, they commenced a seven-day "bed-in" for peace in Room 902 of the Hilton Hotel. Reasoning quite rightly that whatever they did on their honeymoon would make the news, John and Yoko decided to stage what amounted to a commercial promoting peace and love. The fact that they did so from their honeymoon bed ensured that they garnered as much attention as possible.

Sitting in or on top of their large double bed, John and Yoko were surrounded by reporters, friends, flowers, gifts, and a number of hand-drawn posters proclaiming "Peace," "Bed Peace," "Hair Peace" (a typical piece of Lennon word-play), "Remember Love," and "Bagism." In this way the world's most famous newlyweds certainly managed to capture the world's attention. Yet, instead of having their well-intentioned peace campaign taken seriously, their main achievement was to turn themselves into a laughing-stock.

After adopting the middle name of Ono in a formal ceremony on the roof of The Beatles' Apple building in April 1969, John attempted to stage a second "bed-in" with Yoko in America in May. Due to his drug bust the previous year, however, the U.S. authorities refused to grant him a visa, and so the couple instead took their road show to Room 1742 of the Queen Elizabeth Hotel in Montreal. There, on June 1, they—together with various friends and acquaintances—recorded "Give Peace A Chance," the first single to be released by The Plastic Ono Band, the name given to a number of different musicians who would hereafter back John and Yoko on record and in concert.

Later that year, The Plastic Ono Band, featuring John on guitar and vocals, Eric Clapton on lead guitar, Klaus Voormann on bass, and Andy White on drums, would record the single "Cold Turkey," a chilling account of John and Yoko's struggles with heroin withdrawal. This addiction also played a part in John's emotional withdrawal from The Beatles, yet it was by no means his only problem during an action-packed year. At the start of July, he and Yoko were involved in a car crash in Scotland, while vacationing with their respective children Julian and Kyoko. In October, Yoko then suffered a second miscarriage, and in November there was John's infamous returning of his MBE.

*John looks wistful while Yoko eyes up a bouquet of flowers during their "bed-in" for peace at the Amsterdam Hilton in March 1969.*
©Hulton Getty

### Do You Want to Know a Secret?

How about *this* for a piece of choice casting? On December 3, 1969, young British songwriters Tim Rice and Andrew Lloyd Webber approached John Lennon to play the lead role in their new musical, *Jesus Christ Superstar*. They planned to stage this in London's St. Paul's Cathedral, and at first John appeared to be perfectly suited to portray the man from Galilee. After all, not only was he sporting long hair, a bushy beard and mustache, but the famous Beatle was also loaded with charisma. The very next day, however, the composers changed their minds, stating that an unknown actor would be more desirable. What a pity. Imagine Jesus singing with that raunchy Lennon voice!

In the middle of all this activity, John somehow still found time to work on The Beatles' *Abbey Road* album as well as he and his wife's avant-garde recordings. In September the two of them, together with The Plastic Ono Band, made a live appearance at a rock and roll festival in Toronto, while in December "The Plastic Ono Supergroup" performed at a *Peace for Christmas* concert in London. As this lineup also included George Harrison, it was the first time that two Beatles had appeared together on a concert stage since August 1966. It wouldn't be the last time, either, but the chances of all four coming together—or even just Paul with either John or George—would prove to be a forlorn hope.

## Paul: Carrying That Weight

If 1969 was a highly adventurous year for John and Yoko, in a professional sense it was a pretty tough one for Paul, since he had to deal with the hard fact that The Beatles were basically finished. Still, it wasn't as if he didn't give things his best shot.

Following the traumatic *Get Back* sessions, which had seen all of his best-laid plans for the band come unstuck, Paul continued to compose, produce, and play on records by a number of other artists. He also dashed the hopes of girls the world over by marrying Linda Louise Eastman in London on March 12, but soon had his domestic bliss disrupted by legal disputes with his fellow Beatles. (Be patient—I'll tell you about this in a few pages.)

Amidst all this unrest, the group recorded *Abbey Road,* an album that Paul largely instigated as another means to get The Beatles to do what they did best: make music. Yet, while all four band members did themselves magnificent credit on the record, and while Lennon and McCartney contributed roughly the same number of songs, it was undeniably Paul who carried the album's most stunning sequence on side two, where tracks merge into one another to produce one of The Beatles' finest recorded achievements. It was also he, incidentally, who came up with the concept for the album's famous cover photo.

The production polish of *Abbey Road* stands in stark contrast to the patchy quality of the *Let It Be* album. However, even though this is partly due to the fact that John, Paul, George, and Ringo managed to collaborate in a more congenial way during the July/August 1969 *Abbey Road* sessions, there were still flare-ups.

Nevertheless, during the fall of 1969 Paul still didn't give up, sticking to his belief that, despite all of their differences, The Beatles might get back on track if they resumed live performances. He continued to come up with suggestions, until a final rebuff (which, I assure you, I'll tell you about before this chapter is out) convinced him that The Beatles were no more. By Christmas 1969, Paul was working on his own solo album, a project that proved to be the straw that broke the camel's back.

# George: Not a Beatle Any More

As you might recall, immediately after the Fab Four performed their last-ever paid concert George Harrison commented that he was "not a Beatle any more." Well, throughout 1969 he stated much the same on several occasions until, wouldn't you know it, he was absolutely right.

I've already told you how George quit the band during the *Get Back* sessions, and, although he returned soon afterwards, things didn't get much better from that point on. Artistically he continued to feel that Paul adopted a condescending attitude towards him, and that John really wasn't interested in recording any "Harrisongs." Certainly, there are two sides to every story—in The Beatles' case there were often four—but there does appear to have been some justification for George feeling short-changed. John was noticeably absent from many of the latter sessions involving the youngest Beatle's compositions.

In early December 1969, George joined the short British and Danish tours of American "white soul" artists, Delaney & Bonnie, playing in the backing band, Friends, alongside Eric Clapton. The "quiet Beatle" enjoyed being able to perform two shows a night just as in the old days, save for the fact that he could do so virtually unnoticed in his long hair and mustache, and that there was no audience screaming to obliterate the music.

Still, he did get together with Paul and Ringo on January 3 and 4, 1970, to record "I Me Mine" and overdub a new guitar solo, harmony vocals, drums, and percussion onto "Let It Be." John was away in Denmark, and so at one point during the January 3 session, referring to a then-popular British band called Dave Dee, Dozy, Beaky, Mick And Tich, George made

**I Should Have Known Better**

Don't assume that all of The Beatles participated on many of the group's later recordings. John, especially during 1969 and early 1970, was often absent from sessions, and for some reason this was particularly the case with regard to George's songs. "Savoy Truffle," "Long Long Long," "Here Comes The Sun," and "I Me Mine," were all recorded without any contribution from John whatsoever.

an announcement over his microphone: "You all will have read that Dave Dee is no longer with us, but Micky and Tich and I would just like to carry on the good work that's always gone down in number two." (You can hear this immediately prior to "I Me Mine" on *The Beatles Anthology 3*.)

The irony of this show of unity in the face of John's withdrawal from the group is that hereafter it would be *Paul* who George steadfastly refused to work with. Go figure!

# Ringo: Celluloid Satisfaction

Shortly after the band stopped touring, and encouraged by the reviews that he had received for his acting in *A Hard Day's Night* and *Help!*, Ringo asked Brian Epstein's NEMS organization to scout for a solo movie role. Several were probably found, but the one that Ringo agreed to was, quite wisely, a small part in a star-studded film: *Candy*, based on the book by Terry Southern. Marlon Brando, Richard Burton, John Huston, James Coburn, and Walter Matthau headed the international cast that also included Swedish beauty queen Ewa Aulin in the title role of Candy—the nymphette who shares her talents with all and sundry at the drop of her panties.

For his cameo as Emmanuel, the Mexican gardener, Ringo had his hair dyed jet-black, and, in December 1967, flew out to Rome for two weeks of shooting. Unfortunately, he would have been better off staying at home—the reviews ranged from lukewarm to hostile. Still, in 1969 Ringo tried again, although this time he was accorded the co-starring role alongside Peter Sellers in *The Magic Christian*. Celebrities ranging from Raquel Welch, Richard Attenborough, and Christopher Lee to John Cleese, Yul Brynner, and Roman Polanski made guest appearances.

Like *Candy*, *The Magic Christian* was based on a novel by Terry Southern. Unlike *Candy*, it managed to be funny… in part. Centering around the exploits of the world's richest man, Sir Guy Grand (Sellers), and his adopted son, Youngman (Ringo), the film demonstrates in a series of episodes the lengths people will go to for money. Apple artists Badfinger scored a hit with one of the movie's featured songs, the Paul McCartney composition, "Come And Get It," yet *The Magic Christian* itself didn't do so well at the box-office.

If nothing else, *The Magic Christian* did provide The Beatles' drummer with some welcome respite from the miserable *Get Back* sessions. He would continue to appear in films throughout the 1970s and early '80s, the most memorable of which—from the public viewpoint—was *That'll Be the Day* (1973) and—from his own viewpoint, since it brought him together with future wife, Barbara Bach—*Caveman* (1981).

# Apple in De-Klein

On December 7, 1967, the same day that Ringo started filming *Candy* in Rome, The Beatles' Apple Boutique opened at 94 Baker Street in the heart of Central London. Earlier that year the group had formed a legal business partnership, The Beatles & Co, and now here it was, moving into the retail business.

*94 Baker Street, former premises of The Beatles' Apple Boutique. Even Sherlock Holmes, who "resided" on this street, couldn't have solved the mystery of the group's finances.*
©Richard Buskin

The Apple Boutique, with its psychedelic exterior mural designed by artists calling themselves The Fool, and its stock of "way-out" clothes, didn't last long. It seemed the public had no interest in the fashionable line, until it was announced the boutique was

closing down and the remaining clothes given away. The night before the closure, The Beatles, their wives, and friends helped themselves to the choice items, and the next day half of London appeared to be standing in line to pick up the remnants. It would prove to be a scary omen of things to come for The Beatles' other business ventures.

As announced by Paul in May 1968, the aim of the umbrella company, Apple Corps Ltd., was "a controlled weirdness... a kind of Western Communism." There would be an Apple Foundation for the Arts, a record division, a film division, an electronics division, a music publishing division, and so on. The possibilities were endless.

In essence, this amounted to providing creative yet needy young people with initiative and the necessary funds. A fine objective, and it would have been okay had the various divisions even been able to simply recoup their costs, let alone create anything of worth. For the most part they didn't. Only Apple Records initially turned a profit, thanks to division head Ron Kass, Jane's brother (and future record producer) Peter Asher, who was in charge of A&R, and a client roster that included James Taylor, Mary Hopkin, Badfinger, Billy Preston... and, oh yes, The Beatles and The Plastic Ono Band. Otherwise, it was a dismal tale.

Another retail store, Apple Tailoring (Civil And Theatrical), did about as well as the boutique; the Arts Foundation quickly became a black hole into which money disappeared along with the "artists" and "innovators" who regularly turned up on the company's doorstep looking for handouts; and, as for the Electronics division—well, that was put in the trustworthy hands of Fab friend Alexis Mardas.

Walking around his laboratory in a white coat, busily scrawling notes and diagrams, "Magic Alex" was so called due to the array of incredible inventions he'd promised to come up with for the new Apple recording studio. After all, what a joke EMI's eight-track facility would be when compared to Apple's *72-track* studio! And as for those cumbersome screens that normally had to be erected around Ringo's drum kit in order to separate it from the sound of the other instruments—why Magic Alex was inventing an invisible force-shield to take care of that!

As it turned out, when The Beatles transferred from Twickenham Film Studios to their own studio during the course of the already-troubled *Get Back* project, they discovered to their horror that Alex hadn't quite managed to achieve his aims. His recording console, hand-carved and featuring an old oscilloscope in the center, was likened by studio engineers to the control panel of a B-52 bomber. Also, the fact that 72 little loudspeakers had been tacked around the studio didn't mean they could make 72-track recordings.

In fact, as Alex hadn't even remembered to drill holes between the control room and the recording area (for the cables to connect the console to the microphones and amplifiers), it wasn't possible to make any recordings at all. The holes were eventually drilled and The Beatles did try to make a recording, but all that came out was a load of noise. The console was junked and George Martin had to call EMI to borrow a pair of four-track consoles.

Alex was never given the chance to try out his force-shields.

The Apple studio was in the basement of the plush building at 3 Savile Row in central London, where The Beatles' company HQ had relocated to from nearby Wigmore Street in July of 1968. And what a money pit *that* turned out to be. While the executives bought cars on expense accounts, the staff managed to run up exorbitant food and liquor bills, and office furniture literally went out the front door. The Beatles were being robbed hand over fist.

> **I Want to Tell You**
>
> "Hell's Angels will be in London within the next week, on the way to straighten out Czechoslovakia… They will undoubtedly arrive at Apple and I have heard they may try to make full use of Apple's facilities. They may look as though they are going to do you in but are very straight and do good things, so don't fear them or uptight them."
>
> —Part of George Harrison memo to Apple staff, December 1968

John and Paul took turns going into the office to direct operations, but this was about as successful as their efforts at editing *Magical Mystery Tour*. The group members had launched the company with a £1 million ($2.4 million) investment, but within months this was all gone and they were racing into the red. Outside help was desperately needed.

At the start of 1969, Paul turned to the New York law firm of Eastman & Eastman, whose partners, Lee and John, were the father and brother respectively of Paul's girlfriend Linda. For their part, John and Yoko met with strong-arm New York businessman, Allen Klein, and were so impressed by his tough strategy that they subsequently convinced George and Ringo that he should "sort out" Apple. Normally The Beatles only did things that were agreed upon unanimously. This time, however, John, George, and Ringo didn't want to align themselves with the Eastmans, who they considered to be looking out for Paul's best interests. Paul was out-voted three-to-one.

Klein immediately fired many of Apple's top personnel, while others handed in their resignations. So much for the easygoing philosophy that had helped launch the company. Still, the books had to be balanced, and so, in May 1969, John, George, and Ringo appointed Klein's company, ABKCO, to manage The Beatles' various business interests. It was at this point that the band suffered an irreversible fracture. Paul, neither liking nor trusting Allen Klein, refused to sign any such agreement. He did, however, put his signature to a Klein deal that secured the group a vastly improved royalty rate on record sales.

In 1969, due to miscalculations on their own part and betrayals on the part of certain trusted business associates, The Beatles lost their controlling interest in Brian's old NEMS organization, and also in Northern Songs, the company that published the priceless catalogue of Lennon-McCartney compositions. By year's end, they had completely sold out their interest in both. Now others would make decisions and earn the publishing royalties relating to most of the songs that John and Paul had written.

Yet while everything was falling down around their heads, Paul felt that the band could survive if it put business to one side and got back to making music. In September 1969, during a meeting at Apple, he suggested that maybe The Beatles should turn up unannounced at some small clubs and perform just like they used to in the old days...

# The Split: Sue You Blues

On September 13, 1969, during a flight from London to Toronto (where the hastily assembled Plastic Ono Band were due to play in a rock festival) John informed Allen Klein he intended to leave The Beatles. Klein responded that, with the group's business dealings in such a fragile state, and with a new royalty deal with EMI and Capitol in the works, it would be wise to delay announcing this to the other members. John initially agreed, yet, having decided on his future, he wasn't able to keep the secret for very long.

Back at Apple several days later, Paul made his pitch to the other three Beatles about undertaking some live performances. Ringo reportedly supported the idea while George, though not enthusiastic, didn't reject it outright. John, however, did, telling Paul that he thought he was "daft." When Paul tentatively asked, "What do you mean?" he received a swift answer. "I'm leaving The Beatles," John told him. "I want a divorce."

Stunned by this announcement, Paul nevertheless agreed that it would be best to delay making it public. Possibly he hoped that John would change his mind. But then a situation arose that pushed even this keenest member of The Beatles beyond his limits of endurance.

George had been the first of the Fab Four to branch out on his own musically, composing and producing the soundtrack to the 1968 movie *Wonderwall*. John had started collaborating with Yoko and various other musicians shortly afterwards, and now, at the end of 1969, Paul decided to follow suit, recording tracks for his first solo album, *McCartney*.

Subsequently, around February of 1970, Paul phoned John and informed him that he too was leaving The Beatles. "Good," was John's reply. "That makes two of us who have accepted it mentally." However, things took a definite turn for the worse when Paul learned that Allen Klein, supported by the other three soon-to-be ex-Beatles, was trying to impede the release of *McCartney*. This was so that it wouldn't clash with UA's scheduled release of the film *Let It Be*.

Once again, Paul felt the others were ganging up on him, and when Ringo, the band's diplomat, turned up at his house one night in order to explain the situation, Paul went ballistic. Threatening to finish Ringo off there and then, he ordered him to put his coat on and leave. Things were at an all-time low, and the public didn't have a clue.

All became known on Friday, April 10, 1970, after a self-penned question-and-answer "interview" with Paul had been distributed along with media review copies of the *McCartney* album. In it, Paul made it perfectly clear that there was no future for The Beatles, and that he didn't miss the assistance of John, George, or Ringo when recording the album. "Paul Is Quitting The Beatles" screamed the front-page headline of that morning's *Daily Mirror* newspaper in Britain. John was fuming. Having kept his own mouth shut on the subject for more than six months, he'd now been scooped. "I was cursing because I hadn't done it," he later said. "I wanted to do it, I should have done it."

On April 17, *McCartney* was released in the UK. (It was issued in the U.S. on the 20th.) On May 8 (18th in the U.S.), *Let It Be* hit the stores, and on May 13 the movie of the same name had its world premiere in New York. None of The Beatles attended, and neither did any of them turn up for the simultaneous London and Liverpool premieres a week later. The dream was truly over.

Still, Paul was left with a tough decision. If he didn't want Allen Klein to manage his business affairs, he would have to try to dissolve the legal partnership that bound him together with John, George, and Ringo. On December 31, 1970, he therefore filed a lawsuit in the London High Court seeking the dissolution of The Beatles & Co, and requesting the appointment of a receiver to handle the band's dealings. It was the start of a messy battle that would drag on for years.

# The Least You Need to Know

➤ John and Yoko celebrated their March 20, 1969 wedding with a seven-day "bed-in" for peace.

➤ Even while business disagreements were ripping The Beatles apart, Paul wanted the band to return to live concerts.

➤ George felt (with some justification) that John and Paul weren't as interested in recording his songs.

➤ Ringo's burgeoning film career provided some distraction from The Beatles' troubles.

➤ Paul wanted his in-laws, the Eastmans, to manage The Beatles, but John, George, and Ringo insisted on Allen Klein.

➤ The Beatles' break-up was announced to the public on April 10, 1970, and Paul instigated their legal dissolution on December 31.

# Free as a Bird: Life after The Beatles

I'm going to try something fairly novel here. I've spent 24 chapters telling you all about The Beatles' backgrounds, their influences, their pre-Fab adventures, their worldwide success, and so on. Now I'm going to compress their solo careers—three of which have spanned far longer than that of The Beatles—into just a few pages.

## John: Soldier of Love

John kicked off the 1970s much the same way as he ended the 1960s, indulging in off-beat adventures with Yoko and gaining plenty of attention in the process. These ranged from having eight erotic lithographs—in which John graphically depicted bedroom scenes from their honeymoon—confiscated by police during an exhibition at the London Arts Gallery, to issuing a hoax press release on April Fool's Day 1970 stating that the Ono-Lennons had entered the London Clinic for a dual sex-change operation.

During the same year, the couple spent four months in Los Angeles undergoing a course of "primal therapy" under Dr. Arthur Janov. In a nutshell, this encourages the patient to relive his or her most painful life experiences and exorcise them by way of "primal screaming," thus letting out all of the anger and frustration that has been bottled-up since childhood. In John's case, this resulted in his landmark album, *John Lennon/Plastic Ono Band*, a harrowing collection of songs in which he vented his feelings against society, his parents, his fans, and his former colleagues.

With this album, John's artistic integrity shines through not only because of the gripping song material and stark instrumentation, but also his directness exploring his emotions. It was almost as if he was having a private conversation with the listener.

The *Imagine* album, released the following year, managed to express many of the same themes in a far more lush and melodic way. The title song has gone on to be a classic, summing up John's hopes for a united world full of peace and love, but these sentiments contradict a number entitled "How Do You Sleep?" In this, John (supported by George on lead guitar!) delivered a full-scale verbal attack on Paul, accusing his former friend of everything from making vacuous muzak to being responsible for The Beatles' break-up. It was a song that not only managed to hit its target where it hurt, but also served to demonstrate that its author was a man of sharp contradictions.

On September 3, 1971, John and Yoko flew to New York. Ostensibly intended as just a short visit, it evolved into a permanent stay. The couple had managed to garner little more than ridicule in the British press, and felt much more comfortable in the Big Apple, where they soon fell in with a crowd of left-wing political radicals and activists. Having preached all about love and peace, John was soon advocating "Power To The People."

In 1972 he and Yoko issued an album, *Some Time In New York City*, that managed to espouse a whole range of then-fashionable political causes. Most of these dealt with American issues, but one song, "The Luck Of The Irish," also took the British to task for their involvement in the affairs of the Emerald Isle. This stance angered many of John's former countrymen and women, who resented being preached to by someone who they'd enabled to live very comfortably on the other side of the Atlantic.

*Some Time In New York City* turned out to be a bad move, as people opined that the artist's deeply held beliefs couldn't possibly be stretched across such a wide range of topics. John's response to the poor sales was to return to the more tried and trusted themes of peace and love on the *Mind Games* album in 1973, yet by then his personal life was starting to come apart at the seams. For one thing, President Nixon's regime had taken note of the "politically subversive" former-Beatle's left-wing activities, and was now using his 1968 drug rap as a means to deport him. John was fighting to stay, suing the U.S. government while asserting (correctly, as it turned out) that he was being subjected to FBI surveillance and phone-tapping. However, this struggle, together with a number of other personal problems, was putting a strain on his marriage to Yoko.

In October 1973 the couple separated and John flew off to Los Angeles with secretary May Pang (reportedly at Yoko's instigation, since, she reasoned, if her husband was going to have an affair, then it should be with someone who she knew and trusted!). The brief split, however, turned into a 15-month "lost weekend" (as John would later describe it), during which time he went completely off the rails, consuming large quantities of drugs and alcohol, and ultimately pining for his estranged wife. Concurrently, he managed to record a couple of well-received albums, *Walls and Bridges* and *Rock 'n' Roll*, and produce another entitled *Pussy Cats* for friend and fellow-imbiber, Harry Nilsson, before returning to Yoko at their Dakota apartment in New York in January 1975.

## Do You Want to Know a Secret?

In late 1973, John began recording an album of rock oldies in Los Angeles produced by Phil Spector. However, after the sessions disintegrated amidst drink and drugs, Spector disappeared with the tapes. John wouldn't recoup them until June 1974, after which he'd finish the *Rock 'n' Roll* album in New York and release it in early 1975. In the meantime, the 1973/74 "lost weekend" in LA was characterized by wild scenes at the Santa Monica home that John shared with fellow carousers Keith Moon and Ringo Starr. In one notorious incident at the Troubadour Club, John was ejected for hurling insults at the stage act, the Smothers Brothers, and for allegedly assaulting a waitress. (At one point he also emerged from a bathroom sporting a Kotex on his forehead, but that didn't amuse too many people either.)

Soon afterwards, Yoko became pregnant. On October 7 the New York State Supreme Court voted to reverse the deportation order against John, and two days later, on his 35th birthday, Yoko finally gave birth to their first (and only) child, Sean Taro Ono Lennon. In July of the following year, John won his four-year battle to obtain a Green Card, entitling him to reside in the U.S. His life was turning around, and the former hellraiser decided to hang up his guitar (figuratively speaking, at least; he never stopped writing songs) and become a househusband, attending to the needs of his new son while Yoko took care of business.

That's pretty much how things remained until the summer of 1980, when, having kept to his five-year commitment to care for his child, John and Yoko began recording songs for a new album. Entitled *Double Fantasy*, it was released in November 1980 and revealed a couple apparently living in a state of domestic bliss. The reviews were good, and John, at age 40, seemed energized and full of life in a number of interviews. He also appeared to be up to his old tricks, posing nude for the cover of *Rolling Stone* magazine.

Then the unimaginable happened. At around 11:00 the night of December 8, John was shot five times at close range by a deranged "fan" named Mark David Chapman, who had been waiting in the shadows of the Dakota entrance as the Lennons returned from a recording session at the Hit Factory. A police car rushed John to the nearby Roosevelt

269

Hospital, but he'd already lost too much blood. After frantic attempts to revive him, he was pronounced dead. Ironically, only the year before, John and Yoko had contributed $1,000 to a fund providing New York City police with bullet-proof vests.

The global outpouring of grief was immediate and on an unparalleled scale. A man of peace had suffered a violent death, and on Sunday, December 14, 1980, at 2:00 p.m. EST and 7:00 p.m. in the UK, people around the world observed 10 minutes of silence in memory of John Lennon, the founder of The Beatles, and one of the most beloved artists of all time.

*A life-sized bronze statue of John Lennon by Brett-Livingstone Strong. This stood outside Los Angeles City Hall during the early 1980s before being returned to the artist.* ©Richard Buskin

During the ensuing years an entire industry has grown up around John's name, work, and image. Books have been written, films have been made, plays have been staged, tribute songs have been recorded, and many of his own unreleased recordings have been issued or broadcast. At the time of writing, others are still in the pipeline.

# Paul: Knight of the Realm

In August 1971, having already released the solo albums *McCartney* and *Ram*, Paul plunged himself back into a band setup when he announced the formation of Wings with Linda on keyboards, American drummer Denny Seiwell, and ex-Moody Blues guitarist/singer Denny Laine. Almost immediately, however, Paul had to deal with critical barbs regarding the inclusion of his wife—a photographer who had no innate musical skills—in the group's lineup.

Next, having been verbally attacked on record and in the press by John, Paul was further embarrassed when Wings' first album, *Wild Life*, was vilified by critics for its insipid pop content. Still, things could only get better, and they did. Henry McCullough was added to the band lineup on lead guitar, and in early 1972, Wings did what Paul had long wanted The Beatles to do; they turned up unannounced at numerous British universities and performed to the students for a basic admission price. Later that year, buoyed by the success of this venture, they undertook an indoor tour of Europe, followed by a more upscale British one in 1973.

Also during that time, Paul's compositional skills, which had seemed to desert him, started to make a comeback on a series of singles as well as the album *Red Rose Speedway*. Clearly, Paul often manages to come up with the goods when his back is to the wall. Such a situation arose on August 9, 1973, when, just before flying to Lagos, Nigeria, to record Wings' next album, Henry McCullough and Denny Seiwell both quit. Paul, Linda, and Denny Laine carried on regardless, with Denny taking over on lead guitar and Paul filling in on drums. The result was *Band On The Run*, by far Paul's most accomplished post-Beatles work up to that time and, some may say, to this day.

## Do You Want to Know a Secret?

Here are a couple of tidbits about the *Band On The Run* album:

One night, while they were in the Nigerian capital of Lagos for the recording sessions, Paul and Linda were held up by armed robbers. With a gun being aimed at her husband, Linda pleaded, "Please don't shoot him! He's a Beatle!" No guns were fired.

On the album cover, Paul, Linda, and Denny Laine pose alongside British chat-show host Michael Parkinson, singer/comedian Kenny Lynch, chef-turned-politician Clement Freud (grandson of Sigmund), actor Christopher Lee, and boxer John Conteh.

In one fell swoop, Macca had projected himself back to the top of the pop tree, and, with a constantly evolving band lineup, he would consolidate this position with a steady stream of hit singles, best-selling albums, and a mammoth, sold-out world tour in 1975 and 1976. For the former Beatle it was like a second coming. Never again would he recapture the heights that he scaled during the mid-1970s.

### Do You Want to Know a Secret?

In 1974, while visiting Los Angeles, Paul got together at the Record Plant recording studio with John. Paul played drums and John was on guitar as the two of them jammed on rock standards such as "Lucille," "Stand By Me," "Cupid," and "Chain Gang" with Stevie Wonder, Harry Nilsson, and various session musicians. John was seeking inspiration for his *Rock 'n' Roll* album, yet, judging by his offer of "a snort" and "a toot" to Stevie Wonder—not to mention the appalling standard of musicianship—John and some of his colleagues were evidently wired on cocaine. *A Toot and a Snore in '74* is the appropriate title of one of the bootleg releases of this disappointing session.

After a 1979 Wings tour of Britain, the band was scheduled to play 11 concerts in Japan between January 21 and February 2, 1980. Due to the McCartneys' previous busts for possession of cannabis, the Japanese authorities had twice refused them permission to tour there. Now they had relented and the long-awaited tour was sold out. Yet on January 16, when customs men at Tokyo's Narita Airport made a routine search of Paul's suitcase, to their amazement they discovered a large stash of cannabis inside his toiletries bag.

The Japanese tour was off, but that was the least of Paul's immediate problems. Thrown behind bars, he was informed by the local British consul that the Japanese authorities might make an example of him and slap him with a seven-year prison sentence. This was no joke, and Paul realized that, for once, his celebrity might actually work against him. Fortunately, after sitting in a bare cell for eight days, he was released and instantly deported back to England.

### I Should Have Known Better

After Wings officially split, Denny Laine asserted that the cancellation of the Japanese tour due to Paul's drug bust had been the final straw. However, the band, which also comprised drummer Steve Holly and guitarist Laurence Juber, continued to record until October of 1980, when they worked on a never-released album of outtakes and other material entitled *Hot Hitz and Kold Kutz*.

John's death at the end of 1980 put the cap on what had been a bad year for Paul. Dispirited, Wings broke up shortly afterwards, and Paul embarked once again on a solo career, releasing a succession of solid, if unspectacular, albums through the 1980s. Arguably the best among these were *Tug*

*Of War, Pipes Of Peace,* and *Flowers In The Dirt.* There were also several commercially successful collaborations with artists such as Stevie Wonder, Michael Jackson, and Elvis Costello.

However, during the same decade Paul's career took another nosedive when, against colleagues' advice, he decided to take another stab at moviemaking. He wrote the script and composed the songs for his own starring vehicle, *Give My Regards to Broad Street;* yes, it was like *Magical Mystery Tour* all over again. Clearly, Paul hadn't learned his lesson from that debacle. The film was savaged by critics for its non-existent storyline, and it bombed at the box-office.

*June 23, 1982: Linda bangs her tambourine while Paul sings and plays bass during the shoot of the "Take It Away" promo video.* ©Richard Buskin

Since then Paul has continued to record and make live appearances (undertaking two highly successful world tours), while dabbling in classical music. (Sample *The Liverpool Oratorio* and *Standing Stone*.) Meanwhile, other pet projects for this workaholic ex-Fab have included the production of short animated films; the transformation of his former school the Liverpool Institute into the Liverpool Institute for the Performing Arts (LIPA); and, with Linda, serving as a leading spokesperson on environmental issues. In 1997, in recognition of all that he had achieved over the past 35 years, Queen Elizabeth II bestowed a knighthood upon him.

So, now he's *Sir* Paul McCartney, even though I'm sure the title that'll stick the longest will still be that of "former Beatle."

# George: Dark Horse Traveler

The breakup of The Beatles came as a welcome relief to George. For one thing, he had fallen out of love some time ago with being a member of the world's most famous supergroup, and for another, he was sick of playing third fiddle to John and Paul. Now he was free to record all of his own songs, which he did on the very successful 1970 triple-album *All Things Must Pass*. However, during the early 1970s, little else went right for The Beatles' former lead guitarist.

For starters, his worldwide smash-hit single, "My Sweet Lord," immersed George in hot water when Bright Tunes, the copyright owners to the old Chiffons record, "He's So Fine," sued him for plagiarism. The case dragged on for years, until the courts finally ruled that George had "subconsciously" plagiarized "He's So Fine," and he had to make a deal with Bright Tunes... which in 1978 was purchased by Allen Klein!

**I Want to Tell You**

"To get a peaceful life I always let Paul have his own way, even when it meant that my songs weren't recorded. But I was having to record Paul's songs and put up with him telling me how to play my own guitar."

—George Harrison, 1971

Anyway, we're getting a few years ahead of ourselves. Back in July of 1971, Klein was quite happily sitting next to George at a New York press conference announcing the staging of two all-star concerts to aid the famine in Bangladesh. These took place at Madison Square Garden on August 1, and, besides George, others who performed for free included Ringo, Ravi Shankar, Bob Dylan, Eric Clapton, Leon Russell, and Billy Preston. There had been rumors of a Beatles reunion, yet John had pulled out when it became clear that Yoko wasn't invited. Reportedly, Paul also declined.

Still, it was all for a good cause, even if there were problems releasing the revenue from the shows and the resulting live album while the American and British tax authorities had their say. Unbelievably, while the money was only ever intended to help feed starving people in Africa, in 1974 George ended up having to pay £1 million ($2.4 million) in taxes to the British government.

It wasn't a good time for George. His marriage to Pattie had hit the rocks and she went to live with his best friend, Eric Clapton (whose song "Layla" was supposedly written as an ode to her). Then, after forming his own label, Dark Horse Records, George recorded an album (also entitled *Dark Horse*) and undertook a full-scale concert tour of the U.S. The only problem was that a severe throat infection had badly affected his singing voice, prompting critics to dub the album "Dark Hoarse" and fans at the sold-out concerts to openly boo and jeer.

George nevertheless continued to make records, even though his audience diminished as the 1970s wore on. In 1981, he was back in the singles charts with a musical tribute to John, "All Those Years Ago," which included contributions from Paul and Ringo; yet by now George was doing nothing to promote the release of his albums. Quite simply, he was more interested in pursuing other interests such as motor racing, his collaborations with Ravi Shankar, and gardening in the enormous grounds of his Friar Park Mansion in Henley-on-Thames. (During the early 1970s, he'd also purchased a huge property in Letchmore Heath, just north of London, for fellow disciples of the Hindu faith.)

**With a Little Help**
If you watch the movies that were produced by George's company, HandMade Films, you'll often see him make a small cameo appearance. He actually had a tiny speaking role in *Life of Brian*, but this was cut and George just appears as an extra. On the other hand, in *Shanghai Surprise* (starring Madonna) he performs as a nightclub singer.

Despite all this, during the late 1970s and '80s, George gained the most publicity for his success as co-director of HandMade Films, a production company he initially formed to bail out Monty Python's *Life of Brian* when it ran into financial difficulties. Investing £4 million (about $10 million) of his own money, George ensured that the film was completed and released, and thereafter he and partner Dennis O'Brien involved themselves in the production of numerous British motion pictures. Sad to say, several box-office failures eventually put a strain on HandMade, and a major falling-out occurred between the two partners, with George alleging that O'Brien had been living the high life on company money. He sued and was subsequently awarded extensive damages.

In 1987, George released his last solo album under his deal with Warner Brothers. Entitled *Cloud Nine*, it was an unexpected international bestseller, while the album's first single, "Got My Mind Set On You," topped the U.S. charts. Shortly afterwards he enjoyed further chart success as part of "supergroup" The Traveling Wilburys, alongside Roy Orbison, Tom Petty, Jeff Lynne, and Bob Dylan, while in 1991 "the Quiet One" undertook a short tour of Japan backed by Eric Clapton and his band.

One thing appeared certain. George wouldn't ever get together with both of his former Fabs in order to make some new "Beatles" recordings…

# Ringo: All-Starr Jet-Setter

In a surprising turnabout, after The Beatles' break-up, it was actually Ringo who appeared to best find his own niche and establish himself as an all-round showbiz operator. By the end of 1973 he'd managed to direct a movie about "glam-rock" star Marc Bolan and T. Rex entitled *Born to Boogie*; he'd received terrific reviews for his realistic performance in the 1950s nostalgia film *That'll Be the Day*; and he also had a string of hit singles to his name, not to mention an album riding high in the charts.

## Do You Want to Know a Secret?

*That'll Be the Day* contains a number of parallels to The Beatles' story: The main character, portrayed by David Essex, is a poetic singer/ songwriter/bandleader whose father deserted home at an early age. (Shades of John.) He and Ringo's character, Mike, work at a holiday camp much like Butlin's, where Ringo himself had played with Rory Storm and the Hurricanes during the early-1960s. There, the flamboyant resident singer is called Stormy Tempest (subtle, eh?), and he's portrayed by Billy Fury, who, back in 1960, had watched The Silver Beetles fail an audition as his backing band. Halfway through the movie, Ringo asked to be written out. He was replaced by Adam Faith in the sequel, *Stardust*.

Simply entitled *Ringo*, this last-named item featured the Starr man performing catchy pop songs, assisted by the skills of Messrs. Lennon, McCartney, and Harrison, as well performances by a multi-talented cast that included Marc Bolan, Harry Nilsson, Martha Reeves, Steve Cropper, Billy Preston, and The Band. The fact that John, George, and Ringo played together on the Lennon song "I'm The Greatest" quickly fueled reunion rumors. To others, the fact that Paul at no point collaborated with John or George confirmed quite the opposite. Still, "I'm The Greatest" was the closest that the world would get to in terms of a Beatles reunion during the 1970s.

*Ringo* would also prove to be an all-time high in the recording career of the ex-Fab drummer. Thereafter, he attempted to repeat the formula on numerous albums, but the novelty soon wore thin (as did the material suited to Ringo's voice) and by the early 1980s, he couldn't even get his efforts released in Britain or the U.S. Not that he was without friends or things to do.

Shortly after splitting up from Maureen in 1973, Ringo became an international jet-setter, partying all over the

### I Want to Tell You

"I don't mind talking or smiling, it's just I don't do it very much. I haven't got a smiling face or a talking mouth."

—Ringo Starr, 1963

world and enjoying his own version of the "lost weekend" in Los Angeles with musical cronies John Lennon, Harry Nilsson, and Keith Moon. However, while Hollywood was fun for a while, where do the top glitterati often like to hang out? That's right, Monte Carlo! Which is where Ringo decided to set up home and become a tax exile. He has since lived in America and Britain with second wife Barbara Bach, but, at the time of writing, Monaco is still their permanent base.

In the meantime, while Ringo has continued to drum for other artists, his distinctive voice has lent itself to radio broadcasts, records, televison ads, and narration of the hugely successful children's TV show, *Thomas the Tank Engine and Friends*. Also, following his well-publicized and successful battle with alcoholism, Ringo has returned to touring the U.S. and Europe, headlining successful shows with his own "All-Starr" bands.

The featured players in these lineups have ranged from Joe Walsh, Jack Bruce, Billy Preston, Todd Rundgren, Dr. John, and Nils Lofgren, to Levon Helm, Rick Danko, John Entwistle, Clarence Clemons, Jim Keltner, and Zak Starkey. Some take a turn performing their own hit songs, yet inevitably the main man himself, with his unique brand of charm, draws the crowds, proving once and for all that he is more than capable of getting by... with a little help.

# The Least You Need to Know

➤ After an active solo career and a five-year hiatus from show business, John Lennon was killed on December 8, 1980.

➤ Paul enjoyed a renaissance with Wings during the 1970s, but his career was hampered by a 1980 drug bust in Japan and the failure of his 1984 movie *Give My Regards to Broad Street*.

➤ As his interest in the contemporary music scene has waned, George has devoted his time to a variety of other pursuits.

➤ While Ringo's recording career has wound down, he now fronts his own "All-Starr" bands on concert tours.

# Part 6
# Oldies But Goldies

*Throughout the 1970s, there were incessant rumors about The Beatles getting back together. The separate participation of all four ex-members on the 1973* Ringo *album started the ball rolling. This was helped along when John and Paul both made comments that didn't confirm an imminent reunion, but didn't rule out the possibility.*

*With the success of the musical* Beatlemania, *American promoters Sid Bernstein (who had been responsible for the landmark 1965 Shea Stadium show) and Bill Sargent each tried to lure The Beatles into reuniting for just one show, offering them sums reportedly ranging from $25 million to $100 million. The Fabs didn't succumb, although they were tempted when, as a joke,* Saturday Night Live *producer Lorne Michaels offered them a massive $3,000 live on air to get together on his show!*

*Then, in 1994—just over 13 years after John Lennon's death—there was an unexpected event. "The Threetles"—as Paul, George, and Ringo were now dubbed—headed back into the studio. In this section of your* Complete Idiot's Guide, *I'll tell you all about the massive success of that mammoth project, while also filling you in on desirable and bogus Beatles collectibles, how to hook up with like-minded fans, and where to go on your magical sightseeing tours.*

# Can I Have a Little More?— The Beatles Anthology

Ever since the early 1970s, The Beatles had been planning to produce a documentary that would recount the band's story in their own words. Tentatively titled *The Long and Winding Road*, the project suffered the same fate as many of the group's other dealings after the breakup: John, Paul, George, and Ringo could never seem to agree on what, why, and how things needed to be done. Furthermore, there were outstanding lawsuits and royalty deals to settle, and countless solo projects they appeared to attach more importance to. As a result, *The Long and Winding Road* amounted to all talk and little action and remained on the shelf while other documentary-makers did their thing—only to be criticized by The Beatles for failing to tell "the real story."

By the late 1980s, Paul, George, and Ringo finally decided that the time was right for their own enterprise to go into production. Besides, all the signs indicated that it would be a cash bonanza. Eventually retitled *The Beatles Anthology*, it evolved from a straightforward, tell-all documentary into a clear-the-decks project that also involved the simultaneous release of many of The Beatles' outtakes and previously unissued tracks. A number of these had already been bootlegged, but others had never seen the light of day. What's more, in conjunction with Yoko, the three surviving Fabs formulated an idea that sounded ridiculous in theory, but turned out to be the *Anthology's coup de grâce*. It wasn't the first time that The Beatles had taken an "ill-advised risk" only for it to hit the proverbial jackpot.

# Back in the Studio

It was quite a concept: Instead of just Paul, George, and Ringo reuniting to make a few new recordings to tie in with the *Beatles Anthology*, they would do so in conjunction *with John*. Not easy, of course, given that he was no longer around. However, aware that during his five-year "retirement" in the late 1970s John had continued to write and record demos of new compositions, George asked Yoko whether she would loan some of these to the "Threetles." The idea was to utilize John's lead vocals and overdub proper bass, drums, guitars, and backing vocals to produce, in effect, new Beatle recordings. After all, on the *White Album* and *Abbey Road*, the Fab Four had hardly recorded together anyway.

The germ of this idea had actually formulated in George's head shortly after Roy Orbison's death in 1988. Since The Traveling Wilburys (which George and Roy were both a part of) were about to record a second album, George, Bob Dylan, Tom Petty, and Jeff Lynne started to search for a replacement... and came up with Elvis Presley! That's right, they'd utilize his voice (under the guise of "Aaron Wilbury") in conjunction with a new recording. The Presley estate approved wholeheartedly of Elvis' new venture and provided the band with the rights to one of his songs, but there was a change of heart when George said that perhaps the idea was too gimmicky. Still, he happened to talk about it to Yoko and she was quite taken by the notion of perhaps "reviving" John for a Beatles reunion. Shortly afterwards, she came up with one of his demo tapes.

George Martin, meanwhile, didn't share Yoko's enthusiasm. Even though he was producing and directing the compilation of the three *Anthology* double albums, he made it clear that he didn't want to be involved with the new recordings. Jeff Lynne therefore got the call to produce them, with engineers Geoff Emerick and Jon Jacobs sitting behind the mixing console at Paul's home studio in Rye, Sussex. The first sessions were set for February 1994, and the initial song to be worked on was John's 1977 composition, "Free As A Bird."

In a 1995 interview in his own fan magazine, *Club Sandwich*, Paul talked about the attitude that he, George, and Ringo decided to adopt. "We got this scenario going of 'He's

**I Want to Tell You**

"That man who offered us five million dollars each was supposed to also promote a match between a man and a shark, so my suggestion was that he fight the shark and the winner could promote the Beatles concert."

—George Harrison, on Bill Sargent's 1976 attempt to reunite the group for one show asked us to finish a tape.' And the key words for me were, I imagined him saying, 'I trust you. Just do your thing. I trust you.' And the trust was what I needed to know. So I made up a fiction and believed it and it was fine. I went in there—I think we all did—fully believing that this is something John would have wanted us to do."

In the same interview, Paul also stated that newspaper articles questioning the wisdom of such an enterprise only served as a challenge for him to prove the doubters wrong. However, achieving that wasn't totally straightforward. John's recording, made on a mono cassette, featured him singing and playing a piano. Even with current computer technology, there was no way to separate the voice from the keyboard, and so Paul played another piano on top of John's, and he and George added acoustic guitars. That brought them to the next problem; since John only recorded a home demo as a means of working out the song's structure, he hadn't concentrated much on the tempo. As a result, he tended to speed up and slow down, and Paul and George had difficulty playing along to the recording. At this point the computers *did* come in handy, enabling John's voice and piano to be transferred to multi-track tape in perfect time.

> **With a Little Help**
> Tying in with George's ukulele part at the end of "Free As A Bird," John's backwards statement (played forwards) is "turned out nice again." This was the catchphrase of George's hero, British music hall comedian/ukulele player, George Formby. However, if you listen to the actual backwards recording, John's garbled message sounds uncannily like "Made by John Lennon"! A fantastic coincidence or just Fab magic?

Still, the song's bridge section had never been completed by John, so Paul wrote some new words for it. George didn't like them, and neither did Jeff Lynne; but although a spot of *Let It Be*–type tension was threatening to rear its ugly head, adjustments were made and a compromise was agreed upon. Phew! Paul had probably been tempted to say, "I'll write whatever words you want me to write, and I won't write at all if you don't want me to…"

After that, Paul's piano, his and George's acoustic guitars, Paul's bass, Ringo's drums, Paul and George's harmony vocals, and George's rhythm guitar and slide solo were overdubbed, in that order. "It sounds like a Beatle record!" exclaimed Ringo when the harmony vocals had been added. Finally, just to top things off, George played a small ukulele part, and, in true *Sgt. Pepper* fashion, a snippet of John speaking was played backwards and mixed in right near the end.

A year later, in February 1995, much the same process was applied to "Real Love," a song that John had made a demo of at home in 1979. (An alternate version was also featured in the 1988 documentary film, *Imagine: John Lennon*, and on the accompanying soundtrack album.) Once again, the hiss, hum, clicks, and static on the original cassette were removed before overdubbing took place. Paul played two different basses this time— an electric one, and the upright double-bass that once belonged to Elvis Presley's original bassist, Bill Black.

So, these would be the new Beatles singles: "Free As A Bird," credited to John Lennon, Paul McCartney, George Harrison, and Ringo Starr, released in 1995 (November in the UK and December in the U.S.), and "Real Love," credited to John Lennon and released in March 1996.

### Do You Want to Know a Secret?

Paul, George, and Ringo worked together on several songs in 1995. While a Lennon demo of "Grow Old With Me" (similar to the one on his posthumous *Milk And Honey* album) was passed over, the Threetles attempted a third collaboration with John by overdubbing his demo of "Now And Then" (aka "Miss You"). Dissatisfied with the results, they ultimately discarded that, too. "Now And Then" was one of the few unreleased Lennon compositions not to be aired on the syndicated Westwood One Radio series *The Lost Lennon Tapes*. It does, however, appear on the bootleg CD *The Dakota Beatle Demos*. Paul and George reportedly also worked on a co-composition entitled "All For Love," but this remains unfinished.

As for the three *Anthology* double-albums, these amounted to six CDs of material, ranging from some of the band's earliest amateur recordings, a few Hamburg recordings, and part of their Decca audition to alternate takes of well-known songs, false starts, TV and radio appearances, concert performances, demo recordings, and certain songs that had never been released before.

Nevertheless, only *The Beatles Anthology 1* was compiled at the time of its release in 1995. Paul, George, and Ringo waited to monitor public and critical reaction before embarking on the other two. One thing was for sure: They didn't have to worry about there being enough hype to plug the first installment.

## Back on Film

During the 1970s, Apple President Neil Aspinall oversaw the production of the *Long and Winding Road* documentary, but this was rejected because, according to Ringo, "it was mainly airplanes landing and taking off." Then, when the project was resurrected around 1989, Chips Chipperfield was brought in as the producer, and he in turn enlisted the services of Geoff Wonfor as director and Bob Smeaton as the writer.

Between 1993 and 1995, Paul, George, and Ringo went before the cameras and recounted The Beatles' story as they each saw it in a series of interviews with Jools Holland. The only others invited to voice their recollections were George Martin, Neil Aspinall, and press officer Derek Taylor; John's contribution came from interviews done of the course of his career (many of them during his solo years).

*The Beatles: The most successful group in the history of popular music.*
©Hulton Getty

This small lineup led to obvious drawbacks: First, with no one but The Beatles and three of their intimates telling the story, the overall result was extremely subjective. Secondly, whereas Paul, George, and Ringo provided insights into their legend from the mature perspective of men in their fifties, John's mostly originated from when he was in his twenties and early thirties.

Furthermore, when the surviving Fabs viewed the separate interviews, it was clear that they didn't always recall events the same way. Ultimately, compromises had to be reached so that sensibilities weren't offended, especially with regard to still-touchy subjects such as the events leading up to the band's breakup. Diplomacy won the day, so viewers end up being presented not with the definitive, warts-and-all story of the meteoric rise and acrimonious split of the world's greatest supergroup. Rather, it is a celebration, with some trademark Lennon and Harrison cynicism thrown in to at least provide some sense of balance.

On November 19, 22, and 23 of 1995, *The Beatles Anthology* aired in three two-hour episodes in America; it was split into six one-hour episodes for its

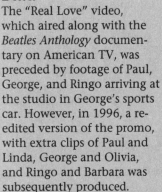

**I Should Have Known Better**

The "Real Love" video, which aired along with the *Beatles Anthology* documentary on American TV, was preceded by footage of Paul, George, and Ringo arriving at the studio in George's sports car. However, in 1996, a re-edited version of the promo, with extra clips of Paul and Linda, George and Olivia, and Ringo and Barbara was subsequently produced.

subsequent broadcast in the UK. Since the U.S. broadcasts contained more advertising breaks, the UK version of the series was actually longer. Still, when the documentary was released on video and laser disc in 1996, it extended to just under 10 hours wherever it was purchased, featuring extra interviews, concert footage, home movies, TV broadcasts, and so on. Surprisingly, however, while the promo video for "Free As A Bird" was also included, the one for *Real Love* wasn't.

Both songs received their world premieres on ABC TV in America in November 1995. "Free As A Bird," an absolutely stunning computerized collage that melded old footage of the band into brand-new surroundings and referenced numerous Beatles songs, was broadcast at the end of the first episode; "Real Love," a more straightforward compendium of old clips interspersed with some very welcome 1995 footage of Paul, George, and Ringo at work in the studio, aired at the end of the second episode.

So much for all the details. Suffice it to say that, thanks to the massive publicity campaign surrounding the entire *Anthology* project, public expectations regarding the TV documentary ran *much* higher than they did for *Magical Mystery Tour*. Fortunately, this time around the masses weren't disappointed.

## Back in the Spotlight and Back on the Charts

It was just like 1964 and 1965 all over again. Well, not quite, but in the build-up to the transmission of the documentary, the first airing of the new single, and the release of the *Anthology 1* double-CD set, The Beatles' names, their images, and their music were all over TV screens, radio airwaves, newspapers, and magazines around the world. Without a doubt, more than a quarter of a century after the band's demise, John, Paul, George, and Ringo were still massive news.

Major newspapers everywhere published special editions, with whole pages devoted to the Fab Four, both past and present. There were also magazines, with titles such as *Life*'s "Reunion Special—The Beatles From Yesterday To Today" and "Beatlemania Is Back!" on sale everywhere. Even *TV Guide* published a "Special Collectors' Edition" for the week commencing November 18, 1995, featuring an updated version of the *Sgt. Pepper* album photo on the front cover, and interviews with Paul, George, and Ringo inside.

**I Want to Tell You**

"We were always waiting to see who was going to be bigger than The Beatles, and it was The Beatles."

—Paul McCartney, 1997

As it turned out, Dave Marsh interviewed Paul and Ringo in person for *TV Guide*, but George simply responded to his questions by fax! Even after so many years, George was adamant that, aside from posing for a set of official "reunion" photos taken by Linda McCartney and being interviewed for the CD-ROM included in *Anthology*'s "electronic press kit" (not to mention Dave Marsh's fax), he wouldn't do one iota of promotion relating to The Beatles. Not wishing to go it alone, Paul and Ringo generally felt obliged to follow the same course, save for just a few solo interviews.

Still, they managed to get by. Billboards and record store posters bore reproductions of the *Anthology* artwork, conceived by Klaus Voormann, the Hamburg friend and former Plastic Ono Band bassist who had designed the *Revolver* album cover. The top of the Capitol Records building in Hollywood was adorned with enormous reproductions of the four famous faces. TV news shows were continually drumming up items with some sort of link (however tenuous) to the Fabs, and ABC, the network transmitting the *Anthology* documentary in America, dubbed itself "ABeatlesC"(!). (Back in February of 1964, New York radio station WABC-AM had also christened itself with that name.)

The only things missing were the hysterical fans, the more ludicrous merchandise... and The Beatles themselves. Three of them set the ball rolling; everyone else picked it up and ran like mad.

In America, "Free As A Bird" peaked at #6 on the *Billboard* "Hot 100" chart (it climbed to #2 in the UK), while "Real Love" went to #11 in the U.S. and #4 in the UK. Also, as I told you right near the start of this book (and as I'm *sure* you remember), *The Beatles Anthology 1* clocked the biggest ever first-week sales of a double album, shifting 855,473 copies during November 21–28, 1995 in the U.S. alone. What's more, with three consecutive albums topping the charts within a 12-month period, and an estimated 33 million copies of these *Anthology* sets being purchased in addition to their vastly popular back-catalogue, The Beatles were setting records and attaining sales figures in 1996 that they hadn't even achieved during their 1960s heyday.

"You can't re-heat a soufflé," Paul had once asserted when asked about the viability of a Beatles reunion. Oh yeah?

**I Should Have Known Better**

The *Beatles Anthology* project ignited fresh rumors about Paul, George, and Ringo reuniting for a concert or even a tour. These continue to circulate every time a multi-star show is set to take place or when any of the former-Fabs is expected to appear on stage. However, treat these stories with extreme skepticism. The chances of a "Threetles" live performance are little to none.

# And the Winner is... More Grammy Awards

As you might imagine, The Beatles have been feted with a number of awards down the years, ranging from the Ivor Novello to the Oscar, yet there are some categories in which it's hard (and unfair) to compare their achievements with those of today's rock superstars.

For instance, back in the 1960s, gold and silver records were awarded for higher volumes of sales than they are today, and platinum discs weren't awarded at all. (Nevertheless, Paul was once honored with a rhodium disc for his achievements, which outstrips the value of either silver, gold, or platinum.) And then there are the annual Grammy Awards.

Three Beatles-related Grammys were handed out in 1997, for Best Pop Performance By a Duo or a Group with Vocals ("Free As A Bird"), Best Music Video, Short-Form ("Free As A

Bird"), and Best Music Video, Long-Form (*The Beatles Anthology*). These brought the grand total of Grammys with a Fab connection to 14 (not all were awarded directly to the band), which is hardly insignificant, yet these days certain artists find themselves being nominated for that amount in one year alone. Furthermore, when you consider how long The Beatles were record-industry leaders and how much they achieved during their years together, then 11 Grammys between 1965 and 1971 doesn't sound like much at all. The problem lay with the attitude of the voters.

Even though rock music was at its peak during the 1960s, many among the industry *cognoscenti* still didn't consider it as worthy as the product that had preceded it. Therefore, even though artists such as Frank Sinatra and Tony Bennett weren't exactly burning up the charts, they were the ones who were scooping the awards. Ludicrous but true. Still, I bet *they* never received MBEs! (They couldn't. They were American.)

Now, for all of my connections, I can't correct this injustice. I can, however, at least set you straight with regard to what the 11 original Beatles-related Grammys were awarded for. So, here goes:

➤ **1965—Best New Artist:** The Beatles

**Best Vocal Group Performance:** *A Hard Day's Night*

➤ **1967—Song of the Year:** "Michelle" (awarded to John Lennon and Paul McCartney)

**Best Contemporary Solo Vocal:** "Eleanor Rigby" (awarded to Paul)

**Best Album Cover:** *Revolver* (awarded to Klaus Voormann)

➤ **1968—Album of the Year:** *Sgt. Pepper's Lonely Hearts Club Band*

**Best Contemporary Album:** *Sgt. Pepper's Lonely Hearts Club Band*

**Best Album Cover:** *Sgt. Pepper's Lonely Hearts Club Band* (awarded to Peter Blake and Jann Haworth)

**Best Engineered Record, Non-Classical:** *Sgt. Pepper's Lonely Hearts Club Band* (awarded to G.E. Emerick)

➤ **1970—Best Engineered Record, Non-Classical:** *Abbey Road* (awarded to Geoff Emerick and Phillip McDonald)

➤ **1971—Best Original Score:** *Let It Be*

Well, that's it, and, you have to admit, it's pretty hard to believe. In fact, it just serves to negate any importance that was attached to the Grammy Awards during those years.

# The Least You Need to Know

➤ Originally titled *The Long and Winding Road*, *The Beatles Anthology* documentary project began in the early 1970s and wasn't completed until more than 20 years later.

➤ Paul, George, and Ringo worked on some old John Lennon cassette recordings to produce the new Beatles singles, "Free As A Bird" and "Real Love."

➤ There was massive hype surrounding the CDs' release and the documentary's TV broadcast, yet George, Paul, and Ringo didn't partake very much in the publicity campaign.

➤ The popularity of all three *Anthology* CD sets enabled The Beatles to sell more records than during any one year back in the 1960s.

➤ The *Anthology* project earned three Grammy Awards in 1997, bringing the Beatles-related total to 14.

# Rattling Those Valuables

Immediately after John Lennon's death, prices of Beatle-related collectibles shot through the roof. Beforehand, Fab Four autographs, artwork, acetates, clothes, gold discs, trading cards, tour programs, ticket stubs, posters, and all of the other paraphernalia were certainly much desired among the die-hard fans, but few (if any) were prepared to shell out huge sums of money for them. (Certainly not me. In 1976 I was offered a John Lennon signed lithograph for £25/$50... and I turned it down!) In fact, in 1979 EMI Studios in Abbey Road decided to auction off a lot of old equipment, including the two four-track tape machines that had been used to record *Sgt. Pepper*. Each went for just £400 ($800), while a batch of EMI-stamped toilet rolls (unused) that The Beatles had reportedly rejected(!) was snapped up for a bargain £85 ($170).

When John died, everything changed. Major auction houses such as Sotheby's and Christie's began marketing the goods, professional dealers entered the fray, and between them they forced the prices up and out of reach of the vast majority of true Beatle People. I mean, $2.29 million for John Lennon's psychedelic Rolls-Royce, or a mere £161,000 ($230,000) for Paul's handwritten lyrics to "Getting Better"? I kid you not! These are the kind of prices that have been fetched at auction! Still, much of the most interesting

"Beatlerabilia" has actually been purchased by the worldwide chain of Hard Rock Café restaurants, where they are on permanent display to the public, so at least some good has come out of all the wheeling and dealing.

While this information may be interesting, you're probably seeking to collect far less pricey items. Therefore, in this chapter I'll tell you about some of the choice objects that you can search out *without* having to rob a bank. (I say *some*, as there are entire books dealing with merchandise.) There will also be some tips on how to do this (sniff out the collectibles, not rob a bank), as well as warnings about forgeries intended to line the pockets of unscrupulous rip-off merchants.

Never mind that line about "the best things in life are free." If you want to acquire some Fab Four goodies, you'll have to open your wallet. However, one collector's honey pie may be another's yellow matter custard. Monetary value doesn't always equate with desirability, for there is also sentiment and personal taste to take into account.

# Rare and Juicy Records

This is a massive market and it basically divides into two categories: the official and the unreleased. The latter sub-divides into tape or acetate demos and test mixes, made for The Beatles and their recording staff to listen to; promo records sent to radio stations; and illegal bootleg releases of material that the general public was never *supposed* to hear.

The prices of such collectibles vary wildly, ranging from virtually worthless damaged goods to gems such as the *Yesterday And Today* album's "Butcher" cover (which I told you about in Chapter 22). In *near-mint* (perfect) condition, stereo versions of this record inside the "Butcher" sleeve have fetched from $7,000 to $20,000 for a sealed copy. In mono, the asking price is around $3,000. Pasted-over covers (featuring The Beatles gathered around a steamer trunk) that haven't been peeled off are only worth about $1,500 (stereo) and $550 (mono), while those with the "trunk" cover very skillfully removed rise slightly to $1,600 (stereo) and $600 (mono).

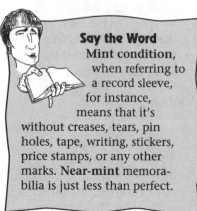

**Say the Word**

Mint condition, when referring to a record sleeve, for instance, means that it's without creases, tears, pin holes, tape, writing, stickers, price stamps, or any other marks. **Near-mint** memorabilia is just less than perfect.

The Tony Sheridan single "My Bonnie"/"The Saints" featuring The Beatles as the backing band was pressed for release by Decca in the U.S. and then never issued. As a result, depending on its condition, a copy of this can be worth anywhere from $1,400 to $8,000. On the other hand, there's the vinyl version of the *White Album*, each copy of which had a seven-digit number embossed on the cover, together with a prefix consisting of either a black dot, the letter "A," or the designation "No." (for "Number"), or no prefix at all. Well, according to market experts Perry Cox and Joe Lindsay, the standard value of a near-mint copy is multiplied by 50 percent if that number is below 10,000, three times if it is below 100, and eight times if under 10. If, however, you happen to be in possession of the double album *The Beatles* that has the number A0000001, sit down and have a drink! In near-mint condition this little beauty is worth 1,000 times the usual $100 asking price…or $100,000!

Closer to earth, there are the picture sleeves that Capitol Records issued in America with virtually all of The Beatles' 45 rpm singles. These sleeves have considerably more value than the records themselves, which in most cases are only worth about $5. The rarest Capitol sleeve is the one for "Can't Buy Me Love," which, in mint condition—including no *ring wear*—can fetch from $400 to $600. The reason? Well, the picture on the sleeve is exactly the same as the one for the Capitol single "I Want To Hold Your Hand." As a result, back in 1964 most teenagers threw away the "duplicate" sleeve, thus creating an instant rarity!

**Say the Word**
**Ring wear** refers to the circular mark created on record sleeves by the pressure of vinyl discs being stored very close together. To prevent this, store the sleeves separately, and place the records in plain sleeves.

The Veejay, Swan, Tollie, Atco, and MGM label picture sleeves are also worth around $150 to $300. However, remember that even the slightest blemish can mean a reduction in value of $50 to $100 or more. For instance, a ½-inch tear, together with a crease and slight ring wear on a "Can't Buy Me Love" sleeve can bring its price down to $100, even if the record itself is in mint condition and never been played before. $5 to $10 is all that's worth.

You could, however, rake in (or lay out, depending on whether you're buying or selling) between $250 to $350 for "little LPs." These are 7-inch records that play at $33\frac{1}{3}$ rpm and were at one time used in juke boxes. They're usually in stereo, have three songs per side, and normally come with a hard cardboard picture sleeve, three 1.75-inch miniature copies of the album cover, and five pre-printed title strips. There were three Beatles little LPs, for *Meet The Beatles!*, *The Beatles' Second Album*, and *Something New*.

**With a Little Help**
If you're interested in the American collector's market relating to The Beatles' records, check out *The Beatles Price Guide for American Records* by Perry Cox and Joe Lindsay, as well as *Goldmine* magazine's publications *Rock 'n' Roll 45 RPM Record Price Guide* and *Collectible Record Albums*. Meanwhile, for records issued in the UK, *Record Collector* magazine publishes a *Rare Record Price Guide*.

Then there are the Christmas flexi-discs that the Official Beatles Fan Club issued free from 1963 to 1969 (from 1964 in the U.S.) to all paid-up members. Flexi-discs were so paper-thin that you often had to tape a small coin onto them to make them play, but when they did they emitted specially recorded Christmas messages from the Fab Four. Each of these are worth between $200 to $400, depending on whether they're in their original sleeves and have the accompanying fan club newsletters. In 1970, American fan club members also received a "Not For Sale" LP issued by Apple Records, featuring all seven of the Christmas messages in a multi-picture sleeve. This too is worth $250 to $350.

Like the Christmas messages, promo discs are much desired and widely bootlegged. Among the many sought-after items are the white-label promo of "She Loves You," the one for "Penny Lane" (which has a slightly different ending from the released single), and two 7-inch, 33⅓-rpm, open-ended interview discs dating back to 1964. (These feature The Beatles giving answers to questions that radio deejays would insert in the blank spaces, thus creating the illusion of an exclusive interview.)

The $400 to $700 range applies to these kind of collectibles, yet if you want to hear different mixes of Beatles recordings without laying out the big bucks, then you should just take a listen to some of the Capitol albums released in the U.S. during the 1960s. A number of tracks sound very different to the versions released in the UK, with some of them boasting plenty of echo which, although it sounds good, was never approved by either The Beatles or George Martin. The Capitol execs just figured that American fans would prefer hearing the songs that way.

# Bogus Discs

Okay, there are plenty of these—gold records that were supposedly presented to The Beatles, the individual members, or others associated with them… yet never were. While you may come across them in a variety of different places, the most obvious locations are at Beatles conventions. All I can say is that, if a framed disc takes your eye at a dealer's stand, be really careful before you commit.

The first thing to look out for is a small gold-plated circle or square stating that the record is 24-carat gold. This kind of assertion *never* appears alongside a gold record. Secondly, if a gold album's inscription plate says that the award is to commemorate the sale of 1,000,000 records, then it's also phony. The sale of 1,000,000 records are rewarded with platinum discs today, but they never existed back in the 1960s. Instead, gold albums were awarded for the sale of 500,000 units, and gold records for the sale of 1,000,000 singles. So, read the inscription plate carefully, and also, for American awards, take note of the RIAA (Recording Industry Association of America) emblem. If it isn't embossed, it isn't real. In Britain, there still wasn't a recognized industry body when The Beatles were together, so there they were awarded both gold and silver records (for 250,000 sales) by *Disc* magazine. Silver records were never handed out in the U.S.

The point is that sometimes all of the different components may appear to be real: The gold record has the correct label, the inscription plate has an embossed RIAA or *Disc* emblem, and, in the case of American awards, the miniature record album cover is perfect. However, if the frame that they are assembled in doesn't look like other gold record frames from that era (compare it with others to make sure), you're probably staring at a worthless piece of junk. Also, take a look at how the record is mounted. Is it lop-sided or drooping? It shouldn't be.

*The Beatles Shop in Mathew Street, Liverpool, situated just a few feet away from the original site of The Cavern.*
©Richard Buskin

Another item to look out for is a record company stamp or sticker on the back of the award, bearing the specific number of the record. This doesn't always appear even on genuine silver or gold discs, but if there is one then you can probably rest easy. If, on the

other hand, the dealer is asking $150 for it because he needs to pay his grandmother's medical bill or bail his son out of jail, don't bite. Record awards don't come cheap unless they've been manufactured in somebody's basement.

Be especially wary of a dealer who happens to have 20 or 30 very similar-looking awards. And remember, 1960s awards have different frames to ones from the 1970s, which in turn are very different to those from the 1980s and '90s. As for the 45 rpm singles awards, these never contained a miniature picture sleeve or a photo of the artist, yet many of the fakes produced today look incredible. In fact, they often look more attractive than the real thing, since they boast a gold 45, an inscription plate, and a picture sleeve all framed together, sometimes even with the sheet music. Very nice, but worthless.

In the final analysis, if you want to know what the proper awards really look like, pay a visit to the Hard Rock Café. There you'll see original silver and gold discs adorning the walls, so take a pen and paper and make some notes.

Other bogus discs include phony versions of the more valuable records that I've already told you about: the "Butcher" album; the U.S. "Can't Buy Me Love" single; the U.S. "Christmas Messages" LP; and so on. In the case of "Can't Buy Me Love," for example, George's head is cropped on the bootleg sleeve photo. As for the Christmas LP, the bootleg has a title on the label that is 2.5 inches long instead of 2.25 inches, while the album cover—instead of being flimsy with an extremely sharp photo—feels more like a normal cover while the photo's a little blurred.

So, always check the sleeve printing to make sure it's sharp, and also ensure that the vinyl doesn't have any bubbles or pock marks. And remember, acetates may look authentic but the fakes are extremely easy to produce… and produced they are, in very large quantities.

I've only provided you with a few examples of how the bootlegs differ from the originals (this is another subject that could consume an entire book), but I'm just trying to convey how complicated record collecting can get. You should carefully study the market before parting with the big money.

# Mad Merchandise

Fairly early on, it became clear that The Beatles were capable of selling far more than just records. In 1963, young Brit males who wanted to look like them could buy Beatle Wigs, collarless Beatle jackets, and Cuban-heeled Beatle boots. Other teen favorites included Beatle belts, T-shirts, handkerchiefs, hats, jigsaw puzzles, bedspreads, pens, pencils, and shoulder bags. For the younger kids, there were the plastic imitation Beatle guitars and drum kits, while Mom could wear her Beatle kitchen apron to wash her Beatle crockery. Dad, on the other hand, could munch on some Beatle chewing gum and redecorate the home with Beatle wallpaper.

Aside from the wigs, boots, and jackets, all of the aforementioned items were invariably adorned with an obligatory photo (or drawing) of The Beatles, as well as their four "signatures." Brian Epstein's company, NEMS Enterprises, owned the copyright to the band's name, and he duly inspected much of the merchandise. Still, those manufacturers who wished to bypass his authority would simply produce goods bearing caricatures of insects, instruments, or moptop hairstyles, perhaps even with the misleading word "Beetles."

*Brisbane fan Jack Bonwell (right), hands over a set of hand-decorated "Beatle boomerangs" to The Beatles' press officer, Derek Taylor, during the 1964 Australian tour.*
*©Hulton Getty*

It wasn't easy to control the merchandising, and, in the beginning, there seemed to be little point anyway. Brian regarded most of it as just a means of publicizing the group and keeping the fans happy. Then he came to realize just how much money was being generated and he started to take matters a little more seriously. In late 1963, Brian's lawyer, David Jacobs, assigned a Londoner named Nicky Byrne to handle the licensing. Byrne and several business partners subsequently set up of a company named Stramsact to license Beatles merchandise in the UK, along with a subsidiary named Seltaeb—Beatles spelled backwards, didn't you know?—for business in the U.S.... should there be any. As for the deal? Stramsact Seltaeb would scoop 90 percent of all profits, leaving only 10 percent for The Beatles!

### With a Little Help

If you have Beatles collectibles or are thinking of acquiring some, an invaluable reference is *The Beatles Memorabilia Price Guide*, by Jeff Augsberger, Marty Eck, and Rick Rann. Published by Wallace-Homestead, this provides descriptions, current values, and, in some cases, photos of "more than 1,000 Fab Four collectibles" that have been produced down the years, be they official, unlicensed, or counterfeit.

Transactions such as this later prompted John, Paul, George, and Ringo to conclude that Brian Epstein not only earned them a fortune, but lost them millions as well. After all, as soon as the band hit America in February 1964, the merchandise orders went off the scale. REMCO Industries produced 100,000 Beatle dolls, Beatle Wigs were being manufactured at the rate of 35,000 per day, and Woolworth's and Penney's were arranging to install special Beatle counters in all of their stores. The *Wall Street Journal* estimated that $5 million worth of Beatles goodies would be sold in the U.S. alone by the end of the year.

It has to be said that, for sheer imagination (or lunacy), some American merchandisers really outdid everyone else. Perhaps one of the most famous creations was "The Beatles Flip Your Wig Game," produced by the Milton Bradley Company. The object of this "threat to Monopoly" was to travel around a board and collect "Beatle Cards" and "Wig Cards." If you managed to attain a complete set of matching cards—Ringo's drums with Ringo's wig, Paul's bass with Paul's wig, and so on—you were pronounced the winner and entitled to, er, flip your wig!

Then there were the "delicious ice cream Beatle Bars covered with chocolate crunch," manufactured by the Hood Ice Cream Company. These were sold in four- or six-bar boxes, which, in mint condition, can today fetch around $400. Add an individual wrapper and that loads another $90 onto the current price. Which brings us to one of the golden rules of buying or selling memorabilia: For a piece to fetch its optimum value, it not only needs to be in excellent condition, but it also should be in its original container. After all, how often have *you* bought a loaf of bread (or Ringo Roll!) and held onto the wrapping?

Fab Four fans could also stay super-clean with Colgate's "Beatle-Beatle" bubble bath (or "personality bath," as it was grandly titled). This came in two different bottles—one in the shape of Paul, and the other looking like Ringo. (Hence the "Beatle-Beatle" name, I suppose.) "Yeah! Yeah! Yeah! It's New! It's Wild! It's Pink Mild!" screamed the ads for this delightful addition to anyone's bathroom. They should also have announced, "It's Not Going To Be on the Market for Very Long!"

Once Beatlemania wound down, so did the amount of merchandise. Drastically. There was an avalanche of it coinciding with the release of *Yellow Submarine* in 1968, but otherwise, after the band quit touring, there just wasn't the same demand for bubble-gum cards, key chains, hair pomade, or perfume bearing the band's name and image. As I explained in the "Generation Game" section of Chapter 1, that image had changed and the fans' perspective had shifted. After The Beatles split, it would shift yet again.

Today, among the more sought-after items of Beatles memorabilia are concert programs. These are worth more money if they pertain to historic shows such as those at Carnegie Hall, the Hollywood Bowl, Shea Stadium, and so on. Then there are the concert tickets, which again may be valued according to the shows they were associated with, but which, if unused and bearing a photo of The Beatles, can be worth up to 15 times more than a torn-off stub that only has the group's name printed on it.

Other fun commodities include the toy instruments boasting the band's image and signatures, that were manufactured at the height of Beatlemania. These range from guitars, drum kits, and harmonicas to banjos and even bongos! Before you scoff, let me tell you that the Beat Bongo manufactured in the USA by Mastro, for instance, can now fetch as much as $900 if in its original box and in near-mint condition.

Another company named Select-O-Pack, on the other hand, cornered the market for America's more studious Beatle People. Assignment books, folders, pencil cases, and school report covers were among the many helpful goodies school kids could buy—and if they learned anything it was to hold onto such memorabilia. A Beatles pencil case, for example, would have cost them a bargain 49¢ back in 1964. Today, it can be worth as much as $300!

One item that has perhaps appreciated the most over the years is the Beatles four-speed record player. Licensed by Brian Epstein's NEMS Enterprises, approximately 5,000 were manufactured during the mid-1960s. Today they're worth up to $1,800 in mint condition, and more than half again if in the original box.

Today, there is a whole line of merchandise officially endorsed by Apple—anything from posters, plates, and T-shirts, to ties, boxers, socks, mugs, towels, trading cards, belt buckles, and baseball caps. At the same time, there is also a very large market for all of the original memorabilia. So, dig around your attic and see if you can come up with anything. You may strike gold!

**With a Little Help**
Original Beatles sheet music can still be found at local music stores. This has a photo (not a drawing) on the cover, normally in full color, and the list price is usually between 75¢ and $1.50. If you can pick one up for this price you're doing well, as it's now worth at least $10 each, and $15 to $20 for sheets of the early songs.

**With a Little Help**
If you're looking to collect original 1960s Beatles bubble-gum cards, there were four sets: three in black-and-white, each with 165 autographed photos; and one in color, consisting of 64 pictures with questions and answers on the reverse side. Try to get them in their original boxes, although I'm not sure how the value will be affected if the bubblegum's still in there.

# Fool's Merchandise

Once again, there are certainly plenty of fakes around. Official Beatles merchandise was endorsed by Brian Epstein's company, NEMS Enterprises, until late 1963, when two companies were then set up to handle licensing. What were they called? Well, if you remember from just a few pages ago and have done your homework, you'll know there was Stramsact in Britain and Seltaeb in America. Items with any of these names stamped or embossed on them are normally the real thing, as are any of the multitude of Beatles-related goodies dating back to the 1960s. It's just that those with a NEMS, Stramsact, or Seltaeb trademark are often the ones that have increased most in value.

In 1967, after The Beatles formed Apple Corps Ltd., the familiar green-apple logo started to appear on all licensed merchandise. Look for this on the cards that Beatles pins, cufflinks, necklaces, brooches, buttons, combs, and charm bracelets are mounted onto. If they don't have a card, stay away from them, especially the pins and buttons, since many forgers have simply purchased Beatles picture books, cut out the pictures, and manufactured their own pins and buttons. They may look good, but don't be fooled into thinking they're original.

Next we come to a particularly dicey area: autographs. For one thing, John, Paul, George, and Ringo's signatures aren't all that difficult to copy—I've been at Beatles conventions where, just prior to an auction, I've actually seen people busy scribbling "Fab Four autographs" onto record labels and sheets of paper before putting them up for sale! And then there's the fact that, during the 1960s, The Beatles often had their roadies, Neil and Mal, autograph photos for them.

First, of course, you should familiarize yourself with what the real signatures look like. Again, you can do this by visiting the Hard Rock Café. Also, note that John amended his signature towards the end of the 1960s. Having done that, there are some obvious precautions you can take. For instance, if an autograph dates back to the 1960s but you don't know the whereabouts of the person for whom it was signed, ask for a written money-back guarantee so that you can have the item verified by an art dealer.

If the vendor won't agree to this, you may be well advised to let him or her hold onto the autograph. Of course, it's often pretty difficult to confirm where, when, and who the signatures were made for, but be sure of one thing: *Any record issued after 1980 and signed by all four Beatles is phony.* (John died on December 8, 1980.) Some records have a date of manufacture as well as release, and this is especially handy as you may be looking at a 1960s Beatles album or single that was manufactured far more recently. I mean, certain "dealers" have somehow even managed to lay their hands on copies of John's posthumous 1983 album, *Milk And Honey*, signed by the man himself!

# The Least You Need to Know

➤ Beatles' merchandise was at a high 1963–1965 and tailed off until there was another surge when *Yellow Submarine* hit the screens.

➤ The prices of Beatles-related merchandise soared following John Lennon's death.

➤ The condition of records and memorabilia is vital to the monetary value, as is the existence of an item's original container.

➤ It's worthwhile visiting the Hard Rock Café to check what authentic collectibles look like, before investing your money in costly goods.

➤ Today Beatles merchandising is a thriving business, with Apple Corps. licensing everything from Beatles ties to Beatles boxer shorts.

# Chapter 28

# Dig It (Especially on Holidays and Weekends)

## In This Chapter

➤ The origins and current state of the fan conventions

➤ The inside track on the main Beatles mags

➤ How to chat with Beatle People using your home computer

➤ How to start planning those fab sightseeing trips

Okay, so you're interested in The Beatles. You love listening to their records, watching their movies, and learning all there is to know about them (which includes reading this book, of course). But then you try to share your interest with friends and family, and what do they do? Either they say a few polite words and change the subject, or they put on that "you'll-get-over-it" look and go back to watching the TV. Yeah, life can be pretty hard, but don't get too down about it. There are others just like you—well, they share some of your musical tastes, at least. They read the fan magazines (or "fanzines") and meet up at conventions geared towards the same glorious subject: The Beatles.

That's it—Beatles, Beatles, and more Beatles! No matter how much you want to discover, discuss, buy, sell, or celebrate regarding the achievements of John, Paul, George, and Ringo, you'll be more than satisfied. The resources are just waiting out there—you just need to know how to access them. Well, read on and I'll not only explain what to do, but, as an added bonus, I'll tell you about all the Beatle sites that any self-respecting fan should visit.

# Beatlefests

In Britain they are known as "Beatles Conventions"; in the States they are widely referred to as "Beatlefests"; and in other countries... Hey, what do you think I am? A linguist?

Whatever they're called, they're all pretty much the same: a chance for Beatle People both old and new to come together. There they can chew the fat over the latest Fab Four gossip, gush about how great The Beatles were (and still are), watch the film clips, sing and air-guitar along to the songs, peruse the dealers' stands for the most interesting Fab Four collectibles, dance to a band of Beatle imitators, listen to the recollections of those who actually knew them (The Beatles, not the imitators), and generally have "a splendid time."

The first such gathering took place in Boston, Massachussetts, in July of 1974, and was organized by Joe Pope, who ran a fan magazine entitled *Strawberry Fields Forever*. Then, a couple years later, the first British Beatles convention took place in Norwich, in the East of England. Both were considerable successes, yet when another larger-scale bash was put on at London's cavernous Alexandra Palace on December 18–19 of 1976, it was a monumental flop. Billed as "Europe's First Christmas Beatles Convention," it also turned out to be the last.

From then on, the Europeans staged their own small conventions in their respective countries, while the English staged theirs mainly in the most obvious setting: The Beatles' hometown of Liverpool. There the fans could not only attend the festivities but also visit the hallowed Fab Four sites. Today there are a number of meetings all over Britain, but since the late 1970s it has fallen to Liverpool to host properly organized conventions on an annual basis.

**With a Little Help**

Beatlefests take place every March in the New York area (actually it's the Meadowlands Hilton in New Jersey), August in Chicago, and November in Los Angeles. If you wish to attend call 1-888-9BEATLES. For merchandise call 1-800-BEATLES. Worldwide, you can also inquire by e-mail to mark@beatlefest.com, or by writing to Beatlefest, P.O. Box 436, Westwood, NJ 07675. Finally, there is also the website: **www.beatlefest.com**.

The Liverpool attendance figures are pretty steady, as they are at similar gatherings all over the world, yet easily the most successful ones are the "Beatlefests" produced in America by Mark and Carol Lapidos. In February 1974, Mark placed a two-line ad in *The Village Voice*, asking if anyone would be interested in attending a New York City convention. At first, 200 people responded that they would. But then, when the New York *Daily News* reported on his little venture, Lapidos received over 2,000 letters in two days.

So far, so good, but Mark wasn't finished yet. He managed to make contact with none other than John Lennon, and, after gaining the ex-Beatle's blessing, he received a number of choice donations for the convention's charity auction: signed guitars from John and Paul, a tabla from George, and a set of drumsticks from Ringo. The effort paid off. On September 7–8, 1974, more than 6,000 people attended the Beatlefest at New York's Commodore Hotel—a story sufficiently newsworthy to make the cover of *Rolling Stone* magazine.

Today, nearly a quarter of a century later, and with more than a quarter of a million dollars raised for charity, Beatlefest has turned into a full-time occupation for Mark and Carol Lapidos. Fans fly in from all over the world to attend the conventions, and the records continue to be smashed. There were over 10,000 people at the 1996 Chicago Beatlefest, and 8,500 at the 1997 one in the New York area, but this is only part of the story. Official merchandise that has been licensed by Apple is featured in Beatlefest's full-color catalog, and the result is more than 100,000 items mailed out each year. Now, does that suggest that the group's popularity is on the wane?

# Fan Clubs and Fanzines

In the old days, Beatle People who wanted to receive the most up-to-the-minute news on their idols usually belonged to the fan clubs—both official and unnofficial—that were dotted around the globe.

The Official Beatles Fan Club was established in Liverpool in 1961 with Freda Kelly as its President. As the band's popularity spread, the club expanded to take in the rest of Britain, while branches were endorsed in other countries to take care of those territories. In the States the main club was Beatles (USA) Limited. While The Beatles' meetings with club members were mainly limited to their early years, they nevertheless always made sure that they were offered items that were not available to the general public. Chief among these were the special Christmas messages The Beatles recorded from 1963 to 1969, and were issued on 7-inch vinyl discs to all paid-up members. In 1970, with the group having disbanded, the club then put together a compilation album of these same messages.

In August of the following year, Paul McCartney issued a formal statement to all club members. In it he stressed that he no longer wanted to be involved with "anything that continues the illusion that there is such a thing as The Beatles." Yet, it took another seven months for the message to really hit home. On March 31, 1972, the Official Beatles Fan Club closed down.

Since then, various unofficial operations have raised their heads, including ones dedicated individually to either John, Paul, George, or Ringo. The only official one among these is the Paul McCartney Fun Club; its glossy, full-color newsletter, *Club Sandwich*, really highlights how Beatle People keep themselves clued in today.

The fanzines basically combine the twin functions of fan-club newsletters and magazines. The first and most popular of these has been the UK-based *Beatles*

**I Want to Tell You**
"Nothing is left of The Beatles, only memories."

—Paul McCartney, 1976

*Book* monthly magazine, which was officially endorsed by the group from 1963 to 1969. It resurfaced as *The Beatles Book Appreciation Society Magazine* in 1976, with several new pages wrapped around reproductions of the original mags. Then, when this had run its course, it reverted to its original title and a full complement of new material. It's still popular today, while others that have been around since the 1970s include *Beatlefan* in the U.S. and *Beatles Unlimited* in Holland.

Beatles fanzines are currently being published in many different countries. Here now are details of some of the more popular English-language ones that you may wish to search out:

*Beatlefan*
The Goody Press
P.O. Box 33515
Decatur, GA 30033

*The Beatles Book*
Diamond Publishing
43-45 St. Mary's Road
London W5 5RQ, England.

*Beatles Unlimited*
P.O. Box 602
3430 AP nieuwegein
The Netherlands

*Beatles Video Digest*
P.O. Box 13322
Des Moines, IA 50310

*Beatletter*
P.O. Box 13
St. Clair Shores, MI 48080

*Club Sandwich*
P.O. Box 4UP
London W1A 4UP, England
[Paul McCartney]

*Good Day Sunshine*
12545 Pacific Avenue #1
Mar Vista, California 90066

*The Harrison Alliance*
67 Cypress Street
Bristol, CT 06010

*The Working Class Hero*
3311 Niagra Street
Pittsburgh, PA 15213
[John Lennon]

# The Beatle-Infested Web

So far in this chapter, I've provided you with some pretty traditional means of communicating with fellow Beatle fans and gleaning info about the group. However, as we approach the 21st century, there's now also a state-of-the-art device that can help you out in this respect. It may not be quite as fulfilling as attending a convention, but it's a very powerful tool that will bring you into contact with fans in all four corners of the earth. It's the personal computer.

Linked to a modem and utilizing an online software package, the computer enables people to catch up with the latest news, relay info, and even discuss different topics with one another. Needless to say, one of the hottest topics is Beatles trivia. There's always an immense number of Beatles Websites, where you'll find fans perhaps appraising Beatles product, asking questions, answering queries, or just indulging in Beatles small-talk.

On the other hand, you may want to subscribe to Usenet newsgroups. Again, each Web browser operates differently, but all of them allow access. In this regard the relevant groups are: "rec.music.beatles," "rec.music.beatles.info," and "rec.music.beatles.moderated."

**With a Little Help**
It's one thing for me to talk to you about Websites and browsers, but what if you're not familiar with computer technology or terminology? Just switching a computer on could be an ordeal. Well, if you're nodding your head, don't panic. Just take a look at *The Complete Idiot's Guide to the Internet*, and all will be revealed.

## Places of Interest

During the Beatle years, fans would often hang around outside the band members' homes, their office building in Central London, or perhaps the EMI recording facility in Abbey Road. Some would even pay visits to John, Paul, George, and Ringo's immediate relatives. Yet while the activity of Beatle-spotting has declined sharply since the group's demise, the number of popular Beatle-related tourist haunts has increased dramatically. These days, the places where they once lived, worked, played, or even passed through have turned into virtual shrines where the faithful pay homage.

Of course, some are of particular note. My aim here is not to provide you with a comprehensive list of all of the places that the avid fan should visit. There are entire books specializing in that. Instead, I am just going to list the more important and/or interesting locations in three major cities: Liverpool, where John, Paul, George, and Ringo grew up and launched themselves as musicians; London, where they spent a lot of their time once they had achieved success; and New York City, where they experienced some of the most overwhelming symptoms of Beatlemania, and where John Lennon is immortalized.

**With a Little Help**
While "Beatles" or the names of any of the Fab Four are obvious and productive searchwords when trying to locate Beatles Websites, you should also try entering the names of the record companies and labels that have released the group's product. Capitol, EMI, and Parlophone all have their own Websites, and if you check them out you'll sometimes find that they feature special Beatles-related pages.

This should get you started on your travels. Then, if you get the taste for searching out the sites, your curiosity will take you further.

(Please note: Aside from the high-profile Dakota building where Yoko Ono still resides, for reasons of privacy none of The Beatles' current homes are listed here.)

## On the Mersey Beat

Here are the Liverpool addresses where John, Paul, George, and Ringo lived during the 1940s and '50s:

*"Mendips," the house in the pleasant Liverpool suburb of Woolton where John grew up with his Aunt Mimi and Uncle George.*
©Richard Buskin

➤ **John:**

➤ 9 Newcastle Road, Wavertree (with mother, Julia).

➤ 251 Menlove Avenue, Woolton (with Aunt Mimi and Uncle George Smith).

➤ 3 Gambier Terrace (with art-college students, including Stuart Sutcliffe).

➤ **Paul:**

➤ 72 Western Avenue, Speke.

➤ 20 Forthlin Road, Allerton.

➤ **George:**

➤ 12 Arnold Grove, Wavertree.

➤ 25 Upton Green, Speke.

➤ 174 Mackett's Lane, Woolton.

➤ **Ringo:**
  ➤ 9 Madryn Street, Liverpool 8.
  ➤ 10 Admiral Grove, Liverpool 8.

The following are some (but not all) of the educational establishments that The Beatles attended:

➤ Dovedale Road Infant and Junior School, Dovedale Road, Liverpool 18. (Attended by both John and George.)

➤ Quarry Bank Grammar School (now Calderstones Community Comprehensive School), Harthill Road, Liverpool 18. (John.)

➤ The Liverpool Institute (now LIPA, the Liverpool Institute for the Performing Arts), Hope Street/Mount Street. (Paul and George.)

➤ Liverpool College of Art, Hope Street/Mount Street. (John.)

## With a Little Help

If you wish to tour the Beatle sites in an organized way or visit a Fab museum, here are some handy phone numbers. (If you're dialing from inside the UK, omit the "+44" and replace it with a "0.")

➤ Magical Mystery Tour bus/Cavern City Tours Ltd: +44-151-236-9091
➤ The Beatles Story (Museum): +44-151-709-1963
➤ Merseyside Welcome Center: +44-151-709-3631

The Quarry Men and The Beatles, in all of their various guises, performed at many, many local venues. Here are some of the more notable ones (several of which no longer exist, even though the sites still remain):

➤ St. Peter's Church. Church Road, Woolton. (Where Paul first saw The Quarry Men and met John.)

➤ Casbah Coffee Club, 8 Hayman's Green, West Derby. (Basement venue in the family home of onetime drummer, Pete Best.)

➤ Jacaranda Coffee Bar, 23 Slater Street, Liverpool. (City centre venue run by early Beatles booking agent, Allan Williams.)

➤ Aintree Institute, Longmoor Lane, Aintree. (A popular Beatles haunt.)

➤ Town Hall Ballroom, Hatton Hill Road, Litherland. (Venue where, on December 27, 1961, the band first experienced the frenzied crowd reaction that would later be known as Beatlemania.)

➤ Cavern Club, 10 Mathew Street, Liverpool. (Legendary basement venue where The Beatles made nearly 300 appearances. Long gone, it is now memorialized by the Cavern Walks shopping precinct just a few feet away from the original.)

➤ The Grapes, Mathew Street, Liverpool. (The pub—close to The Cavern—where The Beatles and their friends drank. The Cavern didn't serve alcohol.)

The following are some other places in Liverpool where you may wish to have your photo taken:

**I Should Have Known Better**

Although The Beatles song "Strawberry Fields Forever" takes its title from the Salvation Army home where John and his friends used to attend summer fetes during the late 1940s and early '50s, the place itself is actually named Strawberry *Field*. The building is no longer there, but the entrance and sign have been preserved for the benefit of tourists and fans.

➤ Penny Lane, Liverpool 18. (As in the song of the same name, you'll actually see "the barber's shop," the fire station, and "the shelter in the middle of the roundabout.")

➤ Strawberry Field, Beaconsfield Road, Liverpool 25. (The Salvation Army home, not far from where John lived on Menlove Avenue, which lent its name to one of his most famous songs.)

➤ 197 Queen's Drive, Childwall. (Brian Epstein's family home.)

➤ NEMS, 12-14 Whitechapel. (The city center music store run by Brian Epstein when he was first informed about The Beatles.)

➤ John Lennon Drive, Paul McCartney Way, George Harrison Close, Ringo Starr Drive. (Streets named after the Fab Four on the Kensington Fields Estate, Liverpool 6.)

# Swinging Around London

As has already been thoroughly documented elsewhere, there are more than 400 Beatles sites in the vast London area and close by. If you only have a day or two to search some out, then stock up with a few rolls of film and try to take in these places:

➤ Abbey Road Studios, 3 Abbey Road, St. John's Wood, NW8. (Perhaps *the* most popular Beatles site. And remember, if you are facing towards the front of the building, the relevant zebra-striped pedestrian crossing is the one just to the left of you!)

➤ 7 Cavendish Avenue, St. John's Wood, NW8. (Where Paul lived from 1966 to 1978, around the corner from Abbey Road.)

➤ Marylebone Station, Grand Central Street, NW1. (Pronounced "marry-le-bone," this is the train station featured at the beginning of The Beatles' movie *A Hard Day's Night*.)

➤ EMI House, 20 Manchester Square, W1. (Formerly the HQ of EMI Records, inside which The Beatles posed for the cover of their first album, *Please Please Me*.)

➤ Apple boutique, 94 Baker Street, W1. (The Beatles' former clothes store, now an employment bureau.)

➤ Apple Corps, 3 Savile Row, W1. (Site of The Beatles' former company HQ, where fans would gather and where, on January 30, 1969, the group was filmed performing on the roof for the *Let It Be* movie.)

**I Should Have Known Better**

If you're thinking of being photographed in a similar pose to The Beatles on the cover of their *Please Please Me* album, as well as those of the *1962–1966* and *1967–1970* compilation sets (known, respectively, as the "Red" and "Blue" albums), then you won't have much luck standing outside 20 Manchester Square. The Fab Four, you see, were looking down towards the entrance from a location on the *inside* of the building!

➤ Prince of Wales Theatre, 31 Coventry Street, W1. (Location of The Beatles' most famous British concert, the 1963 Royal Command Performance.)

➤ Scala Theatre (demolished), Tottenham Street, W1. (Now replaced by a different building, the Scala was where the TV concert scenes in *A Hard Day's Night* were shot. The rear entrance to the Scala was in Tottenham Street, and adjacent you may recognize the Charlotte Mews alley out of which The Beatles run in the film.)

➤ Hammersmith Odeon (now the Apollo), Queen Caroline Street, W6. (The cinema-turned-concert-venue where The Beatles performed their "Christmas Show" and some gigs in 1964 and 1965. Walk around to the back of the building and you'll see an iron staircase. This is the fire escape that the Fab Four run down in the film *A Hard Day's Night*, commencing the famous "Can't Buy Me Love" sequence. Note: The field into which they run is not here, but in a completely different location.)

➤ 24 Chapel Street, SW1. (The principal London residence of Beatles manager, Brian Epstein. He died here on August 27, 1967.)

➤ "Kenwood," Wood Lane (off Cavendish Road), St. George's Hill Estate, Weybridge, Surrey. (Home, from 1964 to 1968, of John, Cynthia, and Julian Lennon.)

➤ "Sunny Heights," South Road, St. George's Hill Estate, Weybridge, Surrey. (Home of Ringo and his family, 1965–1968. Some of the *Magical Mystery Tour* film footage, tying in with the song "Blue Jay Way," was shot in the garden here.)

➤ "Kinfauns" (now "High Walls"), 16 Claremont Drive, Esher, Surrey. (Home of George and Pattie Harrison, 1965–1969. This housed a studio in which The Beatles recorded demo tracks for the *White Album*.)

➤ "Tittenhurst," London Road, Sunningdale, Ascot, Berkshire. (Home of John and Yoko, 1969–1971, and owned by by Ringo Starr, 1973–1988. It was here, on August 22, 1969, that The Beatles posed for their last-ever photo session, and it was also where John's 1971 *Imagine* album and videos were produced.)

## Some Time in New York City

Here are some New York sites that are significant to the whole Beatles story and beyond:

➤ Plaza Hotel, 5th Ave at 59th St. (The hotel where fans laid siege during The Beatles first U.S. visit in February 1964.)

➤ Ed Sullivan Theater, Broadway & West 53rd St. (The TV studio from which, on February 9, 1964, The Beatles were introduced into more than 23 million homes across America.)

**I Want to Tell You**

"Dear Paul, I am 8. I saw you on Ed Sullivan. I think you are wonderful. My mother wants to know why you came to America."

—Letter from Diane P., Ann Arbor, Michigan, 1964

➤ Carnegie Hall, 7th Ave & West 57th St. (Legendary concert venue where The Beatles performed two legendary shows on February 12, 1964.)

➤ Shea Stadium, 126th St & Roosevelt Ave, Queens. (Home of the New York Mets baseball team, where a then world record 55,600 hysterical fans saw The Beatles perform on August 15, 1965.)

➤ 105 Bank Street, Greenwich Village. (Where John and Yoko lived in a two-room apartment on their move to New York in 1971.)

➤ The Dakota, 1 West 72nd St. (Apartment building where John and Yoko moved to in 1972, and outside which John was gunned down on December 8, 1980.)

➤ Roosevelt Hospital, 428 West 59th St. (The hospital to which John was rushed, and where he was pronounced dead, after being shot.)

➤ Strawberry Fields, Central Park West. (The portion of Central Park, facing the Dakota building, dedicated to John's memory.)

*The mosaic center-piece to Strawberry Fields in New York, bearing the message that has become part of John Lennon's legacy.*
©Richard Buskin

## The Least You Need to Know

➤ Beatlefests and conventions are a great way to hook up with other Beatle People.

➤ You can catch up on all of the latest news and gossip via fanzines and the Internet.

➤ You'll need to travel far and wide if you want to take in all of the Beatles-related sights in Liverpool, London, and New York.

# Beatles Chronology

Below you'll find a selective listing of events that, in one way or another, had a significant impact on The Beatles and/or their careers together and separately. Only a few items relating specifically to the group are listed after 1969.

**May 20, 1930:** Harold Harrison and Louise French, parents of George, are married.

**September 19, 1934:** Brian Samuel Epstein, The Beatles' future manager, is born.

**1936:** Richard Starkey and Elsie Gleave, parents of Richard Starkey (Ringo Starr), are married.

**December 3, 1938:** Alfred Lennon and Julia Stanley, parents of John, are married.

**June 23, 1940:** Stuart Sutcliffe, future Beatle, is born in Edinburgh, Scotland.

**July 7, 1940:** Richard Starkey (Ringo Starr) is born at the Royal Liverpool Children's Hospital.

**October 9, 1940:** John Winston Lennon is born at Oxford Street Maternity Hospital, Liverpool.

**November 24, 1941:** Randolph Peter Best (Pete Best) is born in Madras, India.

**Spring 1941:** John is left in the care of his aunt, Mary Smith (Aunt Mimi), and Uncle George.

**1941:** James McCartney and Mary Patricia Mohin, parents of Paul, are married.

**April 1942:** Alfred Lennon, having been away at sea for long periods, leaves Julia for good, while she moves in with her new man, John Dykins.

**June 18, 1942:** James Paul McCartney (Paul McCartney) is born at Walton Hospital, Liverpool.

**February 25, 1943:** George Harrison is born at 12 Arnold Grove, Wavertree, Liverpool.

**1943:** Ringo's parents divorce.

**July 1946:** Freddie Lennon takes John on a holiday to Blackpool, trying to convince him to leave the country with him. Julia turns up and the parents then ask the child to choose between them. After initially choosing his father, John changes his mind and opts for Julia.

**April 17, 1953:** Ringo's mother, Elsie, marries Harry Graves.

**June 5, 1955:** John's uncle, George Smith, dies suddenly.

**October 31, 1956:** Paul's mother, Mary Patricia McCartney, dies suddenly.

**May 1956:** John's world is turned around when he hears Elvis Presley's recording of "Heartbreak Hotel" for the first time.

**March 1957:** John forms The Black Jacks skiffle group with sidekick Pete Shotton, before renaming it The Quarry Men after a week and recruiting other schoolmates.

**June 9, 1957:** First official Quarry Men engagement, auditioning in Carol Levis' "TV Star Search" at Liverpool's Empire Theatre.

**July 6, 1957:** Paul attends a Quarry Men performance at the St. Peter's Church Garden Fete in Woolton, Liverpool, where he meets John for the first time.

**July 20, 1957:** Paul is invited to join The Quarry Men. He accepts but doesn't make his debut for several weeks.

**August 7, 1957:** The Quarry Men perform at Liverpool jazz venue, The Cavern Club.

**October 18, 1957:** Paul makes his Quarry Men debut at the New Clubmoor Hall in Liverpool, but flunks his lead guitar solo. Hereafter he plays rhythm.

**February 6, 1958:** The probable date of George Harrison's first encounter with The Quarry Men, at Wilson Hall in Garston, Liverpool.

**July 15, 1958:** While she is crossing Menlove Avenue after visiting Mimi, John's mother, Julia, is killed when she is struck by a car being driven by a drunken, off-duty policeman.

**Mid-1958:** The Quarry Men, comprising John, Paul, George, and pianist John "Duff" Lowe, but without a drummer, tape amateur recordings of Buddy Holly's "That'll Be The Day" and the Harrison-McCartney composition "In Spite Of All The Danger" at a home studio owned by Percy Phillips.

**August 29, 1959:** The Quarry Men, now comprising John, Paul, George, and Ken Brown on bass, but without a drummer, play at the opening night of the Casbah Coffee Club, owned by Mona Best, mother of Pete.

**October 10, 1959:** After a furious row Ken Brown quits The Quarry Men, leaving the hardcore trio of John, Paul, and George.

**October-November 1959:** The band changes its name to Johnny and the Moondogs before reverting to The Quarry Men.

**January 1960:** John's Art College friend, Stuart Sutcliffe, joins The Quarry Men as their bass player.

**Early May, 1960:** The Quarry Men become The Beatals.

**May 10-early June:** The Beatals become The Silver Beetles.

**May 10, 1960:** The Silver Beetles audition to back Billy Fury, but Fury's manager, Larry Parnes, books them to tour Scotland behind another of his singers, Johnny Gentle.

**May 20-28, 1960:** The Silver Beetles, featuring "Long John" Lennon, Paul "Ramon" (McCartney), "Carl" Harrison, Stu de Stael (Sutcliffe), and Tommy Moore on drums, tour Scotland with Johnny Gentle.

**Early-mid June, 1960:** The Silver Beetles become The Beatles before reverting back to The Silver Beetles.

**Early July, 1960:** The Silver Beetles become The Silver Beatles.

**July 1960:** The Silver Beatles back a stripper named Janice at the New Cabaret Artistes club, owned by booking agent/manager Allan Williams. For a short time afterwards the band is joined by Norman Chapman on drums.

**August 12, 1960:** After a quick audition Pete Best joins The Silver Beatles in time for their first trip to Hamburg.

**August 16, 1960:** The band changes its name permanently to The Beatles and sets off for Hamburg.

**August 17-October 3, 1960:** The Beatles play at the Indra Club on Hamburg's Grosse Freiheit.

**October 4-November 30, 1960:** The Beatles play at the nearby but larger Kaiserkeller Club.

**October 15, 1960:** John, Paul, George, and Ringo record together for the first time, along with bassist Walter Eymond of Rory Storm and the Hurricanes, in the tiny Akustic Studio located behind Hamburg's train station.

**November 21, 1960:** George is deported from West Germany for being underage and therefore ineligible for nightclub work after midnight.

**November 29, 1960:** Paul and Pete are thrown in jail for supposedly "setting fire" to their living quarters at the Bambi Kino.

**November 30, 1960:** Paul and Pete are released from jail but then deported from West Germany. John leaves voluntarily on November 10, but Stu remains in Hamburg to be with his new love, Astrid Kirchherr.

**December 27, 1960:** A performance at the Litherland Town Hall in Liverpool incites the first scenes of Beatlemania.

**February 9, 1961:** The Beatles perform the first of nearly 300 gigs at The Cavern Club. The Quarry Men also appeared here more than three years earlier.

**April 1-July 1, 1961:** The Beatles make their second trip to Hamburg and perform at the Top Ten Club on the Reeperbahn.

**June 22-23, 1961:** The Beatles play in a professional recording studio for the first time, backing singer Tony Sheridan and performing a couple of numbers without him for producer Bert Kaempfert.

**October 28, 1961:** According to Brian Epstein's later recollections, a Liverpool youth named Raymond Jones walks into the Epstein family record store, NEMS, and asks for a copy of "My Bonnie," as recorded by Tony Sheridan and The Beatles.

**November 9, 1961:** Accompanied by his assistant, Alistair Taylor, Brian Epstein visits the Cavern during a lunchtime session and sees The Beatles for the first time.

**December 3, 1961:** The Beatles and Brian Epstein hold their first business meeting.

**December 6, 1961:** The Beatles agree in principle to Brian Epstein becoming their manager. They meet again on December 10 to discuss the terms.

**January 1, 1962:** The Beatles audition for Decca Records A&R man Mike Smith, recording 15 songs.

**January 4, 1962:** The Beatles top a popularity poll in the local music paper *Mersey Beat*.

**January 24, 1962:** The Beatles sign a management contract with Brian Epstein. Brian himself doesn't add his signature until October of 1962.

**Early February, 1962:** Decca Records turn down The Beatles.

**February 13, 1962:** Brian Epstein meets George Martin, EMI Records' head of A&R, and plays him the recording of The Beatles' failed Decca audition.

**March 7, 1962:** The Beatles make their radio debut, performing at Manchester's Playhouse Theatre, where they appear in suits for the first time.

**April 10, 1962:** Stuart Sutcliffe dies of a brain hemorrhage at the age of 21.

**April 13-May 31, 1962:** The Beatles make their third trip to Hamburg, performing at the newly opened Star-Club on the Grosse Freiheit.

**May 9, 1962:** George Martin meets Brian Epstein for a second time and offers The Beatles a recording contract dependent on an audition/recording session scheduled for June 6.

**June 6, 1962:** The Beatles visit the EMI Studios in Abbey Road for the first time, performing an audition/recording session. On the strength of this they are formally offered a record deal.

**August 15, 1962:** Ringo Starr is approached to join The Beatles. He accepts.

**August 16, 1962:** Pete Best is sacked as The Beatles' drummer.

**August 18, 1962:** Ringo Starr makes his debut as a Beatle, at Hulme Hall in Port Sunlight, Birkenhead.

**August 22, 1962:** The Beatles perform before TV cameras for the first time when they are filmed at The Cavern by Granada Television. Deemed unsuitable, the footage is shelved until the group becomes famous the following year.

**August 23, 1962:** John marries Cynthia Powell at Liverpool's Mount Pleasant Register Office.

**September 4, 1962:** The Beatles return to Abbey Road for their first formal recording session with Ringo Starr.

**October 5, 1962:** The Beatles' first single, "Love Me Do"/"PS I Love You," is released in the UK. It eventually peaks at #17.

**October 17, 1962:** The Beatles make their TV debut with a live appearance on Granada Television's *People And Places*.

**November 1-14, 1962:** The Beatles make their fourth trip to Hamburg, playing at the Star-Club.

**December 18-31, 1962:** The Beatles make their fifth and final trip to Hamburg, playing at the Star-Club.

**January 2-6, 1963:** The Beatles travel around Scotland for their first concert tour.

**February 2, 1963:** The Beatles undertake their first proper package tour of Britain.

**February 11, 1963:** The Beatles record 10 new tracks for their first album, *Please Please Me*, in just under 10 hours.

**Late February, 1963:** The "Please Please Me" single tops the *New Musical Express* and *Disc* magazine charts, even though it peaks at #2 on the BBC chart.

**March 9, 1963:** The Beatles embark on their second British concert tour.

**March 22, 1963:** The Beatles' first album, *Please Please Me*, is released in the UK. It will be the first of 11 Beatles albums to top the British charts during the next seven years.

**April 8, 1963:** A son, John Charles Julian, is born to John and Cynthia Lennon.

**April 12, 1963:** The Beatles' third single, "From Me To You," is released in the UK. This will commence a cycle of eleven consecutive singles by the band to top the British charts through 1966.

**May 18, 1963:** The Beatles embark on their third British tour.

**August 3, 1963:** The Beatles play for the last time at The Cavern Club.

**October 13, 1963:** The Beatles' live appearance on the network TV show, *Val Parnell's Sunday Night at the London Palladium*, causes a sensation across Britain.

**October 23, 1963:** The Beatles fly to Sweden for their first-ever foreign concert tour.

**October 31, 1963:** Thousands of fans gather at London Airport to greet The Beatles on their return from Sweden. On hand to witness the pandemonium is Ed Sullivan.

**November 1, 1963:** First night of *The Beatles' Autumn Tour* of Britain.

**November 2, 1963:** Britain's national *Daily Mirror* newspaper coins the term "Beatlemania."

**November 4, 1963:** The Beatles appear at the *Royal Command Performance*, where John asks the glitterati to rattle their jewelry.

**January 3, 1964:** A clip of The Beatles performing is shown on *The Jack Paar Show* in the U.S.

**January 15, 1964:** The Beatles perform in Versailles, France prior to commencing a two-week season at the Olympia Theater in Paris.

**January 16, 1964:** The Beatles learn that, in the January 25 edition of America's *Cashbox* magazine, "I Want To Hold Your Hand" has jumped 43 places to top the singles chart.

**February 7, 1964:** The Beatles arrive at Kennedy Airport in New York.

**February 9, 1964:** The Beatles make their landmark television appearance on *The Ed Sullivan Show*.

**March 2, 1964:** The Beatles commence shooting their first feature film, *A Hard Day's Night*.

**April 3, 1964:** The Beatles hold the top six positions in a local singles chart in Sydney, Australia.

**April 4, 1964:** The Beatles have the top five positions in America's *Billboard* singles chart.

**June 3, 1964:** Ringo collapses with tonsillitis and pharyngitis just prior to The Beatles' first "World Tour." He is replaced in Denmark, the Netherlands, Hong Kong, and Australia by 24-year-old session drummer, Jimmy Nicol.

**June 15, 1964:** Ringo rejoins The Beatles in Australia, and performs with them there and in New Zealand.

**July 6, 1964:** *A Hard Day's Night* receives its royal world charity premiere at the London Pavilion cinema.

**August 18, 1964:** The Beatles leave London Airport for their first North American concert tour.

**February 11, 1965:** Ringo marries Mary (Maureen) Cox.

**February 22, 1965:** The Beatles fly to the Bahamas to begin shooting their second film, later to be titled *Help!*

**May 20, 1965:** The Beatles record their last-ever music session for BBC Radio.

**June 11, 1965:** At midnight it is announced that The Beatles are to be awarded with MBEs.

**July 29, 1965:** *Help!* receives its royal world charity premiere at the London Pavilion.

**August 15, 1965:** The Beatles open their second U.S. tour with a landmark concert at New York's Shea Stadium, witnessed by a then-record audience of 55,600.

**August 27, 1965:** The Beatles meet Elvis Presley at his Beverly Hills home on Perugia Way.

**September 13, 1965:** A son named Zak is born to Ringo and Maureen Starkey.

**October 26, 1965:** The Beatles receive their MBEs from the Queen inside the Great Throne Room at Buckingham Palace.

**December 3, 1965:** The Beatles embark on what turns out to be their last-ever UK tour.

**January 21, 1966:** George marries Patricia (Pattie) Ann Boyd.

**March 4, 1966:** London's *Evening Standard* newspaper publishes an interview with John in which he states that The Beatles are "more popular than Jesus now..."

**May 1, 1966:** The Beatles give their last-ever British concert performance.

**July 5, 1966:** The Beatles run into major problems in the Philippines after being accused of "snubbing" the First Lady, Imelda Marcos.

**July 29, 1966:** American teen magazine *Datebook* publishes John's *Evening Standard* interview, asserting that he said The Beatles are "bigger" than Jesus. Uproar ensues, especially in the country's "Bible-belt" region.

**August 29, 1966:** The Beatles give their last-ever concert performance at San Francisco's Candlestick Park.

**November 9, 1966:** John attends a private preview of Yoko Ono's art exhibition, *Unfinished Paintings and Objects*, at London's Indica Gallery.

**March 30, 1967:** The famous cover photo for the *Sgt. Pepper's Lonely Hearts Club Band* album is shot by Michael Cooper.

**April 19, 1967:** A legal business partnership, The Beatles & Co, is formed to bind the group together until 1977.

**May 20, 1967:** The BBC imposes a radio and TV ban on "A Day In The Life" due to the song's overt drug references.

**May 26, 1967:** First release, in the UK, of the landmark *Sgt. Pepper* album.

**June 25, 1967:** The Beatles perform "All You Need Is Love" before a worldwide television audience.

**August 19, 1967:** A second son, Jason, is born to Ringo and Maureen Starkey.

**August 24, 1967:** The Beatles, wives, and friends, attend a lecture by the Maharishi Mahesh Yogi at London's Hilton Hotel.

**August 25, 1967:** The Beatles and their entourage travel to Bangor, North Wales, to attend a weekend seminar by the Maharishi.

**August 27, 1967:** Brian Epstein is found dead in the bed of his London home.

**August 29, 1967:** Brian Epstein's funeral is held in Liverpool. Strictly a family affair, it is not attended by The Beatles.

**September 11, 1967:** The Beatles start shooting their own TV movie, *Magical Mystery Tour*.

**December 5, 1967:** John and George attend a party heralding the opening of The Beatles' Apple Boutique two days later.

**December 25, 1967:** Paul and Jane Asher end more than four years of speculation by announcing their engagement.

**December 26, 1967:** BBC1 Television transmits the world premiere of *Magical Mystery Tour*.

**Mid-February, 1968:** The Beatles and their entourage fly to Rishikesh, India, to study Transcendental Meditation under the Maharishi Mahesh Yogi.

**May 11, 1968:** John and Paul fly to New York for five days, during which time they announce the setting up of their Apple business venture, and John also takes the opportunity to denounce the Maharishi.

**May 22, 1968:** John and Yoko Ono appear in public for the first time, attending a launch party and press conference for another Apple boutique.

**July 17, 1968:** The Beatles' animated feature film, *Yellow Submarine*, receives its world premiere at the London Pavilion.

**July 20, 1968:** Jane Asher announces that her relationship with Paul is over.

**July 31, 1968:** The Beatles' Apple Boutique on Baker Street closes down, while they also relinquish control of their second clothing store.

**August 22, 1968:** Cynthia Lennon sues John for divorce on the grounds of his adultery with Yoko Ono.

**August 23, 1968:** Ringo quits The Beatles during recording sessions for the *White Album*.

**September 3, 1968:** Ringo rejoins The Beatles.

**September 30, 1968:** Hunter Davies' authorized biography, *The Beatles*, is published in the UK.

**October 18, 1968:** John and Yoko are charged with possession of cannabis and obstructing the police.

**November 29, 1968:** John and Yoko's controversial *Two Virgins* album is released in the UK.

**January 2, 1969:** The Beatles begin filming their troubled *Get Back* project (eventually re-titled *Let It Be*).

**January 30, 1969:** The Beatles' give their last-ever live performance, atop the roof of their Apple office building in Central London.

**February 3, 1969:** Allen Klein becomes The Beatles' business manager.

**February 4, 1969:** The New York firm of Eastman and Eastman is appointed as general counsel to Apple Corps.

**March 12, 1969:** Paul marries Linda Louise Eastman, and George and Pattie are busted for cannabis possession.

**March 20, 1969:** John marries Yoko Ono in Gibraltar.

**March 25, 1969:** John and Yoko commence their seven-day "bed-in" for peace at the Hilton Hotel in Amsterdam, Holland.

**April 22, 1969:** John formally changes his middle name to Ono during a ceremony on the roof of the Apple building.

**May 8, 1969:** Paul refuses to sign his name to a contract appointing Allen Klein's company, ABKCO, as business manager of several of The Beatles' own companies.

**May 26, 1969:** John and Yoko commence their second "bed-in" for peace, at the Queen Elizabeth Hotel in Montreal, Canada.

**August 8, 1969:** The Beatles are photographed walking along the zebra-crossing outside the EMI Studios in North London, for the cover of *Abbey Road*.

**August 20, 1969:** All four Beatles are together for the last time inside a recording studio, when they attend a mix and album running-order session at Abbey Road.

**August 22, 1969:** The Beatles are photographed together for the last time, in the Tittenhurst Park grounds of John's home in Sunningdale, Ascot.

**August 28, 1969:** A daughter, Mary, is born to Linda and Paul McCartney.

**Mid-September, 1969:** John decides to quit The Beatles. He tells the group of his decision shortly after returning from Toronto, Canada, where he has performed a concert with The Plastic Ono Band.

**November 25, 1969:** John returns his MBE to the Queen.

**January 4, 1970:** The Beatles, minus John, participate in their last-ever recording session... during John's lifetime.

**April 10, 1970:** Newspapers around the world carry Paul's statement that The Beatles will never work together again.

**May 13, 1970:** The Beatles' film, *Let It Be*, receives its world premiere in New York. None of the group members attend.

**July 7, 1970:** George's mother, Louise, dies.

**November 11, 1970:** A daughter, Lee Parkin, is born to Ringo and Maureen Starkey.

**December 31, 1970:** Paul files a lawsuit in the London High Court seeking dissolution of the partnership, The Beatles & Co, as well as the appointment of a receiver to handle the group's affairs.

**February 19, 1971:** The hearing for the dissolution of the Beatles & Co partnership commences in the London High Court.

**September 13, 1971:** A second daughter, Stella Nina, is born to Paul and Linda McCartney.

**March 31, 1973:** Allen Klein and ABKCO reach the end of their term as business managers of Apple and other Beatles companies.

**August 14, 1974:** The first Beatles-related stage show, *John, Paul, George, Ringo...and Bert*, opens in London.

**January 9, 1975:** The Beatles & Co partnership is formally dissolved in the London High Court.

**July 17, 1975:** Ringo and Maureen Starkey are divorced.

**October 9, 1975:** A son, Sean Taro Ono, is born to John and Yoko.

**January 5, 1976:** The Beatles' former assistant, Mal Evans, is shot and killed by Los Angeles police.

**January 26, 1976:** The Beatles' recording contract with EMI expires.

**March 18, 1976:** Paul's Father, James, dies.

**April 1, 1976:** John's father, Freddie, dies.

**January 10, 1977:** All outstanding litigation between Allen Klein and The Beatles is settled.

**May 4, 1977:** A live album, *The Beatles at the Hollywood Bowl*, is released in the U.S. (May 6 in the UK.)

**May 25, 1977:** *The Beatles Live! At the Star-Club in Hamburg, Germany, 1962* is released in the UK. (June 13 in the U.S.)

**May 1978:** George's father, Harold, dies.

**June 9, 1977:** George and Pattie Harrison are divorced.

**September 12, 1977:** A son, James Louis, is born to Paul and Linda McCartney.

**August 1, 1978:** A son, Dhani, is born to George and his girlfriend, Olivia Arias.

**September 2, 1978:** George and Olivia marry.

**May 19, 1979:** Paul, George, and Ringo reunite for a jam session at a garden party celebrating the marriage of Eric Clapton to the former Pattie Harrison.

**December 8, 1980:** John Lennon is shot dead at the age of 40.

**December 14, 1980:** At 2:00 p.m. EST, 7:00 p.m. GMT, 10 minutes of silence is observed around the world in memory of John Lennon.

**May 15, 1981:** George's tribute to John, "All Those Years Ago," featuring backing by Paul and Ringo, is released as a single in the UK.

**April 9, 1984:** Liverpool opens its first permanent tribute to the Fab Four, the Beatle City exhibition center.

**March 29, 1986:** Beatles recordings are officially released in the Soviet Union for the first time.

**February 26, 1987:** The first four official Beatles compact discs—*Please Please Me, With The Beatles, A Hard Day's Night,* and *Beatles For Sale*—are released by EMI.

**June 1, 1987:** On the 20th anniversary of the official release date of *Sgt. Pepper's Lonely Hearts Club Band*, Granada Television in the UK screens a two-hour documentary entitled *It Was Twenty Years Ago Today*, featuring interviews with Paul and George.

**December 5, 1991:** John's aunt, Mimi Smith, dies.

**November 30, 1994:** The Beatles album, *Live At The BBC*, is released in the UK. (December 6 in the U.S.)

**November 19, 1995:** The three-part, six-hour documentary, *The Beatles Anthology*, starts airing on ABC-TV in the U.S. (It airs in six parts in the UK during December.)

**November 21, 1995:** The double album, *The Beatles Anthology 1*, is released worldwide.

**December 4, 1995:** The new Beatles single, "Free As A Bird," is released in the UK. (December 12 in the U.S.)

**March 4, 1996:** The second new Beatles single, "Real Love," is released in the UK. (March 12 in the U.S.)

**March 18, 1996:** The double album, *The Beatles Anthology 2*, is released in the UK. (March 19 in the U.S.)

**September 5, 1996:** The extended eight-part, ten-hour version of the *Beatles Anthology* documentary is released on video and laser disc in the U.S.

**October 28, 1996:** The double album, *The Beatles Anthology 3*, is released in the UK. (October 29 in the U.S.)

# The Beatles on the Charts

## Single Releases and Chart Positions

Following are the singles that were released by EMI in the UK between 1962 and 1970, and the two *Anthology* singles, as well as the chart positions published by the widely recognized *Record Retailer* and, after February 13, 1969, British Market Research Bureau.

| Single | Release Date | Position |
| --- | --- | --- |
| Love Me Do/<br>PS I Love You | Oct. 5, 1962 | 17 |
| Please Please Me/<br>Ask Me Why | Jan. 11, 1963 | 2 |
| From Me To You/<br>Thank You Girl | April 11, 1963 | 1 |
| She Loves You/<br>I'll Get You | Aug. 23, 1963 | 1 |
| I Want To Hold Your Hand/<br>This Boy | Nov. 29, 1963 | 1 |
| Can't Buy Me Love/<br>You Can't Do That | March 20, 1964 | 1 |
| A Hard Day's Night/<br>Things We Said Today | July 10, 1964 | 1 |
| I Feel Fine/<br>She's A Woman | Nov. 27, 1964 | 1 |

| Single | Release Date | Position |
|---|---|---|
| Ticket To Ride/<br>Yes It Is | April 9, 1965 | 1 |
| Help!/<br>I'm Down | July 23, 1965 | 1 |
| We Can Work It Out/<br>Day Tripper | Dec. 3, 1965 | 1 |
| Paperback Writer/<br>Rain | June 10, 1966 | 1 |
| Eleanor Rigby/<br>Yellow Submarine | Aug. 5, 1966 | 1 |
| Strawberry Fields Forever/<br>Penny Lane | Feb. 17, 1967 | 2 |
| All You Need Is Love/<br>Baby, You're A Rich Man | July 7, 1967 | 1 |
| Hello, Goodbye/<br>I Am The Walrus | Nov. 24, 1967 | 1 |
| Lady Madonna/<br>The Inner Light | March 15, 1968 | 1 |
| Hey Jude/<br>Revolution | Aug. 30, 1968 | 1 |
| Get Back/<br>Don't Let Me Down | April 11, 1969 | 1 |
| The Ballad Of John And Yoko/<br>Old Brown Shoe | May 30, 1969 | 1 |
| Something/<br>Come Together | Oct. 31, 1969 | 4 |
| Let It Be/<br>You Know My Name<br>(Look Up The Number) | March 6, 1970 | 2 |
| Free As A Bird | Dec. 4, 1995 | 2 |
| Real Love | March 4, 1996 | 4 |

Following are the singles that were released by Vee Jay, Swan, Tollie, and Capitol in the U.S. between 1963 and 1970, and the two *Anthology* singles, as well as the chart positions published by the widely recognized *Billboard* magazine.

| Single | Release Date | Position |
|---|---|---|
| Please Please Me/ Ask Me Why | Feb. 25, 1963 | (Didn't chart) |
| From Me To You/ Thank You Girl | May 27, 1963 | 116 |
| She Loves You/ I'll Get You | Sep. 16, 1963 | 1 |
| I Want To Hold Your Hand/ I Saw Her Standing There | Dec. 26, 1963 | 1 |
| Please Please Me/ From Me To You | Jan. 30, 1964 | 3 |
| Twist And Shout/ There's A Place | March 2, 1964 | 2 |
| Can't Buy Me Love/ You Can't Do That | March 16, 1964 | 1 |
| Do You Want To Know A Secret/ Thank You Girl | March 23, 1964 | 2 |
| Love Me Do/ PS I Love You | April 27, 1964 | 1 |
| Sie Liebt Dich/ I'll Get You | May 21, 1964 | 97 |
| A Hard Day's Night/ I Should Have Known Better | July 13, 1964 | 1 |
| I'll Cry Instead/ I'm Happy Just To Dance With You | July 20, 1964 | 25 |
| And I Love Her/ If I Fell | July 20, 1964 | 12 |
| Matchbox/ Slow Down | Aug. 24, 1964 | 17 |
| I Feel Fine/ She's A Woman | Nov. 23, 1964 | 1 |
| Eight Days A Week/ I Don't Want To Spoil The Party | Feb. 15, 1965 | 1 |

*continues*

| Single | Release Date | Position |
|---|---|---|
| Ticket To Ride/<br>Yes It Is | April 19, 1965 | 1 |
| Help!/<br>I'm Down | July 19, 1965 | 1 |
| Yesterday/<br>Act Naturally | Sep. 13, 1965 | 1 |
| We Can Work It Out/<br>Day Tripper | Dec. 6, 1965 | 1 |
| Nowhere Man/<br>What Goes On | Feb. 21, 1966 | 3 |
| Paperback Writer/<br>Rain | May 30, 1966 | 1 |
| Eleanor Rigby/<br>Yellow Submarine | Aug. 8, 1966 | 2 |
| Strawberry Fields Forever/<br>Penny Lane | Feb. 13, 1967 | 1 |
| All You Need Is Love/<br>Baby, You're A Rich Man | July 17, 1967 | 1 |
| Hello, Goodbye/<br>I Am The Walrus | Nov. 27, 1967 | 1 |
| Lady Madonna/<br>The Inner Light | March 18, 1968 | 4 |
| Hey Jude/<br>Revolution | Aug. 26, 1968 | 1 |
| Get Back/<br>Don't Let Me Down | May 5, 1969 | 1 |
| The Ballad Of John And Yoko/<br>Old Brown Shoe | June 4, 1969 | 8 |
| Something/<br>Come Together | Oct. 6, 1969 | 1 |
| Let It Be/<br>You Know My Name<br>(Look Up The Number) | March 11, 1970 | 1 |
| The Long And Winding Road/<br>For You Blue | May 11, 1970 | 1 |
| Free As A Bird | Dec. 12, 1995 | 6 |
| Real Love | March 12, 1996 | 11 |

# EP Releases and Chart Positions

Following are the four-song extended-play records that were released only in the UK, as well as the chart positions published by *Record Retailer*. (Note: *Magical Mystery Tour* had six songs. )

| EP | Release date | Position |
|---|---|---|
| *Twist And Shout* | July 12, 1963 | 1 |
| *The Beatles' Hits* | Sep. 6, 1963 | 1 |
| *The Beatles (No 1)* | Nov. 1, 1963 | 2 |
| *All My Loving* | Feb. 7, 1964 | 1 |
| *Long Tall Sally* | June 19, 1964 | 1 |
| *Extracts From The Film A Hard Day's Night* | Nov. 6, 1964 | 1 |
| *Extracts From The Album A Hard Day's Night* | Nov. 6, 1964 | 8 |
| *Beatles For Sale* | April 6, 1965 | 1 |
| *Beatles For Sale (No 2)* | June 4, 1965 | 5 |
| *The Beatles' Million Sellers* | Dec. 6, 1965 | 1 |
| *Yesterday* | March 4, 1966 | 1 |
| *Nowhere Man* | July 8, 1966 | 4 |
| *Magical Mystery Tour* | Dec. 8, 1967 | 1 |

# Album Releases and Chart Positions

Following are the albums that were released by EMI in the UK between 1962 and 1970—the only versions that The Beatles took an active interest in—a live album in 1977, and the three *Anthology* sets, as well as the chart positions published by *Record Retailer*. (After 1970 no compilations of previously released material are included. )

| Album | Release Date | Position |
|---|---|---|
| *Please Please Me* | March 22, 1963 | 1 |
| *With The Beatles* | Nov. 22, 1963 | 1 |
| *A Hard Day's Night* | July 10, 1964 | 1 |
| *Beatles For Sale* | Dec. 4, 1964 | 1 |
| *Help!* | Aug. 6, 1965 | 1 |
| *Rubber Soul* | Dec. 3, 1965 | 1 |
| *Revolver* | Aug. 5, 1966 | 1 |

*continues*

| Album | Release Date | Position |
|-------|--------------|----------|
| *A Collection Of Beatles Oldies* | Dec. 9, 1966 | 7 |
| *Sgt. Pepper's Lonely Hearts Club Band* | June 1, 1967 | 1 |
| *The Beatles* | Nov. 22, 1968 | 1 |
| *Yellow Submarine* | Jan. 17, 1969 | 3 |
| *Abbey Road* | Sep. 26, 1969 | 1 |
| *Let It Be* | May 8, 1970 | 1 |
| *The Beatles At The Hollywood Bowl* | May 6, 1977 | 1 |
| *The Beatles—Live At The BBC* | Nov. 30, 1994 | 1 |
| *The Beatles Anthology 1* | Nov. 21, 1995 | 1 |
| *The Beatles Anthology 2* | March 18, 1996 | 1 |
| *The Beatles Anthology 3* | Oct. 28, 1996 | 1 |

Following are the albums that were released by Capitol, UA, and Vee Jay in the U.S. between 1963 and 1970. Prior to the release of *Sgt. Pepper* in 1967, each of these consisted of tracks culled from various sources (including albums with identical names to those in the UK), and The Beatles took little or no interest in how they were compiled. Thereafter, with the exception of the *Magical Mystery Tour* and *Hey Jude* albums, the U.S. and UK releases were identical. There's also the live album released in 1977, and the three *Anthology* sets, as well as the chart positions published by *Billboard* magazine. (After 1970 no compilations of previously released material are included. )

| Album | Release Date | Position |
|-------|--------------|----------|
| *Introducing The Beatles* | July 22, 1963 & Jan. 27, 1964 | 2 |
| *Meet The Beatles* | Jan. 20, 1964 | 1 |
| *The Beatles' Second Album* | April 10, 1964 | 1 |
| *A Hard Day's Night* | June 26, 1964 | 1 |
| *Something New* | July 20, 1964 | 2 |
| *The Beatles' Story* | Nov. 23, 1964 | 7 |
| *Beatles '65* | Dec. 15, 1964 | 1 |
| *The Early Beatles* | March 22, 1965 | 43 |
| *Beatles VI* | June 14, 1965 | 1 |
| *Help!* | Aug. 13, 1965 | 1 |
| *Rubber Soul* | Dec. 6, 1965 | 1 |
| *"Yesterday"... And Today* | June 20, 1966 | 1 |
| *Revolver* | Aug. 8, 1966 | 1 |

| Album | Release Date | Position |
|---|---|---|
| *Sgt. Pepper's Lonely Hearts Club Band* | June 2, 1967 | 1 |
| *Magical Mystery Tour* | Nov. 27, 1967 | 1 |
| *The Beatles* | Nov. 25, 1968 | 1 |
| *Yellow Submarine* | Jan. 13, 1969 | 2 |
| *Abbey Road* | Oct. 1, 1969 | 1 |
| *Hey Jude* | Feb. 26, 1970 | 2 |
| *Let It Be* | May 18, 1970 | 1 |
| *The Beatles at the Hollywood Bowl* | May 4, 1977 | 2 |
| *The Beatles—Live At The BBC* | Dec. 6, 1994 | 3 |
| *The Beatles Anthology 1* | Nov. 21, 1995 | 1 |
| *The Beatles Anthology 2* | March 19, 1996 | 1 |
| *The Beatles Anthology 3* | Oct. 29, 1996 | 1 |

# Films, Videos, and Biopics

## The Beatles' Films

*A Hard Days Night* (1964)
*Help!* (1965)
*Magical Mystery Tour* (1967)
*Yellow Submarine* (1968)
*Let It Be* (1970)

## The Beatles' Official Promo Videos 1965–1970 and 1995

1965: "We Can Work It Out" (three versions)
"Day Tripper" (three versions)
"Help!"
"Ticket To Ride"
"I Feel Fine" (two versions, one unreleased)

1966: "Paperback Writer" (four versions)
"Rain" (three versions)

1967: "Strawberry Fields Forever"
"Penny Lane"
"A Day In The Life"
"Hello, Goodbye" (four versions, one unreleased)

1968: "Lady Madonna"
"Hey Jude" (two versions)
"Revolution" (two versions)

1969: "Get Back"
"Don't Let Me Down"
"The Ballad Of John And Yoko" (two versions)
"Something"

1970: "Let It Be"

# Video Releases

The following is a selective list of *Beatles*-related documentaries and other video releases, both good and bad, some of which are not presently available on videocassette or laser disc:

*All This and World War II* (1976)—War documentary entirely set to Beatles music.

*The Beatles* (1992)—Documentary.

*The Beatles: Alone and Together* (aka *The Legend Continues*) (1990)—Documentary.

*The Beatles Anthology* (1995/96)—The Beatles' official version of their own story.

*Beatles Concert at Budokan 1966* (1993)—Japanese concert footage and documentary.

*Beatles Firsts*—Documentary.

*The Beatles Live In Japan* (1984)—Tokyo concert footage.

*The Beatles Live!—Ready, Steady, Go! Special Edition* (1989)—The band's musical performances from the 1964 TV show *Around The Beatles*.

*The Beatles Story* (1995)—Documentary without music.

*The Beatles: The First U.S. Visit* (1991)—Apple documentary of the February 1964 American trip.

*The Beatles Unauthorized*—Concert and press-conference footage.

*Biography: The Beatles*—Documentary.

*The Compleat Beatles* (1982)—Documentary.

*Fun with the Fab Four* (1987—Newsreel footage plus the Shakespearean sketch from *Around The Beatles*; no music)

*History of The Beatles*—Concert, TV, and newsreel footage.

*Imagine: John Lennon* (1988)—Official documentary of John's life and career, both as a Beatle and a solo artist.

*John Lennon: The Beatles and Beyond*—Beatles and solo concert/interview footage.

*The Making of A Hard Day's Night* (1994)—Authorized documentary.

*Ready, Steady, Go!—The Beatles*—Japanese compilation of all of The Beatles' appearances on the 1960s British TV pop show.

*Yesterday—The Beatles*—Newsreel footage.

# Biopics

Here's a selective list of some of the films featuring actors portraying The Beatles during the band years:

*Backbeat* (1994)—Feature film dramatization of The Beatles' pre-fame years and their relationship with Stuart Sutcliffe.

*Beatlemania* (1981)—Film musical based on the stage show.

*Birth of The Beatles* (1979)—TV dramatization of the band's early years.

*I Wanna Hold Your Hand* (1978)—Feature film about The Beatles' first visit to the U.S. and their appearance on *The Ed Sullivan Show*.

*The Rutles—All You Need Is Cash* (1978)—The most celebrated of all Beatles spoofs, conceived by—and starring—Eric Idle and Neil Innes, with a cameo appearance by George Harrison.

# Recommended Reading

Here's a selective bibliography dealing with some of the other noteworthy books relating to the band, many of which were utilized while researching this *Complete Idiot's Guide.* (The titles and publishers listed are British, unless otherwise stated.)

Baker, Glenn A., *The Beatles Down Under: The 1964 Australia & New Zealand Tour* (Australia: Wild & Woolley, 1982).

Best, Pete and Patrick Doncaster, *Beatle! The Pete Best Story* (Plexus, 1985).

Braun, Michael, *Love Me Do: The Beatles' Progress* (Penguin, 1964).

Brown, Peter and Steven Gaines, *The Love You Make: An Insider's Story Of The Beatles* (Macmillan, 1983).

Buskin, Richard, *John Lennon: His Life and Legend* (U.S.: Publications International, 1991).

Buskin, Richard, *Beatle Crazy!—Memories and Memorabilia* (Salamander, 1994).

Carr, Roy, *Beatles at the Movies* (HarperPerennial, 1996).

Carr, Roy and Tony Tyler, *The Beatles: An Illustrated Record* (New English Library, 1975).

Castleman, Harry and Wally Podrazik, *All Together Now* (U.S.: Pierian Press, 1975).

Castleman, Harry and Wally Podrazik, *The Beatles Again?* (U.S.: Pierian Press, 1977).

Castleman, Harry and Wally Podrazik, *The End of The Beatles?* (U.S.: Pierian Press, 1985).

Coleman, Ray, *John Winston Lennon, Volume One 1940-1966* (Sidgwick & Jackson, 1984).

Coleman, Ray, *John Ono Lennon, Volume Two 1967-1980* (Sidgwick & Jackson, 1984).

Coleman, Ray, *Brian Epstein: The Man Who Made The Beatles* (Viking, 1989).

Coleman, Ray, *McCartney: Yesterday and Today* (Boxtree, 1995).

Davies, Hunter, *The Beatles* (Heinemann, 1968).

Di Franco, J. Philip, *A Hard Day's Night: A Complete Pictorial Record of the Movie* (U.S.: Chelsea House, 1977).

DiLello, Richard, *The Longest Cocktail Party* (Charisma, 1973).

Dowdling, William J., *Beatlesongs* (U.S.: Simon & Schuster, 1989).

Epstein, Brian, *A Cellarful of Noise* (Souvenir Press, 1964).

Evans, Mike, *The Art of The Beatles* (Anthony Blond, 1984).

Friede, Goldie / Robin Titone / Sue Weiner, *The Beatles A to Z* (Eyre Methuen, 1980).

Harrison, George, *I Me Mine* (Genesis, 1980).

Harry, Bill, *Mersey Beat: The Beginnings of The Beatles* (Omnibus Press, 1977).

Hertsgaard, Mark, *A Day in the Life* (Macmillan/Delacorte, 1995).

Howlett, Kevin, *The Beatles at the Beeb: The Story Of Their Radio Career, 1962-1965* (BBC, 1982).

Howlett, Kevin and Mark Lewisohn, *In My Life: John Lennon Remembered* (BBC, 1990).

Kozinn, Allan, *The Beatles* (U.S.: Phidon, 1995).

Lewisohn, Mark, *The Beatles Live!* (Pavilion, 1985).

Lewisohn, Mark, *The Beatles: 25 Years in the Life* (Sidgwick & Jackson, 1987).

Lewisohn, Mark, *The Complete Beatles Recording Sessions: The Official Story of the Abbey Road Years* (Hamlyn, 1988).

Lewisohn, Mark, *The Complete Beatles Chronicle* (Pyramid, 1992).

Lennon, Cynthia, *A Twist of Lennon* (Star, 1978).

MacDonald, Ian, *Revolution in the Head* (4th Estate, 1994).

Martin, George, with Jeremy Hornsby, *All You Need Is Ears* (Macmillan, 1979).

Martin, George, with William Pearson, *Summer of Love—The Making of Sgt. Pepper* (Macmillan, 1994)

McCabe, Peter and Robert D. Schonfield, *Apple to the Core: The Unmaking of The Beatles* (Martin Brian & O'Keeffe, 1972).

Miles, *The Beatles in Their Own Words* (Omnibus, 1978).

Norman, Philip, *Shout! The Beatles in Their Generation* (Elm Tree, 1981).

Pawlowski, Gareth L., *How They Became the Beatles*, (U.S.: E.P. Dutton, 1989).

Schreuders, Piet / Mark Lewisohn / Adam Smith, *The Beatles' London* (Hamlyn, 1994).

Sheff, David and G. Barry Golson, *The Playboy Interviews with John Lennon and Yoko Ono* (Playboy Press, 1981).

Shotton, Pete, and Nicholas Schaffner, *John Lennon: In My Life* (Coronet, 1984).

Southall, Brian / Peter Vince / Allan Rouse, *Abbey Road* (Omnibus, 1997).

Stannard, Neville, *The Beatles: The Long & Winding Road—A History of The Beatles on Record* (Virgin, 1982).

Sulpy, Doug and Schweighardt, *Drugs, Divorce and a Slipping Image* (The 910, 1994).

Taylor, Alistair, with Martin Roberts, *Yesterday: The Beatles Remembered* (Sidgwick & Jackson, 1988).

Taylor, Derek, *As Time Goes By* (Davis-Poynter, 1973).

Taylor, Derek, *Fifty Years Adrift* (Genesis, 1984).

Turner, Steve, *A Hard Day's Write* (Carlton, 1994).

Wenner, Jann, *Lennon Remembers* (Penguin, 1973).

Wiener, Allen J., *The Beatles: The Ultimate Recording Guide* (Bob Adams, 1994).

Williams, Allan and William Marshall, *The Man Who Gave The Beatles Away* (Elm Tree, 1975).

**341**

# Index

# D

# M